D1602228

THE NORTHERN
GAME

BASEBALL THE CANADIAN WAY

BOB ELLIOTT

THE NORTHERN GAME

BASEBALL THE CANADIAN WAY

SPORT CLASSIC BOOKS

www.sportclassicbooks.com

Published in the United States of America by Sport Media Publishing
Inc., Wilmington, Delaware, and simultaneously in Canada.

For information about permission to reproduce selections from this book,
please write to:
Permissions
Sport Media Publishing, Inc.,
21 Carlaw Ave.,
Toronto, Ontario, Canada, M4M 2R6
www.sportclassicbooks.com

This book is set in Garamond.

Cover design: Paul Hodgson
Interior design and layout: Greg Oliver

ISBN: 1-894963-40-7

Library of Congress Cataloging-in-Publication Data

Elliott, Bob, 1949-
   The northern game : baseball the Canadian way / Bob Elliott.
      p. cm.
   Includes index.
   ISBN 1-894963-40-7 (hardcover)
   1. Baseball—Canada—History. I. Title.
   GV863.15.A1E44 2005
   796.357'0971—dc22
                                                2005006806

Printed in Canada

TABLE OF CONTENTS

Dedicated to all the players I've had the honor of coaching, including my son, as well as all the volunteers from coast to coast who rake fields, hammer in bases, drag infields, dig into their pockets to pay umpires, spend summer weekends on the road and who leave the game to those it was meant for: kids with dreams who put on the uniforms.

FOREWORD
BY DON CHERRY

Hockey is my life but it's never been my only sporting passion. Like many Kingston boys, I spent my winters on ice and my summers on ball fields. So I'm sitting here now feeling nostalgic about my youth and baseball, and my father.

No one loved baseball like Del Cherry. My dad was a natural, and a local hero on the diamonds around Kingston during the 1920s and '30s. He was a 6-foot-4, 234-pound centre fielder who could hit for power and average, and run like a deer. And, boy, was he strong. He had a 17-inch neck and 32-inch waist. He'd grip the bat right at the end of the handle and rip home runs that people would talk about for days.

They still talk about the time at the Cricket Field in Kingston when he cranked one that went beyond the trees in left field and hit the old, gray courthouse on the second bounce. Someone measured it once at 500 feet! One year he led the league in batting average, home runs, slugging percentage, RBIs, stolen bases and fielding percentage. My dad could do it all.

He was a master electrician by trade, and turned down an invitation to play in the International League at Syracuse because taking to the road in the minor leagues was no way to raise a family. Instead, he became a legend in the Central Ontario Baseball League, which was pretty good ball in those days. Sunday sports were banned in Ontario back then. So on the Sabbath my dad would hop on a motorcycle with his buddy, Teddy Gallagher, a left-hand pitcher, and cross the border to places like Watertown or Syracuse, where, playing under assumed names to protect their amateur status, they'd hire themselves out to the local team on Sunday afternoons.

They say Del Cherry was the best ballplayer to ever come out of Kingston, with one possible exception—a catcher by the name of Bob Elliott.

It's funny how life works. The author of this book is the son of Bob Elliott the catcher. I remember the dad. Some people called him Mr. Baseball. Even after he retired from playing, he managed and coached local teams for years. So I was delighted to be invited to contribute to *The Northern Game*.

And I was particularly happy to learn that one of the themes of this book was a look at how Canadians play baseball with a hockey mentality. It's true, of course.

A kid that comes out of the southern U.S. or from Latin America, places where baseball can be played year round, may have an edge in some of the pure skills. But Canadians compensate with grit and heart. I've often heard old-time ballplayers players describe a player they like by saying he plays "Canadian." And we all nod and know exactly what that means. You see it all the time. Larry Walker will run through the wall to make a catch. Corey Koskie will eat dirt before he lets a ball get by him. Eric Gagne has the nerves of a goalie when the game is on the line. Jason Bay will gladly take a ball in the ribs to get on base.

What these guys have in common is that they played hockey as kids. And to succeed in hockey, you need to have that go-for-broke mentality. You need to be tough and determined. You have to put the team first. You have to be willing to pay a price and stand up for your teammates. And you have to be willing to play hurt. Sometimes, the mentally tough kid will go farther in sports than the kid with pure talent.

I'm not saying Canadians aren't talented. Larry Walker is an MVP. Eric Gagne won a Cy Young. Ferguson Jenkins is in the Hall of Fame. Obviously, they have talent. But they also have a huge heart. Bobby Orr was the greatest hockey player ever, but what made him truly special was not just his skill—and, boy, was he skilled—but Bobby also had the biggest heart in a Boston Bruins locker room that was full of heart. The same goes for players like Walker, Gagne and Jenkins.

I loved playing baseball as a kid. I was a good hitter and fielder but I didn't have a very good arm, probably because I had broken a shoulder playing ball when I was young. When I was 17, I was invited to attend a Brooklyn Dodgers prospect camp in Welland, Ontario. They liked what they saw and offered me a spot on their Double-A team in Florida, which was pretty heady stuff for a 17-year-old. But, by then, hockey was my life, so I asked them to give it to me straight: Was I going to make it to the big leagues? They told me I'd certainly go to Triple-A, but I probably didn't have the arm to go to the majors. I told them no thanks.

The next summer, playing baseball at the Cricket Field in Kingston, I slid into second base and broke my ankle. My dad had become a legend at Cricket Field. And me? That's where my NHL career effectively ended. But I never lost my love of baseball.

One summer when I was unemployed, after finishing my hockey career in Rochester, I attended every one of the Triple-A games of the Rochester

Red Wings. When I coached in Boston I'd go to Fenway Park whenever I could. The announcer, Sherm Feller, was an all-time favorite of mine.

I remember one time I was at Fenway with my son, Tim, to see the Yankees and Red Sox. Reggie Jackson was having one of those games where he wasn't trying and where he kept going over to talk to the fans. I said to Tim: "If he keeps this up there's going to be trouble." Well, Billy Martin finally had enough, and he took Reggie out of the game during the middle of an inning. The next thing you know they had to be separated in the dugout by Elston Howard or they would have slugged each other.

I couldn't blame Billy. If one of my players had acted that way, I'd want to slug him, too. But hockey players aren't likely to be found chatting up the fans. The game is too fast and too intense for that. And if it did happen, one of the guy's teammates would probably take care of it before the coach.

That's just how it is in hockey. It's a completely different mentality from baseball. And that's what makes Canadian baseball players special. They play baseball with a hockey attitude.

Introduction

A GOLDEN ERA

As the calendar turned to 2005, Canadian baseball was a paradox: healthy yet sick, rich yet poor.

For the first time since 1976, Canada is home to only one major-league team. Reports of the Montreal Expos demise are no longer greatly exaggerated; they've gone to Washington, D.C. The Toronto Blue Jays? They're struggling at the gate and in the standings to return to the glory days. In the minor leagues, Canada will field just two teams in 2005—Triple-A Ottawa and Rookie-Class Vancouver—compared with eight in 1992, when there were Triple-A clubs in Calgary, Edmonton, Vancouver; a Double-A team in London; Single-A franchises in Hamilton, St. Catharines and Welland; and Rookie-Class in Medicine Hat.

You don't need to be Columbo to read the signs: pro baseball in Canada is circling the drain and heading south. Yep, and rapidly.

But the news is not all bad. While the pro game in Canada is close to flat-lining, Team Canada, composed of minor-league pros, came within a double play ground ball of being four outs away from playing Australia for gold at the 2004 Summer Olympics in Athens. Canadian prospects, meanwhile, have been heading south like flocks of strong-winged Canada geese:

Outfielder Jason Bay of Trail, British Columbia won the 2004 National League Rookie of the Year Award with the Pittsburgh Pirates. First baseman Justin Morneau of New Westminster, British Columbia might have won the American League honors had he logged two fewer days of service for the Minnesota Twins in 2003, thereby preserving his rookie eligibility in 2004.

A total of 20 Canadians appeared on the rosters of major-league teams in 2004. Don't credit expansion; the majors hasn't bumped its 30-team enrollment since 1993. The total is the highest since 1884 when 28 Canucks played for 33 teams in what constituted the majors back then: the National League, the American Association and the Union Association.

Eight Canadians were on post-season rosters in 2004: Corey Koskie, Jesse Crain and Morneau of the Twins; Larry Walker and Cody McKay of the St. Louis Cardinals; Eric Gagne of the Los Angeles Dodgers; Paul Quantrill of the New York Yankees and Chris Reitsma of the Atlanta Braves.

A total of 114 Canadians were on minor-league rosters in 2003, an increase of 75 percent from the 1998 total of 65. The number dipped slightly to 106 in 2004 due to a change in U.S. policy that put a cap on the number of visas issued to foreign workers.

There were 648 Canadians playing college baseball south of the border in the spring of 2004, compared to 490 in the spring of 2000, a growth of 30 percent. In 2003-2004, 564 NCAA hockey players were Canadian. Who would have thought Canadians have a better shot at going to the U.S. on a baseball scholarship than on a hockey ticket?

We are on the cusp of a golden era for Canadian baseball.

In 1994, less than six months after the Blue Jays won their second consecutive World Series, Baseball Canada reported 232,281 registered players. For the 2004 season, registration was 257,514, an increase of 10.9 percent. Still not close to Hockey Canada numbers—538,152 registered players—but respectable, and growing.

Remo Cardinale, Baseball Canada coach of the year in 2001 and the first Canadian the Jays ever signed, believes the numbers indicate a positive trend for the future. "It will take a few years," he said, "but Canadians have been heading to the U.S. on baseball scholarships since about 1992 and now there are more than 600. These guys who love baseball will come home, get married, have kids and will take their kids out to the park or the back yard for a game of catch. A lot will want to coach their kids in baseball. I truly believe registration will take off down the road."

From father to son.

When lefty Jeff Francis made his debut Aug. 24, 2004 for the Colorado Rockies, he became the 218th Canadian—native born Canadians plus a handful of foreign-born players who became Canadian citizens—to appear in the majors, according to Canadian baseball historian William Humber. For many years, Mike Brannock was believed to be the first Canuck, but new American research has transfered that honor to Jimmy Wood (hometown unknown), a second baseman who debuted in 1871 with the Chicago White Stockings of the National Association.

This book is about baseball in a country where hockey dominates; about the Olympic experience, how close and yet so far; about hardworking coaches; about the passion we have for baseball and baseball's heritage in Canada, which runs deeper than the roots of a sturdy maple tree or a giant Douglas fir.

It's about Hall of Famer Fergie Jenkins; Tip O'Neill; fathers and sons; the baseball hotbed known as British Columbia; Claude Raymond (proudest Expo of all) and our own Moonlight Graham of *Field of Dreams* fame, Eric MacKenzie.

It's about a pitcher named Ron Taylor, who became Dr. Taylor; about a failed starter, Eric Gagne, who became the game's most dominant closer; and about Mr. Baseball Canada, back-flipping infielder Stubby Clapp, part of Team Canada that won the World Youth Championships in 1991.

It's about Danny Klassen, who went from breaking greenhouse panes to the majors; about Chris Begg, who wore the same underwear from bantam to Triple-A; about the prairie experience led by Corey Koskie and Terry Puhl, and it's about Shawn Hill, who got to pitch for the Expos and his country in the same season.

It's about fathers and sons, like Gerry Reimer and Kevin Reimer; like Bill Zimmerman and his major-league sons, Jeff and Jordan; about what can happen during a day at a ballpark in Canada; and it's about Larry Walker, the only Canadian MVP winner, and his father.

And it's about how Canadians play the game differently, with a hockey mentality, unselfish, tough and determined. How are we different? Well, when the St. Louis Cardinals eliminated the Los Angeles Dodgers in the 2004 National League Championship Series, they crossed the diamond and shook hands with the Dodgers—not unlike the custom in the NHL playoffs each spring. This baseball innovation was the brainchild of Cardinals' slugger Walker. The idea came in 1995 after his Colorado Rockies were eliminated by the Atlanta Braves in the NL Division Series. At the end, Walker felt like something was missing. He would have liked a chance to shake hands with the Braves and wish them well.

"I always thought it would be nice to try and have that approach the next time," Walker said. "You see it in hockey all the time. They go out, beat up on each other the whole series, but in the end they shake hands. I thought, 'That's great for kids to see, the fact that the two teams can compete and try to beat each other, but when it is over, there is a respect between the two sides.' This won't hurt the game. It's something that brings a more human element to the game."

Before the first round of the 2004 post season, Cards' manager Tony LaRussa discussed Walker's idea with his Los Angeles Dodgers' counterpart, Jim Tracy, a former Expo coach. When the final out was recorded, the Cards put their celebration on hold and exchanged post-game pleasantries with the Dodgers.

Walker called the dugout-emptying scene "a little sloppy," adding, "We can work on it." Dodgers' closer Eric Gagne, a Montrealer, hugged Cards' Albert Pujols and told him he was "one of the best hitters in the game, now go win the World Series."

Think of Canadian baseball as a crackling campfire, and the subjects of this book are gathering around it to tell their stories. The tales are endless and stretch back more than a century. Baseball has always been as American as apple pie. It was that way in 1900 and remained so in 2004, when the Boston Red Sox broke their 86-year streak of futility by finally winning the World Series for the first time since 1918. But baseball is Canadian too, eh?

Woven throughout the fabric of America's pastime are the red and white of Canucks, from the early stars like Tip O'Neill, George (Moon) Gibson, Jack Graney, Russ Ford, and George (Twinkletoes) Selkirk to post-war big leaguers like Ron Taylor, Fergie Jenkins, Terry Puhl, Larry Walker and Eric Gagne.

Canadian baseball is different. Canadian baseball players are different. They have brought a nation's rich hockey culture into ballparks, and they play baseball as if they're going into the corners, elbows up.

"Bobby Prentice told me years ago: don't be interested in Canadian kids unless you've heard they've played hockey," said Chris Buckley, the former Jays scouting director, relating advice from the original Jays director of scouting. "Bobby told me to go with that rule because a hockey player knows how to compete. He's been through regimented practices. They have that toughness and they liked to compete. Long before Larry Walker, they all wanted to grow up to be Bobby Orr."

This book also answers an oft-asked question aimed at your correspondent: "Why does someone from Canada have such passion for baseball rather than hockey?"

Easy.

I grew up with baseball. My affection for the game and everything that goes with it is rooted in my childhood.

My father loved baseball and shared his passion for the game with me. From father to son. It's as simple as that.

MADE IN CANADA

1

As they waited in line to pass through an airport metal detector, not one of them would stand out—unless, of course, they were to drop a loonie into the change tub. Similarly, they'd be indiscernible stepping sleepy-eyed from a bus after a six-hour trip from Macon, Yakima, Wilmington or Cedar Rapids—unless, of course, they were to greet the driver with, "Great day, eh?"

Yet, once the game starts ... Well, it becomes easy to pick out the Canadians.

"I remember scouting Corey Koskie when he was a kid," said Bill MacKenzie, a former major-league amateur scout, talking about the Anola, Manitoba native who joined the Blue Jays in 2005 after seven seasons with the Minnesota Twins. "He was so tough playing third base, he'd block balls with his face and then throw guys out. You see the way Derek Jeter plays the game; he has a Canadian mentality, jumping into the seats chasing foul pop-ups."

In the minors, labels are dispensed more readily than meal money. They're handed out by scouts, general managers, minor-league managers, and the biggest gossips of all, trainers. It can take five minutes to earn a label and five years to get rid of it ... if it's a bad one. There are lots of labels: "good field, no hit," or "no hustle" or "ill-tempered" or "he's lazy AND he sulks." Then there is the 'Canadian' label. In baseball, it's a term of respect.

Take it from Pete Laforest, a catcher in the Tampa Bay Devil Rays organization and a member of Canada's 2004 Olympic team.

"All I hear in the minors when a roving instructor or a minor-league coach comes into town and asks 'what about Pete Laforest?' The answer is always, 'Oh, he's Canadian.'" With the Devil Rays, that was it, that was all. He's Canadian. 'Nuff said. The Canadian tag is like the *Good Housekeeping* seal of approval. "Finally, I asked someone what exactly does it mean when you say, 'He's Canadian?' Like what does that mean? I was told it means 'he does what is expected, he plays hard, he'll run through a wall for you. He plays hard, works hard and doesn't cause any problems. He's Canadian.'"

It's like when a new pitching coach is introduced to a writer in the club-house. The coach looks over his shoulder to see another coach give a thumbs up. That's all that is needed.

"The Canadian mentality is different," Laforest said. "I've heard coaches say we have a hockey mentality. A hockey mentality means a player pushes the envelope, dives in the dirt for a ground ball, breaks up two, does whatever is needed. Some players don't like it, because they don't like hockey and it's a wide statement made by an American, but it is meant as compliment."

Finesse lefty Mike Kusiewicz, the second Canadian chosen over-all in the 1994 draft behind Jason Dickson, has heard the hockey analogy. "I couldn't skate to save my life," says Kusiewicz, who has pitched 10 years in the minors after signing with the Colorado Rockies. "I don't like it. Why not just say 'he's a competitor,' or 'he can pitch.'"

Scout Dick Groch, known as The Legend, says that the term 'hockey mentality' is not a generalization.

"When you go to watch a young man play hockey in Canada you can see his physical and mental toughness," says Groch, who covers Canada for the Milwaukee Brewers. "In the United States we can see his toughness either on the football field or the basketball court. When you go to Canada you find corner players, infielders and outfielders, plenty of left-hand hitters, raw-boned pitchers, both left and right. Scouts should not expect to find a runner or a finesse position player. Canadians were always known for their rough style of play. Tough kids play in tough weather."

Still, growing up playing baseball north of the border is distinctive. The Canadian baseball player is like the American hockey player in Tennessee or Texas. A minority. Back-of-the-sports section type news. They hear whispers that they're in their sport because they couldn't succeed in the country's No. 1 game. Yet their passion is genuine. And, whether it's hockey in the south or baseball in the north, they're flocking to facilities that weren't around 15 years ago.

Are Canadian baseball players bucking long odds? For sure. But if they make it, which more and more of them are doing, the rewards are immense. Larry Walker, cut by the Regina Pats of the Junior-A Western Hockey League when he was a teenager, earned $12.66 million from the Colorado Rockies and St. Louis Cardinals in 2004. Eric Gagne, a so-called hockey goon who was good enough to be offered a scholarship to the University of Vermont, earned $5 million closing for the Los Angeles Dodgers in 2004. Corey Koskie, a failed goalie who excelled at volleyball at the University of Manitoba before attending Des Moines Area Community College, signed a three-year, $16.5-million contract with the Toronto Blue Jays in December 2004.

To American baseball fans, the Canadians are not identifiable at first glance because they're not a visible minority, the way that Latins or Asians are—but they definitely are a minority. Of the players on the 2004 opening day major-league rosters, including the disabled lists, 27.3 percent were born outside of the United States, hailing from 13 other countries and Puerto Rico. The Dominican Republic led with 79 players, followed by Venezuela (45) and Puerto Rico (36). Canada was fourth with 20 players, four more than Mexico and 10 more than Japan and Cuba. Of the 6,117 minor-league players signed to 2004 contracts, 47.6 percent were from outside the U.S. Again, the Dominican led with 1,442 players, followed by Venezuela (803), Puerto Rico (127), Canada (106) and Mexico (102). U.S. visa restrictions in 2004 saw a decrease in Canadians in the minors for the first time since 1994.

The most obvious explanation for the relatively small number of Canadians playing professional baseball is that, unlike aspiring pros from the U.S. south and the Caribbean, players north of the 49th parallel don't enjoy 12 months of warm weather. You can't take infield drills when the ball fields are covered in snow. When Pete Laforest started playing baseball in his native Quebec his season consisted of 20 games. Then, he went to the Academie Baseball Canada in Montreal and played a 50-game schedule. But compare that, says Laforest, to the story of his agent, Myles Shoda of Atlanta. "His son is 16, playing for East Cobb, and they play 100 games a year," Laforest says, shaking his head. "The more you play, the more repetitions, the more game situations you are exposed to, the better you become. Canadians are always playing catch up."

Yet, some Canadians do succeed. Their secret weapon? Canadians have taken their hockey mentality and applied it to baseball. In hockey, the real players go into the corners, they battle in front of the net, they don't complain when the coach puts them through stops and starts, and, above all else, they compete. Bernie Beckman, who grew up in Toronto, was signed by Detroit Tigers scout Bobby Prentice and pitched nine seasons in the minors, reaching Triple-A in 1975 with Wichita. After retiring, he was hired by Pat Gillick to instruct in the Jays minor-league system and, from 1986 to 1993, he ran Team Canada. He's a subscriber to the theory that hockey is good training for baseball, and points to Matt Stairs, a 12-year major leaguer from St. John, New Brunswick, who twice topped 100 RBI for the Oakland A's, as an example of a player who successfully crossed over. "He was a good hockey player," said Beckman. "He was hard nosed and he took his hockey instincts out onto the field with him. When he was turning a double play you'd think he was going into the corner for the puck." Stairs, of course, bats left, common for Canadians.

The Los Angeles Dodgers, under scouting director Logan White, have an affinity for Canadian players. In 2004, the Dodgers had Cy Young winner Eric Gagne and Russell Martin on their 40-man roster, plus six other Canucks in their system. "You hear the term hockey mentality bantered around and it's definitely meant as a compliment," said White. "Canadians have a blue-collar, working-man's mentality: self is second and team is first. I'm sure there are selfish Canadian players and even some who aren't the most competitive, but we usually see the cream of the crop."

White says an advantage Canadian ballplayers have, although they may not realize it, is that they play a lighter schedule at younger age groups. Whereas many talented Americans get burned out in their teens as a result of too many games and practices, not to mention the pressure exerted by well-meaning, but zealous, coaches and parents, there is less pressure on Canadians at an early age. Canadian kids today are playing more, but their season is still relatively short compared to Americans in hotbeds like California, Texas and Florida.

"The Canadian players I've been around are of a quiet confidence, humble, and of a strong mental makeup," White said. "I'm sure it's a combination of so many things—upbringing, genetics, environment and weather. All I know is I have yet to see a Canadian player not make it due to his head or makeup. It's usually lack of physical ability or injury."

Scouts look for mental toughness in prospects. To advance through a minor-league system to a major-league team often takes much more than raw talent. The hours are long, the pay is rotten and the travel, usually by bus, is mind-numbingly boring. Homesickness is common. Nagging aches and pains and minor injuries are an everyday occurrence, yet players can't afford to spend too much time with the trainers or medical staff for fear of being labeled soft. There is always someone eager to take your job, or an unfriendly manager willing to give it away. Some players can get by on pure ability but most need something extra. Call it perseverance or doggedness or toughness. Whatever. By and large, Canadians seem to have it.

"Canadians are all mentally tough," said Bill MacKenzie, Baseball Canada's original technical director. "Go ahead, lay the names all out on a table. All the Canadians who have succeeded at the game are mentally tough. I've often been in Florida scouting Canadian teams against high school teams. There would be a threat of rain, the grass was really long or it would be drizzling and the Florida kids didn't want to play. Well, the Canadians just wanted the chance to play. These kids don't whine. Upstate New York kids have the same makeup."

Today, MacKenzie sells bats for his pal Sam Holman, founder of the Original Maple Bat Company. In a unique way, they have been putting a made-in-Canada stamp on the American game.

MacKenzie and Holman were sharing a pint—how Canadian is that?—and watching the Chicago Cubs on TV at Ottawa's Mayflower Pub in the spring of 1996. When the game was delayed as yet another bat splintered, they came up with the bat idea.

MacKenzie: "Why do so many bats break? Why not build a bat that won't break?"

Holman: "You're not going to build a better ash tree."

A former set maker at the National Arts Centre, Holman made a few attempts at building bats from maple rather than the traditional ash. The first maple bat, made by architect Sam Roberts and Holman, was too heavy. Eventually, Holman found a lighter maple wood from Shawinigan, Quebec. The dealer specialized in top-grade hardwood used in guitars. The Sambat was born.

Holman then made inroads with the Montreal Expos and the Toronto Blue Jays. When Jays slugger Joe Carter was signed as a free agent by the Baltimore Orioles Dec. 12, 1997, he took his stockpile of Sambats with him. Around the batting cage, when players hear a 'whack' they become like kindergarten kids wanting to try a schoolmate's new box of crayons. Then Carter was dealt to the San Francisco Giants on July 23, 1998. Barry Bonds used Carter's bat, liked it, and hit homers No. 600 and 700—and the 99 in between—with the made-in-Canada Sambat.

The Sambat aside, Canada's contributions to baseball have largely come on the field and, there, are often measured by attitude. In some cases, this hockey mentality comes in a Philadelphia Flyers' persona, as it did when former Blue Jays general manager Gord Ash made his best deal ever, acquiring Paul Quantrill from the Philadelphia Phillies for minor-league third baseman Howard Battle in 1995. We remember asking a Phillies coach why they had traded Quantrill. The coach said his team was short on starters and used Quantrill in the rotation when actually he was a better reliever. So, no warts, we asked? "Well," said the coach, "he does have a problem if one of our guys gets hit in the foot accidentally with a 62-mile-an-hour curve ball. He'll want to stick up for his hitters by giving one of their guys a bow tie. Noble concept if their guy had buzzed our guy up around the head, but not on a curve ball that got away."

Generally, you run into problems when you generalize. Nevertheless, there are a few points to be made about Canadian ball players:

• The best Canadian pro prospects are usually left-handed hitters or pitchers. Scouts who see Team Canada at the world junior championships or on their annual spring trip to Disney's Wide World of Sports are often heard saying: "Does Canada not have any right-handed hitters?"

According to Team Canada's Peter Orr: "It's because most everyone shoots left playing hockey, so they hit left in baseball." When Bernie

Beckman was running Team Canada, he says opposing managers routinely used a left-hand pitcher—any lefty on the staff—to counter his left-hand hitting lineup. "It got to the point where I never asked an opposing manager who they were throwing—it was always a lefty," he said. "The reason we have so many left-handed hitters is hockey. We also don't run well. That is an offshoot of hockey, too." Canadian Olympian Todd Betts has his own theory: "I think it's because of the way we shovel snow," he said, prompting laughter. "No, think about it," he protested, as he rose in a restaurant in Anzio, Italy and began to shovel imaginary snow, stopping a waiter in his tracks.

• Canadians might not be the fastest running to the wall, but they will generally run through it.

• Canadian batters might not have the best mechanics when it comes to keeping their hands back and taking an outside pitch the other way, but they will outlast any hitting machine loaded with baseballs in an effort to improve.

• Canadians might not get the best jump when leading off first, but there is no telling what could happen when they're intent on breaking up two at second base, or when the ball and runner arrive at home plate at the same time.

• Canadian pitchers might not be the best at getting to their balance point, but they will throw an extra bullpen session to straighten out mechanics.

These generalizations seem to hold up when applied to just a small sample of recently-drafted Canadians:

• Joey Votto of Etobicoke, Ontario, a second-round pick (40th over-all) by the Cincinnati Reds in 2002, who has been switched from catcher to first base and is impressing coaches with his work ethic, bat speed and steady improvement.

• Scott Thorman of Cambridge, Ontario was the first Canadian high schooler ever drafted in the first round, taken in the 2001 draft by the Atlanta Braves. His instructional league manager in the fall of 2002 was future Jays manager Carlos Tosca, who raved about Thorman's attitude. "Once on a close play at second he almost knocked the shortstop into left field," said Tosca. "He was a joy to manage."

• Lefty Jeff Francis, of North Delta, British Columbia, the ninth over-all pick in 2002 by the Colorado Rockies, and the second-highest Canadian selection ever, caused Rockies farm director Bill Geivett to comment: "Let's put it this way, he's too old to marry my daughter. He's just a great, great person first and foremost and very down to earth."

• Russ Martin of Montreal was drafted in the 17th round by the Los Angeles Dodgers as an infielder. Converted to catcher, Martin hit .250

with 15 homers and 64 RBIs at Single-A, and in November 2004 he was placed on the Dodgers 40-man roster. Logan White, Dodgers scouting director, calls Martin an outstanding young man who's "really getting better behind the plate."

• Right-hander Scott Mathieson of Aldergrove, British Columbia was chosen in the 17th round by the Philadelphia Phillies. He pitched at Single-A Lakewood and, according to manager P.J. Forbes, "his work ethic was the best on our team."

What has been a boon to Canadians are the talent showcases held annually in the United States. A showcase gathers elite high school players—most are invited and pay for the chance to have their talent assessed—at camps in places like Fort Myers, Florida, Long Beach, California, or Wareham, Massachusetts run by outfits called TeamOne, Perfect Game and Blue Chip Prospects. Players run a 60-yard dash, show off arm strength, and take a turn on the mound or in the batter's box, and are evaluated by an audience of 100 or more professional scouts and college recruiters. It can be a make-or-break weekend for players. The showcases are valuable for the scouts because they bring together the top players from small towns and schools and match them up against the known talent from the big-city programs. Or, to put it another way, the big fish from the small ponds are tossed into the same pool with the barracudas and the sharks, while the game wardens watch and evaluate.

Many Canadians have benefited from the program, often landing college scholarships but occasionally catching the eye of pro scouts. "The thing about showcases," said Greg Hamilton, director of the highly successful Team Canada junior national program, "is that kids are no longer playing against guys from their hometown. They go all over to face high-quality competition, they're being challenged and a lot of them are meeting the challenge."

One such example is Adam Loewen of Surrey, British Columbia. Loewen was first identified as a prospect in Grade 9. He excelled with Team Canada at two world junior championships, and played with minor-league pros at extended camps in the U.S, as well as Rookie-Class Dominican teams. At Major League Baseball's June 2002 draft, he was selected fourth over-all out of 1,050 high schoolers and collegians picked, by the Baltimore Orioles. After a year at Chipola College—and at the 11th hour before he would have become re-eligible for the draft—Loewen received a major-league deal from the Orioles worth $4.02 million.

In many respects, major-league scouts hold Canadians and Australians in similar high regard. Chris Buckley, former scouting director of the Toronto Blue Jays, says "Australians and Canadians are big strong people," who generally come from solid school systems. They also hold in common a fondness for physical sports, hockey in Canada and Aussie rules football down under, which provides the mental toughness required to succeed in any professional sport. Also, unlike Latin players, who face language and cultural obstacles, the transition is relatively easy for Canadians and Australians who go to the United States to play minor league baseball.

One significant difference between players from the two Commonwealth countries, says Buckley, is that "it's a $2,500 plane ticket to get to Australia and they're all free agents once you get there."

Either out of necessity (due to Canada's short season or a typically late migration to the sport) or because it's in their essential nature (due to their hockey mindset, or their upbringing) Canadian players are almost invariably lauded for their work ethic.

Calgary's Ryan Radmanovich, who began his pro career in 1993, has played on 12 different minor-league teams in the United States and Mexico, and played 27 games with the Seattle Mariners in 1999. He has crossed paths with dozens of Canadians and says he has never seen one who does not work hard. "I don't know if it is because there are so few of us, but it is the Canadian way. We have respect for the game, we're taught from Little League on up to respect others and it carries over as to how we go about our business. I've played with American players, some who are like us when it comes to work ethic, some who aren't. I've played with Venezuelans, some just like us, some who aren't. I've played with Dominicans who play hard and some who don't. But every Canadian I have ever seen plays hard."

Radmanovich told the story of being in downtown Athens with his teammates, all of them wearing Canada gear. "We were loved walking through the streets," Radmanovich said, "and we weren't loved because we were baseball players. People in Athens loved us because it said 'CANADA' on our shirts. That's because of Canadians who have traveled the world and respected other people's customs. It's like when in Rome, do as the Romans. Have you ever heard the term The Ugly Canadian?"

Canadians work hard, execute a head-first slide, do the little things right because they have to in order to make it. They will do anything to win … and it's not just about being physically tough. Evidence? Ask Italian Davide Dallospedale. At the 2004 Athens Olympics, after Dallospedale flared a single into short right field, Canadian catcher Pete Laforest noticed the Italian had used a bat called a Bombat, which is banned in the Olympics because it has metal rods inside, making it more like an aluminum bat than one made of pure wood. "Italy used them during the (pre-Olympic) tournament in Italy and I thought to myself I'd have to remember that when we get to the Olympics." Laforest said. He yelled to manager Ernie Whitt, who persuaded the ump to check out the bat. It was found to be illegal, Dallospedale was called out, and Canada rolled to a 9-3 win.

Olympian Jeff Guiel has spent eight years in the minors and, like Radmanovich, believes the common denominator for Canadian players is work ethic. "They always bust their butts," Guiel said. In 2003, an instructor with the Anaheim Angels mentioned to Guiel that the Angels had brought in a Canadian amongst a group of newcomers, prompting Guiel to boldly predict he'd be able to pick out his countryman just by looking at the new arrivals. "I picked him out immediately," Guiel said. "I could see how hard he worked, and I went up and introduced myself." The player was Ryan Kenning of North Vancouver.

Canadians are always looking up other Canadians in the minors. In 2003, Guiel was playing for the Triple-A Salt Lake Stingers, the Anaheim Angels' top affiliate. Players can select the music to be played as they come to bat and Guiel's song that year was *New Orleans is Sinking* by the Kingston, Ontario band The Tragically Hip. The song was played one night when Salt Lake hosted the Sacramento RiverCats. A few weeks later, Salt Lake was in Sacramento and Guiel was in the outfield when a RiverCat approached him:

"You Canadian?" he asked. Guiel nodded yes.

"Hi, I'm Mike Kusiewicz," said the lefty, "and so am I."

Not so Tragically, they became joined at the Hip, so to speak—in Panama and in Greece—as members of Team Canada.

The team formerly known as the Montreal Expos used to take a special interest in Canadian talent, just as the Jays used to do. "I'd sit up and take notice in meetings when it was mentioned a kid was from Sarnia or Stratford," said the late Larry Bearnarth, an American who pitched for the New York Mets and then was a pitching coach with the Expos and the Rockies. "In organizational meetings with the Expos, no one would ever say this guy's from Odessa, Texas, or Bowling Green, Ohio, or Staten Island, New York. We paid attention to Canadians. Why? Because the average Canadian has more guts than the average American."

But guts and glory don't always come as a package. We remember talking to Dave MacQuarrie in the mid 1970s. The right-hander was signed by the Expos in 1973 by farm director Mel Didier and Bearnarth after starring for Art Neilson's Ottawa-Nepean Canadians. MacQuarrie spent six seasons in the minors, made it to Double-A Memphis and went to spring training with the Cleveland Indians before retiring in 1979. "Minor league pitching coaches and instructors tell me the same thing," MacQuarrie said in 1975. "They say I'm 'pretty good ... for a Canadian.' What I'd like them to tell me is that I'm pretty good. Period."

Three decades later, MacQuarrie's wish is coming true. Not for him, of course, but a new generation of Canadians is being recognized as being pretty good. Period. The evidence is to be seen in the likes of major leaguers such as Larry Walker, Eric Gagne, Corey Koskie and Jason Bay. But it was also evident in Canada's hard-working 2004 Olympic team that came oh-so-close to advancing to the gold medal game. Said Radmanovich of his fellow Olympians: "What kind of guys are on this team? Every one of the guys on this team are the one and two guys on every club who are first to the ballpark, that takes batting practice serious, that takes his ground balls during BP serious. That's what this team is all about."

Radmanovich played college ball in California for coach Andy Lopez with the Pepperdine Green Wave. "He always used to say 'look like you belong.' He was very big on running out ground balls. His point was it doesn't take any talent to hustle. Coach used to say how the scouts were watching and they'd say 'look at that, he grounded out to second ... AND ... he didn't even hustle.' Or, you could make them say 'look at that ... he grounded to second ... AND, MAN ... did he fly down the line.' It was a good lesson."

And, for Canadian ballplayers, a lesson they usually heed.

THE SWING

2

The game was almost too nerve-wracking to watch. No, not for members of Team Canada, who leaned on the railing of the first base dugout at the Helliniko Complex's Olympic Stadium in Athens—but for CBC viewers across Canada! It was Tuesday, Aug. 24, a clear, warm evening in Athens, and Canada trailed Cuba 8-5 in the top of the ninth in the 2004 Olympic semi-final. The temperature was about to rise.

Canada had runners on first and second, with two out and the potential tying run coming to the plate. Team Canada manager Ernie Whitt sent up the left-handed hitting Simon Pond to pinch-hit for his fifth-place hitter, Andy Stewart.

"It was certainly do or die and you could only think of the journey those Canadians had been on to get to that point," Bill Hurley, a Mississauga sandlot coach, said, watching the game at the Heron Point Golf Club in Ancaster, Ontario.

Cuban manager Higinio Velez countered by bringing in lefty pitcher Noberto Gonzalez.

Seven time zones away, former Toronto Blue Jays president Paul Beeston was so nervous he went out into the yard to hit golf balls.

Whitt countered by calling back Pond and sending in switch-hitter Kevin Nicholson to pinch-hit. Whitt told him: "All we need is a base hit." Nicholson, from Surrey, British Columbia, had been the starting shortstop in the 2003 Olympic qualifying tournament in Panama, but had watched most of the Olympic competition from the bench, as Danny Klassen played. The first Canadian ever selected in the first round of the major-league draft, Nicholson was an eight-year minor-league professional—plus 24 games with the San Diego Pardres—who now faced the daunting task of getting on base in order to keep alive Canada's gold-medal dream.

"When he headed to the plate I thought of seeing him at Team B.C. tryouts and how he hit several home runs from both sides of the plate and how it would be justice if he hit one now," said Ron Mace, watching from his living room in Nelson, British Columbia.

Cuba's outfielders were playing deep. As Nicholson walked to the plate, he thought, "There looked like there was so much room." He was looking for a pitch to drive up the middle. He took a borderline first pitch, down and away. A strike or a ball? Plate ump Vincente Troudart of Panama said ball ... 1-0.

"With two on and Nicholson up, I thought we had a chance. We were a swing away from evening it up," said Greg Brons, watching from his office in Saskatoon with eight others.

Gonzalez checked the runner at first and went into his delivery. "I'd never faced him before," Nicholson said. "Not that I was looking for a walk, but I was going to see a strike from this guy before I swung."

Toronto Blue Jays centre fielder Vernon Wells was watching the game in the Jays' luxurious clubhouse at SkyDome. "I played with Kevin in Peoria in the Arizona Fall League in 1999. I was rooting for him," Wells said. "He's such a great guy, I'm thinking how nice will this be for him to get a big hit in this situation."

Gonzalez threw a cut fastball on the inside portion of the plate, which Troudart called a strike ... 1-1.

Like most baseball-loving Canadians, Clyde MacLeod was in front of his TV, taking in the Greek drama at Abbotsford, British Columbia. "I was watching with a couple of fellas, Chris McGregor and Jay Andrew, who played with Kevin and knew him from Surrey."

Nicholson would say later that he didn't think Gonzalez had over-powering stuff. He took a pitch away for a ball ... 2-1.

In St. Marys, Ontario, home of Canada's Baseball Hall of Fame, president Tom Valcke recalled Nicholson hitting a home run in Ottawa at Jetform Park, home of the Triple-A Ottawa Lynx, to win a national championship for British Columbia in 1993. "From the right side, too" Valcke thought.

Now, Gonzalez came in with his cut fastball, this one over the middle of the plate. Nicholson fouled back and broke his bat ... 2-2.

Neil Srivastava, who works at the University of Guelph, was in his living room multi-tasking: watching the game as he chatted on his laptop with friend Andy Wilson from Brock University, who was also watching the nervy ninth: "I guess Canada could still score four in the ninth."... "Not likely."... "Not likely, but stranger things have happened."

Nicholson headed to the bat rack in the first-base dugout. The TV showed he was smirking. "Funny thing was, I had only one bat, my others were in the clubhouse," Nicholson said.

Jeremy Ware was near the bats and asked: "Where's your bat?"

Nicholson replied: "That was it. I'm out. You pick one for me to use."

Ware: "No way, you pick it."

Nicholson: "No, you pick."

With so much at stake the two Team Canada veterans were going back and forth like a couple of pre-schoolers: Did not. Did so. Did not. Finally, Nicholson grabbed a new bat belonging to second baseman Stubby Clapp, because they swing "pretty much the same bat."

Ten time zones away, in Surrey, British Columbia, Dennis Springenatic was now off the couch and standing. Nicholson's former coach in the British Columbia Premier League was too nervous to sit. "The guy came back inside on Kevin and he was ready," Springenatic said, "I thought it was gone."

The swing.

"When I saw his swing, with a slight upper cut, I thought it was out of the park and I immediately jumped up and yelled 'it's gone!'" Brons said.

"When Nicholson swung, it was a smooth sweet swing," Hurley said. "I thought it was out."

The ball began to climb ...

"I thought it was out," MacLeod said. "Everyone I was with thought it was out. We were out of our seats and making noise like we were at a bantam game. It was crazy."

The ball soared into the wind blowing in off the Gulf of Saronikis.

"All I could think was that Kevin Nicholson's going to make a ton of money on the rubber chicken circuit if this goes out," said Dan Mendham, a scout for the Major League Baseball Scouting Bureau, as he watched in his living room in Dorchester, Ontario. "Stubby Clapp was booked to every speaking engagement in Canada after he hit a bloop single to beat Team USA in the Pan-Am Games in 1999."

"GET UP, BALL!" screamed Clapp from the Team Canada dugout. In the stands, a crowd of 6,033 followed the flight of the ball. Cuban fans gasped. Canadian supporters began to cheer.

"At the golf club at that moment, we weren't golfers, we were Canadians," Hurley said. "Half the room held its breath, the other half yelled 'Go, go, go!'"

"I watched the ball carry and carry, I was on the edge of my seat," Mace said.

"I jumped off the couch when the ball left his bat thinking it was gone," Valcke said.

And then, as Tommy Lasorda, former Los Angeles Dodgers manager, used to say: "You know you're in trouble if that ball comes down." The ball came down—eight, maybe 10 inches from the top of the wall. Cuban left fielder Frederich Cepeda leapt against the wall and made a game-saving catch. Game over. The jubilant Cubans poured onto the field while Team Canada and its supporters fell into a stunned silence. Beyond left field, the flags—those damned flags—were whipping in towards home plate, standing at attention as if an anthem were playing. But there was no music, only the whistling of the wind.

"I knew he got it, well, I thought he got it all," said right fielder Ryan Radmanovich. "It was what, about 10 inches short of tying up the game?"

Later, Whitt would say, "The baseball gods were against us." But maybe the manager's beef is with the gods of physics. Baseball is a game of inches. Or 1/64th of an inch ... if Nicholson's bat had made contact with the ball a fraction of an inch higher or lower, maybe he'd have created the force to produce the velocity to overcome the wind. Instead ...

Watching the replay of his blast, Nicholson noticed that, as the ball soared toward the outfield, Cuban third baseman Michel Enriquez was standing with his head down. He, too, thought it was gone. "I watched the at-bat maybe 10 times when I got back home," Nicholson said. "I kept thinking: 'Maybe it will go out one of these times.'"

Heading into Athens, depending who you asked, either Canada or Chinese Taipei was favored for the bronze medal. The favorites for gold were Cuba and Japan. Cuba fielded a powerhouse, having won Olympic gold in 1992, when baseball rejoined the Olympics as a medal sport, and gold again in 1996, before losing the 2000 gold-medal game to Team USA. Japan fielded a so-called Dream Team that included up to two players from each of its major-league teams. And then there was Canada, fielding a team comprised mostly of career minor-leaguers, save for prospects like outfielder Adam Stern, Peter Orr and Shawn Hill.

Still, this was the best international team Canada had ever assembled. Despite the loss of two star players—Justin Morneau and Jeff Francis— just prior to the Games, Team Canada arrived in Athens with a team that, by Canadian standards, was high in talent and, of course, loaded with heart. The higher talent level was a testament to the developmental programs across the country that, in recent years, have become a signifi- cant source of players for university, minor professional and, on occasion, major-league teams. Also, improved co-operation with Major League Baseball helped to ensure that, for the most part, Canada's best players were available for Athens.

Canada had qualified for the Olympics by virtue of an 11-1 semi-final victory over Mexico in November 2003 at a qualifying tournament in Panama. Two teams were slated to advance to Athens from the Americas and, heading into Panama, the favorites were Cuba and the United States. Cuba made it through, but Team USA, in a major upset, was eliminated in the sudden-death quarter-finals by a 2-1 loss to Mexico. For Canada, its previous Olympic baseball appearances came in 1984 in Los Angeles and 1988 in Seoul, when baseball was a demonstration sport. (Canada did not participate when baseball was an exhibition sport at the Olympics in Paris in 1900, Stockholm in 1912, Berlin in 1936, Melbourne in 1956 and Tokyo in 1964.) So 2004 was Team Canada's first Olympics since baseball became a medal sport in 1992.

Few would have envisioned Canada in the Olympics when Bill MacKenzie took over at Baseball Canada. In 1978 he picked his national team without the benefit of a tryout camp or a scouting network in order to send a team to a tournament in Italy. "I was introducing myself to players on the flight," he said. "We didn't even have a budget for equip- ment." In those early years, MacKenzie exhibited the wisdom of Solomon and patience of Job to obtain complimentary equipment from the Blue Jays and the Expos. He remembers one year when the Expos agreed to provide bats, caps and warm-ups jackets, while the Jays said they'd pay for uniforms and 10 dozen balls. "But when the Jays learned that the Expos were involved, they reneged on their offer." So MacKenzie phoned Jim Fanning of the Expos, told him the situation and explained that, "on the record" the Expos could not be involved, "but send the stuff." Fanning agreed to the under-the-table deal, and when MacKenzie told the Jays the Expos were no longer involved, the Toronto team got back on side.

Before MacKenzie, Baseball Canada did not have any full-time employees. Among his first tasks was to create a bonafide development program so that Baseball Canada would qualify for federal funding. In 1986 the National Baseball Institute in Vancouver opened and by 2004 it had produced 14 big-league players. The development of a strong junior national program, due largely to the efforts of Greg Hamilton, and the strengthening of the National Team program not only produced a string of solid results internationally, but provided reachable goals for Canada's most talented players. The junior program has also provided a platform for Canada's brightest talents to be seen by college and professional recruiters, opening doors for many of them to go south to hone their game. In 2003, 114 Canadians were playing minor-pro ball, compared to 59 in 1992, which was almost double the count from 1990. And today, many of these players not only dream of a career in the majors, but of representing Team Canada at world championships and the Olympics. Of the 24 Canadian players in Athens, 23 had worn the Team Canada jersey before, including 10 who had played for the National Youth team.

• • •

Team Canada arrived in Athens to play on fields constructed on top of the old Athens Hellinikon airport, located in the shadow of a hill where Patriot missile launchers pointed skyward. They came to the land of Greek gods, of Aphrodite, Apollo, Hades, Hermes, Persephone, Poseidon and Zeus ... and were felled by the gods of baseball.

The gods of baseball play by simple rules. Some examples:

• On-the-screws line drives that find the shortstop's webbing—the ball resembling the top of a vanilla ice cream cone as it crests the top of the glove—are an out. But bloopers that kick up chalk down the foul line are doubles. Which ball was hit harder? Doesn't matter, the baseball gods say. Everything evens out.

• A bad strike call by the plate umpire? Not to worry, he'll miss one in your favor four innings later. Everything evens out.

• A botched double play ball that prevented Canada from being just four outs away from playing for an Olympic gold medal? No big deal, say the baseball gods ...

Well, actually, there may be reason to worry. There's no telling when, or if, Canada will be in position again to allow the baseball gods to even things out. Baseball is on Beijing's 2008 Olympic calendar, but you have to ask: can Canada qualify again? Will Team USA fail again to qualify?

Will Cuba cede its spot to Canada? With only two teams from the Americas guaranteed a berth in the Olympics, Canada must get past one of the baseball superpowers (although, for 2008, up to two additional spots could be earned by teams from the Americas through an additional wild-card qualifier). And after Beijing, who knows? As the Olympics keep growing larger, calls for fewer events become louder. Baseball is frequently listed among the expendable sports.

So 2004 may someday be remembered as Canada's best chance for glory. Canada went into its semi-final against Cuba looking for its first ever baseball medal, and Canada's first team-sport medal of any kind since 1936, when Canada lost to the United States in basketball to earn silver. This was the year. This was the time. But, ultimately, it will be remembered as the night the bullpen failed to hold a lead, and the potential tying run died on the track. Canada's 8-5 loss to Cuba—the product of six Cuban runs in the eighth followed by Nicholson's game-ending out at the wall—was a crushing blow. Canada had entered the game confident that Cuba could be beaten; after seven innings, it seemed they could be right.

"We got the match-up we wanted," Whitt said. "We know more about Cuba than Japan. Cuba had a good team, but they were beatable. Six outs from competing for gold or silver. ... Disappointing, disappointing."

• • •

Team Canada had assembled Aug. 1 at Toronto's SkyDome and headed to Baltimore for an exhibition game against Greece, then to Italy for a pre-Olympic tournament and then on to Athens. In all, Canada played 14 games, losing just four, twice each to Cuba and Japan's Dream Team.

In Italy, the Canadians learned that their No. 1 starter, lefty Jeff Francis, wouldn't be joining the Olympic team. As the Games began, Francis was pitching for the Colorado Rockies Triple-A farm team in Colorado Springs. Rockies general manager Dan O'Down refused to let Francis go to Athens, and instead, after two additional Triple-A starts, promoted him to the big club, where he would make his major-league debut in Atlanta on the day of the Olympic gold-medal game. The Francis disappointment came on the heels of Canada losing its clean-up hitter. Major League players were not eligible for the Olympics. To qualify for Athens, players had to be in the minors at the cut-off date, July 31. On July 10, Canadian Justin Morneau was elevated from Triple-A to hit in the No. 4 spot for the Minnesota Twins.

So the Canucks, missing their best pitcher and their best hitter, began their Olympic odyssey as 15-1 longshots, behind Cuba, the 4-5 favorites, and even-money Japan. They understood that their hopes rested not on individual performances, but on how they could play as a team. To that end, the lavish opening ceremonies became a unifying event, providing a boost of confidence and nationalism.

"Walking into that stadium is about coming out together as Canadians," Radmanovich said. "My first major-league home run was great, but this was something else."

In the massive mingling of athletes from around the world, Radmanovich met U.S. hoops star Lisa Leslie and tennis star Andy Roddick. Peter Orr and Chris Begg had pictures taken with NBA stars Yao Ming and Tim Duncan. Orr and Phil Devey bookended tennis legend Martina Navratilova in a photo. Adam Stern had his picture taken with Nigerian boxers, Kenyan runners and Team USA volleyball players. "We were all so proud to be Canadian at that moment," said Jeremy Ware.

The adrenaline rush of opening night was a prelude of things to come. The Canadians were anything but intimidated by the eight-team field. They had beaten Greece in an exhibition game in Baltimore, and in Italy they'd beaten The Netherlands, Cuba, Italy and Chinese Taipei. That success carried over to Athens, where Canada opened the round-robin at 4-0 with wins over Chinese Taipei, Italy, The Netherlands and Greece. After losses to Cuba (5-2) and Japan (9-1), Canada closed the round-robin on a high note, whipping Australia 11-0 to finish with a 5-2 record to set up their sudden-death semi-final against Cuba to decide who would play for gold.

Canadian ballplayers hate the Cubans. There is no other way to put. For many years, when Canada was a struggling baseball nation, the powerful Cubans delighted in running up scores and showboating. In 1967, after a rare Canadian win over Cuba at the Pan-Am Games, infielder Maurice Oaks of Gladstone, Manitoba strode to the mound and played taps on his trumpet. Almost four decades later, the ill will remained. When Canada thumped Cuba 9-1 in a pre-Olympic game, left fielder Jeff Guiel had a run-in at the plate with Cuban catcher Ariel Pestano, which led to Guiel getting plunked by the Cuban pitcher in the eighth and Canadian Chris Mears retaliating in the ninth. Over the years there had been many similar incidents, so it was not in the true spirit of Olympic brotherhood that they lined up in Athens.

Cuba jumped to a 2-0 first-inning lead before starter Shawn Hill, who had made three starts for the Montreal Expos earlier in the season, settled down to hold the Cubans to just one hit and no runs over the next five innings. Canada finally got on the scoreboard in the third, courtesy of a two-out single by Andy Stewart that scored Peter Orr. Stewart was an unlikely hero. The day before the semi-final, when the hitting groups were posted for batting practice, Stewart saw that he was listed in the first group, which meant he would be starting against Cuba. Whitt had been going with the left-handed hitting Simon Pond at DH, but switched to the right-handed hitting Stewart.

It had been a lot of time between hacks for the 24-year-old Stewart. In 1999, he was the hero of the Pan-Am Games in Winnipeg, as the gritty baseball team, thanks largely to Stewart, became the story of the Games. In the opener, he hit a three-run homer to help Canada to an improbable 7-6 win over Team USA in 11 innings. In all, Stewart hit four homers and knocked in 15 runs, more than four other countries scored, as Canada won the bronze medal.

For the next two seasons Stewart was the bullpen catcher for the Toronto Blue Jays. Then he managed Single-A Williamsport, of the Pittsburgh Pirates organization, in 2002-03. When Canada qualified for Athens in November of 2003, Stewart wanted to make a comeback, so he signed with the Winnipeg Goldeyes of the independent Northern League and eventually worked his way onto the Olympic team. Canada, noted for its left-handed hitters, had qualified in Panama with seven left-handers. Asked at the time if he considered other options, Whitt replied: "Well, I could have gone with eight left-handed hitters." Adding Stewart to the lineup against Cuba gave Whitt three right-handed hitters, Stewart, short-stop Danny Klassen and left fielder Jeremy Ware.

Cuba held its 2-1 lead until the fifth, when Adam Stern knocked in two runs with a single to right-centre to put Canada ahead, 3-2. Canada was forced to make a pitching change after six innings when Hill reached 84 pitches. Hill was coming off an elbow injury and the Expos had given him permission to participate in the Olympics on the condition that Team Canada agree to limit him to two starts and adhere to a pitch count of 85 to 90 pitches an outing. So Chris Begg took over and worked a scoreless seventh.

As the Cubans came to the plate in the bottom of the eighth, Canada ahead 3-2, we were sitting four rows behind the backstop across the aisle from Gary Hughes, executive assistant to Jim Hendry, general manager of the Chicago Cubs.

"Well, kiddo, what do you think?" we wondered aloud.

"As I say to Jim Hendry about five nights a week, it's awfully hard to win a ball game," Hughes replied. Canada was about to find that out.

The eighth opened with Cuban shortstop Eduardo Paret touching Begg for a single. Begg needed a double-play ground ball, and he got it—the ground ball, that is. Third baseman Peter Orr, normally a sure-handed infielder, fielded the ball and threw to second, hoping to start a double play, but feeling certain to get at least one out. Instead, the throw sailed into right field. With one errant throw, the complexion of the game was suddenly changed. Instead of possibly two out with none on, there were two on and none out. The next batter, Yulieski Gourriel, Cuba's No. 3

hitter, singled to left to tie the game. Whitt turned to reliever Chris Mears to face clean-up hitter Osmani Urrutia, and the Canadian got a strikeout for the first out. But three consecutive base hits moved Cuba into a 6-3 lead. Canada got its second out with a force at the plate, and almost got out of the inning when Klassen and Orr both came within a stride of catching a foul pop-up. But, given a second life, Paret hit a two-run single and Cuba took an 8-3 lead into the ninth.

In the disastrous eighth, the Canadians had given up six hits and six runs, while making one error. Time to warm up the bus? Not quite. Remember what we said about the character of Canadian baseball players? They sometimes fall short on talent, but never on desire. The ninth inning was going to put that maxim to a test. The first sign came early, and it wasn't subtle. Ryan Radmanovich led off with a homer to right.

"It would have been easy for our guys to go down 1-2-3," Whitt said. "A lot of teams would have folded after the six-run eighth. Like I've always said, this is a blue-collar team."

Todd Betts and Orr followed with singles before Cuba got two outs, Stubby Clapp on a ground ball and Klassen on a strikeout. One out from elimination, Canada made it 8-5 when Betts scored on a passed ball. Then Laforest worked a walk to bring Nicholson, representing the potential tying run, to the plate for Canada's fateful final at-bat.

As heart-breaking, kick-in-the-stomach Olympic experiences go, the Nicholson blast that died on the track was as painful to watch as someone tripping over the first hurdle in the 100-metre final, as Canada's Perdita Felicien did the same night.

Who to blame? Orr, who made the error in the eighth that led to three unearned runs? Begg, who allowed five singles to the eight hitters he faced? Whitt, who allowed Begg to go too long?

As for Orr ...

"The play is still in my head; it sucks," Orr said. "I didn't field it clean. I thought I had the ball in my fingers to make a good throw, but I was wide right. We probably wouldn't have got two, but getting the guy at second would have made things easier for us."

On the eve of the semi-final, seven games into the tournament, Whitt was asked to name his biggest surprises to date. "Pete Orr has been outstanding, both ways. He might have been our best player in Italy, and Danny Klassen has been so solid."

Prior to that fateful eighth inning in the semi-final, Orr had handled 26 chances flawlessly in the Olympics, plus 10 more opportunities in the pre-Olympic tournament in Italy. He came to the Olympic team with a reputation of sure-handedness. At Triple-A Richmond, he made just three errors in 114 games in 2004, handling 470 chances, a

.994 fielding percentage.

As for Begg …

"It's my job to get outs," Begg said. "The ground ball hurt, but it was not irreparable damage. At the time, I'm thinking. 'It's not any big deal. I'll just get another ground ball.' It was all my fault. I failed to get another ground ball, so we could turn two."

As for Whitt …

Did the manager stick with Begg for too long in the eighth? "They're entitled to say that, I'm the manager," Whitt said. "But Chris Begg did his job. He got us a ground ball." If that ground ball had been fielded cleanly and had Canada turned the double play, Canada would have been four outs away from playing for the gold medal. Begg certainly was not over-extended. It was his seventh outing for Canada and it the sixth time he was asked to work two innings.

Maybe no one is to blame. Baseball can be very unfair for the way it zeroes in on one play, one at-bat, or one swing in a close game. Often over-looked are the at-bats that preceded the crucial moment. For instance, forgotten amid the hits off Begg and the error by Orr was that Canada stranded nine base runners, including coming away with nothing in the second when it had runners on first and third with one out. In all, Canada was 2-for-11 hitting with men in scoring position, and had just two two-out hits. The talent-rich Cubans, on the other hand, were 6-for-15 with runners in scoring position and had 13 hits over-all.

And then there was the wind. What if it hadn't been blowing so hard? Or been blowing in? Or what if the pitch Nicholson hit was traveling at just one more mile-per-hour of velocity, or Nicholson's swing was a millisecond quicker, or struck the bat a millimeter higher or lower?

Cuban manager Higinio Velez said afterwards on watching Nicholoson's swing: "I thought it was a home run."

"I thought it was a home run, too," Whitt said. "That ball Nicholson hit reminded me of Jim Sundberg's against (the Blue Jays) in the deciding game of the American League Championship Series against the Kansas City Royals in 1985." But Sundberg's ball kept carrying, hitting the top of the fence for a triple that eliminated the Jays.

Nicholson's blast missed by inches, and the loss meant Canada had to get ready to play Japan, 1-0 losers to Australia in their semi, in the bronze-medal game. It was like losing the deciding game of the World Series and being told to be ready for a game at 10 a.m. the next morning. Worse still, had Japan beaten the Aussies, Canada could have lost to Cuba and gone into a game against Australia with an excellent shot at a medal.

"We got back to the village at 2 a.m. and had a 6 a.m. wake-up. I know we're all professionals, but it was tough to bounce back from that,"

Radmanovich said. "We were taking batting practice before the bronze-medal game and no one wanted to look out to the left-field wall. It's not a memory you want to keep in your mind, but I'll always see the Cuban left fielder snow-coning that ball for the third out."

Japan beat Canada 11-2 in front of 4,145 fans as the Japanese pros scored six times in 2 1/3 innings against starter Mike Johnson, who had beaten Mexico twice to get Canada to Athens. He had done his part. A few hours later, Cuba, as expected, beat Australia 6-2 in the final, but by then the Olympics were already just a memory for the Canadians. But what kind of a memory?

There are 135 countries registered with the International Baseball Federation. Canada finished fourth out of 135. Yes, it was the dreaded fourth, one step from the medal podium. Yet it was an achievement worth noting because it showed the world how far Canada has progressed in the past 20 years. Just by qualifying for Athens, Team Canada achieved more than any national team before it.

"The Olympics were mostly a high note," Whitt said. "It's a good memory, a great memory, even though we were so close and let it slip away. Think of it, qualifying out of the Americas with all those good countries. Qualifying in Panama was quite a feather in the cap for Canada. Canada has some great young players. Hopefully, it won't be the last time Canada qualifies for the Olympics."

There are the memories of Panama, Italy, Athens, the nine straight wins, the six-run eighth and the Nicholson blast. It's difficult to quantify the long-term impact on Canadian baseball as a result of Canada's Olympic experience, or what the impact could have been had Nicholson's blast gone over the wall, but with large television audiences fueling coast to coast interest, it seems likely that in households across the country a future generation of Olympians (and major leaguers?) was taking notice. The Canadians failed to win a medal but they fought for one to the final swing of the bat. On a blustery night in Athens, Zeus, the Greek god of weather, conspired with the baseball gods to command that Nicholson's ball stay in the park. After making giant strides, Team Canada came up inches short. But they played hard to the end, demonstrating passion, grit and determination. The Canadian way.

3

SATURDAYS AT BERT VINCE'S SMOKE SHOP

Growing up in Kingston, Ontario meant a Saturday morning, winter ritual—a leisurely visit to Bert Vince's Smoke Shop on Princess Street that might last two or three hours. My father would shoot the breeze with Vince, a speedy outfielder who once played for the Kingston Ponies in the Central Ontario Baseball League but who now manned the cash register in his store. When not tending to customers, he'd match father story for story, memory for memory and laugh for laugh.

"Remember the night ..." was the way one sentence after another would start. Or during a lull in the conversation someone would say, "How 'bout the time ...?" The tales went far beyond being repetitive, but there was a gentle rhythm to what was said. A left-right, left-right cadence ... not of a platoon of soldiers marching in boot camp but of two friends strolling down memory lane.

On Sundays we'd attend Cooke's United Church, but these Saturday stories were my hymns. They'd clank around my cranium until they found a home. They're still there, evoking warm feelings, a father welcoming a son into such wonderful memories.

From father to son.

Often, American seam-head friends who write about baseball ask how does a Canadian get a passion for baseball when everyone in Canada is so hockey minded. The love affair began in Kingston, Canada's first capital. The baseball roots go back to grandpa, Edwin (Chaucer) Elliott.

Chaucer played for Concord and Lowell, Massachusetts in the New England League in 1899. Then he played for the Kingston Ponies and, in 1902, was signed by Ed Barrow, who later ran the New York Yankees, to play for the Toronto Maple Leafs of the Eastern League. Released, he returned to play in Kingston. The *Toronto Telegram* wrote: *"Looks to me like a Canadian has no chance. Looks to me like the motto is chuck the Canadians but hang onto the hired men from across the border, whether they are good or not. If Elliott had been dealt with fairly he would have been given the chance to show what he could do in warm weather. Elliott is quite as good as many who have graced the field and a good deal better than some."*

Chaucer headed south again and played outfield for Concord in the New England League, hitting .182 in seven games, as well as with Amsterdam, Johnstown and Gloversville in the New York State League in 1904. Then he moved on to Knotty Lee's Brantford team in the Western Ontario League in 1905. (This was the same Knotty Lee whose hotel in Smiths Falls became our stopping-off point on the way to Ottawa Rough Riders football games in the 1950s.) The next year, Chaucer was with Oswego, New York, of the Empire State League and, named manager in 1907, he hit .275 in 71 games to guide Oswego to the Empire League championship. In 1910, he helped organize the Canadian League, and in 1911 was playing manager of the St. Thomas Saints, where he hit .287 in 87 games.

Baseball, apparently, didn't take up all his time. Chaucer was inducted into the Hockey Hall of Fame in Toronto in 1961 as a referee. He studied medicine at Queen's University in Kingston, where he was also captain of the Golden Gaels football team for two years. It was at Queen's that my grandfather earned his nickname Chaucer in recognition of his scholarly ability to quote the classics and his knowledge of the English language. He passed neither talent to his grandson. Chaucer's love of baseball caused him to leave university a year before graduation when Kingston entered a team in the New York State League. Chaucer also played football for the Kingston Granites, who won the Canadian championship in 1899, and coached football, the Toronto Argos in 1906, and later the same year took the Hamilton Tigers to a Dominion championship, where they defeated the McGill University Redmen. Never one to stay in one place, Chaucer was named coach of the Montreal Amateur Athletic Association football team in 1907 and a year later was named advisor for all sports for the Montreal AAA.

Chaucer excelled at football and baseball and played some hockey, but it was officiating hockey where his reputation as a "true sportsman" grew. He began refereeing in the Ontario Hockey Association in 1903 and for 10 years was an in-demand official called in to work series marred by fighting. He suffered a groin injury working an OHA final between Orillia and the Toronto Canoe Club in 1912, and a short time late was diagnosed with cancer. A New York doctor suggested amputating his leg, but Chaucer refused. He died March 13, 1913 at age 34. Obituaries appeared in newspapers from Brantford to Hamilton to Toronto to Kingston to Oswego to Montreal.

Father was three years old.

"Chaucer was a debonair dresser as a referee," said Bill Fitsell, official historian of the International Hockey Hall of Fame in Kingston. "I have a clipping from a Montreal paper and the cartoon shows him wearing a blue serge suit and a caveat tie. You could say he was the Don Cherry of his day."

Grandpa's athletic genes went right to father. He was good at everything—basketball, baseball, football—everything but hockey, although on a bet he did make the Golden Gaels hockey team one year. He played flying wing for the football Gaels in 1929, 1930, 1931 and 1934, winning titles in every year but 1931. (He missed the 1932 and 1933 seasons when he lost his left eye after a player threw some mud after practice at George Richardson Stadium and it hit him in the eye.)

Father later coached the Gaels in 1945 and 1947, and was inducted into the Queen's Hall of Fame. (Me? I got lost a few times and drove by the university.) Father also curled in the 1960 Brier in Port Arthur, Ontario, as vice for Jake Edwards' Ontario rink, which went into the final day tied with Ernie Richardson's Saskatchewan rink before losing the national title. Yet, despite success at football, playing basketball at Queen's and curling, baseball was my father's game.

After playing for Kingston teams until 1928, he was good enough by age 19 to land summer jobs in mining towns that had baseball teams, towns like Delora in 1929-30 and Creighton Mines, 1931-92. He was with Brockville in 1933 and the Smiths Falls Railroaders in 1934-35.

Father never kept scrapbooks. The type of clippings my mother or aunt would paste in a scrapbook, father saved in his memory. One night my sister Elizabeth found a small poster in an old trunk, the kind shopkeepers used to stick in their store windows. It read:

Sunday 1 p.m.
Auburn vs. the Railroaders
Playoffs
BOB ELLIOTT WILL PLAY
The last line was deliberately set in larger type. The story goes that, at the time, father was recovering from the loss of his eye. He was a right-handed hitter without a left eye, his lead eye when standing in the batter's box, which caused him to struggle at the plate. The team owner had planned to drop him from the playoff roster, but the rest of the team said they wouldn't play without him. The owner relented. Hence, the additional line on the poster.

"Ah, I went hitless," we remembered him saying.

He returned home to play for the Kingston Ponies until 1938 and continued managing and coaching for the next three decades while filling out his days as a manager at the Alcan forge plant.

"Your father was Mr. Baseball in Kingston from the 1920s to the 1960s," Ron Bearance, who played for father, once told me. Ron and his brother Elmer ran a grocery story on Union Street, one more stop where my father and his friends would trade stories and debate.

My job as a sports writer has taken me to every major-league park on the continent, but Kingston is where I learned the game. I learned it at the Cricket Field from Keith Weese or Billy Kyle. Or at Megaffin Stadium with Clyde Harris, Bobby Gilmour and Guy White. Mostly, though, I learned while sitting in the back seat of a car returning from Belleville or Peterborough, listening to Cliffy Earl and father discuss the whys and wherefores of the recently concluded game. I remember one time listening to father convince Tom Carty he should switch positions to make the team stronger. Carty said he agreed after 10 minutes, but the talk lasted almost two hours.

For the vast majority of Canadians who play the game of baseball, it's all about friendships and memories. Father made many of both, which he shared with his son, as I now share with mine. As a boy, one of my favorite places was the bottom rung of the newsstand, the latest copy of *The Sporting News* on my lap, looking for Wigwam Wisps, the paper's notes on my favorite team, the Milwaukee Braves. Walking and chewing gum was easy. Reading about Hank Aaron and Eddie Mathews and Warren Spahn and Lew Burdette while listening to a Hewitt Smith/Mickey Compeau story for the 54th time and making sure not one line was left by the wayside, was not easy. The stories rolled on like a gentle stream. Everyone already knew the final destination. There couldn't be any detours, so I read and listened.

"Remember the time," one of the adults would say, "we were playing Peterborough, a drunk kept yelling at Mickey Compeau when they were making a pitching change?"

Both men would laugh. I'd chuckle. I knew where we were headed (as father would often say to friends like Earl or Butsy Gray, "Bet you saw that one coming like a yellow cab driving the wrong way on a one-way street with its lights on, both doors open and its blinkers flashing"). The yellow cab in this story was Compeau, a smooth fielding shortstop who normally Hoovered infields from Kingston and Belleville to Oshawa and Peterborough, whether they had been dragged or were a garden of pebbles. Yet, if rowdy fans got under Compeau's thin skin, well, the Ponies might as well play without a shortstop. Ground balls to short were fielded by the left fielder.

"You stink Compeau, you rotten, no good ----". Remember, this was the early 1930s. Times were different. They called them the dirty thirties for lots of reasons. You fill in the blank.

On this particular day, third baseman Hewitt Smith, the on-deck hitter, walked over to the loud-mouth drunk behind the plate and told him to shut the hell up. "Smitty told him off with a string of four-letter words," my father would say, doing a poor impression of Foster Brooks before any of us knew who Foster Brooks was, "and the drunk slurred and says 'whooooo's (burp) going to (belch) make me?'"

As the story was building towards its peak, I lay down *The Sporting News*. Mathews and Aaron could wait.

"Smitty said, 'Look, shut your yap. I'm not telling you again,' and the silly drunk, still behind the regular screen, leaned around and placed his face up against this little old rusty screen mesh, like you'd find at a cottage, and yelled 'let's see (burp) youuuuu (belch) try old man.' Smitty didn't need to be invited twice. He popped the guy right in the kisser. The drunk was cut and bleeding with little checkerboard squares on both cheeks, his nose and his forehead. That was the end of that. Mickey had a hell of a game."

And Vince would interject, "until we told him after the game what had happened and then he got mad at Smitty, telling him 'I don't need any help from you, ya big palooka. I can look after my own self.'"

And then, there would be an argument about whether Gerry Arniel, grandfather of future NHLer Scott, knocked in the winning run on a 2-1 pitch or a 1-1 count. Eventually, either Bert or my father would yield: "Didn't matter. We beat those lugs."

Those were the times. Words that were originally spoken in the 1930s were repeated 30 years later as if they'd been carefully preserved and transported by a time machine. Usually, after a particularly good yarn like the Smitty story, father would buy a Cola-Cola and, after a long sip and a look out the window, he'd start again.

"Remember the night, after winning the Central Ontario Baseball League final, we went to London for the Ontario final ...?" They'd debate the score of the opener, how they'd won in Kingston and how the best-of-three series moved to London. It was either decided by Vince saying "you're right Knobber," "you're wrong Knobber," or "Knobber, it doesn't really matter."

Father was called Knobber because of his knobby knees.

"We lost the second game when Joe Corkey was charged with a passed ball," he would recall. The loss meant an overnight stay for Game 3. The small-towners headed to London's Western Fair Raceway. They knew little of handicapping. They knew a lot about omens. About the third or fourth race, they spotted a long shot named Joe's Mistake.

Catcher Joe Corkey's passed ball was the reason they were there. It was fate.

"So, we're gathering up money to plunk it all down on Joe's Mistake," Bert would say, "and then Yip Radley, the only one of us who had been to the races more than once, starts knocking the horse, how he had no chance and how he was moving up in class. Eventually, he talked us into betting on the horse he liked."

Time again to put down *The Sporting News*. The story was peaking.

"So, what happens? Joe's Mistake wins at 25-1 and the horse we bet is up the track. How many times did we mention that to Yip on the drive from London to Kingston?"

Eventually, it would be time to move on, usually because the store would get busy, so father and I would walk up to the corner, turn right, and right again onto Queen Street to arrive at Harv Milne's Bicycle Repair Shop. Neither one of us had ever ridden or owned a bike, so we weren't going in to get one fixed. But Milne had played for the Ponies, coached by my father. So we were off on Round 2. "Afternoon Harvest," father would say to Harv, for he never ever called anyone by their real name.

Father did a little bird-dogging in the old days for the Cleveland Indians. He even had a business card, which was the extent of his reimbursement. He tipped the Indians off on right-hander Jack Stone, who was signed and went to Marianna in the Single-A Florida State league in 1950. Stone, or "Stoney" as he was called, could also hit.

"Remember the day we were all in Cain's pool hall on the corner of Montreal and Princess and someone ran in with the latest issue of *The Sporting News* from Bert Vince's?" Milne would begin. "What a day that was."

Everyone crowded around the paper to check the Class-D league leaders. This was pre-Internet days. So what if the paper was two weeks old? It was great reading.

"Yep, there was Stoney, the sixth best earned run average in the league. Then someone spotted him seventh amongst the Top 10 hitters. They had him catching when he wasn't pitching. Were the fellas ever excited for Stoney."

All the boys celebrated with a bottle of Coke and toasted Stoney's success.

Then "the fellas" told stories about Stoney getting them out at the Cricket Field on that nasty fastball, which he could locate the way kids today fire pitches on Nintendo. Others told of the night they thought they had second base stolen "easy," on a curve ball in the dirt ... yet Stoney, catching, back handed the ball, recovered and threw out the runner at second. But, whereas Smitty popping a drunk left them feeling proud and cheerful, and Joe's Mistake left them laughing at themselves, the Stoney hymn did not have a happy ending. We always wished the ending could change, but it was like watching *Old Yeller* or any movie with a sad ending. It never did.

Usually, there was a short silence before the story shifted into its second chapter. From Cain's pool hall, the boys moved out to the street to start heading for home. They were still giddy over seeing Stoney, one of their own, having so much success in Florida and being recognized in that old issue of *The Sporting News*.

"How far did you walk that day Knobber, four blocks?" Milne would ask, shaking his head. We all knew what was coming.

"Naw, it was only three," father would say, wondering what might have been. "I get to the corner of Barrie and am waiting for the light. The light changes, I'm walking across and there, coming towards me, was Stoney. I stopped dead in my tracks."

Stoney had been stricken by a common baseball disease: homesickness. So he quit the game, came home and took a job driving a bus for Colonial Coach. It was difficult to fathom. The boys would have given just about anything for a shot at a pro baseball career. Left unasked was the question on the lips of every one of them: Was the pro ball lifestyle that rough or was Stoney that lonely?

"Your pop was upset with me at first, real upset," Stoney told me years later after he'd made a comeback in 1971 with the Ponies. "I never saw anyone that upset until I used to make the Toronto-Montreal run in the snow, arrive six minutes late, and get yelled at by the people waiting to pick up relatives. It might have been clear in downtown Montreal, but from Oshawa to Dorval was a snowstorm. Anyway, a couple of days later your father said that if I thought it was the right decision for my life, then it was the right decision to come home. He said it didn't matter what anyone else thought."

One morning reading *The Sporting News* we fell in love with the word "of." There, in 1958, was Ted Bowsfield, "of" Vernon, British Columbia, pitching for the Boston Red Sox. Canadians could play in the majors? Wow! We didn't know that. Then came Claude Raymond *of* St. Jean, Quebec with the Chicago White Sox, followed by Georges Miranda *of* Levis, Quebec with the San Francisco Giants, and then Ken Mackenzie *of* Gore Bay, Ontario with the Milwaukee Braves.

When father and his friends told stories it reminded us of a scene from a movie in which the elders of a native Indian band were sitting and talking about memorable battles ... and every story had to start at the start. Likewise, the baseball stories never started off with talk about a player's best game. They'd start at the start ("his parents lived on York Street, didn't they?"), then the background ("played for the Circle Six, no it was the Kingston Giants and then the Aluminum Co.") to reach the end ("and he joined us in 1928").

One year the Ponies added a right-hander, Bud Clancy, an import from Philadelphia. Wally Elmer, Vinnie McQuaide, father and others met him in New York to bring him north. This was a regular hymn and a racy one at that.

"We get there and we're supposed to meet Clancy the next day at our hotel," father said. "So, we're walking along and we see the sign that Cab Calloway is singing at Minsky's Burlesque. We're seated in the second last row of the balcony. Vinnie said to someone 'what kind of dang costumes are those dancin' gals wearing, it looks like they aren't wearing nothin'.' Someone said 'Vinnie they aren't costumes.'"

McQuaide, later the bravest member of the Kingston police force, was one of the quickest outfielders ever to play in Kingston. If we'd heard the Minsky's story once, we've heard it 50 times and it always ended the same way: "No one ever saw Vin move so quick; he went right down to the front row of the balcony. The usher tried to move him and he gave him two bits to let him sit in the aisle."

No place was out of bounds for storytelling, including our house at the corner of Johnson and College. Ted Reeve would stop by for some Hudson's Bay or Myers rum and talk Queen's football. Jack Adams, who ran the Detroit Red Wings and spent his summers in nearby Napanee, would visit to talk baseball. National Hockey League referee Eddie Powers would come by after working a pre-season or Eastern Professional Hockey League game to talk baseball. Former players father coached and players father played with all had their own hymns, but they loved the oldies.

"Tell the one about Smitty popping that guy when you guys were playing Oshawa," we remember Justin Sullivan asking one night on the front steps. Oshawa? My heart skipped. This was not the verse I had learned.

"Ah, wasn't it against Peterborough?" I asked, shyly.

"Yes, it was Peterborough. Anyway some drunk is yelling at Mickey ..." and on the story would roll. Back on track. My first foray into the story-telling world of adults had been a success.

If there wasn't a game or practice Saturday afternoon, we remember watching Dizzy Dean and Pee Wee Reese on the *Game of the Week*. ("Dad why do they call it a foul pole, if the ball is a home run if it hits it?") We remember Nellie Fox of the Chicago White Sox hitting a lead-off triple in the bottom of the 10th, and me proclaiming confidently that the game was over, the Sox were about to beat father's hated New York Yankees.

"You just jinxed them," father said.

The Yanks walked the next two hitters, Sherman Lollar hit a come-backer for a 1-2-3 double play and the next hitter popped up. Bobby Richardson's single over the outstretched glove of Fox won it the next inning for the Yanks. "Not only are the Yanks good, but they are so damn lucky," father said.

We remember watching John Romano of the Cleveland Indians arguing with the plate ump for a number of innings. Eventually someone hit a foul ball that Romano had no chance to catch. Yet Romano turned as if intent to chase down the ball and bowled over the ump. "Man," I said, "did Romano every misjudge that." "No," said father, "I think he hit the target he was looking for, the umpire."

In football season, we'd make road trips to Ottawa to see the Rough Riders of the Canadian Football League. Mother seldom came, saying "I can't fathom how you two can turn a two-hour, one-way drive into an eight-hour trip." Actually, four hours was a quick trip one way. We'd stop in Smiths Falls, either at Bill Cowley's Rideau Hotel or George (Knotty) Lee's Lee Hotel. Sometimes we'd stop at both, and sometimes we'd go 0-for-2. Cowley was the former Boston Bruins centreman, spending 12 seasons in Boston. He loved talking baseball. He was good friends with Johnny Pesky. Father's favorite team was the Boston Red Sox and his favorite player was Ted Williams.

"Five years! Five years in the prime of his career because he was serving his country," father or Cowley would say, referring to two stints by Williams in the U.S. armed forces. "Who knows how many homers he would have finished up with?" the other would say.

Lee ran a number of teams and was in Cooperstown July 9, 1939 for the first minor-league all-star game. At the time he was managing the Ogdensburg Colts. A favorite tale about Lee involved the time he was running Peterborough's team and the Kingston Ponies eliminated them from the Central Ontario Baseball League playoffs. After the final game, Kingston's Joe Daley, seeing his team was running low on bats, strolled across the diamond to see if he could buy a few from Peterborough. Lee picked up as many of the thick-barreled pieces of lumbers that he could in his two hands and tossed them onto the field.

"Take 'em, take for free," Lee hollered, then he turned to his dugout. "There sure as hell aren't any hits in them, least none that these jaybird hayseeds could find."

Leaving the Falls, where father played for the Railroaders, we always stopped at Gibson's Drive-thru for a chilled mug of root beer. Hymns I had not heard before would be recited. Questions would be asked. Occasionally we'd talk about the Rough Riders. At the time, Russ Jackson and Ron Lancaster, a pair of future CFL Hall of Famers, shared quarterbacking duties. A fan would jump up after a Jackson incompletion and yell: "Put in Lancaster!" Two unsuccessful passes later the same fan would yell even louder: "Put Jackson back in!"

Summers revolved around baseball.

• Fielding ground balls on College Street. We used rubber balls on loan from George Binnington's batting cage, which, come to think of it, have yet to be returned. You learned quickly to get your rear end down because, unless the rubber ball was on an angle so it hit the curb or a car, it would roll for a block and a half.

• Playing second base for Jimmy McLaughlin's Tigers in the Kingscourt Little League.

• Joining father at his team's practice, working as a foul ball chaser, and then being promoted to bat boy at father's games. I'd try to stay out of the way, but I couldn't get much closer to the action than this. Father was coaching the Kingston Dunbricks of the Kingston Baseball Association. About four games into the 1964 season, players were talking about Buddy Aylesworth's reaction to a missed strike call followed by the next pitch that knocked off his cap, just like Charlie Brown. Aylesworth must have lost the ball in the twilight because he didn't react until after the ball had sailed by him. But unlike the stories from years gone by, the Aylesworth incident had happened just two nights previous. A new hymn was written and sung for the first time, and I'd seen it unfold and could sing it myself.

It was a wonderful gift that father gave son, to come to practice, lug the bats, put in the bases and line the field. It was heaven.

During batting practice I'd stand behind the pitcher and catch the throws in from the outfield. If it was a left-handed hitter, I stood on the third base side, right-handed hitter on the first-base side. Best to stay out of harm's way. Afterwards some oldtimer would say "you Knobber's kid?" And I'd nod. Then, he'd explain how years before he'd been at the Cricket Field when father smashed a ball that sailed up the gently sloping hill in left field and through the trees before it splashed down in the courthouse fountain.

In 1965-66, father coached the Edwards Ford Mustangs, a junior team playing in the Kingston Baseball Association, which was comprised mostly of senior teams. They took their lumps to start with, especially playing the Wolfe Island Bridge Boosters. Kingston to Wolfe Island was a ferry ride of about 25 minutes. One night we pulled off an upset on Wolfe Island. Most of the excited players went to the back of the boat where it was cooler and where father was telling stories. Even some new ones.

Just as we pulled into Kingston, father said: "This reminds me of the night we played in Toronto and it must have been over 100 degrees. I'm catching. We go out for the 12th or 13th, no it was the 12th, no wait a sec' it was the 13th, ah, it doesn't matter. We had a chance to score and didn't, so everyone is upset. Our guy, who is running out of gas, throws the first pitch, a perfect strike, right down the middle and just as the ball is about 10 feet from the plate, the ump screams 'TIME, TIME, TIME!!!' I turn around and get right in his face: 'How can you call time, my guy is working his butt off to throw a strike in this heat, and then he does and you have the gall to call TIME?"

Father chuckled and then laughed aloud.

"What happened," asked right-hander Elwood Johnston. "Why did he call time?" wondered second baseman Bobby Gilmour.

"Well," father said sheepishly, "in the heat, I had forgotten to put on my mask and the ump didn't want the guy swinging, fouling one back and hitting me smack in the puss. He didn't want me to lose my good looks. He did me a favor. It was a long, long walk to the bench to get my mask."

Laughter enveloped our group but, rather than subsiding as you'd expect, it grew louder and louder. The man they looked up to was human and made mistakes. Suddenly, the laughter stopped. The ferry's engines were firing. We had cast off from Kingston and were headed *back* to Wolfe Island. So enthralled was our group by father's story that we had sat through the docking, unloading and re-loading of the ferry. So we settled in for another ferry ride, and for more stories.

First baseman Guy White asked father: "What's your greatest accomplishment in baseball?" Father told of the Ponies playing an exhibition game at Camp Drum, a U.S. Army base near Watertown, New York, in 1944. Red Schoendienst was the best on the Army team.

"Our knuckleballer, Jake Edwards, was pitching," father said, "and I threw Red out attempting to steal on a knuckleball." That was big news. Schoendienst went on to play 19 years in the Major Leagues and is in the Hall of Fame. But it was unlike father to boast, so we suspected a punch line might be coming. "Yep," he continued about his greatest accomplishment, "it had to be throwing out a future Hall of Famer at second on a knuckler ... or making two return trips to Wolfe Island with you bunch of lumps."

The ball talk was endless, the debates nonstop, swirling around places like Megaffin Stadium or the Cricket Field. One of most persistent debates concerned father. The late Gord Wood, who played first base for father and won four Memorial Cups (three with the Cornwall Royals and one with the Ottawa 67s), used to say "the prime debate was over who was the best player Kingston ever produced: Knobber Elliott or Del Cherry."

Del Cherry, whose son Donald S. went on to some fame as an NHL coach and TV commentator, was a 6-foot-2, 234-pound outfielder who covered a lot of ground. Long before Don, I had heard of Del. His was a Kingston legend and his story was a bonafide hymn. One year at the Cricket Field, playing for the Ponies, he won $1,000 worth of prizes for leading the Kingston Baseball Association in average, homers, RBIs and slugging percentage.

Del passed his baseball genes to his two sons. Don and Dick both excelled at baseball and were "players of great promise," according to Brooklyn Dodgers scout Hal Southworth. Don turned down a minor league spot in the Dodgers chain to focus on hockey. But he broke a leg sliding into second at the Cricket Field in July of 1953. The injury cost him a chance to make the Bruins blue line, but he had a long minor league hockey career before his years as coach of the Boston Bruins. Dick, too, opted for a hockey career and proved to be the best hockey player in the family, spending two years with the Philadelphia Flyers.

"The best player I ever saw was either Lorne Ferguson or Charlie Pester," Donald S. told us. "Goose hit them a long way and so did Ferg."

Ferguson played parts of 10 seasons in the NHL with the Boston Bruins, Detroit Red Wings and Chicago Black Hawks. Pester was signed by the Toronto Maple Leafs baseball team, sent to Dubuque, went to camp with the Toronto Argos, once scored 100 points in a basketball game and some of his high school track and field marks at Kingston Collegiate still stand.

And where do the sons of Knobber Elliott and Del Cherry stand on that greatest Kingston athlete debate?

"I never saw my father play," Cherry said.

Ditto.

● ● ●

Friends often ask what's the most exciting game I've ever seen. Was it the night in Atlanta when Mike Timlin fielded Otis Nixon's bunt and threw to Joe Carter for the final out to give the Blue Jays their first World Series in 1992? Or was it a year later when Carter homered off Mitch Williams to end the 1993 World Series, only the second World Series to end on a homer?

No and no.

The most exciting game I ever saw was Arty Leeman pitching a no-hitter for father's Kingston Lakeview Indians in Oakville to wrap up the Ontario Baseball Association semi-final in straight games at Wallace Park in 1967. Leeman took the mound with a 2-0 lead, thanks to a home run by Charlie Pester. At the end of Leeman's warmup, first baseman Guy White rolled the infield ball in towards the bench. It wound up at father's feet and he nudged it to Mikey Goodridge, so he could flip it to White at the end of the inning.

After Leeman pitched a 1-2-3 first, the White-to-father-to-Goodridge ritual was repeated after each inning. About the sixth inning, White's roller wound up closer to Goodridge than father. When Goodridge started to reach for it, father almost spiked him as he toed Goodridge's arm out of the way so he could kick the ball to him.

Leeman went 26 up, 26 down, including Bobby Hull's Chicago Black

Hawks teammate Murray Hall (soft hands, no bat), who played first for Oakville. Facing the final batter, and the count at 3-2, Leeman watched the batter take a pitch on the corner. The ump raised his right arm about half way up, ready to signal a game-ending strike, but changed his mind and yelled: "Ball four!"

The perfect game was gone, the no-hitter was in jeopardy and, given the short left-field fence at Wallace Park, the lead wasn't real safe, either. But the next batter lined a ball down the third-base line and Don Goodridge, making like Graig Nettles, dove towards the foul line and speared a sure double. Leeman had his no-hitter.

There were tears and beers and the day ended with everyone in the cars, but no Pester. He was still in the communal shower, buck naked, screaming at the buck naked plate ump, calling him "gutless" for not calling strike three on the next-to-last hitter.

When I moved to Toronto in 1987, I was told that Wallace Park was no more. My son played in the Mississauga system and when we made trips to Oakville, I always hoped it would be to the Wallace Park I remembered from 20 years earlier. Then, in 2003, helping coach a peewee team, I was driving past the left-field fence and I was struck by the familiarity of the park, although it was too shallow in centre and right field to be the same place. But the curling rink was there, so were the tennis courts. After asking around, I was told that the tennis players, realizing that love means nothing but a baseball to the noggin hurt, complained about foul balls landing on the court. So the backstop and home plate were moved forward, thus cutting the field dimensions.

Eureka! The site of Arty Leeman's no-hit, almost-a-perfect-game outing had been found after 36 years. What happened first time back? Mark DeMelo, Gianfranco Diceglie and Billy Hurley of the Mississauga North Tigers combined on a no-hitter in a 14-1 win. Walking to the car I said to some of the kids: "You have no idea the last time I was here." Asked second baseman Michael Cardinale, age 12: "What, in 1922 or 1923?"

In 1968, the spring after Leeman's perfecto, we were playing the Leaside Maple Leafs at Talbot Park in Toronto. It was the top of the second inning. Father collapsed with a stroke in the third base coaching box. Never mind the ambulance. My uncle Sam Sheridan, a paratrooper, a Canadian hero who dropped behind enemy lines on D-Day, drove onto the field, loaded father into the car and sped to Sunnybrook Hospital. My uncle's fast response saved my dad's life. Father spent almost two months in Sunnybook. His left side was fully paralyzed, and he battled pneumonia before returning home to begin an arduous physiotherapy program. (He never coached again but, in curling, he would win his third Ontario Governor-General's.)

The year of father's stroke we played the Hamilton Cardinals in the final. We were eliminated, a one-run loss, despite the fact Keith Weese hit what looked like a three-run homer since the base ump was circling his right hand. Instead, the ball was thrown in and Weese wound up with a run-scoring double. Five or six years later, Brian Coffey and Clyde Harris, who played the outfield that night, third baseman Don Goodridge and myself were seated down the first-base line at Jarry Park watching the Expos.

"You guys weren't with that Kingston team that played Hamilton a few years ago, were you?" Mike Buist said, noticing the jackets.

Someone nodded. Then Buist told the most amazing story about the homer that wasn't a homer. Hamilton centre fielder Larry Cunningham always kept a spare ball in his back pocket. As Weese's ball soared into the darkness and into the girders at the back of Ivor Wynne Stadium, way above the 10-foot-high fence, Cunningham took the ball out of his pocket and flipped it against the fence. The ball came in and one out later we were short-changed two runs. Great story. We liked it so much we all adjourned to Crescent Street.

Father wasn't around to hear that story. He passed away on Victoria Day, May 18, 1970, age 61, following a heart attack. Six months later, mother died at 51; one more heartbreak for me and my younger sister Elizabeth.

At father's funeral, friends and family lined up outside Robert J. Reid & Sons Funeral Home on Johnston Street to say their final goodbyes. Players from all eras stopped by. One we'll never forget was lefty Arnie Jarrell. He'd won 26 games for father's Ponies in 1944 and was signed by the Toronto Maple Leafs the next season. Jarrell came in, pulled up a chair and sat in front of the coffin and cried. After sitting 20 minutes he stood up and said, "I keep expecting him to stand up and yell 'C'mon, lefty, throw a strike.'"

• • •

Newsrooms are now filled with people with degrees from journalism school. When I received my first job offer I was in Grade 12. The *Kingston Whig-Standard*, where I'd worked as a summer student, asked me to become a full-time employee. It was in March and they had an opening. Pete Fowler was the boss and he nearly jumped out of the chair when given my answer.

"When school is out! Are you nuts? We have a four-man department. We aren't going very long with three people. You have two weeks."

Mother was upset. Very upset. My grandfather went to Queen's. My father went to Queen's. Most of my family went to Queen's. I was supposed to go to Queen's. Father was another matter.

"You don't really apply yourself in school, and this opportunity won't be there in June," he said. "Leave it with me."

A couple of days later, he said I could take the job on one condition. Becoming a sportswriter would be allowed as long as I didn't behave like the Red Sox writers who fought with Ted Williams and then left him off the Most Valuable Player ballot in 1941. At the time, harness racing and high school football were my main sports to cover. Major League Baseball? That was a dream in Canada. It was an easy commitment to make.

Not until 1993, when filling out the American League Most Valuable Player Award, did I recall his words. Albert Belle of the Cleveland Indians had acted like a jerk and, come the end of the season, the ballot staring me in the face, I dropped him from second to fifth on my list. But then father's words came back from the 1960s, and the ballot was re-arranged.

From father to son.

THE HALL OF FAMER

4

To paraphrase Hall of Famer Yogi Berra, being a baseball writer is "80 percent watching games and the other half is spent on the phone."

Today, the annual announcement by the Baseball Writers Association of America of the newest Hall of Fame members is made at two o'clock in the afternoon. The announcement is followed by conference calls with the stars and their stories fill the next day's papers. In 1991, that wasn't the case. Back then, the elected players were notified late in the afternoon and asked to attend a press conference the next morning in New York, leaving baseball writers with, literally, a story to chase. On Jan. 8, 1991, the subject of our chase was Ferguson Jenkins.

Jenkins had failed to receive the required 75% support for nomination in his first two years of Hall of Fame eligibility. On announcement day of Year 3, not knowing whether the news for Jenkins was good or bad, we phoned him at his farm in Guthrie, Oklahoma. No answer. We phoned again. Someone told us he'd just left for the airport.

"Headed to New York?" we asked.

"Yes, he was," we were told.

That meant good news for Jenkins.

After finding out that the fastest way to New York was by flying with TWA, with a connection in St. Louis, we tried to intercept Jenkins at the gate in Oklahoma City and then at the gate in St. Louis. Failing twice, our last shot to get Jenkins in time to make the next day's paper was to have him paged at New York's La Guardia Airport. So we phoned the New York Port Authority and talked to a security guard who agreed to meet the plane. He asked for a description of Jenkins and was told he looked "like a Hall of Famer." We learned the guard was only 29, and then asked him the age of his partner. "Oh, he's real old, maybe 50." So, we spoke to the partner.

"Ferguson Jenkins? Sure, I watched him come into Shea and beat my Mets," the guard said. Half an hour later Jenkins was on the phone.

He was excited, and rightfully so. He is the first and, to date, only Canadian elected to the Hall of Fame. The first call he'd made—after learning he'd been elected along with Rod Carew and Gaylord Perry—was

42

to a seniors' residence in his hometown, Chatham, Ontario (pop. 40,000). Ferguson Holmes Jenkins, 82 at the time and suffering with arthritis, was in his room. On one wall he'd hung a picture of his son in a Chicago Cubs uniform. He was wheeled to the phone.

The son said to the father: "Dad, I've been voted into the Hall of Fame. Are you happy?"

The elder Jenkins leaned away from the phone receiver to shout: "My son got into the Hall of Fame! My son got into the Hall of Fame!"

Jenkins was and is a giant in Canadian baseball. To be eligible to participate in the Hall of Fame balloting, voters must have logged 10 consecutive years as BBWAA members. This was our 11th year and our first year voting.

Jenkins needed 333 votes of the 433 cast to hit the magic 75 per-cent mark. In his first two years of eligibility he'd received support of 52.35 and 66.67 percent. But in 1991 he had 334 votes, including my vote, which led to an embarrassing headline in the *Toronto Sun* that touted "Our Man Elliott" helps put Jenkins into the Hall." Without our vote, he still would have gotten in, although his 75.3 percent was the slimmest margin ever for an inductee.

On the day of Jenkins' induction at Cooperstown, July 21, a Sunday, we were covering the Blue Jays in Arlington, Texas. Most of the time writers spend in a clubhouse is spent waiting—waiting for the starting pitcher to ice his arm, waiting for the goat of the game to compose himself, waiting for the star of the game to finish making post-game plans with his agent. On that afternoon, we were watching the ESPN telecast of the induction. Jenkins was speaking ...

"... guys like Bobby Tsukayama, Bob Swift, Paul Brown, Darcy Tuck, Mac Cundle, Kenny Milbourne, Lennie Milbourne," Jenkins said, rhyming off names.

"Who are all those guys?" asked Jays' goofy lefty, David Wells. "Never heard of any them. How good were they? They never played in the big leagues."

No, we told Wells, they were Jenkins' boyhood friends and teammates in Chatham.

"Being from Canada, I had an opportunity to play a lot of different sports and these gentlemen had a factor in it," Jenkins said. "We were competitive in small-town Ontario."

We've heard a dozen or so induction speeches. None touched them all for thank-yous like Jenkins did.

Later that day, Jays manager Cito Gaston was asked how he fared during his days with the San Diego Padres against Jenkins, the Chicago Cubs workhorse.

"He got me out some and I got him a few times," Gaston said. "But we did have a thing going. One hot afternoon at Wrigley, he hit a sharp one-hopper to me in right. I looked and he'd let up coming down the first-base line, so, I tried to throw him out at first."

Jenkins sped up and beat the throw. "That was in 1970 I think. Every time after that when he faced me, he knocked me down once an at-bat," Gaston said. "I wasn't trying to embarrass him, I thought I could make a play. That's the type of competitor he was. And he had a long memory."

Ferguson Arthur Jenkins was born Dec. 13, 1942 in Chatham to Delores Jenkins, who lost her sight giving birth, and his father, also named Fergie but known as Hershey because of the candy bars he used to carry in his pocket. The Jenkins family had a strong Baptist background. The baseball background was pretty strong too; his father had played semi-pro in Ontario and Pennsylvania.

Growing up, Jenkins excelled at basketball, hockey and baseball. For a time, he believed pro basketball would be his calling. He was a fan of the NBA's Cincinnati Royals, who featured future Hall of Famers Oscar Robertson and Jerry Lucas. By high school, as he grew to 6-foot-5, he'd routinely score 40 points a game. "I thought I was the next Oscar Robertson," he said. "I'd come home from school and read the clippings to my mother."

In hockey, he was a defenseman who enjoyed the rough going and took a lot of penalties, collecting several stitches and losing several teeth along the way. "I wasn't a star. I played because I liked it," he remembers, although he did make "a few all-star teams in midget." Jenkins said. His hockey hero was Montreal Canadiens Hall of Fame defenseman Doug Harvey. Jenkins went as high as Junior-B, playing for the Chatham Maroons, but after suffering a hip injury he heeded advice from his mom and a baseball scout named Gene Dziadura to give up hockey.

It was Delores who steered Jenkins towards baseball. "My mother always thought hockey was too rough," he said. "She was a guiding force and told me that potentially baseball was my best sport, not hockey and not basketball." Hershey would bring Delores to their son's baseball games and, although she couldn't see him, "she liked the atmosphere at a baseball game the best of all."

The other guiding force in Jenkins' life, besides his parents, was the scout, Dziadura. The two were brought together by high school teacher Gerry McCaffery in 1959. McCaffery asked Dziadura if he'd drive from Windsor to Chatham's Turner Park to look at two players, Jenkins and infielder Mel Wakabayashi, who went on to play hockey at the University of Michigan and coach in Japan.

"First time I saw Fergie?" Dziadura said. "He was about as loose an athlete as I'd ever seen. He was skin and bones. He had a fluid motion. It looked like he had a lot of potential as long as he had some adult weight."

Dziadura filled out a scouting card on Jenkins detailing his vital statistics, and mailed it off to Philadelphia scout Tony Lucadello. Dziadura then decided to stick around Chatham, eventually taking a job as a teacher at Chatham Collegiate. His own playing career had come to end in 1958, after three seasons in the Chicago Cubs' minor league system. Playing for Class-C Lafayette, he was beaned in a game. A month later, at Class-B Burlington, he collapsed attempting to steal second. The beaning had left him with a spinal injury, a compacted lumbar, and he was done as a player. Returning home, Dziadura graduated from the University of Windsor.

"I knew how difficult it was to go down there as a Canadian and compete with an American," he said. "Players from, say, Arizona and Florida, were 400 players ahead of us and they probably had better coaching. Even though you had the talent, Canadians were still behind. There would be 40 guys trying out for one team."

Dziadura taught history at Chatham Collegiate for 34 years. He taught a Hall of Famer for three years, three to four nights a week. "When I first saw him in games he was striking out 16 of 22 throwing curveballs to 4-foot-11 guys," Dziadura remembered. In the gym, Dziadura got Jenkins to only throw fastballs. They worked on velocity, throwing strikes and throwing over the top.

Before Dziadura, what Jenkins knew about control came from the time he spent throwing rocks at passing freight trains in the east end of Chatham. "The Chesapeake and Ohio railway ran near our place and we'd throw rocks at the box cars," Jenkins said. "It was a challenge throwing them right through the open box cars of a train moving 50-60 miles an hour."

Under Dziadura, Jenkins improved his control thanks to a contraption the scout constructed. He built a large, wooden frame and stretched two strings across it horizontally and then attached two more strings vertically to form a strike zone. In Japan, bullpen catchers sit on three-legged stools, normally used to milk cows, in order to save wear and tear on their knees. Dziadura, suffering a bad back, spent countless nights catching Jenkins while sitting on an overturned wastebasket. "One time he threw a ball and it knocked the can out from under me," Dziadura said. "An inch or so higher and I wouldn't be here. The basket was dented. An inch higher and … " Instructor and student both laugh at the memory and still enjoy telling that story.

In addition to teaching him to pitch, Dziadura prepared Jenkins for pro baseball in several other ways. The scout passed to Jenkins a set of rules he'd learned many years earlier from Lucadello: work hard, never discuss your contract, walk to the hotel to build up your legs and "don't get messed up with women or you're done." He also advised Jenkins to run to build stamina, to do eye exercises and to strengthen his wrists by lifting a three-pound mallet while watching TV or chopping wood. Jenkins chopped until his wood was gone and neighbors would bring more.

Before long, Jenkins was eliciting interest from several teams. In addition to the Philadelphia Phillies, he heard from the Cleveland Indians, Chicago White Sox, Pittsburgh Pirates, Boston Red Sox and Detroit Tigers. "Writers will always ask me how tough is it to sign out of Canada, and I always say it's tough to get signed period," Jenkins said. "You have to have some kind of ability. I had a raw ability." Jenkins signed with the Phillies on June 15, 1962 and received a $10,000 signing bonus, which he gave to his parents to apply to the family house on Adelaide Street. It was a gesture of thanks from a son who remembered that his father always made sure the young pitcher got to the park, whether it was a trip to Windsor, Hamilton, St. Catharines, Peterborough or London. For his part, the father deflected any credit for his son's success.

"My wife Delores made that young man, her and Gene Dziadura," the father said at the time.

• • •

By far the most popular 'of' and the most often 'of' we read in Canadian Press stories was ... "Ferguson Jenkins *of* Chatham, Ont." Jenkins made his major-league debut Sept. 10, 1965, on my 16th birthday, although we didn't read about it until the next day. Recalled from Triple-A Arkansas, he pitched 4 1/3 innings of relief as the Phillies edged the St. Louis Cardinals 5-4 in 12 innings. His rise to the majors had been remarkably fast. Jenkins started pitching when he was 16, was signed by the Phillies at age 19 and made his major-league debut when he was 22. He was a quick study in the minors and believes that if not for Phils pitching coaches Al Widmar (later the Jays pitching coach), and Calvin Coolidge Julius Caesar Tuskahoma McLish (later the Montreal Expos pitching coach), he never would have made the majors. Joe Becker and Hall of Famer Robin Roberts also helped mould Jenkins.

"To sign right out of high school and be in the majors that quickly, I consider myself fortunate," Jenkins said.

And in Kingston, we had another Canadian to follow.

Baseball gives you friendships, memories and lessons in geography. For instance, why was there an "Ont." after Chatham in Ontario papers, we wondered growing up? Chatham is near London, Ont., which is between Windsor, Ont. and Toronto, Ont. and we could go Ont. and Ont. Later we learned there was a Chatham, N.B., which Miss Smith failed to teach us in Grade 5 geography at Rideau Public School in Kingston. It was Jenkins who introduced us to Chatham, Ont., and right-hander Jason Dickson who introduced us to Chatham, N.B.

Jenkins was not an instant success in Philadelphia. He came up as a reliever and the manager, Gene Mauch, told him he'd never win in the majors with "that fastball." (Hey, Hall of Fame manager Tommy Lasorda said Pedro Martinez was too frail to be a starter.) So, Jenkins and his 14 2/3 innings of major-league experience in eight games with the Phillies was dealt to the Chicago Cubs, along with outfielders Adolfo Phillips and John Herrnstein, for popular starters Bob Buhl and Larry Jackson, April, 21, 1966. A headline in a Chicago paper read: "Ferguson Who?"

Two days later, Jenkins came on in relief and hit a home run to help the Cubs blank the Hall of Famer Don Sutton and the Los Angeles Dodgers 2-0. A short time later Cubs coach Whitey Lockman met with manager Leo Durocher and asked: "Where is it etched in stone that Fergie has to be a reliever?" "Well, the rest is history," said Lockman. Halfway through Jenkins' first season in Chicago, with the Cubs' starting rotation in tatters, Jenkins was inserted into the rotation for the final 12 starts. He got six wins in 1966 and followed that up with six straight 20-win seasons.

"It didn't take long before you knew when you walked onto the field you were going to win (with Fergie on the mound)," said former Cubs third baseman Ron Santo. "Never have I had that feeling with another pitcher. Fergie wasn't overpowering, but he got it done."

There were indications right from the start that Jenkins was special. A durable and competitive pitcher, in his first year as a starter, 1967, he was 20-13 with a 2.80 ERA in 38 starts. With 20 complete games, he logged 289 1/3 innings, walking just 83 and striking out 230. By mid-season he gained enough notice to be named to the National League team for the All-Star game at Anaheim Stadium. A live crowd of 46,309 fans, plus a TV audience, including Canada, in the millions, saw Jenkins replace Juan Marichal in the top of the fourth and pitch his way into the record book. After he got Rod Carew on a fly ball to centre, Tony Oliva singled and Harmon Killebrew struck out looking. The inning ended when catcher Joe Torre threw out Oliva attempting to steal. Jenkins started the next inning by striking out Tony Conigliaro. He allowed a double to Carl Yastrzemski, when Hank Aaron missed a shoestring catch and, after getting Bill Freehan to pop to third, Mickey Mantle came on to pinch-hit.

"Manager Walter Alston came out to the mound and said to me, 'Do you know who this is?' I told him of course I knew—Mickey Mantle," Jenkins remembered. "Then my catcher Joe Torre said I better treat this man with respect. So I threw him strikes. Got him on four pitches."

In his third inning, Jenkins struck out Jim Fregosi and gave up a solo homer to Brooks Robinson, tying the game 1-1. Jenkins then struck out Carew and Oliva to end his night. The Nationals won 2-1 in 15 innings when Tony Perez homered off Catfish Hunter. "I ended up throwing three pretty good innings and striking out those six great batters," Jenkins said. The six strikeouts—against future Hall of Famers Killebrew, Mantle and Carew, as well as Conigliaro, six-time all-star Fregosi and three-time batting champion Oliva—tied the all-star record held by Carl Hubbell, Johnny Vander Meer and Larry Jansen.

In 1968, the Harlem Globetrotters made their annual visit to the Kingston Memorial Centre. Usually Curly Neal or Meadowlark Lemon would arrive a week before to promote the event. This time, Delores Jenkins, Fergie's mom, came to town. The picture in the *Kingston Whig-Standard* that ran atop the story of the Globetrotters visit was of the blind Delores Jenkins and my father, who had lost an eye playing football. Proceeds for the game went to the Canadian National Institute for the Blind. Delores had another connection with the Trotters. Her son Fergie toured with them for the 1967-68 season. He would tell people that after spending his summers with the Cubs he had to go somewhere in the winter where he could win. He estimates he played 150 games against the New York Nationals and the Washington Generals—and never lost.

Jenkins was not the star of this show. Meadowlark Lemon, Curly Neal and Showboat Hall were the headliners. Jenkins would watch from the bench as the Globetrotters went through their warm-ups to the whistling strains of *Sweet Georgia Brown*. He would usually take the court in the third quarter and be involved in three skits. Some nights, depending on the city, the announcer would tell fans that a special guest, a 20-game winner from the majors, was in the arena and ready to pitch to any Globetrotter. "People would look around, everyone on the bench would look to their left and right," Jenkins said. "Then, they'd introduce me to cheers."

Jenkins warmed up a little and then he'd pitch a basketball to Meadowlark. The first pitch was always taken by Lemon and always ruled a called strike by ump Curly Neal. Jenkins would always hit Lemon with the second pitch, which Neal always called "steeee-rike two!" Lemon would argue, "It wasn't a strike, it hit me!" And Neal would say, "It *struck* you ... so it's 0-2." On the next pitch, Lemon would put his hands together and hit the ball. Then he'd take off around the bases only to have the ball arrive at home before him, to Neal, ready to make the tag, who would yell: "I got you tonight!" Then Lemon would yell: "Hey Curly, there's Superman!" When Neal turned and looked up, Lemon would hook slide in safely.

Next, Lemon would try a hook shot from wherever he was on the court. "My job," says Jenkins, "was to sneak down the court. Usually Meadowlark made the shot, but if he missed I threw the ball back and he gave it another try. If he missed a second time I'd dunk it."

In his third skit, the ref would call a traveling violation and give the ball to Jenkins so he could in-bound it from the sideline. Jenkins would playfully toss it back to the referee, who, startled to receive the ball, would toss it back to Jenkins beneath the basket. Jenkins would dunk the ball. "Fans were surprised to see a baseball player with the ability to dunk."

"Meadowlark was the inventor of most of the skits," recalls Jenkins, "but it never got old. We'd see the same thing night after night and be on the bench laughing. Like when we'd bring a little kid out of the crowd to shoot a free throw and he'd get all set and then we'd turn him around and tell him: 'No, no, the other basket.'"

Looking back on his 19 major-league seasons, Jenkins ranks 1968 as his best. He went 20-15 with a 2.63 ERA in 40 starts, including a remarkable 20 complete games, working 308 innings with only 65 walks against 260 strikeouts. Five of the losses were 1-0 decisions, a major-league record. Further, the Cubs were blanked in nine of his 15 losses. "With a little luck, I might have won 26 or 27 games," Jenkins said. "That seemed to be the story of my career."

Over the next four years Jenkins won 21, 22, 24 and 20 games. His 24 wins in 1971 led the National League and earned him the Cy Young Award. That year he made 39 starts, pitched 325 innings and compiled a 2.77 ERA, while walking 37 and fanning 263. He received 17 of 24 first-place votes to finish ahead of the Mets' Tom Seaver and the Dodgers' Al Downing.

"Fergie was blessed with a lot of talent," said Dr. Ron Taylor, a reliever who watched Jenkins work. "He was a great competitor and had a very strong work ethic."

Cubs' outfielder Billy Williams remembers one game in particular. "We played St. Louis Opening Day 1971, at Wrigley Field—Bob Gibson against Fergie," he said. "We play nine and we're tied 1-1. Then we go to extras. First game of the year and neither pitcher will come out. In the 10th, with the sun going down and it getting colder, I hit a home run. I had to. My buddy deserved the win. He only gave up three hits, didn't walk a man and struck out seven. He out-pitched Gibby (who allowed seven hits, four walks and struck out five)."

In 1973, John McGregor High School in Chatham could boast three alumni who were pitching professionally: Jenkins, Doug Melvin in the Pittsburgh Pirates system and Billy Atkinson of the Montreal Expos. Melvin, a few years younger than Jenkins, used to make the eight- or nine-hour drive from Chatham with his buddies to see Jenkins pitch at Wrigley Field. "Fergie was a fast worker. I'll bet he had a lot of games over in under two hours," Melvin said. "On the mound he was a good example for young kids to follow on how to pitch."

Despite six straight 20-win seasons and leading the Cubs in wins in seven consecutive seasons, Jenkins was traded to the Texas Rangers for Bill Madlock and Vic Harris after going 14-16 in 1973. Moving to the American League proved to be no problem for Jenkins; he went 25-12 for the Rangers with a 2.82 ERA and 225 strikeouts, finishing second in the 1974 Cy Young Award voting behind Catfish Hunter of the Yankees. In the final game of the season, against the Minnesota Twins, Jenkins singled to break up Jim Hughes' no-hit bid and sealed his 25th win, 2-1, by striking out pinch hitter Harmon Killebrew, making his final at-bat as a Twin, for the game's final out.

After going 17-18 for the Rangers in 1975, Jenkins was dealt to the Boston Red Sox for Juan Beniquez, Steve Barr, Craig Skok and cash. It was a familiar story for Jenkins on opening day 1976; he dropped a 1-0 loss to Baltimore's Jim Palmer. Returning to his home and native land, Jenkins threw the first shutout ever in Toronto's Exhibition Stadium, as Boston blanked the Blue Jays, 9-0. Jenkins pitched two years in Boston, going 22-21 over-all, and then was traded back to Texas, where he regained his form, averaging 15 wins a year for three seasons. In the 14 seasons from 1967 to 1980, Jenkins' led all major-league pitchers with 251 victories, ahead of four-time Cy Young winner Steve Carlton (246), three-time Cy Young winner Tom Seaver (245), and two-time Cy Young winner Gaylord Perry (244).

His consistency and longevity were probably attributable to many factors, but first among them was Jenkins' work ethic. At the end of each season he'd return to Chatham and pick up the routine that made him a major leaguer in the first place. "The thing I liked about Fergie is that every year he'd come home, take October and November off, and come December we were back in that gym," Dziadura said. "He did it until he retired. Maybe he didn't start up until January, but there he was in the same gym, working on the same things."

The low-mark of Jenkins' career came Aug. 25, 1980 when he was arrested for possession of illegal drugs after customs officials discovered an estimated $500 worth of cocaine and marijuana in his suitcase. Commissioner Bowie Kuhn suspended Jenkins indefinitely, but arbitrator Raymond Goetz overturned Kuhn's ruling on Sept. 22. The courts were equally forgiving. Jenkins was convicted on cocaine possession charges Dec. 18, but the verdict was immediately erased by Judge Gerald Young because of Jenkins' years of "exemplary" conduct. The episode was hard on

Jenkins, and especially hard on his father. The elder Jenkins had been just as proud of his son's outstanding character as his on-field accomplishments.

"For a long time, he didn't believe that the drugs weren't mine," said Jenkins. "I told him that I was his only son and that he had to believe me. But he's a serious, religious man. It was hard for him. My father suffered more than anyone." The rift was finally healed and, eleven years later, when Jenkins was elected into Cooperstown, the father was bursting with pride once more. "He's probably as proud as I am right now," said Jenkins when he arrived in New York. "That means a lot to me."

After making only 16 starts with the Rangers during the strike-marred 1981 season, Jenkins went home to Chicago, signing with the Cubs as a free agent in 1982 and going 14-15 and logging 217 innings, the 13th time in 16 seasons he'd worked more than 200 innings. That's the standard now. But from 1968 through 1971 Jenkins pitched more than 300 innings a season. His final season came in 1983 when he went 6-9 in 29 starts for the Cubs. His 664th and final appearance in the majors was Sept. 26, 1983 at Wrigley Field when he worked the top of the ninth in a 5-2 loss to Philadelphia.

His old mentor and coach, Dziadura, tried to convince Jenkins to keep going because the pitcher was only 16 wins shy of the magic 300 number. He remembers a talk he had with Jenkins in the parking lot of a fitness centre. "He said I think I've had it," Dziadura said. "I was telling him he should keep pitching because he was so close to 300 wins." But Jenkins said 300 wins didn't matter to him much—"whatever I've done was enough." And who could argue with that?

Jenkins retired as the only pitcher in history with the dual accomplishment of more than 3,000 strikeouts (3,192) and fewer than 1,000 walks (997). He pitched 49 shutouts. In 45 of his 226 career defeats, his team was held scoreless.

• • •

After retiring, Jenkins returned to Chatham and began farming. He became just another member of a close-knit community, rising at dawn and slipping into his boots and overalls to tend to chores. In 1988 he remarried (his first marriage had ended in divorce) and moved to Guthrie, Oklahoma where he was hired as pitching coach for the Texas Rangers' Triple-A team. A few days before the 1991 Hall of Fame announcement, his wife, Mary-Anne, was seriously injured in an automobile accident. Driving alone at night in a 1991 Ford Explorer, a tire blew and the car rolled, tossing Mary-Anne through the window. She suffered a broken neck, clavicle and hip, as well as three broken ribs and a punctured a lung. She was in hospital when he received news of his induction into the Hall of Fame. She died four days later.

So, it was with a heavy heart that Jenkins arrived in Cooperstown the following July. As commissioner Fay Vincent stood at 3:50 p.m. to read Jenkins' Hall of Fame plaque before making the presentation, about 100 red and white Maple Leaf flags shot into the air from among the attendees at the ceremony. The Jenkins plaque, which today hangs between Jim Palmer and Gaylord Perry in the hallowed Hall, reads:

> *Philadelphia of the National League, 1965, 1966; Chicago of the National League, 1966 to '73 and again 1982, '83; Texas of the American League, 1974, '75 and again 1978 to '81 and finally Boston of the American League, 1976 to 1977. Canada's first Hall of Famer. 284 wins, 226 losses lifetime with 3,192 strikeouts and an earned run average of 3.34. Despite playing 12 of his 19-year career in hitter's ballparks, Wrigley Field and Fenway Park, won 20 games, 7 seasons including six consecutive years 1967 through 1972. The Cy Young Award winner in 1971. Trademarks were pinpoint control and changing speeds.*

In his speech, Jenkins said that honor reflected athletic excellence "and I must share it with others." He thanked the people of Chatham and all the cities in which he played. "To my first country, Canada, the nation where I was born, I owe a great deal. Thank you," Jenkins said. "My love for Canada is immeasurable and, to the second country, the United States, (that) gave me the opportunity to play here and to learn the sport of baseball. Thank you." He touched them all, thanking his high school teachers, the Gerry McCaffrey family, Gene Dziadura and his family, along with scout Tony Lucadello. He thanked his parents, Delores Louise (who passed away in 1979) and Fergie Jenkins, Sr., saying: "They taught me ... to strive for excellence and to reach my potential.

"My parents were both loving, strong, powerful individuals. They encouraged me to play as many sports as possible. They instilled in me strong values and solid work ethics. My mother knew before I did that the sport of baseball is what I should play. Although she was blind and never saw me play, she always knew that this was the game that I wanted to do whole heartedly. Thank you very much mother. I know you're here."

Jenkins looked down from the microphone to speak to his father, Hershey, sitting in a wheelchair some 20 feet away. Hershey was a chauffeur in Chatham, then a cook in the merchant marine and later a chef at the William Pitt Hotel and Holiday Inn.

"My father played outfield from 1925 to the 1940s in the Ontario Baseball League and in the Negro Leagues," Jenkins said. "His opportunity to play pro ball was limited by the history of that era. Fortunately, he outlived history and witnessed this change. His sacrifice in baseball has been my reward."

Jenkins said the day belonged to his father, his first teacher, who inspired him. His father taught him to be conscientious and responsible. "My father instilled the love of baseball in me so on this day I'm not only being inducted alone. I'm being inducted on July 21, 1991 with my father, Fergie Jenkins, Sr. 'Hershey.'"

That was the end of the speech.

From father to son.

•••

Late in 1992, Jenkins accepted a minor-league pitching assignment with the Cincinnati Reds for the following season. Then, on Dec. 17, tragedy struck once again. Jenkins' despondent girlfriend, Cynthia Takieddine, took her own life and that of Jenkins' three-year-old daughter, Samantha. They were found dead in their car from carbon monoxide poisoning 50 kilometres north of Jenkins' farm in Guthrie. Three deaths in two years had left Jenkins alone to raise his 12-year-old son Raymond.

In 1996, Jenkins was in downtown Toronto for a Canadian Baseball Hall of Fame fundraiser. We first met Jenkins during the ill-fated Senior Professional Baseball Association one December night in 1989. He reached out and my right hand was swallowed by his big meaty paw. His long middle finger extended up my forearm. Nolan Ryan and Roger Clemens won because of their powerful legs and thighs. Our guess was that the baseball felt like a Titlest in Jenkins' right hand. Seven years later, his grip was still strong. He was attending the Toronto dinner with Milwaukee Braves lefty Hall of Famer Warren Spahn and the right-handed portion of the Braves' 1-2 punch, Lew Burdette. Dave Stieb of the Blue Jays and Steve Rogers of the Expos were there, too, joined by Dave Stewart and former Dodgers all-star Don Newcombe. Also in attendance were Canadian Hall of Fame members Claude Raymond, Phil Marchildon, Ron Taylor and Ron Piche. The illustrious head table had under its collective belts 1,668 major-league wins. Despite the fact that he didn't win 300 games or blank the Yankees in Game 7 of the World Series at Yankee Stadium like Spahn, Jenkins found himself surrounded by the crowd. That's common. At the Canadian Baseball Hall of Fame in St. Marys, he still attracts the most autograph seekers.

"I played almost 20 years, you hope people will remember," Jenkins said. "The years with the Cubs still stand out. I pitched in Detroit (as a visitor with the Texas Rangers), which was close to my hometown and I still have the game ball as the first Canadian to beat the Blue Jays and the first Canadian to beat the Expos. It's nice that people still remember."

The day Jenkins was inducted into Cooperstown, the runner-up to Jenkins for the best speech was respected writer Phil Collier of the *San Diego Union*. Collier was presented with the J. G. Taylor Spink Award, given annually to a member of the print media. "Someone once said that God gave us a mind so that we could remember roses in December," Collier said, taking a moment to glance at the Hall of Famers on stage with him. "Ladies and gentlemen, these are my roses."

Although Ferguson Jenkins' life has not been without thorns, he is one of baseball's roses. Canada's best.

OF J.J., TIP AND FRIENDS

Officially, the Curse of the Bambino ended at 10:40 p.m. Central time on Oct. 27, 2004 at Busch Stadium in St. Louis. At that moment, Boston pitcher Keith Foulke fielded Edgar Renteria's comebacker and threw to first for the final out of the World Series, sending the Red Sox and their fans into a celebration of the four-game sweep of the Cardinals.

Members of the Red Sox Nation are taught the litany of Sox near misses the way children learn their A-B-Cs. The club hadn't won a World Series since the end of World War I. Every time they'd been close, disaster struck. They'd made it to the Series four times since 1918 and lost each time in agonizing fashion in the seventh game. So, even with their Sox one out away from ending the skid in St. Louis, they weren't going to relax until the final out was made. Truth be told, some of them probably feared disaster would strike again.

Christopher Tunstall wasn't among the nay-sayers. He had predicted in June that the 2004 season would be different. He claims his confidence was unwavering, even when the New York Yankees had closer Mariano Rivera on the mound and were an out away from sweeping the Sox in the American League Championship Series. For starters, Tunstall never believed in the curse of the Bambino. The Bambino, of course, was Babe Ruth and his curse was supposedly inflicted on Boston after Red Sox owners sold Ruth's contract to the Yankees in 1920 for $100,000 cash plus a $300,000 mortgage on Fenway Park. Following the trade, the Yanks became a dominant franchise, winning 26 World Series, while the Sox, winners of five of the first 15 World Series, had not won since the Babe departed.

But, says Tunstall, the Babe had nothing to do with it. "I've always thought of it as the curse of J.J." Tunstall said. That would be J.J. Lannin, a Canadian and former owner of the Red Sox, who, suggests Tunstall, has haunted the Red Sox because he never received the recognition he deserved. Lannin, born in Beauport, Quebec, purchased the Red Sox in 1914 and owned the Sox for three seasons. Under him, the Sox won the World Series in 1915 and 1916. And, oh yes, it was Lannin who signed a wayward Baltimore teenager named Herman "Babe" Ruth.

Tunstall is the great-grandson of Lannin. And he has never understood why the accomplishments of great-gramps have been whitewashed from baseball history. While the name of Harry Frazee, the Boston owner who eventually traded Ruth, rolls easily from the lips of Red Sox fans, the name of the person who signed him is all but forgotten.

"The more I read about the man, the more I became fascinated with J.J.'s life," Tunstall said. "Yet, every time I saw an article or documentary on Babe Ruth, the only owner mentioned was Harry Frazee. J.J.'s involvement was gleaned over. When the Ken Burns baseball documentary came out (in 1994), I thought, finally, some people will learn about J.J. But that wasn't the case."

Lannin remained a footnote in baseball history until January 2004, when he was voted into the Canadian Baseball Hall of Fame. At the induction ceremony that July in St. Marys, Ontario, Tunstall predicted that: "Now that my great-grandfather has been recognized ... I think Boston will win a World Series." And like the man said, Boston won.

Lannin's story is just one example of Canada's contribution to baseball's rich history. Other stories abound: Like that of third baseman Mike Brannock of Guelph, the first Canadian to play in the majors with the Chicago White Stockings in the National Association in 1875. ... Like the Guelph Maple Leafs, winners of the World Semi-Professional championship in 1874 at Watertown, New York. ... Like the Hamilton Standards, Kingston St. Lawrence, London Tecumsehs, Guelph and Toronto, which comprised the Canadian League in 1886, its inaugural season. Or there is the story of the first documented game in Canada, played on June 4, 1838. That game was recalled in 1988 by Nancy Bouchier and Robert Knight Barney in *The Journal of Sports History*. They uncovered a letter—published on May 5, 1886 in *Sporting Life*— from a Dr. Adam Ford of Denver titled: "A game long ago which closely resembled our present National Game." Ford described a game played by southwestern Ontario's Oxford County residents on Militia Muster Day, June 4, 1838. The game was played between teams from Beachville and Zorra. The Zorra team was comprised of a detachment of Scottish volunteers from the 3rd Oxford Regiment under the command of Colonel J. Barwick from Zorra. In his letter, Dr. Ford included diagrams that show territory for fair and foul struck balls, or, as Ford described them, a "fair hit" and "no hit." As well, there was a common "striker stone" and "home base." The game was played in a pasture field behind Enoch Burdick's shops as Ford recalled:

"I well remember a company of Scotch volunteers from Zorra halting as

*they passed the grounds to take a look at the game. The ball was made
of double and twisted woolen yarn, a little smaller than the regulation
ball and covered with good honest calf skin, sewed with waxed ends by
Edward McNames, a shoemaker.*

*"The infield was a square, the base lines of which were twenty-four yards
long, on which were placed five bags, thus the distance from the thrower
to the catcher was eighteen yards; the catcher standing three yards behind
the home bye. From the home bye, or a "knocker" stone, to the first bye
was six yards. The club was generally made of the best cedar, blocked out
with an ax and finished on a shaving horse with a drawing knife. A
wagon spoke, or any nice straight stick would do.*

*"We had fair and unfair balls. A fair ball was one thrown to the knocker
at any height between the bend of his knee and the top of his head, near
enough to him to be fairly within reach. All others were unfair. The
strategic points for the thrower to aim at was to get near his elbow or
between his club and his ear."*

Ford's description continued with some familiar concepts about the
game, even including the guideline that the game should be "between six
and nine innings."

For many years, baseball's origins were thought to date to 1845, when
the New York Knickerbockers formally organized a baseball club and
played under a set of rules drawn up by Alexander Cartwright. Dr. Ford's
account predates Cartwright's rules by seven years. So does that make
Canada the birthplace of baseball? Well, no. In 2004, respected baseball
historian John Thorn uncovered evidence that trumped the Beachville
game. In 1791 the town of Pittsfield, Massachusetts passed a bylaw aimed
to protect the windows in Pittsfield's new meeting house by prohibiting
baseball, among other games, within 80 yards of the building. Other
evidence has suggested the first real game was played in Hoboken, N.J., in
1846, or in Manhattan in 1823. The Hall of Fame in Cooperstown says it
is almost impossible to pinpoint where the first game was played—it
largely depends on your definition of baseball—but it regards all docu-
ments as additional pieces of the puzzle that make up the grand old game.

And many of those pieces come from Canada. Baseball has been alive
in Canada for more than 160 years, whether in the form of leagues that
are amateur, semi-professional, minor professional or, since 1969, the
major leagues. For instance, the name Maple Leafs is a Canadian tradition
that dates back long before Conn Smythe attached the name to his famous
hockey team. In 1885, Toronto's Eastern League team was renamed the
Maple Leafs. And then there's second baseman Bill Galloway, who played
for Woodstock of the Canadian League in 1899. Prior to Jackie Robinson

in 1946, Galloway was the last African-American to play in an integrated professional league. The list is long of Canadians who headed south in the late 19th and early 20th century to earn a living at baseball, and includes men like Bill Phillips, Arthur Irwin, Pop Smith, George (Moon) Gibson, Jack Graney and Frank (Blackie) O'Rourke, all of whom played more than 1,000 games in the majors in the early years. It also includes Tip O'Neill, who some believe should have been the first Canadian into the Hall of Fame, ahead of Ferguson Jenkins.

Let's take a brief look at their stories:

Bill Phillips of Saint John, New Brunswick appeared on the scene with the 1879 Cleveland Blues, becoming the first Canadian major leaguer who was not born in Ontario. In 1880 he became the first Canadian to hit a home run in the National League, and went on to play 1,038 games over 10 seasons, for Cleveland, the Brooklyn Grays and the Kansas City Cowboys.

Arthur Irvin of Toronto made his debut with the 1880 Worcester Ruby Legs. He played 13 seasons, mostly at shortstop for Worcester, the Providence Grays, the Philadelphia Quakers, the Washington Nationals, the Boston Reds and the Philadelphia Phillies. His career covered 1,010 games.

Pop Smith of Dibgy, Nova Scotia made his debut in 1880 with the Cincinnati Reds. The second baseman played 1,112 games over 12 seasons with the Cleveland Blues, the Buffalo Bisons, the Worcester Ruby Legs, the Philadelphia A's, the Louisville Eclipse, the Columbus Buckeyes, the Pittsburgh Alleghenys, the Boston Beaneaters and the Washington Statesmen.

Moon Gibson of London, Ontario broke in with the Pittsburgh Pirates in 1905 and played 14 seasons with the Pirates and the New York Giants, appearing in 1,213 games, and played on the 1909 World Series winners, a year in which he knocked in 59 runs. Gibson caught his 112th consecutive game Sept. 9, 1909 to break Chief Zimmer's 1890 record (and eventually ran his streak to 140 games), and then he was behind the plate in every game of World Series as Pittsburgh beat Ty Cobb's Detroit Tigers 8-0 in the seventh and deciding game. For 11 years, Gibson was the Pirates catcher on a full-time basis, or in a platoon situation, catching 1,113 games from 1905 through 1916. After his playing days, he had a couple of managing stints with the Pirates, plus 26 games with the Chicago Cubs, with a .546 career winning percentage.

Jack Graney of St. Thomas, Ontario made his debut with the Cleveland Indians in 1908 as a pitcher, working two games. Two years later he was converted to an outfielder, playing 14 seasons and 1,402 games, a record for Canadians that stood until Houston's Terry Puhl broke it on June 13,

1989. At 5-foot-9 he didn't tower over opposing pitchers, but he circled them pretty quick, leading the AL in doubles in 1916 and in walks in 1917 and 1919. Graney's .241 batting average in 1917 was the lowest average for a walks leader until Oakland's Gene Tenace batted .211 with 110 walks in 1974. He is also remembered for some other notable firsts: He was the first hitter Babe Ruth ever faced in the majors, July 11, 1914, and a year later he became the first player to wear a uniform number in the 20th century. He later became the first player to head to the broadcast booth, and today the annual media award handed out by the Canadian Baseball Hall of Fame is named in his honor.

Frankie O'Rourke of Hamilton made the big leagues in 1912 with the Boston Braves. An infielder, he played 1,131 games over 14 seasons with the Brooklyn Robins, Washington Senators, Boston Red Sox, Detroit Tigers and St. Louis Browns. After winning the starting job at second with the 1926 Tigers, a case of measles knocked him out of the lineup and rookie Charlie Gehringer took over and went all the way to Cooperstown. After his playing career, O'Rourke managed in the minor leagues before becoming a big-league scout, first with the Cincinnati Reds, from 1941-1951, and then the New York Yankees, from 1952-1983, where, among many others, he signed Al Downing, who pitched 17 seasons, including a 20-win season for the Los Angeles Dodgers. He retired in 1985, ending a 73-year career in baseball.

Canada's first big baseball star—and perhaps the nation's best position player ever before Larry Walker—was James Edward "Tip" O'Neill of Woodstock, Ontario. He could hit for power and average, and was a master at fouling off pitches in order to draw a walk or to set up something he could drive, which led to the nickname "Tip."

In 1887, playing with the St. Louis Browns of the American Association, O'Neill had a season for the ages. The Woodstock Wonder won baseball's first-ever batting triple crown (leading the league in average, home runs and RBI), as well as leading the majors in runs, hits, doubles, triples (tie), on-base percent, and slugging percentage. Writing about O'Neill today reminds us of working the 1985 World Series in St. Louis and seeing a caption beneath a photo of Willie McGee in the *St. Louis World* that read: "Willie had many doubles, a few triples and some homers." Talk about not spoon-feeding the reader. We're not vague when it comes to O'Neill's 1887 stats: He had 52 doubles, which certainly counts as "many," 19 triples, which is definitely "a few," and 14 homers, which is unquestionably "some."

His average was .485, breathtaking by today's standards but only astounding by the rules of 1887. For that season, the lords of baseball decreed that a walk was as good as a hit. Literally. And this was long before

Money Ball. If a hitter had one hit and two walks in five plate appearances, he was credited with a 3-for-5 day. O'Neill worked 50 walks that season that counted as hits. Recalculating O'Neill's average to eliminate walks leaves him at .435, the second-highest single-season average ever, behind Hugh Duffy's .438 for the 1894 Boston Beaneaters. And O'Neill didn't just have one fantastic year. He had an outstanding 10-year career as one of the game's top power hitters, retiring in 1892 with a .326 lifetime average.

Yet, O'Neill is seldom listed among the pantheon of baseball's greatest players. He is one of only 12 players in major-league history to win the triple crown, joining Nap Lajoie (1901), Ty Cobb (1909) Rogers Hornsby (1922 and 1925), Jimmie Foxx (1933), Chuck Klein (1933), Lou Gehrig (1934), Joe Medwick (1937), Ted Williams (1942 and 1947), Mickey Mantle (1956), Frank Robinson (1966), and Carl Yastrzemski (1967). Eleven out of 12 triple-crown winners are in the Hall of Fame. The exception is O'Neill.

In the early 1990s, two of O'Neill's relatives campaigned to have their great-uncle inducted into Cooperstown. Mark O'Neill and his sister, Liz, wrote letters to politicians and the Hall of Fame, but to no avail. "I sort of gave up in 1994 after Tip was elected to the Canada Sports Hall of Fame," said O'Neill, vice-president of affairs for strategic planning at the Canadian Museum of Civilization in Ottawa. "We've heard that they are no longer nominating players from before the 1900 season."

As a member of the Baseball Writers Association of America (BBWAA) board-appointed historical overview veteran's committee, we were in Cooperstown in November of 2001 and 2003. At the time, the Hall of Fame was retooling its nomination process for players who had been retired for more than 21 years and were not previously elected by the BBWAA. A 10-person committee was asked to compile a list of 200 candidates, which was then pared down to about 25 names. Efforts to get O'Neill on the ballot were unsuccessful. It turned out that none of the veterans we nominated received the 75 percent of votes required for induction.

"I'm not anti-American," Mark O'Neill said. "But he's the only one (triple-crown winner) not in the Hall of Fame. Tip was without question one of the all-time greats of his day."

How good was O'Neill? Well, he led the Browns to four successive American Association championships from 1885 to 1888. And how popular was he? Well, think of the way young major leaguers named their first-born sons Nolan or Ryan, after the Hall of Fame fireballer. If you were Irish and your last name was O'Neill, chances were your nickname was "Tip".

"In St. Louis, Tip was larger than life," said Mark O'Neill. "Kids competed for the chance to carry his bag to the ballpark; they painted on the side of the team train: 'Greatest Hitter of Them All.' He did have some marks against him—he left to join the Players League and he wasn't in favor of having black players in the league. It was part of the context of his time."

In addition to Canada's Sports Hall of Fame, O'Neill is a member of the Canadian Baseball Hall of Fame, which, since 1984, has presented the Tip O'Neill Award to the best Canadian player of the year.

● ● ●

Throughout the 20th century, Canada turned out a steady stream of major leaguers. There were men like ... outfielder Jeff Heath of Fort William, Ontario, who hit .340 in 1941 for the Cleveland Indians and collected 199 hits, six more than Joe DiMaggio in the year of his magical 56-game hit streak, and 14 more than AL batting champ Ted Williams ... Right-hander Dick Fowler of Toronto, who returned in 1945 after three years in the Canadian Army to pitch a no-hitter for the Philadelphia Athletics ... Phil Marchildon of Penetanguishene, Ontario, who spent nine months in a German prisoner of war camp after his plane was shot down in 1944 before returning to the Athletics and winning 19 games in 1947.

In addition to the Canadian-breds, Canada's minor pro teams helped hone dozens of Americans for major-league jobs. Minor league baseball has a rich history in Canada. Over the past century, 74 different Canadian cities and towns have fielded minor-pro teams, according to baseball historian and author William Humber (humbersports.org). There have been teams in the big cities of Toronto, Montreal, Vancouver and Calgary, and dozens more in small and mid-size communities like Cornwall, Granby, Red Deer, Brandon, Dartmouth and Charlottetown. It is in many of these smaller centers that baseball interest flourished and, particularly in the early part of the century, large crowds were not uncommon. And the caliber of play was often quite high. In 2002, baseball historians Bill Weiss and Marshall Wright compiled a list of the Top 100 minor-league teams of all time and it included eight Canadian clubs. The Toronto Maple Leafs held five of the eight spots, 21st over-all (1920), 39th (1926), 45th (1918), 76th (1902), and 87th (1960). The other three were the London Tecumsehs, 52nd (1920), the Montreal Royals, 84th (1946), and the Quebec Braves, 96th (1950).

The most celebrated U.S. born minor leaguer to come through Canada is probably Jackie Robinson, who graduated from the Montreal Royals to the Brooklyn Dodgers in 1947. But fans of the old Toronto Maple Leafs may remember Elston Howard. After the Yankees optioned the power-hitting catcher to Toronto in 1954 he was voted the International League's Most Valuable Player. Howard went on to become the Yankees first

African-American player and the American League's MVP in 1962. He never forgot the Tip Top Tailors "hit sign, win suit" billboard in Maple Leaf Stadium. He used to say that sign kept him and his father "in suits for years."

We began this chapter with a discussion of Red Sox owner J.J. Lannin and the curse of the Bambino. But besides the connection between Lannin and Babe Ruth in Boston, there is another Canadian twist to the story. But first there is more to learn about the Canadian entrepreneur who once owned one of baseball's most famous franchises.

Lannin, the ninth of 10 children, was born in 1866 and orphaned at age 14. Penniless, he walked from Quebec City to Boston, following the old fur trade route, in search of a new life. He took a job as a bellhop at the Adams Hotel for three dollars a week and, through hard work and good fortune, parlayed his meager wage into a $1-million windfall in commodities by picking up tips from wealthy hotel guests. Eventually, he bought the hotel. Only in America. Only by a Canadian.

In 1914, Lannin paid $200,000 to buy the Sox. It happened that Lannin had a friend, Jack Dunn, who owned the Baltimore Orioles of the International League. Despite having one of the top gate attractions in minor-league baseball, a young pitcher named Babe Ruth, Dunn's team was a bust at the gate and he ran into financial difficulty. In stepped Lannin with an offer to purchase the contracts of right-hander Ernie Shore and Ruth, a lefty, who also played the outfield, for roughly $30,000. It was an offer Dunn was in no position to refuse. The deal closed in early July and, by then, Ruth already had 14 wins in Baltimore, prompting the Red Sox to immediately add him to the big-league lineup. He won his first game, 4-3, but a month later he was dispatched to the Providence Grays of the International League, which is where the story takes a Canadian twist. On Sept. 5, in a game at Toronto's Hanlan Point, Ruth hit his first professional home run. He also pitched a one-hit shutout for the win.

Ruth opened the next season with the Red Sox and, winning 18 games in 1915 and 23 in 1916, helped Lannin's Sox win back-to-back World Series. After the season, Lannin sold the Sox to Harry Frazee for a reported $1 million and walked away from baseball.

Lannin was inducted into the Canadian Baseball Hall of Fame in June 2004. His great-grandson, Christopher Tunstall, who lives in Asheville, N.C., threw out the first pitch before the Sox played host to the Minnesota Twins on June 22, 2004. "Even though J.J. was on my father's side of the family, it was my mother who knew the family background and told me all the stories," Tunstall said. "I became fascinated with his life. In 1989, I moved from California to New York to hit the libraries and research J.J.'s life, before the Internet arrived."

J.J. Lannin died in 1928 at age 61 after falling from the 10th floor of his Granada Hotel in Brooklyn. Depending on which version of the story you believe, he either slipped while checking an awning or he was murdered. His great-grandson leans towards the murder theory, although there is no proof either way.

When *Sports Illustrated* named the Red Sox as its 2004 Sportsmen of the Year, it did a two-page photo spread of the history of the Red Sox. The 48-page section included photos of six owners, but there was no sign of Lannin, the Canadian who, to this day, is the only owner in Red Sox history to win two World Series championships.

THE MVP

6

The goalie equipment—the wet pads, mask, blocker and other gear—was tossed into a corner and forgotten. He was through with hockey. There'd been years and years of early morning practices in cold arenas. There'd been hundreds of games in dozens of arenas across the province. There'd been countless hours of blocking tennis balls and pucks in the driveway of 21642 River Road in Maple Ridge, British Columbia. But no more. Larry Walker was moving on. But hockey's loss was baseball's gain. The kid who grew up dreaming of appearing on *Hockey Night in Canada* instead matured into the greatest position player in Canadian baseball history, a five-time all-star, seven-time Gold Glove winner and a National League Most Valuable Player winner in 1997.

Baseball, though, was far from his thoughts in the fall of 1983 when the Regina Pats of the Western Hockey League drafted Walker. In his first camp, coach Bob Strumm rated Walker as the third-best goalie and told him to, "Go home, have a great year, come back and we'll keep you next fall." Walker returned the next year and was cut after one scrimmage. He then received a tryout with the Kelowna Rockets, a Tier II Junior-A team. Walker and his father Larry had breakfast with the Kelowna coach and were told that, because the Rockets had three goalies in camp, each would play one game over the coming weekend. But before the weekend, Walker played one period in a scrimmage, allowing two goals on 11 shots, and was cut. He never played hockey again.

"He threw the hockey equipment in a corner and there it sat. To my knowledge, that's the last time he touched it," said Walker's father. "We might have said a few angry words to the coach before we left, too."

The anger didn't last long.

"Baseball found me," said the junior Walker. "When I smile, these aren't my teeth."

Fast forward to July 2004, when a handful of Denver writers are waiting in the Colorado Rockies clubhouse when Larry Walker, smiling, walks by.

"So, let me ask you guys," he says, "does Team USA play Canada in the first or second round of the Olympics next week?" The joke, of course, is that the U.S. didn't even qualify for the Athens Games, while its northern neighbor was seeded fourth in the tournament. Score one for the Canadian.

Walker has hit home runs for the Montreal Expos, the Rockies and the St. Louis Cardinals, and while all his pay checks are in U.S. dollars and he has played longer south of the border than north of it, few are as proudly Canadian as Walker. Born, bred and fed in Maple Ridge, Walker could be a spokesman for one of those Molson's Canadian "I Am Canadian" commercials. (Of course, Walker, who shies away from endorsements, would first have to agree to do a commercial.) There is a Canadian flag above his locker and most games he wears a Canada t-shirt under his jersey. "Larry has lived in West Palm Beach and Denver," says his dad. "But any time he is interviewed, he always says 'I'm from Maple Ridge.' I appreciate the way he talks about being Canadian."

There was never any question which sport Walker, Sr. liked. "I always preferred baseball, never played much hockey," he said. A lefty, he was signed by the Vancouver Mounties and assigned to Class-B Yakima in 1954. "I had pretty good control; their rotation was set by the time I got there, so I pitched in relief," he remembered. He was 2-1 with a 4.49 earned run average. Eventually, he began work at Haney Builder Supplies in Maple Ridge and was there for 44 years before retiring as manager in 2001.

Today, he frequently attends games at Larry Walker Field Complex in Maple Ridge. Like at every sandlot park across the country, there are good games, so-so games and bad games at the Larry Walker Field Complex. As always there is 'ball talk' as parents and ball fans lean against a chain-link fence.

"Man, has the third baseman grown since last year?"

"I heard the lefty had two scholarship offers."

And of course 100 sentences that begin with "remember the night?"

Pops roams the two-field complex, Hammond Stadium and Larry Walker Field, the way Walter Gretzky tours the Wayne Gretzky facility in Brantford, Ontario. The field was re-named early in Walker's career, after his fourth season with the Expos. The mayor was on hand. Walker was asked to throw out the first pitch. He chose as his catcher long-time friend Ron Crawford, confined to a wheelchair since age 10 after being involved in a motorcycle accident. To this day, the biggest thrill for Walker's father occurs when he attends sandlot games at the Larry Walker Field Complex. "What makes me very proud, as the father, is when I'll be talking to a parent of a 12-year-old at a game, and either right off or five minutes into the conversation, he'll say 'You're Larry Walker's father! My son idolizes your son. My son wants to grow to up be like your son, that's his goal.'

When it happens—and it has happened more than a few times—it makes my heart pound. I really believe that my son is a baseball pioneer."

Larry and Mary Walker had four children and played the name game as well as Shirley Ellis, who sang: *Shirley, Shirley, bo-birley / banana, fanna, fo-firley ... Shirley!* Barry, their eldest, sells medical supplies in Kelowna, British Columbia. Carey installs ceramics in Vinton, Virginia. Also a goalie, Carey won the 1977 Memorial Cup under Ernie (Punch) MacLean with the New Westminster Bruins and was selected in the 12th round of the National Hockey League draft in 1977 by the Montreal Canadiens. He played eight years in the minors. Gary lives in Maple Ridge and owns a fish wholesale company. Larry, the baby of the family, was born Dec. 1, 1966.

The Walkers played a typical Little League 14-game schedule in Ridge-Meadows, a league made up of players from the Maple Ridge and Pitt Meadows communities. "I recall some of my games and things I did, like hitting the ball into a public swimming pool that was well past the right field fence." When Larry turned 15 he joined the Coquitlam Reds, 10 kilometres away. Counting exhibition games, coach Don Archer's team played 60-70 games, often traveling south of the border to play teams in Washington State. Coaches Lorne Upstell and Paul Hamlin and, of course, Walker's father, were his biggest supporters in the early years. He was good enough at baseball, with the bat and the glove, to be invited to play for Team Canada in 1984 at the world junior championships in Kindersley, Saskatchewan. He was playing shortstop at the time.

Scouts from 15 teams, including two from the Blue Jays, were there with their stopwatches and radar guns. The question they asked themselves after eyeballing each and every prospect was the same: Where is this guy going to be four or five years down the road? "He was awkward fielding the ball and he was awkward throwing the ball, but man, that son of a buck, when he swung the bat, he could hit it a long way," said Jim Fanning of the Montreal Expos. He was there with area scout Bob Rogers, a former longshoreman in Seattle who turned to scouting after losing his hand in an accident on the docks.

Most scouts didn't spend a lot of time on Walker, since he made little contact. "I remember him from that tournament," said Bill MacKenzie, who ran Baseball Canada in the mid-1980s. "His swing had a lot of holes, but he had the kind of mental makeup where he said: 'I'm going to keep swinging until I get it right.' He would take some ugly looking swings in batting practice. Every so often he'd get into a groove and his swing would light people's eyes up."

A month after the world championships, Larry Seminoff, who ran a senior cash tournament in Grand Forks, British Columbia, phoned Wayne

Norton, executive director of Baseball B.C. Seminoff was in trouble. A team had dropped out of his annual Labor Day tourney three days before the first pitch. Clubs made up of college players were coming from New York, Washington state, Japan, Korea and Taiwan. Vancouver-area senior teams had shut down for the season, so Norton phoned the coach of the B.C. Selects, for whom Walker had played that summer, to suggest that they attend. "I knew they'd be overmatched," Norton said of his young team. "We were going with 17 and 18-year-olds. Larry went even though he hadn't played in three or four weeks."

Here was Walker's chance against more established and experienced pitching. Jack Hays of Portland, Oregon, a scout with the Detroit Tigers, wasn't there that day, but he has heard the stories. "Walker had a bunch of homers and hit .400 in the tournament," said Hays. "Since it was mostly older players, collegians, the only guy there was Bob Rogers." Under Fanning's orders, Rogers phoned Walker's father a few days later and asked if he could come from Portland for a meeting. "I was refereeing hockey at the time," Walker said. "I remember it vividly. I checked my schedule and I had the next night free and then I wouldn't have an off night for two weeks." So, Rogers showed the next night, the Walkers meeting him at the Airport Inn in Richmond, B.C.

"I asked Larry, 'Do you want to play professional baseball?' Larry said yes," recalls Walker's father. So, with a $1,500 (U.S.) signing bonus, Walker was heading to spring training in 1985. It is one of the greatest amateur free-agent signs ever. He wasn't good enough for the Regina Pats, but plenty good enough for the Expos.

Walker spent the 1985 season at Single-A Utica. One of the more memorable moments from his first year as a pro came on a hit-and-run play. Walker was doing the running and sped past the shortstop before he picked up the third base coach pointing up—the ball was in the air. Translation: RETREAT! NOW! And so Walker did, returning to first. However, he ran from shortstop directly across the mound—without re-touching second—and was called out. Walker had never been told he had to re-touch because the situation had never arisen. And it never happened again. In fact, he would become the complete five-tool player—he could run, hit for average, hit for power, throw and field—with base running and base stealing ability listed as two of his better attributes.

Walker started slow, hitting .223 with two homers and 26 RBIs in 62 games at Utica. "I could barely hit the ball out of the cage when I first started!" Walker said. He says being Canadian didn't make it more difficult to climb the ladder. "There weren't any real barriers, really. It was the same for everyone, no matter where you were from. If you have the willingness to learn, practice and play the game with all your might, one got the same opportunities as the next guy. You can never give up though. It is a long process."

The fact that the Expos signed Walker, and not the Jays, is a sore subject in Toronto. In 1984, before Canadians were eligible for the draft, it was a case of first come, first sign. The Jays thought they had the country covered on the amateur level and had overtaken the Expos in scouting and signing Canadians. When the Jays used to care about Canadian prospects, they would often say, "if he burps we know about it."

"All I remember about Walker," said an ex-Jays scout now with another club, "is that one time I asked: 'What happened? Where were we, why weren't we on this guy?' The room went silent. I was afraid to ask that again."

Walker started the 1986 season in Single-A Burlington, Iowa, splitting time between third base and first base. At Burlington, the Expos made the decision to convert him to an outfielder. Pop remembers the phone call home very well. "He was very despondent when he called ... he wanted to quit. I told him to think of all the outfielders that are big-time hitters. Besides, when you're playing the field it's more relaxing; you aren't into every pitch like in the infield and you can think more about hitting. Larry said 'Okay, I'll try it.' He hit .406 that first week and was player of the month in the Mid-West League."

When he returned home that winter, he showed pop videos of him taking ground balls in right field and then throwing to the bases. "Well, that's not too bad," the father observed. "I like your arm action on that one." Replied the son: "Only one thing wrong with it dad ... that throw you liked so much? The ball wound up in the parking lot."

In all, Walker hit 29 homers in 95 games as a 19-year-old, leading the league with 74 RBIs despite the fact he was promoted to Single-A West Palm Beach in mid-July. Walker hit .289 before the promotion to West Palm, where he had four homers and 16 RBIs in 38 games. Next stop was Double-A Jacksonville in 1988, where Walker earned Southern League post-season all-star honors. At Jacksonville, he developed a fondness for the number three: he wears No. 33, takes three practice swings before each at-bat (if he's not loose he takes six or nine swings, not five or seven) and when he sets his alarm he doesn't set it for 8 o'clock but 8:03. Why? "It's tough to explain superstitions because they are superstitious."

After the season Walker flew to Toronto to be presented the prestigious James 'Tip' O'Neill Award, presented annually by the Canadian Baseball Hall of Fame to the Canadian who has excelled in individual achievement. It was the first of nine times he would win it.

When Walker was at Jacksonville and West Palm Beach, he shared the outfield with Canadians Andy Lawrence of Mississauga, Ontario and

Scott Mann of Oshawa, Ontario. Walker hit .287 with 26 homers and 83 RBIs in 128 games at Jacksonville. That winter, playing winter ball for the Hermosillo Orangemen, Walker damaged his right knee in the Mexican dust after stepping on a bat at the plate. It was a long road back: his leg was in a cast for eight weeks and he re-habbed for seven months. And it was a longer road back to being in playing shape, as he missed the complete season and then headed to West Palm Beach for instructional league. The only bright spot for Walker was that, because he was on the Expos 40-man roster, he received credit for a year's service time and was paid the major-league minimum of $62,500.

Walker started the 1989 season at Triple-A Indianapolis—a stubbed toe away from the majors, as the saying goes. He got the big-league call after hitting .270 with 12 homers and 59 RBIs in 114 games, and made his major-league debut with the Expos Aug. 16 under manager Buck Rodgers at Olympic Stadium. The opposition was the San Francisco Giants and 24,719 fans were at the Big O.

"You don't ever forget your first game in the big leagues," Walker said. Facing Mike LaCoss, Walker walked in the second, walked in the fourth, led off the seventh with a single to left and walked against reliever Steve Bedrosian to score in the three-run eighth. On his third walk, when he reached first base Will Clark of the Giants said: "It's your first game in the big leagues and they're pitching you like you're Babe Ruth." Final score: 4-2 Expos.

Four days later, pop was in Montreal to see his son play. Was dad misty-eyed? Not really. Walker was promoted while his father was on his annual sojourn to Seattle to see the Mariners play the Texas Rangers. The highlight at the Kingdome wasn't Nolan Ryan winning his 14th game of the season before 16,873 fans. While watching the Mariners, Walker read on the scoreboard that his son got his first hit.

Pop had remained dry-eyed when he saw his son's first big-league hit announced on the Seattle scoreboard, and again when he watched his son for the first time in Montreal, but he shed a tear the next year on Montreal's first trip to Los Angeles. "That was the first time I got emotional to the point of teardrops," pop said. "I grew up a Dodgers fan and to see him in right field at Dodger Stadium … it was a very special feeling. I was on a cloud nine." By then, Walker was in the major leagues to stay.

For Walker, the 1990 season was his first full year in the big leagues, although, technically, he had been credited with a year of service while recuperating from the injury he suffered in Mexico two years previous. That should have meant he was ineligible for the rookie of the year ballot, but the Baseball Writers Association of America, ruling a player should not lose his rookie eligibility due to injury, reinstated his status in a vote at a meeting at the all-star game in Chicago. The wording in the rookie rule was clarified (and is now called the Larry Walker rule) to give Walker back his rookie status. He then went out and hit 19 homers and 51 RBIs in 133 games, and tied for seventh in the voting, won by Atlanta's David Justice.

As the 1991 season began, a situation occurred that would be the first sign of trouble to come between Walker and Montreal fans. Pre-game ceremonies at home openers at the Olympic Stadium in Montreal are unpredictable because of the often-volatile political climate in the province of Quebec. On April 15 the American anthem was played, not sung, because singers won't take the gig, and went off smoothly. Then the Canadian Armed Forces band began the strains of *O Canada*. This was during the Persian Gulf War. As soon as the Canadian anthem began, boos rained down from one section of the stadium. But the boos were quickly drowned out and several young fans unfurled a huge Canadian flag along the base paths. In the left centre-field bleachers, however, a wild fist fight erupted when a fan began to wave a red Maple Leaf.

"When they started booing the anthem, I shook my head," said Walker. "Then when the waves of cheers kept coming and coming, I had shivers up and down my spine." Two years later, the fiercely patriotic Walker would find himself in the middle of another anthem controversy that made him a lightning rod for the anger of some fans and management. But that was in the future. As the 1991 season unfolded, Walker started to blossom and, after the all-star break, was the top hitter in the National League, hitting .338 in 72 games with 21 doubles, 10 homers and 41 RBIs. He also logged 39 games at first base, including a 16-putout day when Dennis Martinez pitched a perfect game at Los Angeles on July 28. He finished the season hitting .290 in 137 games with 16 homers and 64 RBIs.

Walker's breakout year was 1992. He earned his first Rawlings Gold Glove, and Louisville Silver Slugger for offensive performance after a .301 average in 143 games with 23 homers and 93 RBIs. In May, Walker hit a ball into uncharted territory, striking a speaker suspended high above the field at Olympic Stadium and was awarded a "ground-rule homer" in a win over San Diego. "The IBM Tale of the Tape should have read 310-foot speaker," joked Walker. The homer prompted this chart in the Expos game notes the next night by P.R. man Richard Griffin:

Momentous Homers in Expos history:
May 20, 1978 — Willie Stargell, only homer into the middle deck (Long fly).

April 4, 1988 — Darryl Strawberry, only homer off Stadium rim (High fly).

May 5, 1992 — Larry Walker, only homer off speaker (High fi).

Walker was named to the all-star game at San Diego and won AP and *The Sporting News* post-season all-star honors, while finishing fifth in the NL MVP balloting, behind winner Barry Bonds of the Pittsburgh Pirates. He became only the ninth Canadian ever selected to the all-star team. The others: Ferguson Jenkins of Chatham, Ontario (Cubs), John Hiller of Scarborough, Ontario (Tigers), Terry Puhl of Melville, Saskatchewan (Astros), Goody Rosen of Toronto (Brooklyn Dodgers), reliever Claude Raymond of St. Jean, Quebec (Expos), George (Twinkletoes) Selkirk of Huntsville, Ontario (Yankees), Jeff Heath of Fort William, Ontario (Indians), and Oscar Judd of London, Ontario (Red Sox).

Walker earned his second straight Gold Glove in 1993, teaming with Marquis Grissom to make up two-thirds of the golden NL outfield. He also turned in the first 20/20 season of his career, with 22 homers and 29 stolen bases and became first 20/20 Canadian. After the 1988 injury to Walker's right knee, the Expos had worried about his speed, but it was never an issue with him. "I don't know if it slowed me down," said Walker. "Stole 36 (at Indianapolis) the next year. I wanted to bang up my left knee. Who knows? Might have stolen 72." On Sept. 1 at Cincinnati, he hit his first grand slam against John Roper. He finished the season with a .265 mark, along with 22 homers and 86 RBIs in 138 games.

However, the honeymoon in Montreal was coming to an end. Walker was in the midst of the Expos' cost-cutting days, and the cutting knew no bounds. In the spring of 1994, the Expos cut off their usual spring clubhouse supply of vitamins. Said Walker: "They tell us to take vitamins and drink water down here, so what's next? Are we going to have to bring our own water to the park?" After the uproar, Walker received mail that told him he should have paid the $1,200 for vitamins himself.

The original game plan, first for the Expos and then later the Jays, was the same: find, develop and market a Canadian player. Then step back while fans rushed the turnstiles to watch the home-grown product. In Walker, the Expos had all of that, the best Canadian run producer ever to play. Yet, as Maple Ridge's favorite son entered his free-agent season in 1994, he wasn't treated as a national treasure, but as someone who was moving elsewhere. In mid-season, the Expos sat 30 games above .500, with the best record in baseball, and Walker hadn't had serious talks with management about a multi-year contract. At the same time, the Expos attempted to deal him and, whenever there was trouble, he always seemed to be the lightning rod.

"All the way through the minors, all I ever heard was 'We really need a Canadian to make it,'" Walker said. "Bob Gebhard (former farm director, later the Colorado GM) said over and over: 'We need a left-handed hitting Canadian power hitter.'"

On the eve of St. Jean Baptiste Day, a holiday that has become a celebration day for Quebec nationalists, Walker ripped the organization for its plans not to play the Canadian anthem before the game. As happened in 1991, the Expos feared the anthem would be booed. Walker said it was a bunch of bull; the anthem should have been played. His comments angered sovereignist Quebeckers, but also garnered a lot of support. "I received mail from French people in Quebec, fans in Ontario and New Brunswick thanking me," said Walker. "This is still Canada. Our anthem should be played."

With the Expos leading the Atlanta Braves in the NL East, GM Kevin Malone tried to deal Walker. He also offered him a one-year deal. "It's not that we don't want to keep him. The question is, can we afford to sign him to the long-term deal which he deserves," Malone said. "When players reach a certain level it's a case of cost versus production."

The Baltimore Orioles, the Florida Marlins and the Jays had interest. Meantime, as the Expos peddled Walker, petitions were being signed in cities like Baltimore and Minnesota to keep hometown heroes Cal Ripken and Kent Hrbek during their free-agent years. That's the American way. But not in Canada. The Great Canadian Hope seemed unwanted. The Expos themselves were a paradox in 1994. They were running away from the Braves with one-third of Atlanta's payroll, yet then Expo president Claude Brochu was a hawk on the side of commissioner Bud Selig in stalled contract negotiations with the players. The season was halted Aug. 12 and, when negotiations failed, the World Series was cancelled. The Expos, fighting for a salary cap and revenue sharing, lost a chance at the post-season by insisting on the New Order.

Next they would lose Walker.

"Walker is the most important person in the lineup," Jim Fanning, a Day 1 employee with the Expos, said at the time. "I'm not saying he's the best or most valuable. He's a professional. What they have now is a complete team. I can't imagine them without Walker."

Walker was popular with teammates and, he admits, sampled Montreal's nightlife from time to time. "I did some partying," he said. "I always have, I always will." To the front office, he was a royal, three-leafed pain. "He's vocal," said Malone said. "It's Larry's personality. He says things the team doesn't want said."

During the early 1990s, Tim Wallach was clearly the Expos' team leader. The franchise leader in games played and several batting categories,

Wallach was also a solid third baseman who was team captain when Walker arrived. But the Expos traded Wallach to the Dodgers after the 1992 season and expected Walker to fill the leadership void. "They told me, 'You're our leader.' I can stir it up." Walker remembers. But when Walker showed leadership, it earned him criticism from the front office and the media. "They tell me the French papers buried me a few times," said Walker.

Montreal Gazette columnist Tim Burke used to write that an athlete in Montreal was cursed to be "big, slow and English," when describing the fans booing Bob Bailey, Larry Parrish and Wallach. Walker was never slow, but at times in his final season he was booed. When Walker charged Pittsburgh Pirates pitcher Blas Minor and was suspended for four games, the Expos withheld his pay ($87,000). "Both the league and the team punished me," said Walker. "I was getting it from all sides, wondering whether my mother would get the whip out and give me a spanking." Walker eventually was paid, although the Expos filed a grievance. To make his point, he boycotted batting practice. Said Malone: "He never works hard in batting practice anyway."

Walker's locker that year was an interesting collection of pictures (former Tampa Bay Lightning goalie Manon Rheaume, former Expos Rick Cerone and Ken Macha), Metallica stickers, and a boom box always blasting. But it wasn't a fun season. In addition to the St. Jean Baptiste flap, the labor unrest and other minor issues, Walker was playing with a torn rotator cuff that would require post-season surgery and caused him to be moved to first base. Despite the injury, teams were interested in acquiring him. When the season was ended on Aug. 12, Walker was batting .322 in 103 games with 19 homers and 86 RBIs. He tied for the NL lead in doubles (44), despite his bum shoulder. Dr. Larry Coughlin operated on Walker Oct. 4 at Montreal's Queen Elizabeth hospital. And six weeks later—after Walker was not offered a contract by the Expos—the free agent headed to the Colorado Rockies, signing a four-year, $22.5-million deal, with an option.

"It sucks when you look back and see the way 1994 ended," Walker said, referring to the Expos' failed pennant hopes. "I feel bad for myself and my teammates, but most of all for the people of Montreal. How many years have they been waiting for a team to go all the way?"

In his April 26, 1995 Rockies debut and Coors Field's inaugural game, Walker had three doubles, including one with two out in the ninth that sent the game into extra innings, as the Rockies went on to edge the New York Mets 11-9. He homered in four consecutive May games and hit his 100th career homer May 7 against Los Angeles and righty Hideo Nomo. He showed a playful side on the field when making a catch June 27. With two out in the sixth, San Francisco Giants' Barry Bonds hit a fly ball in Walker's direction and the outfielder couldn't resist an imitation. Using an exaggerated Bonds-like snap at the ball and spreading his arm like a breast-stroker hitting the wall, Walker made the catch.

"I've done it to him before," Walker said. "He styles on me, I style on him. I'm just trying to make ESPN's *Sports Center*."

With the Rockies, Walker went somewhere that the Expos had never taken him—the playoffs. Colorado reached the post-season and Walker hit a game-tying, three-run homer off Tom Glavine in Game 2 of the NL Division Series against the Atlanta Braves. But Atlanta won the best-of-five series in four games. Despite the playoff disappointment, Walker's move to Colorado had been a success: He batted .306 with 36 homers, 101 RBIs, 82 extra-base hits, a .607 slugging percentage and 300 total bases to place seventh in the MVP balloting behind winner Barry Larkin of the Cincinnati Reds.

Early in the 1996 season Walker gave indications that he was ready to elevate his game to superstardom. Playing centre field on opening day, he homered in his first at-bat off Sid Fernandez of the Philadelphia Phillies. On May 21, against Pittsburgh, he set a Rockies' record and established a career high with 13 total bases. He also had six RBIs. The next afternoon, he tied a club record with two triples and, when he added a double, he set the National League record for consecutive extra-base hits with six. About that time Neil Munro released *The Canadian Players Encyclopedia* in which he maintained the best Canadian pitcher of all-time was Hall of Fame righty Fergie Jenkins, but the best hitter was a matter of debate. "Well, it's an argument," said Munro. "Tip O'Neill, Jeff Heath, Terry Puhl, George Selkirk or Larry Walker." It was quite a testament to Walker to be included among such august company after only six full big-league seasons.

Walker was white hot, and turning heads around the league, but injuries again put out the fire. On June 9, a day after going 4-for-4 against the Braves, he slammed into the Coors Field fence and broke his left clav-icle, which cost him the next 60 games. Unable to help the Rockies on the field, Walker devised a cash-reward system, paying out of his own pocket: $20 a hit, $20 a run, $20 a game-winning RBI, $50 a save, $100 a win for a starter, $50 a win for a reliever and $200 a complete game. The bounty was for road games only and the Rockies had to win to be paid. "If we win I'll make money, too," said Walker. "If we win, it means post-season and that means bonus checks." He returned to the lineup on Aug. 15, but less than two weeks later he suffered a shoulder spasm and had only 14 at-bats in the final month. Limited to just 83 games for the season, he hit .276 with 18 homers and 58 RBIs.

Walker returned to the Rockies the next season healthier and hungrier than ever. He was hitting .440, with six homers and 11 RBI after the first week, and kept his average above .400 through July 4. His 11 home runs in April tied a National League record. But, as Walker's amazing season progressed, he had more than baseball on his mind. After the final game before the all-star break, Walker and his girlfriend, Angela Brekken, flew from San Francisco to Cleveland on a private jet along with the Rockies' owners Jerry McMorris and Charles Monfort, GM Bob Gebhard and their wives. At 35,000 feet, somewhere over Iowa, Walker stood up and made a speech:

"Jerry and Charlie, I'd like to thank you for bringing me to Colorado and being so good to me. Geb, I'd like to thank you for allowing me to bring Angela on trips since I've been here, even though she isn't a wife." With that, he turned to his girlfriend. "Angela, it's time you became a wife. Will you marry me?" Walker then gave Angela an engagement ring.

Prior to the all-star break, as Walker went into an 0-for-15 skid before getting four hits in his last six at-bats, he had said that the .400 mark had become a distraction. It didn't help that he had suffered a bout of flu. "I spoke to Rod Carew about his run at .400 (in 1977, when Carew finished at .388)," Walker said. "He said the media pressure took its toll. He told me you have to make sure you allow time to get your work in."

On the workout day at the 1997 all-star game in Cleveland, Walker was asked to look over a list of the top Canadian hitters in major-league history. The list was sprinkled with names like Jeff Heath, Goody Rosen, Terry Puhl and George (Twinkletoes) Selkirk, men who held single-season batting records for Canadian-born players in the major leagues in the 20th century. As he reviewed their records, Walker, in the midst of a phenomenal season, was asked how many of the records were attainable that year. He checked them off one by on—all but doubles and RBIs, he figured at the time. It turned out Walker was wrong. Doubles and RBIs were both among the 13 Canadian single-season records he established. No Canadian has ever had a better season than Larry Walker in 1997.

He led the NL with 49 homers, ranked second to Tony Gwynn with a .366 average and was third with 130 RBIs, behind Andres Galarraga and Jeff Bagwell. He scored 143 runs and had 208 hits, including 46 doubles, as well as 409 total bases, a .452 on-base percentage and a .720 slugging percentage. He also chipped in a Canadian-best 33 steals, and set Canadian-best marks with 76 extra-base hits, 149 extra bases and getting plunked 14 times. It was a dream season and only the eighth time in major-league history that a player topped 41 homers while batting at least .320. Hank Aaron did it three times, and Hack Wilson, George Foster, Ted Kluszewski, Chuck Klein and Barry Bonds did it once. Wilson, Aaron and Klein are in the Hall of Fame, and Bonds is headed that way.

"To have a season like Walker, my God," said San Diego's Tony Gwynn. "He's had a year everybody in this game dreams about. I mean, what a year. What more can a guy possibly do? He's not only the MVP, he's the greatest player in the game."

The BBWAA named Walker the NL Most Valuable Player winner as he finished with 22 of 28 first-place votes—the first time a Canadian had ever won the award. He was within four hits and 10 RBIs of winning the first NL Triple Crown in 60 years and he became the first player since Hank Aaron in 1959 to top 400 total bases.

"I've never seen a year like Walker's," Padres manager Bruce Bochy said. "I've never seen anyone with that kind of consistency, to hit for that high of an average and with that many homers. To top it all, the guy's the best defensive right fielder in the game. He can beat you at the plate, in the field, or on the base paths. This will go down as one of the greatest seasons in history. It's a Babe Ruth season."

There have been plenty of MVP winners over the years, but where does Walker's 1997 season rank? His .720 slugging percentage led the NL and, at the time, was the fifth highest in NL history. He was the 14th player in major-league history to top 400 total bases (with 409), the most since Stan Musial had 429 in 1948. His on-base percentage topped the league and his 33 steals in 41 attempts made him only the fifth player with at 40 homers and 30 steals in one season. Before 1997, of all the players to hit at least 49 home runs, only one, Babe Ruth, had topped Walker's .366 average. To critics who suggested Walker benefited from playing in the thin air of mile-high Denver, Walker responded by leading the league with 29 road homers and batting .346 on the road to rank third among NL hitters.

Walker did all this despite injuring his right knee in the 10th game of the season, and with a sore right elbow, appearing in a career high of 153 games. Walker also won his third Rawlings Gold Glove, committing two errors in 246 total chances, and set a club record with 132 consecutive errorless games. But it was his accomplishments at the plate that turned heads and had Canadian baseball watchers nodding in agreement that Walker, in his eighth big-league season, had earned the title of Canada's best all-time hitter. Mind you, you'd have a tough time getting him to admit it. Asked if he was looking forward to being called the greatest Canadian hitter ever, Walker, in his aw-shucks style, said, "I go out, play and put up the numbers. How people perceive me is out of my control."

Another thing beyond Walker's control were year-end awards, and that led to a sore point. Walker was denied the Lou Marsh Award, given annually to Canada's top athlete. The prize went to race-car driver Jacques Villeneuve, winner of the Formula One championship. Learning the news, there was nothing aw-shucks about Walker's reply. He was angry and hurt, and he let people know it. "I lost to a machine," he said. "It ticked me off, made me angry. I'm the first Canadian to win the MVP in the 128 years the game has been played and I'm not good enough to win the Canadian athlete of the year? I'm sure if Andres Galarraga had won the MVP he would have been the athlete of the year in Venezuela. Or, if Vinny Castilla had won, I am sure he would have been the athlete of the year in Mexico. I was named athlete of 1997 in five provinces but couldn't win it for the country. That's one award I felt I should have won."

Walker had a word of advice for voters in 1998, saying: "If I have a worse year than last year and win it, I won't accept it. That tells you how political it is."

Statistics aren't what motivates Walker, although he admits satisfaction at becoming the career Canadian home-run leader, passing Jeff Heath. He is also the all-time Canadian leader in hits, doubles, runs, RBIs, total bases, stolen bases. "A guy sends me stats of Canadian players each year and every year my name gets higher and higher in the lifetime stats; that's a great feeling," Walker said. "Maybe some day a kid will say, 'I want to be like Larry Walker.' I'd like to read that."

Walker's over-all numbers slipped in 1998, which was to be expected, but he followed his MVP season by becoming the second Canadian to win a major-league batting title. He did it by taking over the lead on Sept. 2 and then hitting a remarkable .528 for the month to finish the season with a .363 average. His September surge saw him become the first player since 1993 to unseat Tony Gwynn for the NL batting title. It also made him the first Canadian batting champ since Tip O'Neill of Woodstock, Ontario batted .435 for the St. Louis Browns to win the 1887 American Association crown.

Despite his accomplishments the previous two seasons, Walker arrived in Tucson for spring training in 1999 wondering whether he was walking into a repeat of 1994, when the Expos traded him in the final year of his contract. But on the morning of the first exhibition game, March 4, he reached agreement with Colorado on a six-year $75-million contract. Then he went out and homered in his first spring at-bat. Four days before the opener, he strained a muscle on the right side of his rib cage and was placed on the disabled list. On April 15, in his first official at-bat, he doubled for his 600th hit in a Rockies' uniform. He hit safely in his first five games, went hitless in the next and then had a 21-game, consecutive-game hitting streak. From April 25-May 21, Walker batted .506, only the eighth time in history a player has batted at least .500 over a streak of 20 or more games.

Three weeks later, Walker had an 18-game streak, making him only the fourth player in the 1990s with multiple streaks of at least 18 in the same season as he went 33-for-70 (hit .471) over the 18 games with 11 homers and 27 RBIs. And from June 18-23, Walker homered five consecutive games, tying Dante Bichette's 1995 club record. One memorable game came at Qualcomm Stadium June 26. After the Padres prematurely set off victory fireworks in the ninth, he doubled through the smoke to score two runs, continuing the streak. He headed for the all-star game in Boston with a .382 average.

In Boston, Walker was one of the first on the scene when an ailing Ted Williams circled the Fenway Park warning track and then headed to the mound. The Boston P.A. announcer said: "and now ... the game's greatest living hitter ... " That was all anyone could hear from the noise of the jammed Fenway Park crowd. The NL and AL rosters were standing along the third and first base line when one by one they headed towards Williams. The whole thing was scripted, but watching from high above or being on the field didn't make it any less moving.

"It was rather emotional," Walker said after the game. "I'm a rather emotional guy and when I got there tears were coming out of Ted's eyes. I had to turn away. It almost brought tears to my eyes. The greatest players in the world surrounded by more great players. Ted was extremely touched."

Walker then proceeded to rack up Williams-like numbers in the second half of the season to win his second consecutive batting title. He ended with a club-record .379 average, the fifth highest in the majors since Ted Williams hit .406 in 1941. Walker also led the majors in slugging (.710) and on-base percentage (.458), becoming the first player to win the percentage triple crown since George Brett in 1980 (the last NL player to lead the league in the three categories was Stan Musial in 1948). He also had 37 homers and 115 RBIs. His .461 average at home is believed to be a major-league record. Elias Sports Bureau, which has tracked home/road splits since 1974, shows Walker's 1999 home mark was 43 points better than any other player in that span.

Walker followed his back-to-back batting titles with a 2000 season marked more by injury than accomplishment. He made two trips to the disabled list with elbow woes and played in only 87 games, batting .309. Still, the season was not without a couple of special moments. On April 19, Walker broke the career-hit record for Canadian-born major leaguers with a fourth-inning single against the Arizona Diamondbacks. It was the 1,148th hit of Walker's career and moved him past Jeff Heath, although Walker got there in 284 fewer at-bats—roughly half a season faster—than Heath, who played from 1936 to 1949. In August, just before his second trip to the DL, Walker played in Montreal and reached base in 10 consecutive plate appearances (six hits, three walks, hit by pitch). Healthy again, Walker opened 2001 with 11 homers in April and maintained a hot bat throughout the season, winning his third NL batting title in four years, hitting .350 with 35 doubles, three triples, 38 homers and 123 RBI, second most in his career.

By 2002, Walker was firmly ensconced among the game's elite. The past decade had shown him to be a player with remarkable talent at the plate and outstanding ability in the field. He'd also proven to be an unselfish team player, as demonstrated in 2000 when he agreed to defer $18-million in salary to free up some cash so the Rockies could sign free agent pitcher Mike Hampton. But for Rockies' rookie manager Buddy Bell it took an unusual play early in the 2002 season to fully appreciate Walker's all-round contribution. Walker hadn't gotten off to one of his fast starts. Nine games into the season he had just two RBIs and no home runs. But playing the Cincinnati Reds, Walker scored from second base on a wild pitch for the Rockies' first run in a 7-5 win. He made the mad dash for home when he noticed Reds catcher Ed Taubensee hesitate for a second because he thought the ball had struck Rockies' batter Todd Helton. That was all the opening Walker needed.

"That," said Bell, "is the reason Larry Walker is the best player in our league. It's not because he is so talented. There's pride involved. He understands the game as much as anyone."

Later that season, the Rockies were playing an intra-league game in Toronto. It was the first time Walker had played in Toronto. When he emerged from the first-base dugout at SkyDome on June 7, a World Series-type crowd of media awaited him. Rockies reliever Todd Jones glanced at the assembled dandelions of Canadian journalism and cracked: "Holy cow! A Canadian who can actually play baseball, either that or it's a line for a Celine Dion concert." At the time, Walker had a few more hits than Dion—1,760, including 320 homers.

Walker, of course, had begun his major-league career in Canada with the Expos, but that experience ended on a sour note, due in part to Walker's fervent patriotism. He was never a good fit in the province of Quebec. But Toronto might have been another matter. As a young player in Montreal, he admits to being envious at the success being enjoyed in Toronto. The Blue Jays won World Series in 1992 and 1993 and they played to nothing but sellouts from the time the SkyDome opened in 1989. That success wasn't lost on the Expos players, just five hours down the highway. "One of the things that stood out to the Montreal players about Toronto," said Walker, "was all the people going to the Jays games. You saw them winning and drawing 40,000, 50,000 a game. That was impressive." So, the question was put to Walker: Did he regret never having the chance to play for the Jays?

"I never had the opportunity, so it's tough to regret something you've never had," he said. Still, Walker concedes that life wasn't always easy for him in a French-speaking province and "it probably would have worked out better for me with the Blue Jays than the Expos. In Montreal if you are not French-Canadian, you aren't Canadian. I'd be more welcome in Toronto being an English-speaking Canadian." There was a time, when Walker was making noise with his bat in the minor leagues in the late 1980s, that Blue Jays management had been kicking themselves for letting him slip through the cracks of their scouting network. Then at one point well into Walker's career the Jays had some interest in making a play for him, but general manager Gord Ash backed off because, he said, "Walker played the game too hard," resulting in injuries. It was an odd statement. A common complaint these days is that "too many guys are going through the motions." Here was a bonafide Canadian superstar who would run through a wall to make a catch, but apparently that made him *persona non grata* in Canada's biggest market.

Baseball has become a nomad profession. The lure of free agency means most veteran players don't stay in one place for long. Walker was an exception. The 2003 season was his ninth with the Rockies. He entered the year as Colorado's all-time leader in average, slugging percentage, on-base percentage, home runs, runs scored, total bases and extra-base hits, and before the year was done he'd added games played, starts, hits, RBIs and doubles to become the franchise leader in almost every offensive category. But it wasn't a banner year. Walker batted .286, his lowest average since hitting .276 in 1996, and added just 16 home runs. After the season he had minor surgery on his right knee and left shoulder.

He came to camp healthy in 2004 but suffered a groin injury that side-lined him for the Rockies' first 68 games. Back in the lineup in mid-June, Walker stood at second base at Coors Field on Wednesday, June 30 with the giant scoreboard behind him blinking "2000" in bold numbers. Walker, in his 16th season, had doubled to become the 234th member of the 2,000-hit club. He is the only Canadian-born player to reach that milestone. He tipped his hat and said it was only the second time he had done so in his career. "I don't tip my hat often. The first was in 1992 when I got my third double in a game in Montreal and they got excited."

Standing on second base, taking in the affection of the Denver fans, those tips of the cap were like bookends to a remarkable 16-year story. "A big, fat Canadian kid has come a long way from scrubbing pins at bowling alleys in Kelowna, B.C.," Walker joked. "Not bad for an injury-plagued career. If I avoided injuries, it could have been easier and more fun, but it is what it is. I'm happy I lasted this long. I would've been better without all the injuries, but as long as this game's been going on, it's an honor to play the game longer than any Canadian player."

Five weeks later, Walker was again overcome with emotion. He had to fight back tears when saying goodbye to Denver on Aug. 6, 2004. After being with Rockies since 1995, the year Coors Field opened, he had waived his no-trade clause to join the playoff-bound St. Louis Cardinals, in the process allowing the Rockies relief on $9-million of the roughly $17-million he is owed through 2005. Among the many tributes received by Walker that day, Rockies first baseman Todd Helton called Walker "the best true athlete I've ever seen or played with." Helton recalled a Coca-Cola ad on the back of a program that showed Walker jumping to catch a ball. "His feet are probably chest-high off the ground," said Helton. "He's 6-foot-3, 245 or 250 pounds, with that type of athletic ability."

Walker had hoped the Cardinals would deliver him the championship that had eluded him throughout his career. Over the final 44 games, he delivered a respectable 11 home runs and 27 RBIs while batting .280 as the Cardinals easily won their division, and he was solid again as the Cards got past the Dodgers and Astros to claim the National League pennant. But 2004 was the year of the Red Sox. They swept St. Louis in four games, despite Walker, in his first World Series, batting .357.

For all his success, perhaps what surprises many people most about Walker is that he has not changed much since the day in 1985 when he showed up in Utica to begin his climb to the majors. When he returns to Maple Ridge, says his father, the first thing he does is call his old buddies to join him for a beer. "His hat size hasn't gone up to a size 12; it's the same as when he left for that first spring with the Expos in 1985. He's a down-to-earth guy and he's still a big kid at heart." And you won't see Walker's face in TV ads. He has never done commercials because, he has said, he doesn't need the money. He will, though, sign autographs—but one at a time. Collectors will send him a stack of Larry Walker cards and he'll autograph one, returning the others with a note promising to sign the rest after the person has made a donation to charity. Originally, he'd ask them to send $15 to the Denver Children's Hospital, but now he requests $25 for the Youth Sports Association, a non-profit organization for kids. When he signed his last contract with the Rockies, it included a joint $3,333,333 donation—there he goes with the 3s again—to children's organizations in British Columbia and Colorado. He has also donated a substantial sum to the Rockies Youth Fields of Dreams Program, which helped open five Colorado facilities.

It was either 1992 or 1993 that the subject of autograph signing put dad in hot water with his son. "I was in Montreal watching batting practice leaning up against the dugout when a man comes with his young son—his boy had his arm in a cast—and he asked me, 'Are you Larry

Walker's father? Do you think he would sign my boy's cast?' I went over and asked Larry. So, we're walking back to the dugout and he says without moving his teeth: 'Dad, don't you ever do this to me again before a game.' As soon as he got there 150 more people showed up." Walker signed for everyone.

When he was with the Rockies, Walker was once asked how he would like to be remembered 10 years after he retired. "Ah, I don't know," he said, wrinkling his face. "It would be kind of neat if 10 years from now I read about some kid who made it and said that growing up, he wanted to be Larry Walker." And if that kid were Canadian, Walker would be even happier. He says he prefers to hear people describe him as a Canadian ball player and not just a ball player. "It gives me that sense of pride knowing that I have done something that so many kids from my country can shoot for growing up."

Ultimately, the greatest compliment for any player is a place in the Hall of Fame. Walker neatly sidesteps the question.

"I remember Jim Deshaies (84-95 won-loss record in his 12-year career) begging people to vote for him for the Hall of Fame, just so he could say he had one vote," says Canada's greatest hitter. "If I get one vote for Cooperstown, I'll be happy."

If he keeps it up, he's got mine.

FARM BOYS

It has been a wonderful ride for Corey Koskie. From the University of Manitoba to Des Moines Area Community College, to the National Baseball Institute, to the Minnesota Twins minor-league system, to the majors and now the Toronto Blue Jays, courtesy of a three-year, $16.5-million contract signed in December 2004. Not bad for a kid from a tiny dot on the map of the Canadian prairies.

Then again, maybe it shouldn't come as that much of a surprise. Despite relatively small populations, the provinces of Manitoba, Saskatchewan and Alberta have produced some of Canada's best and most enduring baseball talent. From Alberta, there is Jeff Zimmerman of Carseland; from Saskatchewan, Terry Puhl of Melville and Reggie Cleveland of Swift Current; from Manitoba, Russ Ford of Brandon and, of course, Koskie, the pride of Anola, a farming community of 300 souls just east of Winnipeg.

"Look up hometowns of our better players, they are mostly from rural Canada," said Tom Valcke of the Canadian Baseball Hall of Fame. "No knock against city kids, but if you didn't do a lot of manual and physical work—loading bales of hay, lifting boxes, whatever—as a kid, it's tough to develop the strength needed for the speed required to play baseball."

The first major-league star, and still the greatest arm, to emerge from the Canadian prairies was Ford. Scouted and signed by fellow Canadian Arthur Irwin, Ford had three 20-win seasons in the majors during his career from 1909 to 1915 with the New York Highlanders (renamed the Yankees in 1913), and the Buffalo Bisons. Ford had a reputation for intentionally doctoring the ball, or scuffing it for more movement. Fifty-five years later, it was Cleveland who picked up the pitching torch, and he was as durable as any prairie farm workhorse. Signed by St. Louis scout Bill Sayles, Cleveland made his debut with the Cardinals in 1969, but still had rookie status in 1971 when he went 12-12 with a 4.01 earned run average to earn National League rookie pitcher of the year honors.

The '71 season was the first of Cleveland's seven straight seasons with 10 or more wins, three with the Cards, and four more with Boston after being dealt in 1973. Cleveland won 13 games for the 1975 Sox in a season where he became the first and only Canadian pitcher to start a World Series game, pitching five innings in Game 5 against the Cincinnati Reds, who won 6-2 and took the series in seven games. Cleveland moved to the Texas Rangers in 1978 and on June 20 was the back end of a Toronto trifecta. He picked up the win over the Blue Jays, the third consecutive game the Jays lost to a Canadian-born pitcher. Detroit reliever John Hiller of Scarborough, Ontario, started the run, followed by Ranger righty Fergie Jenkins of Chatham, Ontario. The following season, Cleveland found himself in Milwaukee, where he wound up his 13-year career in 1981 with lifetime totals of 105 wins and a 4.01 ERA.

By that time, the Prairie baseball faithful already had another hero to discuss each morning at the coffee shop. Like all good prairie stories, the Terry Puhl tale starts on a farm. He was born on July 8, 1956, on a grain farm outside Melville. When he was a toddler, his family moved into the town of 4,600, where his father Frank ran the Massey Ferguson dealership. He began playing ball at age six and never played hockey. Baseball would start in mid-June and finish the middle of August. Nowadays, high schoolers travel to Arizona, Florida, Ohio or Georgia for baseball tournaments. Puhl's team never left Melville, save for the national championships. The 1971 Melville Lions team won the Western Canadian bantam title as Puhl was named Most Valuable Player. In 1973, Puhl was again named MVP as the Melville Elks won the Canadian midget title at Barrhead, Alberta. Earlier that season, the uniqueness of prairie baseball was demonstrated during a game in which Puhl was pitching, setting hitters down 1-2-3, 1-2-3, like the Rockettes, but without the kick. Teammate Jason Schoeffer was playing right field, completely bored by the lack of action. Remembered Puhl, "A gopher popped his head up, Jason picked up a rock and fired it." So much for the gopher, which, at inning's end, Schoeffer scooped up by the tail and brought along as he jogged in to the dugout.

Leading up to the Barrhead tournament, which was played on the Labor Day weekend, Houston Astros' scout Wayne Morgan, a native of Kindersley, Saskatchewan, had a choice to make. "I could have gone to Kamloops, B.C., to see an open-aged tournament with college kids and stayed in a luxury hotel," Morgan said. "Or I could have gone to Barrhead. I went to Barrhead and we stayed in a cabin without running water. We were lucky to get that. It was either that or a tent." After the championship game, in which Puhl pitched and later played the outfield, Morgan asked Puhl if was interested in signing a pro contract. Replied Puhl: "Are you crazy? Of course I would." So Morgan phoned Astros' farm director Pat Gillick, asking for permission to give Puhl a $10,000 signing bonus. "Pat said our budget was shot, but if I really liked him, and I did, to stay around two weeks and look at his arm when it recovered from the tournament," Morgan remembered. Two weeks later, Morgan worked Puhl out at Pirie Field in Melville. The scout put Puhl in right and had him throw to third. Although there wasn't a third baseman to throw to, Morgan watched the trajectory of the ball and "that was good enough for me."

Puhl had only completed Grade 11 when his father Frank and his mother Margaret sat down at the kitchen table after the workout. According to the rules of the time, Canadians couldn't sign until they had finished Grade 12, or had their 17th birthday. Since he'd turned 17 two months earlier, Puhl was able to sign. Morgan managed to get him a $1,000 signing bonus, a new glove and a new set of cleats, and tossed in an incentive bonus which bumped his salary every time he jumped a level in the minors. "I always thought our midget team had a few guys that should have had an opportunity," Puhl said. "Our catcher John Maserek; the Reds wanted to sign him, but it didn't work out. We had about five quality hitters. Playing on a pasture with all the bad bounces we weren't good fielders."

Puhl headed to spring training in Cocoa Beach, Florida, in 1974, not knowing a soul and reckoning he'd be headed home any day. "They were releasing guys one after another; I didn't realize that they had a few years in and, in my situation, I wasn't in jeopardy," he said.

The Astros sent Puhl to play rookie ball in Covington, Virginia; "The culture was a little different, but all you did was play. I never saw a family member for six months. After a road trip, we knew we were close to home when we could smell the saw mill."

Puhl returned home to finish Grade 12 in the fall of 1974. "I needed physics and Mr. Wardle taught physics and happened to be the football coach. He tutored me, I played quarterback for him," Puhl said. The Astros were unaware he was throwing passes and executing the odd quarterback sneak. Three years later, Frank and Margaret Puhl made the drive from Melville to Charleston, West Virginia, to see their son play a Triple-A game. A week before they left, Puhl, not wanting his parents to make the long drive for naught, asked his manager Jim Beauchamp: "Skip, I'm not going anywhere, am I?" Replied Beauchamp: "The Astros have said you'll be here the whole season. You're not going anywhere." After the first game his parents saw, their son was summoned to Beauchamp's office. The Astros needed outfield help and since Puhl's teammate J.J. Cannon was injured, Beauchamp told the Astros that Puhl was his best outfielder. Five days after his 21st birthday, Puhl was in the majors. "My parents went 2,000 miles to see me hit a home run in one game and turned around and drove home," Puhl said. On the drive into Houston from the airport, Puhl drove past the Astrodome and, seeing the lights, suddenly found every-thing "very intimidating." On July 12, 1977, he entered the game in the eighth inning as a defensive replacement, in an 8-0 loss to the Los Angeles Dodgers. The next day manager Bill Virdon posted the lineup and there it was in the leadoff spot: 1. Puhl, LF. Once he stopped shaking, he lined to left against Burt Hooten in his first major-league at-bat and was 0-for-5 when he led off the 13th with the score deadlocked 2-2. Puhl smacked a single to left against Elias Sosa. With two out, he scored the winning run on a double by Bob Watson before 17,755.

So began a 12 1/2-season run as the Astros' leadoff hitter. "I never expected to stay … (but I) did well and stayed and stayed," Puhl said.

He had a good relationship with Virdon, who managed the Astros from 1975-82. As Puhl puts it, "I was Bill's type of player—some say I played the same way he played when he was with the Pittsburgh Pirates: don't make mistakes, keep your mouth shut. We didn't have that many words over the years, but if you did things right you got to play." The manager, a former centre fielder, loved to work the outfielders hard and Puhl loved the work. "He taught me how to play the outfield," Puhl said. "No one could handle a fungo as well as Bill. He was very adamant about throwing to the right base and hitting the cutoff man."

National League manager Tommy Lasorda selected Puhl to play in the 1978 all-star game in San Diego; that season he hit .289 with three homers, 35 RBIs and 32 steals. In 1984, the Canadian Baseball Hall of Fame named Puhl the winner of the Tip O'Neill Award as Canadian player of the year. After batting .303 in 1988, Puhl's average dropped to .271 the next season and in 1990 he was just an extra player, appearing in only 37 games. Puhl wanted to sign with the Jays as a free agent. The feeling was not mutual, so he stayed in the National League, signing with the New York Mets, but was released at spring's end. The Kansas City Royals signed him to fill in for an injured George Brett at first base April 25, but released him June 9 after only 15 appearances.

When Puhl retired, he had played in 1,531 games and had 1,361 hits, the most ever by a Canadian, until Larry Walker surpassed him in both categories. He had a .280 career average with 435 RBIs and 217 stolen bases. Mind you, it's his defense and prairie work ethic that will be best remembered. Playing 15 seasons, he maintained a fielding percentage of .993, making only 18 errors in 2,596 chances, the best average of any outfielder in baseball history.

Not to shabby for a prairie boy who, upon signing his first contract, just hoped to "play Double-A ball some day."

While he was playing, Puhl spent his winters working as a stockbroker. Since retirement, he has moved around the investment business, from E.F.

Hutton to Rotan Mosley, which was purchased by Paine Webber, and now Sanders, Morris and Harris, an investment banking firm. Inducted into the Saskatchewan Sports Hall of Fame and Museum in 1994 and into the Canadian Baseball Hall of Fame in 1995, Puhl had by then made his home in Sugarland, Texas, with his wife Jacqueline, whom he met in 1977 in Melville.

Despite his post-baseball career, Puhl isn't a stranger to the diamond. In 2002, he served as interim head coach of the Fort Bend Baptist High School Eagles, where he coached his son Stephen. He has also continued to be involved in projects in Melville, where baseball almost died out as the new century dawned, according to Puhl. Fastball was knocking at the door for diamond space. "A group of guys my age who all have sons resurrected baseball and they won the Western Canada championship. Now there are a ton of fields," Puhl said.

Like Puhl, Koskie grew up on a farm, filling his summers during the 1980s with prairie baseball, through t-ball, tyke and peewee. Unlike Puhl, he also gravitated toward hockey, good enough as a goaltender to advance up to Tier II Junior-A with the Selkirk Steelers. When he wasn't tending goal for the Steelers, he was playing volleyball at the University of Manitoba. "I was the setter and he was the power hitter," recalled Scott Shipper, Koskie's buddy from kindergarten through the elementary Anola School to Springfield Junior High and Springfield Collegiate. "Some tournaments he'd leave us high and dry because he had a hockey game. We'd get to the final without him and we'd get destroyed."

In the summer of 1992, Koskie visited the office of Manitoba Bisons' volleyball coach Garth Pischke. "I walked in and Garth started to talk about next season, 'this is how we're going to run the offence, it's going to be all around you, here's where we want you,'" Koskie remembered. That's when he broke the news to a shocked Pischke. He wouldn't be playing hockey anymore. But he wouldn't be playing volleyball, either. He was headed to the Des Moines Area Community College in Boone, Iowa, to play baseball. "By the time I got home Garth had phoned my mom to try to get her to talk me out of going to Iowa," said Koskie, whose play had drawn attention at a Major League Baseball Scouting Bureau camp at Giants Field in Winnipeg. There, he had been one of the chosen few asked to stay behind by Canadian scouting director Tom Valcke. Koskie ran a 6.9 in the 60-yard dash, which opened eyes. Cincinnati Reds' scout Bob Szymkowski gave Koskie's name to John Smith, the coach at Des Moines. "John called me every day in May asking 'are you coming?' Sometimes he would call three times," Koskie said. "I can't imagine that school's phone bill. It got to the point where my parents recognized his voice." Koskie admits he probably would not have gone in the end, except that Cam

Croy, whom he played against, was planning to attend. Without a scholarship, Koskie took out a student loan.

The first time coach Smith worked out his Bears, he had 50 to 60 players on the field, including the green Canuck, who had driven down with his parents, Leonard and Maryann, from Anola. "I felt overwhelmed. I was scared and thought 'you're making a big mistake,'" Koskie said. "I'd left all my buddies. What have I done, what am I doing here?" mom said, "try again tomorrow," and he did. Then, Koskie saw a familiar face, or should it be a familiar hat ... his own. There on the same Iowa field was right-hander Curtis Falls, a Mic-Mac Indian from Yarmouth, Nova Scotia, wearing a Manitoba hat. Koskie recognized it from playing in the national championships, when players from competing provinces exchanged hats after the game. Turns out there were five Canadians in the Bears camp. "Canadians are easier to recruit," said coach Smith, who has been at Boone since 1974 and has had more than 40 Canadians on his team. "Talk to an American and they come with an attitude 'how much money (scholarship) will you give me.' The Canadians, they want to play. And most of the time they are better students because their educational system is tougher."

Smith has had three players make the majors: catcher George Williams with the Twins, Paul Wilmet with the Texas Rangers and Koskie. "You know, I never thought he'd play in the big leagues," Smith said. "He was in the right place at the right time and he took advantage. Corey didn't run to first in 3.8 seconds, but he was a big old boy that ran hard to first down the right-field line and he swung the bat hard. He could hit when he got here, so I didn't touch him." Des Moines practiced during the winter and hit in a cage and when spring finally arrived Koskie lit it up and was voted a third-team all-American at Boone, hitting .389 with 12 homers. Returning home to Manitoba, Koskie played for Morgan de Pena and the Tewlon Cardinals seniors to get ready for the 1993 Canada Games in Kamloops, British Columbia.

In Kamloops, John Harr of the National Baseball Institute saw Koskie playing shortstop and offered him a spot on his team for 1993. "I don't remember working that hard in Des Moines; you just played," Koskie said. "Where I really learned how to play third base was at NBI."

Harr, who coached Canada to the 1991 world junior title, had Koskie for two seasons at the now defunct NBI. Koskie calls him the most influential man in his baseball career. Initially, he had trouble learning to throw the way he thought Harr wanted. "Corey!" said Koskie in his John Harr voice, "what are you doing?" "John showed me how to throw the ball and when it carried, it would go straight. I didn't know I could throw that straight, it was such a drastic difference."

In 1994, Twins' scout Howie Norsetter selected Koskie in the 26th round of the major-league draft. After a short season of rookie ball, the spring of 1995 was Koskie's first major-league training camp at Ft. Myers, Florida. "I had the same feeling as Des Moines ... where do I fit in? There were 150 guys, guys from all over the world, from Venezuela and the Dominican Republic who played every day growing up. There were six third basemen in the system." But Koskie held his own and that season, at Single-A, began to hit for power. By 1998 he had worked his way up to Triple-A, where a 26-homer, 105-RBI season for Salt Lake prompted the Twins to promote him in September. Koskie made his debut Sept. 9, going hitless in a 10-8 loss to the Angels at Edison Field in Anaheim.

His best year with the Twins was 2001, when he hit .276 with 26 homers and 103 RBIs. In 2004, his final season before gaining free agency, Koskie hit .251 with 25 homers and 71 RBIs as half of the Twins' Canuck corner duo of Koskie at third and Justin Morneau at first base. He felt very attached to the Twins, who made him a two-year, $8 million contract offer. "One day we were on the phone and Corey said, 'What about all the kids that say Koskie's my favorite Twin?'" said lefty Paul Pavicich, a minor-league teammate from Clarence, New York. "I said, 'Corey, what about all the young kids in Canada who will say you're my No. 1 favorite Jay?'"

Koskie and his wife, Shannon, prayed in the new house they just built in Medina, Minnesota, and spoke to their pastor Tom Lamphere every day. "I'm a Christian and wanted to go where God wanted me to go," said Koskie. "Tom asked 'Do you have a passion in your heart to play for the Twins?' No, I don't. After they didn't offer me arbitration, I knew it was time for me to leave, but I am part of the community and I love it here. Then, Tom asked, 'Where do you feel in your heart you want to go?' I feel the pull from Toronto." Koskie's agent Pat Rooney was hammering out the final details when the Los Angeles Dodgers called and asked if they could talk since it was apparent third baseman Adrian Beltre was leaving. Koskie told Rooney to finish the deal with the Jays. "He has a great opportunity, being Canadian, to play every day for a Canadian team," Pavicich said.

In appreciation of his time in Minnesota, Koskie took out an ad, which ran Jan. 6 in the *Minneapolis Star-Tribune*, thanking the fans, the organization, GM Terry Ryan and coaches. Pavicich says Koskie is a great role model, as a family guy and from the way he plays, "he's not afraid to get dirty. Hey, he's Canadian."

So, how has seven years in the majors and the lifestyle that goes with it changed the kid from Anola?

"He hasn't changed a bit," said Mark Schlosser, who played with Koskie at the National Baseball Institute. "My wife's family are from Minnesota and in 2001 we went to see him. He was driving the same Ford Explorer as before. He's unaffected by fame and money. He's become a better person; he's very strong in his faith. He doesn't have to give me time, or call or leave tickets. He once told me the true measure of a person is how they treat someone who has nothing to offer them."

"He's the same now as he was in the minors," said Pavicich. "The only thing that's changed is his clothes; in the minors he wore shorts, polo shorts and sandals. Now he wears nice suits. A lot of people in this business move on and forget. I'm so glad he made it. He's a family guy, he's a Christian guy, he loves the Lord, loves his family."

Shipper, who has known Koskie going back to when a big day was finger painting and sleep time in kindergarten, hasn't noticed any changes either. "He treats everyone the same as when we were in high school; we're all really proud of him. He still plays tricks like in high school," said Shipper, recalling Koskie's favorite high school prank was to pull his father's truck across the narrow entrance to Springfield Collegiate on Friday afternoons, pop the hood and pretend something was wrong with the vehicle: "It's a Friday afternoon, everyone is trying to go somewhere for the weekend, teachers are honking, Corey's throwing his arms up: 'I'm sorry, I don't know what's going on.' It was typical Corey."

With the Jays, Koskie becomes the team's first everyday Canadian in 27 years, since second baseman Dave McKay played second base way back in the franchise's second season.

"Look at me" says Koskie in amazement. "How did I get to where I am? This really shouldn't be. I'm a Christian and I believe God had a plan."

At his unveiling by the Jays, Koskie told the assembled media of his first trip to Yankee Stadium. "Reporters would come and say, 'What does this feel like? You're in the same place Babe Ruth played,'" Koskie said. "I was 'Cool, but my place is SkyDome, because that's what I grew up watching ... the same place where Paul Molitor, John Olerud and Tony Fernandez played. Those were my heroes.'"

These days, the latest generation of Canadian prairie farm boys has a new hero to root for, one who happens to be one of their own.

A HOLLYWOOD STORY

8

You can just see the imaginary script meeting unfolding. Film folk gather in a room, sitting around a cluttered conference table full of empty coffee cups and a tray of doughnuts. Ideas for a baseball movie are being tossed around. Maybe these are the same people involved with making *The Rookie*, which starred Dennis Quaid as Jim Morris, a coach who bet his players that if they made the playoffs he'd go to a pro tryout camp, and is signed and makes the Tampa Bay Devil Rays at age 36.

"Okay," the screenwriter says. "Let's say we take these teenagers, their pop uproots the family, moves to Texas, one son is drafted and gets a big bonus. The other is ignored for years and winds up in France? FRANCE! He learns a new pitch, has to beg an independent league—an independent league, baby, that's not even in the minors—for a tryout in some out of the way place with snow on the field. Two seasons later he is in the all-star game. Make it a park with history, say Fenway. And oh yeah, as a kicker, the father gets sick, goes into a coma and awakes to see his sons pitch against each other in the majors. Will it sell?"

The room goes silent. One by one, people shake their heads. Not bloody likely. Who in Hollywood would touch such a script? Directors and actors would read it and say, "If this was fiction, I'd never do it. It's too unbelievable."

Yet, as sure as there are three outs an inning, this is a true story.

This is a story about Jeff Zimmerman and the how the Zimmerman family might be the best illustration of Canadian perseverance. It's about Jeff's brother Jordan, about their father Bill. It's how Bill Zimmerman defied medical odds and how his sons defied the baseball gods. Both made the bigs. And Bill was there to see it.

Before we get to the climax we start with Bill, of Oliver, British Columbia, in the Okanagan Valley in the interior of the province. His sons were born in Kelowna, Jeff in 1972 and Jordan in 1975. Then, Bill and his wife Sharon moved the family to Carseland, Alberta (pop. 600) about 30 miles southeast of Calgary, in 1976. Bill's father Eugene wanted his son to help run his Carseland Hotel. Jeff played senior Little League and Big

League sandlot ball in Calgary. When Jeff turned 16, Bill Zimmerman came up with an idea. Why not form a traveling team? The Calgary '88 Selects were born playing under the Baseball Alberta umbrella. The team, which included Jeff, played against teams from both the Alberta and Calgary associations and made regular trips south. To be prepared to play all summer, the Selects worked out throughout the winter. Bill opened an indoor facility, a converted World War II airplane hangar. Batting cages were built, turf was laid. Players were recruited. Some coaches were upset. Like so many great baseball ideas by good baseball men, it ran short of financing. "We didn't have 100 percent of the best players. With so much travel, not everyone could commit," Jeff said. "Parents had to be sold first rather than the kids; they all wanted to play." Bill bought uniforms, equipment, kept some players who couldn't afford to play and picked up the tab for rooms and meals. Bill spent roughly $10,000 for that 1988 season on the road. Which meant that that was the Selects' one and only season.

In 1989, Jeff was back to playing for the Big League Dodgers. In 1990, he pitched at Treasure Valley Junior College in Ontario, Oregon, and in the summer played with the Calgary Royals, who were coached by Bill. Ryan Radmanovich, the first Calgary player to make the majors, was also on the team. "Teams all played short seasons," Radmanovich said. "Bill thought a traveling team was a good idea, going to Montana, Idaho and Washington. Bill was a big influence in my life." In 1991, Jeff transferred to Indian Hills Community College in Centreville, Iowa, under the guidance of coach Rick Mathews and pitching coach Cam Walker of Winnipeg, then transferred to Texas A&M on a half-ride scholarship. However, in August two drafted players decided to return to school rather than sign and turn pro, and Zimmerman saw his offer reduced to 10 percent, which he couldn't afford. Jeff phoned his former coach, Mathews, who lined him up with Texas Christian University "sight unseen" for the same half-ride scholarship A&M had originally offered.

Along about that same time, Bill decided to move with Jordan from Alberta to Texas. Dad figured the exposure, the coaching, the quality of competition and the opportunity to play year round would be good for Jordan. The Texas A&M coaches suggested to Bill that the town of Brenham would be a good place to re-locate. John Peters, owner of a 53 consecutive-game win streak for Brenham High School, put the school on the map when he appeared on the cover of *Sports Illustrated* in 1988. So off went dad and Jordan, with Jordan entering Grade 11 at Brenham High. Recalled Jeff, "Mom ran the hotel in Carseland and dad played Mr. Mom in Texas. They realized it was a sacrifice they wanted to make to help Jordan's baseball career."

In Jeff's second year at TCU in 1993, he put up some decent numbers as a senior, going 8-3 with a 4.50 earned run average. "I was good, not great and had a lot of interest from scouts," Jeff said. But zero phone calls on draft day. He then pitched for Team Canada at the World University Games in Buffalo and the World Cup qualifier in Nicaragua in 1993, with Bernie Beckman managing and Greg Hamilton the pitching coach. Again, no interest, though, at a training camp in Windsor, Ontario, he did get some attention for lighting up a radar gun at 91 miles per hour. With nothing else doing, Jeff accepted Hamilton's offer to head to, of all places, Montpellier, France, to pitch in 1994. "France was a wonderful experience, a relaxing change of pace, I enjoyed the culture," Jeff said. "Baseball in France was very rudimentary. They'd only been playing for 20 years. It was novel. They weren't that familiar with the game, but they played with a passion."

Jeff joked that with his 85-mile-per-hour fastball, he was considered France's Nolan Ryan. But it was a great opportunity to experiment. "I'd never been able to throw a slider. Greg and I tried a few different grips," Jeff said. "Pitching in competitive games you don't want to break out new pitches." The Canuck was so far above the competition he could start out a hitter with three sliders in the dirt to fall behind 3-0 and come back with three straight fastballs for a strikeout.

The French had a unique approach to baseball, shutting down the season for almost two months for a summer vacation and then resuming the remainder of the season at the playoffs. For the break, Jeff flew to Nicaragua to pitch in the World Cup for Canada. Getting ready to face Korea, he warmed up and had to wait out an hour rain delay. When he took the mound he hit the first batter in the head, walked the next two, but escaped the jam and pitched a 3-1 win. When he returned to France, Jeff helped Montpellier beat the Paris University Club in the Division 1 final.

Returning to Canada, Jeff pitched for the Kelowna Grizzlies in 1995 against college players before joining Team Canada for its cross-country tour to the Olympic qualifier in Edmonton, then for the Coquitlam Athletics in 1996 while finishing his master's degree in business administration at Simon Fraser University in Vancouver. In the spring of 1997, he decided to give professional baseball one last try, driving from Carseland to Winnipeg to audition at an open tryout for the Winnipeg Goldeyes of the independent Northern League. Zimmerman arrived to find the city covered in snow, with a Zamboni being pressed into service to remove snow from the Astroturf of Winnipeg Stadium. Used to facing hitters with aluminum bats in college and international competition, the righty wanted to saw off a few hitters, jam them on the hands and break some wooden bats. He went inside and broke so many bats the Goldeyes brought out aluminum bats. Manager Hal Lanier, who ran the Goldeyes, liked what he saw. Jeff signed to play for $700 a month and quickly established himself. He earned Northern League rookie pitcher-of-the-year honors and led the league with a 2.82 earned run average, going 9-2 with 140 strikeouts in 118 innings. "I'd throw a slider two feet in front of the plate and the hitters couldn't check their swings," said Zimmerman, thinking to himself: "Holy cow, this is a pretty terrific pitch. If I'd had this in college it would have been different; this pitch may have saved my career."

Ultimately, the new slider did just that. At season's end, Zimmerman faxed his resume to every team in the majors. "I didn't brag, I just stated in my letter 'I'm Canadian, I'm a late bloomer, I still have a lot of mileage in my arm,'" Zimmerman said. Texas Rangers' scout Reid Nichols called the next day for Lanier's phone number and a contract soon followed.

The Rangers sent Jeff to Single-A Port Charlotte where he remained for just 10 games before getting bumped to Double-A Tulsa, where he was 2-1 with a 1.29 ERA, recording nine saves.

Because of his age and his success, Jeff was being fast-tracked. After appearing in only two games at Triple-A Oklahoma in 1999, he was called up by the Rangers. Jeff came on in relief in the seventh inning against the Seattle Mariners April 13, with a 15-5 lead, and pitched 1 2/3 scoreless innings.

Meanwhile, brother Jordan had pitched at Brenham High in Grade 11 and 12, earning all-district honors twice. Then he went to Blinn Junior College in Brenham and was selected in the 32nd round of 1994 June draft by Seattle. Spurning the Mariners' offer and returning to Blinn for another season, he then signed a letter of intent with Texas A&M but ultimately capitulated and accepted M's scout Bill Young's offer of a $325,000 signing bonus in May 1995. A lower back fracture delayed Jordan's pro debut until 1997 at Single-A Everett. He pitched in only 22 games in his first four seasons due to injuries. His breakthrough came in 1999, when he was recalled from Double-A New Haven by the Mariners on May 13, just 34 days after the Rangers had promoted Jeff. In his debut, Jordan got the final two outs of the eighth inning in a win over Minnesota and he didn't allow a run his next four outings. He went back down to Triple-A Tacoma June 18, but was back with the Mariners 10 days later, four days before Seattle visited the Rangers.

Along the way, Bill and Sharon had divorced; Bill had wed Carol but had also battled cancer, had a heart attack and contracted pneumonia. The season before both sons made the major leagues, Bill was hospitalized and fighting for his life. "Being on the mound was a mental break," Jeff said.

"I wasn't thinking about my father's health, the adrenalin took over."

Bill was strapped to a ventilator for 4 1/2 months and was in a coma for 51 days. "We always knew there were great odds, but he had always beaten all the odds," Carol told John Lott in one of the several wonderful stories Lott wrote about the Zimmermans on his website TruNorth Baseball. It reached the point where doctors said a decision might have to be reached on taking Bill off life support. Carol said no. "I said, 'You may not have anything that can help in your medical journals, but you are not God,'" Carol told Lott. "'God can do anything. He's walked on water. He's divided the seas. I've given this to God, and you all keep telling me that Bill's not going to make it, and every day he does. No, I refuse to give up and I won't sign the papers not to resuscitate.'"

Bill the battler kept battling, and he finally left the hospital. And so it came to pass that on Friday, July 2, 1999, at the Ballpark in Arlington, as the Rangers hosted the Seattle Mariners, father and sons were together. Bill was there in his wheelchair, wearing a red Rangers cap to support Jeff and a blue and green Mariners jacket to support Jordan. "It was not the best color coordinated combo," Jeff said.

That night, both brothers worked in the game. Jeff came on with the score tied 5-5 in the eighth and worked a scoreless inning. Texas took a 6-5 lead in the bottom half against Ken Cloude. The M's tied it in the ninth against John Wetteland. In the bottom of the ninth, Royce Clayton doubled off Cloude and Mark McLemore was intentionally walked. Ivan Rodriguez lined out. Jordan then came on with the game on the line to face the left-handed hitting Rusty Greer. The brothers had never played against each other at any level. Greer lined a high fastball to left-centre for the game winner. It was a good news, bad news Zimmerman night: Jeff extending his scoreless streak to 17 1/3 innings in 15 outings, while Jordan, although he didn't allow a run, giving up the game-winning hit to Greer. "That was really tough. I can't bear to watch Jordan pitch, either that night or when we were together with Team Canada," Jeff said. "I feel so helpless. I want him to do so well. When he gets hit, it's like I'm out there, not doing well. My heart went out to him that night."

For Bill, it was a very special evening. Twice within a few innings, he heard the announcer say, "Now pitching..." and the guy they introduced was one of his sons. The Zimmerman gang gathered that night at T.G.I. Friday's: Jeff and Jordan, Bill and Carol. "My brother wasn't in the best spirits, but my father..." Jeff said. "He kept staring at the two of us with a big grin; he was smiling ear to ear. How unbelievable it was to see both of us pitch in a game. It was strange seeing him that way. He's not an emotional guy, but he was so happy that night." How many nights had Bill lain in hospital unable to sleep, closing his eyes to shut out the pain of the cancer and the respiratory ailments and thinking good thoughts of just such a night?

When it was over, Bill and Carol headed home, Jeff flew with the Rangers to Oakland and Jordan headed for Anaheim with the M's. In Anaheim, Jordan planned on surprising his wife Jennifer. He watched from above when he saw her get out of the cab and then hid. As his wife opened the door, he jumped up to surprise her, only to land on her suitcase with a sprained right ankle. The next day, July 6, the M's placed him in the disabled list. Later that week, American League manager Joe Torre selected Jeff for the all-star game in Boston. The rookie set-up man had pitched 50 1/3 innings, allowing 18 hits, fanning 46 and walking only nine. He was 8-0 with a 0.89 ERA. Jeff came on to work the seventh at Fenway Park before a sold-out crowd of 34,187 fans. The AL led 4-1 when Zimmerman walked the first man he faced, Brian Jordan. Friends and family had gathered along with mom Sharon, watching nervously at the Carseland Hotel. Brad Ausmus then threw Jordan out attempting to steal and Zimmerman walked Jeff Kent. Alex Gonzalez popped to second. Luis Gonzalez reached on a Jose Offerman error. Now, Zimmerman was facing the potential tying run, with runners at first and third with two out. Finally, Jeff induced the Expos' Vladimir Guerrero to ground out, ending the inning as cheers engulfed the Carseland Hotel, otherwise known as the Blue Saloon.

Jeff finished the 1999 season with a 9-3 mark and a 2.36 ERA. He was 4-5 with a 5.30 ERA in 2000 and, in 2001, took over as the Rangers' closer from John Wetteland, going 4-4 with a 2.40 ERA and 28 saves. In January 2002, he signed a $10-million, three-year deal. The celebration was cut short by elbow tendonitis as the season began, and Jeff had Tommy John surgery on his right elbow. Over the next three seasons, he pitched just eight innings while rehabilitating the elbow, and signed a minor-league deal with the Rangers for 2005.

Jordan's career, meanwhile, has had more downs than ups. In 1999, after posting a 7.88 ERA with the Mariners, he was sent to Tacoma. In the spring of 2000, Jordan was demoted on the next-to-last day of camp. Jordan and some other players headed out golfing the next day. His left foot was hanging out of the golf cart he was driving and it got wrapped around the golf ball washer and the back tire of the golf cart, tearing tendons in his left ankle. He missed the whole year, and then resurfaced for one game at Triple-A Omaha in 2002. In 2004, he pitched in 50 games with the Long Island Ducks of the independent Atlantic League, going 3-2, with a 2.28 ERA, and was set to attend spring training with the Houston Astros in 2005.

While he doesn't like to talk about it, Jeff Zimmerman has been

Baseball Canada's No. 1 financial supporter in recent years. He says that the talent with Team Canada has improved since he pitched in 1993. "The program has come so far since I played … and Greg Hamilton has done such a great job. Greg's someone who has made an incredible difference in my life. Greg personifies Baseball Canada and everything it stands for. Over the past 10 years Greg has been my coach, instructor, mentor and role model. He helped me become a better pitcher and most importantly, a better person. I am honored to call him a friend."

As for the man most responsible for the major-league dreams-come-true of two brothers from the British Columbia interior via Alberta and Texas, Bill Zimmerman passed away on July 7, 2000, after fighting the good fight. He had made it known that he wanted to be cremated and have his ashes spread across a ball field. So, Jordan and Jeff and their step-mom Carol gathered at Leroy Dreyer Field at Blinn Junior College, where Jordan had starred and where Bill could still be found watching games after his youngest son had signed and moved on. They spread half his ashes on the mound.

Later, Jordan, Jeff and their mom Sharon headed to the new four-diamond complex in Carseland, which was under construction at the time. Appropriately, one of the diamonds was called Zimmerman Field, named after the town's most famous baseball family. The brothers spread some of Bill's ashes on the mound, then walked to the other three diamonds and spread the remainder on the home plate areas. "Both were very solemn moments; we were alone with our thoughts, contemplating," Jeff said.

One father. Two sons. Two *major-league* sons.

"It was such a miracle we both made the big leagues, to pitch against each other and my dad still to be alive to see us pitch," said Jeff.

Yep, too unbelievable for Hollywood.

AUGUST 4, 1991

9

What has been the greatest single moment for Canadians in baseball?

Would it be Jan. 8, 1991, the day right-hander Ferguson Jenkins of Chatham, Ontario was elected to the National Baseball Hall of Fame? Or July 21 of the same year when he was inducted in ceremonies at Cooperstown, New York?

Maybe you prefer Oct. 26, 1992, or 362 days later when the Toronto Blue Jays won back-to-back World Series titles, the first in Atlanta, the second at the SkyDome? Could it be Nov. 13, 1997 when Larry Walker of Maple Ridge, British Columbia was named the National League Most Valuable Player? Or perhaps you prefer Nov. 9, 2003 when Team Canada qualified for the 2004 Olympics. Or possibly when Los Angeles Dodgers closer Eric Gagne earned the NL Cy Young Award on Nov. 13, 2003?

Whatever your choice is, stick with it. For our money, however, the date to remember is Aug. 4, 1991, a Sunday. While that date may not be imbedded in the minds of a majority of Canadian baseball fans, check it out:

Terry Puhl of Melville, Saskatchewan didn't play for the Houston Astros in a 2-1 win over the Los Angeles Dodgers.

Kirk McCaskill of Kapuskasing, Ontario wasn't on the mound in the California Angels 5-2 loss to the Chicago White Sox.

Rob Ducey of Cambridge, Ontario didn't have an at-bat, though he did enter the game in the eighth inning as a defensive replacement for the Blue Jays' left fielder Mookie Wilson in a 2-1 victory over the Red Sox.

Lefty Denis Boucher of Montreal, Quebec didn't throw a pitch for the Jays.

Mike Gardiner of Sarnia, Ontario didn't pitch for the Sox.

Kevin Reimer of Enderby, British Columbia went hitless in three at-bats for the Texas Rangers, in a 3-2 loss to the Milwaukee Brewers.

Steve Wilson of Victoria, British Columbia didn't work for the Chicago Cubs in an 8-3 win over the New York Mets.

Larry Walker had a fourth-inning, run-scoring single for the Montreal Expos in a 3-2 loss to the Philadelphia Phillies.

Dave Wainhouse of Scarborough, Ontario didn't pitch for the Expos, a day after making his debut against the Phillies.

So, on the day, the four Canuck hitters combined to go 1-for-6 with one RBI and the five pitchers didn't throw a pitch. That's what was happening in the majors.

Meanwhile, in Brandon, Manitoba, a Miracle on Grass was taking place. A total of 5,000 fans crammed into the 3,800-seat Westbran Stadium tighter than a clown car. At least 10,000 have since claimed they were there. There at Westbran, Team Canada won its first and only World Youth Baseball Championship, beating Chinese Taipei 5-2 for the gold, ending a 10-game journey against nine of the world's best teams.

We're not seeking here to diminish the outstanding careers of Jenkins and Walker, the best pitcher and hitter the country has ever produced. The Jays gave Canadian baseball a boost by beating the Atlanta Braves in the 1992 World Series. While the front office—president Paul Beeston, chairman of the board Peter Widdrington, vice-presidents Bob Nicholson and Howard Starkman and assistant general manager Gord Ash—was pure Canadian, on the field it was Toronto's Americans and Latins beating Atlanta's Americans and Latins. The next year, Toronto's Americans and Latins beat Philadelphia's Americans and Latins in the World Series with an assist from Rob Butler of East York, Ontario.

But that day in Brandon, Manitoba's second largest city with about 40,000 residents, Team Canada was A-No. 1, king of the hill, top of the heap, like the song says. Pitcher Daniel Brabant started the final before collapsing in pain throwing a fastball in the sixth. He left to a standing ovation. Jason Birmingham took over and when he fielded a comebacker and flipped to first baseman Troy Croft for the final out of the ninth, all hell broke loose.

"We were all on the mound in record-breaking time," said manager John Harr, who for 13 years was the main man behind the National Baseball Institute, which produced major leaguers Denis Boucher, Steve Sinclair, Rob Butler, Matt Stairs and Corey Koskie. "That stadium had so much emotion that day. After the presentations when everyone boomed out *O Canada* you would think there were 50,000 in the stands."

Team Canada's win was pretty much kept a nationwide secret because Canada had not been expected to play for gold, and the media coverage reflected that belief. Rick Birmingham, Jason's father, who pitched in the Atlanta Braves' minor-league system, was at home in Sarnia, Ontario, trying to find the gold medal game on his TV. He did find the world junior championships that day: Argentina was playing Team USA. From Edmonton. In basketball.

"Greatest day in the history of Canadian baseball?" Harr says slowly as he repeats the question to himself. "Hmmm, I might be a little biased, but I think 1991 was something special. We did something that Canada had never done before and it hasn't been done since."

Canada has fielded 65 teams in international competitions since 1965—in the world juniors (27); the world seniors (15); the Intercontinental Cup (seven); the Pan-Am Games (six); the Olympic Games (three); world university championship (three); junior Pam-Ams (two), the Presidential Cup (one) and the Goodwill Games (one). But only one Team Canada, the 1991 youth team, left the field with gold medals around their necks. A year later, they were inducted, en masse, into the Canadian Baseball Hall of Fame in St. Marys, Ontario.

The Canadians earned the gold by defeating Chinese Taipei in the final, but at least some of the medal's luster could be traced to having beaten heavily favored Team USA 10-6 in round-robin play. Chinese Taipei defeated Canada 9-7 the night before the gold-medal game to claim the top spot in the round-robin competition with an 8-1 mark. Canada and the United States were tied with 7-2 records, but Canada's earlier win over the Americans earned the host team the berth in the final. The U.S. defeated Australia 6-5 to win bronze.

"The 1991 team is the best kept secret in Canada," said Earl Berard, team leader of Canada's entry. Or, as longtime Blue Jay fan Marnie Daly would put it years later, "I remember watching TV after the 1993 World Series, they were talking about whether it was possible for Canada to win the world championship back-to-back-to-back. The other commentator said 'Canada has already won three in a row ... the World Juniors in 1991, then the Jays in 1992-93.'"

The story of the forgotten world title began in July of 1991 at the National Selects championship for players 18 and under. The best players from all 10 provinces gathered in Regina in the midst of a heat wave and a mosquito epidemic. As Stubby Clapp recalled, "They were as big as pterodactyls." Seriously, though, the bugs were so distracting that one Quebec outfielder, tired and frustrated at swatting away the gnats, sprinted off the field in mid-inning and raced, screaming, into the safety of the dugout. "We played one game and they stopped play for 30 minutes while they sprayed the field," said Team Ontario GM Tom Lawson. The final, in which Ontario beat British Columbia 6-1, was played as fires burned in dumpsters strategically placed around the outfield fences, the smoke rising to keep the critters away.

A total of 34 players from the tournament were selected by Team Canada evaluators to board a bus for a 10-day training camp in Kindersley, Saskatchewan.

Canada's eventual roster of 25 included only eight 18-year-olds. Going in, Harr was concerned that it was "a pretty young group." Recalled Birmingham, "We thought we had a pretty good over-all team; we had some hitting, we could pitch and field. We were consistent. We were not dominant. We always knew the Americans and the Cubans were the strongest. We didn't know how we would stack up."

Canada rolled over The Netherlands 10-0 in the opener July 26, a win not everyone was expecting. Canada had played a pre-tourney exhibition against The Netherlands and lost 6-4. Said pitching coach Gary Picone: "I'm thinking 'geez, we can't even beat The Netherlands.' We have to pitch our best, so we can say we at least won one game." Daniel "Bear" Brabant pitched a three-hitter with seven strikeouts to make things easy for the Canadian defense. Oh yes, and he hadn't had his nickname for very long. Brabant had been the only Quebec player to survive training camp. "We felt that he might feel a little uncomfortable," Harr said. "So Gary and I talked it over. The question was, how do we make him feel an important part of this team? We nicknamed him the Bear. Gary told him that he was going to be the tough, growly, grizzly bear when he was on the mound. Within minutes all the kids were calling him 'The Bear' and he felt he was a part of the team. He proved that he was."

In its second game, Canada beat Australia 9-7, but it was one that could have got away and almost did. Which would have been oh so painful considering that the mercy rule was eight runs and in the eighth Canada led 8-1, with the bases loaded and only one out. Instead of being able to push the killing run across, Team Canada had to sweat out a nervy, six-run, bottom-of-the-ninth Aussie rally. With two out and runners on second and third, Aussie Greg Rodgers lined a ball down the line that just stayed foul. Mark Fraser then struck out Rodgers looking. "My heart was pounding in the ninth, we thought the last out would be simple and we almost got beat," said Todd Betts, who went 3-for-5, drove in Canada's first run with a double in the third and added singles in the fifth and ninth innings. Jason Birmingham picked up the victory, pitching 7 2/3 scoreless, striking out five.

Canada's perfect record didn't last long, as the next day, defending champion Cuba beat the Canucks 3-2 in 10 innings. Fans greeted Harr with boos in the eighth after the Canadians failed to score the go-ahead run. With one out and centre fielder Ken Torrance on second, Blaise Laveay lined a ball to the gap in right centre. Coaching third, Harr held up Torrance at third; alas, Laveay failed to pick up the stop sign and chugged towards third. Caught in a rundown, Laveay was erased and Canada failed to score. Starter Joe Young worked 7 1/3 strong innings, allowing two runs on six hits while striking out four. "He opened some eyes," said Harr. "Here was a 16 year old, getting by on strictly fastballs.

He had the Cubans chasing pitches out of the zone. They had a lot of free swingers." Mike McKinlay, after escaping a jam in the ninth, allowed the winning run in his third inning of work, as Daniel Lazo hit a one-out single over a drawn-in outfield.

Canada rebounded from the Cuban loss with a 5-3 win over Brazil, despite a lot of tension in the dugout. Down 4-0, some chirping Brazilian players managed to rattle starter Mark Fraser in the middle innings, prompting Picone to yell at Fraser: "Don't be listening to their bench!" At which another coach, Tony Flood, told Picone, "You can't talk to a kid like that." Shot back Picone, "I'll talk to him anyway I want! We're trying to win a ball game!" Fraser went back out to the mound and rolled along. "I'd tried to be nice and that didn't work, so I took the hard-ass approach," said Picone. "He got angry with me and it worked." Fraser pitched 7 2/3 innings, allowing three runs on five hits, while walking six and striking out two. Kevin Collins was 3-for-3 with a double, two singles, an RBI, two runs scored and two steals in earning game MVP honors.

Collins was at it again in Canada's fifth game, hitting a three-run double as the host ran its record to 4-1 with a 4-1 win over Mexico. Next, against Italy, back-up catcher Jim Curtis made the most of his first start, hitting Canada's first home run of the week in the fourth, a two-run shot to left, on the way to a four-RBI performance and a 10-2 thumping.

Aug. 1 was decision day at Westbran. The doubleheader had Chinese Taipei vs. Cuba and Team USA vs. Canada. All four owned 5-1 records. Former Philadelphia Phillies stars Bob Boone and Greg Luzinski were there to watch their sons, who were with Team USA: third baseman Aaron Boone and catcher Ryan Luzinski. "I was sitting beside them," Doug Betts, Todd's father said. "They left in the sixth."

For a time it looked as if Boone and Luzinski might enjoy the game. Canada and righty Joe Young fell behind quickly, allowing three runs in the first. Another run put Team USA up 4-0 in the second. "We were fast approaching the point where we had to make a decision," said Harr. "Either write the game off or try and stay close. I said 'Get Jason Dickson ready.'" Dickson took over with one out in the second and silenced the American hitters, working 5 2/3 innings and allowing one run as Canada bounced back for a 10-6 win and a first-place tie with Chinese-Taipei, which had beaten Cuba 1-0.

Late in training camp, Dickson had been a long shot to make Team Canada. It wasn't a secret. The coaches knew it and most telling of all, Dickson knew it. So, on the morning of the final day of workouts, hours before the team was to be picked, Dickson approached Harr and asked for a meeting. "Jason asked whether he could speak to me in private," Harr said. "He said, 'you have given me every opportunity to succeed and I haven't shown much. If I could have one more chance, fine, if not I'll understand.'" Harr spoke to pitching coach Picone and asked if Dickson could be worked into the final intra-squad game that day. Picone agreed and Dickson was outstanding. When Harr and his coaches—Gord Leduchowski, Flood and Picone—along with guest coaches Greg Hamilton and Ron Betts, adjourned to pick the 18-man roster, the discussion went long into the night. "We sat up until three or four a.m. discussing our 17th and 18th players," Harr said. "In the end, we cut a player from (the previous year's team) to keep Jason Dickson."

What would have happened had Dickson not had the confidence to approach Harr that final day of camp? "The reason I remember fighting for Dickson was while he'd been less than consistent, with his stuff he could beat anyone—if he pitched well," said Picone. "Going in we didn't think he was one of our best three arms, but he dominated. If he doesn't win we don't play for the gold."

●●●

Like everyone else who succeeds in baseball, whether he's from South Lompoc, California, Waxahachie, Texas, or Chatham, New Brunswick, Jason Dickson had help from a mentor. His was Greg Morris. "Greg was my coach in midget, junior and high school at James M. Hill in Chatham," Dickson said. "He follows baseball real close. Before he would help me with pitching. Now I phone him and ask: 'Which team should I sign with?'" Morris is a retired high school principal and coaches the Chatham Ironmen, perennial contenders for the New Brunswick and Canadian national senior crowns.

Born in London, Ontario, to Royce and Ann Dickson, Jason moved to Chatham as a youngster and turned to baseball when he realized he wasn't the "best hockey player in the world." By July 1997, though, he was sitting in a clubhouse alongside the best baseball players in the world. Dickson was 8-4 with a 3.51 earned run average with the Anaheim Angels when American League manager Joe Torre named him to the all-star team. Though he didn't get in the game, there were still plenty of memories. "Torre said he was sorry, but at the same time he's trying to win a ball game. I understood. I enjoyed the experience. Just being selected, taking part in the festivities, going to the parties, hanging out in the clubhouse— I was rubbing shoulders with guys I grew up watching on the TV—and I found out that they are human like any one else."

Dickson finished third in rookie-of-the-year balloting, behind Nomar Garciaparra and Jose Cruz, and when he went home that winter, "It was pretty crazy. Everyone was excited; I did public speaking and banquet appearances. I'm not a celebrity, but that's the way people at home treated me." After a 10-10 performance in 1998, a torn labrum in his right shoulder cost Dickson the entire 1999 season. He has appeared in only two games in the majors since—he began 2004 pitching for the Somerset Patriots in the independent Atlantic League, then was signed by the Kansas City Royals for the Triple-A team in Omaha—which has made his stints with Team Canada all the more rewarding. In 2004, he pitched five scoreless innings as Canada beat The Netherlands 2-0 in pre-Olympic play. Then, in the Athens Olympics, he pitched six innings in a 9-3 win over Italy and took the loss in a 5-2 setback to Cuba in round-robin play.

Asked for his favorite baseball memory, he admits to having a tough time choosing between two: "Winning the World Youth at Brandon in 1991, with Todd Betts and Stubby Clapp, as well as being named to the 1997 all-star game."

• • •

While the much younger Dickson had kept Canada in the crucial game against Team USA that afternoon in Brandon, it was catcher Blaise Laveay who provided the offensive difference. Right-hander Ken Henderson started for the Americans, coming off a 19-strikeout performance against Chinese Taipei when his fastball was clocked at 97 miles per hour. Laveay hit the first pitch he saw in the sixth for a two-run homer over the left-field fence for a 5-4 Canada lead. Stubby Clapp remembers Laveay rounding third and yelling at Henderson, who had been selected fifth over-all in the first round of the 1991 draft by the Milwaukee Brewers: "Hey Kenny, there goes your contract." "I thought we were going to brawl right there, both benches were yelling at each other," remembered Clapp.

That wasn't the only reason the first-rounder lost his composure. "We had a game plan," Harr said. "He enjoyed working quickly, liked to dictate the pace. He was cocky. We had kids willing to slow him down; they called time once in a while and stepped out. Eventually he lost it; he threw gas, but his strikes were in the middle of the zone." A three-run homer by Todd Betts in the eighth provided a cushion, and Mark Fraser performed some final heroics by striking out Ryan Kjos with the bases loaded in the ninth. "After beating the U.S., we thought we could beat any team," said Jason Birmingham.

Next up was Nigeria, making its first appearance on the international stage. They had taken some serious drubbings, like a 26-0 loss to Team USA in seven innings, but Canada wasn't looking to make matters worse. Harr suggested acting like hosts: no stealing, no going first-to-third on a single, don't take an extra base on an error. Harr gave the ball to outfielder Collins rather than using a pitcher. "Even Stubby Clapp pitched and he couldn't hit 60 miles an hour," Birmingham would later joke. Clapp remembers a number of players heading to the Nigerian dugout during a rain delay. "They had bongo drums with them, they let us try them, guys were giving them chewing tobacco; we completely bonded with them," Clapp said.

"All we really wanted to do was get it over in seven innings," Harr said. "The Nigerians appreciated that we didn't run up the score. At the end of the game, the Nigerians came out of their dugout and saluted us by clapping their hands and pointing to our team. We clapped back."

And they could have clapped for the Aussies, who had upset Cuba, assuring the Canadians of a spot in the gold-medal game. That meant Chinese Taipei had to defeat Canada in the final game of the round robin, or the gold medal game would be a rematch with Team USA. "Going in, we knew it was a nothing game for us. If we'd beaten Chinese Taipei we were in, if we had lost we were in," Harr said.

Chinese Taipei won 9-7, setting up the rematch for gold, but the game had its moments. For one, Stubby Clapp did his acrobatic back flip, a tribute to his favorite player and fellow flipper, St. Louis Cardinals Hall of Famer Ozzie Smith. Then he delivered with the bat: two singles and a double.

• • •

Stubby Clapp and Manitoba go together like his hometown of Windsor and its famous Tunnel Bar-B-Q. Clapp's 1991 trip to Brandon was his first time wearing a CANADA jersey, but not his last. In the opener of the Pan-American Games at Winnipeg in 1999, Team USA led Canada 6-3 in the bottom of the 11th. Andy Stewart hit a three-run homer to tie the game and four batters later, Clapp blooped a ball into shallow left. The ball plopped on the grass between players, and pinch runner Julien Lepine scored the winning run.

Manager Ernie Whitt was asked whether he'd considered pinch-hitting for Clapp, 0-for-5 until his 11th-inning at-bat. "How do you pinch-hit for a guy with a name like Stubby Clapp?" Whitt asked. Stubby-mania was born.

At a Great Big Sea concert, a song was dedicated to Stubby and the Canadian players; a helicopter took him across town for a personal appearance and CNN's *Sports Tonight* signed off with: "I'm Vince Cellini ... and I'm Stubby Clapp."

When the *Toronto Sun*'s Steve Simmons asked him what it was like to be a media darling, Clapp replied: "I don't know about being a darling. I'm not that good-looking." For the week—at least for the week—Stubby Clapp's name was as big in Canadian baseball as Larry Walker.

"Stubby had that little flare to shallow left to beat Team USA and became a household name," Harr said. "People ask me about him and I say, 'He played third for us when we won the worlds in 1991.' Most people say, 'no kidding?' Stubby had so much energy. When he was doing his flips, the crowd loved him."

From afar, the sawed-off human dynamo resembles a pint-sized Pete Rose, when he excelled for the Cincinnati Reds and Philadelphia Phillies. He seldom blinks, doesn't wear batting gloves, but his mouth is usually chirping. His jaw sticks out farther than former Prime Minister Brian Mulroney's. He'd break a store window if he ever walked into one. "Hey Baba!" Clapp yelled across an Olympic courtyard to Baseball Canada executive Jim Baba after Canada beat The Netherlands 3-0 at the 2004 Olympics. "You cut me in 1995 and I'm still here." Another day, another zing, this one directed at the man who coached the Olympic qualifier in 1995, but failed to include Clapp on his team.

Baseball may be an equal opportunity employer—Curtis Pride played for the Montreal Expos when he couldn't hear, Jim Abbott pitched a no-hitter for the New York Yankees after being born without a right hand—but do you not have to be stubborn to make it in the game of baseball when you stand five-foot-eight? How many times has Clapp been told he was too short? Not fast enough? Didn't have enough power? "Stubby was a guy you wanted to have up with the game on the line," remembered Picone, one of Canada's coaches at the '91 world juniors. "Good hitter, but he struggled with the glove." Picone never thought Clapp would make the St. Louis Cardinals, who promoted him for a 23-game stint in 2001. "I was surprised when I heard Stubby made Double-A. I mean Stubby Clapp, that's a hard name to forget. You can imagine what I thought when I heard he was in the big leagues, but good for him. He must have worked his butt off."

Clapp is a survivor with a heart as big as a Canadian map, including the territories. It sometimes seems he lives for the international stage, whether it's the Olympics, the 1999 Pan-Am Games or the 1991 world juniors. Clapp was a 36th-round pick, the 1,058th player chosen by St. Louis in 1996. When Clapp's coach at Texas Tech called him into his office and told him he'd been drafted, the infielder replied: "I can't be drafted, I'm Canadian." Starting at Single-A at age 23, he worked his way up to Triple-A Memphis by 1999. Called up to the Cardinals in 2001, he retired the flip, but stayed a fan favorite, as well as a favorite of manager Tony LaRussa's good friend Bobby Knight, a Busch Stadium regular. When Knight was headed for Texas Tech, where Clapp had played, he asked for a scouting report on Lubbock.

"He'd done his research and knew I went there," Clapp recalled. "So he sought out my opinion on what Lubbock was like, what it was like to live there. I had nothing but good things to say about the city and the university."

Clapp brought the flip out of retirement for the Olympics. "He wanted to leave it in Memphis," said Chastity Clapp, Stubby's wife. "But in the Olympics, how can he hold anything back?" Stubby met Chastity in Memphis, the night of the Mike Tyson-Lennox Lewis fight, June 8, 2002 at an after party hosted by *Stuff* magazine. They were married the next spring training. "He picked me up after a game and we were married," said Chastity. "Then he played another game the next day." The Clapps had a baby in 2003 and named the boy Cooper Wrestles Stubby Clapp. Cooper was Clapp's first baseball glove, Wrestles is his brother's name and of course Stubby is Stubby. As was his father, who nurtured his son's talent—and sense of fun—through Little League and beyond. Watching her 31-year-old husband in Athens, Chastity said, "He's like a little kid again."

Clapp was 1-for-3 in a 5-2, round-robin loss to Cuba in Athens, yet hours later his likeness was bobbing his head in approval back in Thunder Bay, Ontario, where baseball's Canada Cup was being played. During the Quebec-Ontario game, organizers decided to pay tribute to the man who is the face of Baseball Canada on the international stage. They reserved two seats in the stadium: one for a Stubby Clapp bobblehead doll, and the seat next to it so fans could have their picture taken with the doll.

The 29 people wearing Canada's uniform at the Olympics were asked to select the best Canadian player they'd ever seen. Larry Walker of the St. Louis Cardinals was the runaway winner, but Clapp was tabbed as the best by reliever Chris Begg.

"Stubby is Mr. Baseball Canada. I say that part facetiously and part seriously," Begg said. "He's Mr. Baseball and he plays with a great talent, a great abandon. He's well liked by everyone. What he does most of all is exemplify what Canadian baseball is all about. We call him Mr. President."

When Clapp was told someone had picked him, he was silent, as if waiting for a punch line. "I'm flabbergasted," Clapp said. "It's certainly not because of my ability. That's unbelievable for someone to say that about me. If someone says that about me it shows that I was taught to play the game the right way."

The fruits of that labor were evident long before Clapp became a household name across the country. In Brandon, they knew he was a star way back in 1991.

● ● ●

Before the final of the 1991 World Youth Baseball Championship between Canada and Chinese Taipei, there were troubling signs for Canada. Shortstop Todd Betts was hobbled by thigh and ankle injuries and had not played against Chinese Taipei in the final round-robin game. And scheduled pitcher Daniel Brabant had, at least for a few moments, become a doubtful starter after the trainer came to the coaches early in the day and said Brabant couldn't pitch because he was suffering from overuse. "We talked to the kid and he says 'I'm fine,'" pitching coach Picone said. "I don't ever remember a trainer having more say than a manager."

As it turned out, both players emerged as heroes. But not without some difficult moments. Betts made two fourth-inning errors, allowing the first of two Chinese-Taipei runs, and Canada fell behind 2-0. Brabant, who didn't allow a run in two starts during the round robin, allowed just four hits in 5 2/3 innings before collapsing on the mound. Jason Birmingham took over. "When I came in it was sort of a downer; we all thought Brabant had seriously hurt his arm," Birmingham said. Afterward, with his arm in a sling, Brabant said he felt that on his final pitch something in his arm had disconnected. He wasn't seriously injured, though, and a week later pitched for his club team in Montreal.

Clapp walked to lead off the sixth inning and Jason Lee singled to centre. A passed ball moved up the runners and Betts doubled to tie the game. Collins singled home Betts and Canada led 3-2. "That's when we started to believe we could win it," said Birmingham. The 6-foot-4 Troy Croft hit a monstrous line-drive homer over the 400-foot mark in right-centre in the top of the eighth that put Canada ahead 4-2. And proving the symmetry of baseball once again, the home run ball by Croft, the team's only Newfoundlander, was caught by a man from Newfoundland sitting in a lawn chair atop his RV. "He was from Corner Brook and came up to me after the game and introduced himself," Croft said.

Betts drove in another run in the ninth for a 5-2 lead while Birmingham worked 3 1/3 scoreless, recording 10 outs, including the final one, a comebacker that he threw to Croft at first base. The Canadian dugout emptied and the sky filled with gloves tossed in celebration. Coach Tony Flood spotted Croft still wearing his glove. Croft was holding the final out in his hand. Thus, he headed home with two souvenirs: the home run ball caught by a Newfoundlander, and the final out, caught by another Newfoundlander.

In the immediate after-glow of victory, there were still more honors for the Canadians. Second baseman Jason Lee, the 18-year-old Korean who immigrated to Canada from Seoul in 1988, was named MVP of the game after going 4-for-5, with two runs scored, and being involved in seven of the final eight outs. Collins, the right fielder, led all batters in the tournament with 14 RBIs, four game-winning RBIs and 23 total bases. As for Betts, he had knocked in three of Canada's five runs, including the winner. The errors were forgotten.

•••

When Betts arrived home from Brandon, his left hand was in a cast. As his dad Doug recalled, "He broke a bone in his left hand in the eighth inning breaking up two, but he was out there in the ninth when they won it." Doug Betts had been in the stands for Canada's first nine games, but missed the gold medal game because he had to head back east for work. Not that he missed many games over the years.

"He didn't push, but he was always there to drive me to the park," Betts recalled. He coached me until I was about 13. After that, he was always around, always at our games." One of dad's best memories is the time in t-ball in Ancaster, Ontario, when Todd made a highlight-reel play in centre, then ran in to tag the runner at third and the runner at second for an unassisted triple play. "He was a five-year-old playing six-year-olds," Doug Betts remembered.

Jill Betts' favorite memory is seeing her son hit two solo home runs for the Yakult Swallows in a 2-0 win over the Yomiuri Giants before 55,500 at the Tokyo Dome in 2003. For home games at Tokyo's Jingu Stadium, when Betts left the on-deck circle and headed towards the plate, the theme from *Hockey Night in Canada* blared. His theme music used to be *Jump Around* by House of Pain, but then some Canadian visitors stopped by and gave him a CD with the Saturday night theme. Only Murray Westgate and Don Cherry were missing.

When Betts was a tyke, and on up through peewee and bantam, his team would often play Windsor, home of future teammate Stubby Clapp. "Stubby's name always came up," Doug Betts said. It would continue to come up, running parallel with Todd's career, merging every now and then at important junctures, and usually in lock step with Jason Dickson. It's not Tinker to Evers to Chance, but Dickson to Clapp to Betts sure covers some ground.

"When the three of us get together I'd like to think that we haven't missed a beat," said Clapp. "I'd played against Stubby all the way up to midget," said Betts. "Then we were teammates the first time in 1991. No matter what happens off the field, the other two and I are like brothers. You can trust them with anything." Betts and Clapp roomed together in 1991, again in Panama at the world qualifier and again in Greece at the Olympics. "We have a unique friendship," Clapp said. "We started out in basically the same place with Team Canada. In 1991 Todd played short-stop; that was the first time I'd ever seen anyone field a ball on the run and throw. We all ended up in the same place 13 years later due to a lot of persistence. Except Athens was a bigger stage, the head of the class." In Brandon, Clapp played third and Betts shortstop, while Dickson spent most of his time on the mound. In Winnipeg, Betts played third and Clapp second. In Athens, Clapp was at second and Betts at first, while

Dickson took his turn on the mound. "Together again," Betts said. "It's a small world."

Clapp hit the game-winning bloop against Team USA in the Pan-Am thriller, but it was Betts who allowed the game to go into extras with five solid plays at third.

"The U.S. played college teams and beat Notre Dame," recalled Betts. "The U.S. is No. 1 in baseball and for us to come out and win ... woo, there aren't any words to explain that. I still feel that today. I still have the newspapers; I'll always remember that."

• • •

Back in Brandon, Betts, left fielder Todd Schell and second baseman Jason Lee were named to the World Youth Baseball Championship all-star team. Brabant was selected the top pitcher with three wins in as many starts and a near-perfect earned run average of 0.46 in 19 2/3 innings. The next day, the players scattered to their homes to begin the rest of their lives, Canada's first and only international champions. Coach Flood and Croft flew home to St. John's, Newfoundland, arriving around midnight. "My club team was playing that night in our local senior league and in our approach I looked out the window of the plane and saw that the lights were still on at the park," Croft said. "I was wondering if we were winning or losing."

Then, when he stepped off the airplane into the terminal, there were his Gonzaga High School Vikings teammates wearing their grey and navy uniforms and Flood's Mount Pearl High School Blazers in their royal blue and white uniforms. His team had left the park as soon as the game was over to welcome him home. There they stood, dirty uniforms, sweaty faces and all. In a crowd of more than a hundred, Croft locked his gaze on one face. "My father," Croft said. "He shook my hand and hugged me. People still tell the story of seeing him walking home the next day with 20 news-papers under his arm because of the story about me that was in the news-paper."

• • •

Croft and Clapp would continue their careers at the Acadamie Baseball Canada. Betts, Dickson, Mark Fraser and Todd Schell headed to play at Northeastern Oklahoma A&M Mountaineers. During the 1993 Junior College World Series, Betts hit .670, coming within one hit of breaking former Minnesota Twins' centre fielder Kirby Puckett's record for the highest tournament average. Soon after he went in the 14th round to the Cleveland Indians. The Angels selected Dickson in the sixth round, the top Canadian in the 1995 draft. Jason Birmingham, whose father Rick pitched in the first Canada Games in 1967, headed to the University of Ohio. Mike McKinlay went to Oklahoma's Seminole State and was chosen by the Baltimore Orioles in the 20th round in 1993. Joe Young was selected in the third round by the Jays in 1993.

Thirteen years after that magic summer in Brandon, Harr figures he had the right team at the right time. "It might not have been the best team ever talent wise," said Harr, who was with eight Team Canada teams in all. "But it was the best team for chemistry and getting along." Looking back on the scene at Westbran when fans sang *O Canada* at the closing ceremonies, Troy Croft remembers being caught up in all the goings on, not really sure of how to best enjoy the moment.

"Every time I'm watching TV and Canada wins the world junior in hockey, an international competition, or we do well at the Olympics, it's like I am watching guys in the same situation we were in," Croft said. "You can't help but get a bit emotional when you see them take the picture and the joy on the faces. It was a proud moment. Not many Newfoundlanders get to experience what I did—heck, not many Canadians have experienced it."

Gary Picone has been a part of nine National Association of Intercollegiate Athletics national championship teams at Lewis-Clark State, but any time he goes out "anywhere that someone might look at a ring" he wears his Baseball Canada ring from Brandon.

"Anyone who knows me knows I'm not a real warm and fuzzy guy," Picone said. "I don't wear our flag on my sleeve as a real patriotic Canadian. But when all those people began to sing *O Canada* to us and we sang, my whole body just tingled. I have never felt that feeling before or since."

CANADA'S MOONLIGHT

10

Entering the ballpark in Courtright, Ontario for the first time was not as spine tingling as my first visit to Maple Leaf Stadium in Toronto, MacArthur Park in Syracuse, or Tiger Stadium in Detroit. Yet, it was impressive. It was like arriving at a run-down, four-bedroom house and being unimpressed until you enter a room to find a floor-to-ceiling picture window leading out onto a magnificent deck ... and then gazing upon a gorgeous view of a windswept coast with the sun setting in the distance, hues of bright blue and bright orange melting into one. Or maybe it was like standing in a long line at an airport behind a travel group from the Golden Home from the Aged ... and turning to hear Shania Twain ask if you'd mind if she cut in front of you.

We were attending the 1999 Gold Bat juvenile tournament. Our first two games had been played on schoolyard diamonds at Bridgen and Lambton that had stone-dust, slide-at-your-own-risk infields. I went to see my son's team play. The third game was at Courtright, 12 miles south of Sarnia on the St. Clair River, where we came upon the most beautiful amateur diamond we've ever seen in Canada.

Up front we should tell you that 98 days out of 100 we're not romantic about baseball. It is a beautiful game to watch, say, when Andre Dawson or Devon White is legging out a triple, but how often does that happen? And, while the game itself is beautiful, more and more it is showing warts in the form of drug abuse and business greed and salary turmoil. John Robertson, of the *Toronto Sun* and the *Toronto Star*, used to tell of arriving at spring training, driving to the park and startling the egrets as he slid into second base, so excited that another season had begun. Spring training for us? It's a month of getting up early after 40 years of working nights. But coming upon a setting like the ball diamond at Courtright makes you forget all that. I can still picture it in the mind's eye.

Walt Burrows, who travels the country from coast to coast as the Canadian director of the Major League Scouting Bureau, says that the nicest parks he has seen are Nat Bailey Stadium in Vancouver, Norbrock Stadium in Kamloops, British Columbia, Connorvale Park in Etobicoke,

112

Ontario, and Courtright. This field was of major-league quality, from the well-manicured mound, to the red stone dust infield, which could also be found in front of the four-foot brick wall behind home plate, much like at Wrigley Field. I noticed the green hitter's backdrop in centre field. Another parent said it must be a short drive to centre even though the sign read 368 feet from home plate, while left field was only 328 feet away. I tried explaining that the green netting was there to give the hitter a better view of the ball coming out of the pitcher's hand, but the parent would have none of it. "No, no. It's to protect the centre fielder from getting hit in the back of the head by balls hit from the other field."

Frustrated, I went for a walk and asked someone for information about who had built this park. He pointed to a man sitting on his John Deere lawnmower, the same model they used across the river at Detroit's Tiger Stadium. Why, it was Eric MacKenzie, who coached or managed Team Canada for nine years from 1978-1986, including the 1984 Olympics in Los Angeles. MacKenzie was a former major leaguer, born in Glendon, Alberta, in 1932. He was the architect and caretaker of this magnificent diamond.

What was the name of this park anyway? MacKenzie thought it over and replied, "Ah, it really doesn't have a name; guess it's called the Courtright Park." So now, when I think about the park, I see it like a painting that is listed as untitled.

We never expected to bump into Eric MacKenzie. A golfer would compare this meeting to having three members in his foursome cancel at the last minute and the man in the pro shop saying: "There has also been a cancellation in the group behind you. Would you mind playing with Mr. Woods, Mr. Nicklaus and Mr. Palmer?" That's just about what MacKenzie represents to amateur baseball in Canada. This was an unexpected pleasure, an afternoon talking baseball with a Team Canada manager who built this slice of heaven. The smell of fresh-cut grass, the pre-game infield chatter, the bright sun and the light, cool breeze—the only thing missing was the crack of the bat. Instead, we heard the ping of aluminum.

Yes, it was a great day to be alive, talking ball and listening to stories, even if the Erin Mills Eagles lost 4-2 to Scarborough, despite a homer from Fraser Vernon, while Louis Raptopoulos took the loss. Eric MacKenzie was not then nor is he now an "I-did-this," and "then-I-did-that" type of guy. Yet there was a story here, so I headed to the car for a notebook and pen. But what I really needed was advise from my dentist, because getting MacKenzie to talk about himself was like pulling teeth. "Why are you asking me so many questions?" MacKenzie asked. Told I was going to write something about him, MacKenzie snorted and said:

"Huh, I should be worth a sentence."

While he talked and I scribbled, a couple of his pals would walk by, handing over an additional pen: "Just in case he talks so much that you run out of ink."

There is more to MacKenzie than his obvious love of the game. Eric MacKenzie is Canada's version of Archibald "Moonlight" Graham. In the movie *Field of Dreams*, both Kevin Costner's and James Earl Jones' fictional characters see the name of the real life Moonlight Graham flash on the Fenway Park scoreboard. Graham played one game for the 1905 New York Giants, but never had a plate appearance. Off they head to Minnesota to find Graham and, well, you know the rest of the story. Well, okay, Graham never had a major-league at-bat. MacKenzie had one. But you get the picture. So near. So far.

MacKenzie's one at-bat in the big leagues came on a sunny spring day in Kansas City in 1955. You may have heard Wilbert Harrison's song ...

I'm going to Kansas City, Kansas City here I come.
They got a crazy way of loving there
And I'm gonna get me some.

In MacKenzie's case, it was "I'm going to Kansas City ... to get me one." One at-bat in the majors. That's it, that's all.

He has told the story of the at-bat before—when prodded—to his son Lee and daughters Coleen and Christine and her son, Grant Mullen. (Lee has carried on the baseball tradition. Drafted twice but unsigned by the Colorado Rockies, he still plays for the River Bats.) MacKenzie's moment in the sun of the major leagues came courtesy of Kansas City manager Lou Boudreau, who later gained entry to the Hall of Fame for his feats as a second baseman with the Cleveland Indians. MacKenzie was one of the 25 A's farmhands invited to the 1955 camp in February at Stanford, Florida. He still has the letter on official blue paper. Three players were subsequently invited to the main camp at West Palm Beach and MacKenzie impressed enough to be one of them.

"The numbers were against me, but Boudreau had this camp two-to-three weeks before the main camp; it was a big advantage being a catcher," MacKenzie said. "Catchers who already had spots on the team just hit in spring training and play a few innings in the games. They don't do a lot of warming up pitchers in the bullpen. For a catcher in my position, you feel like you are warming up pitchers forever."

As training camp wound down, Boudreau decided to go with three catchers in 1955, Joe Astroth, Billy Schantz and Jim Robertson. MacKenzie was sent to Single-A Savannah on the last day of spring, with the promise that, in the event of an injury on the big club, he'd get the first shot. Robertson was injured and had to go home with personal business.

Help was needed. Savannah manager Clyde Kluttz spoke to MacKenzie and apologized: "I'm sorry, but I have to send you out." MacKenzie asked where and Kluttz, the comedian, answered "Kansas City." MacKenzie didn't phone home. He just went on his way.

"I never phoned home. I shook hands with my dad every year and said 'see you in the fall,'" MacKenzie said. "Nowadays parents go to most of their children's games. When I left home I don't even think we had a phone."

The next day MacKenzie took his first-ever plane ride. He joined the A's, which had a roster featuring Vic Power, Hector Lopez, Clete and Cloyd Boyer, Gus Zernial, Elmer Valo, Art Ditmar, Bobby Shantz, Vic Raschi, Johnny Sain and future Hall of Famer Enos "Country" Slaughter. His one and only at-bat came against the Chicago White Sox and pitcher Harry "Fritz" Dorish, an eight-year veteran, on Saturday afternoon, April 23, his first day with the A's, in front of 18,338 fans at Municipal Stadium. The White Sox were winning 29-6—who says lack of pitching depth is a current phenomenon—when MacKenzie, 22 at the time, pinch-hit for Astroth in the eighth inning. Bill Wilson was on first and two were out. "The score was so lopsided they were throwing only fastballs," MacKenzie said.

As he should, with the deficit that large, MacKenzie took a strike. Dorish then threw a ball. With the count 1-1, MacKenzie pulled a pitch to future Hall-of-Fame second baseman Nellie Fox, who threw to first baseman Walt "Moose" Dropo for the out. And that was it. An interesting sidebar, though, was that when Ozzie Van Brabant of Kingsville, Ontario worked an inning of relief for the A's, the Van Brabant-MacKenzie combo became only the third all-Canadian battery. "I didn't even know he was born in Kingsville until a couple of years later," MacKenzie said. "His family moved across the river to Michigan when he was two years old."

MacKenzie was with the A's for three weeks and most of the time he was called Sergeant Preston or Johnny Canuck. "I didn't expect a lot of playing time as a third-string catcher," said MacKenzie. "I knew I wasn't going to get a lot of playing opportunity that year; it would probably come the next year." But the next year never came.

The major-league life was "crazy," recalls MacKenzie. On meal money of $1 a day they'd hang around hotel lobbies and people-watch. "In those days older people sat in the lobby all day. We'd sit and make fun," MacKenzie said. "And sometime we'd go outside the hotel, and a bunch of guys would look up in the air, and yell and scream. Some guy driving along would stick his head out the window to see what we were yelling about, and he'd forget to put on the brakes and ram into the rear end of the car in front of him." At the time MacKenzie was making $6,000 U.S.

"But you spent more too," he said. "You had to wear a suit and tie to walk through the hotel lobby."

One memory MacKenzie won't forget, as the A's played the Red Sox both home and away during his stint, was watching Ted Williams of the Boston Red Sox. "During batting practice everyone watched him," MacKenzie said. "After we hit, we would go up the tunnel, change our shirts and come back down. It was almost like you were ordered to watch him hit." MacKenzie said he never saw Williams hit a ball that stayed on a line. It would rise or drop because of the spin on the ball, created by Williams' swing.

Not long after MacKenzie's at-bat, Robertson was healthy and MacKenzie was back in Savannah. After three more springs and three more minor-league seasons, MacKenzie, the man with the large paws, retired. "I gave it my best shot," MacKenzie says. "But I was a little short on talent."

MacKenzie, who made only $6,000 in his best year, looks at today's salaries and shakes his head. "I've never been in a union my whole life, but those owners made a whole pile of money the years I was involved and the players had to go home and get a job in the winter," MacKenzie said. "It was good that the union came along; now maybe the pendulum has swung too far."

MacKenzie received his love of baseball and his work ethic from his father Hugh MacKenzie, who grew up and played baseball in London, Ontario. Hugh enlisted in the Canadian army to serve in World War I. Overseas, he met his bride to be and returned home to buy a farm in Glendon, Alberta, northeast of Edmonton. The MacKenzies had six children, a daughter and five sons, with Eric the youngest. "I was born during the depression and life wasn't too good on our farm," MacKenzie recalls from his parents' hymnals. "Let's see ... one year we had grasshoppers, another year we had a drought and another year we froze. My father couldn't make it."

So, Hugh MacKenzie moved east to Leamington, Ontario, and bought another farm when his youngest son was three years old. He had 20 acres to raise tomatoes and another three acres to grow tobacco. "The boys did all the work, and eventually we got a contract to supply tomatoes to H.J. Heinz and my father was able to pay off the mortgage on the farm," MacKenzie said. "As the youngest boy, there was no way there was going to be anything for me on the farm. I grew up wanting to be a baseball player, like everyone else."

Growing up in the 1940s in Leamington, MacKenzie didn't really have a choice of what would be his favorite sport. "We didn't have an arena; if you wanted to play sports, your only hope was baseball," MacKenzie said.

"Few kids from our way at that time made it in hockey. We lived in Ontario's banana belt. We didn't get the same outdoor rinks as say Brockville, Belleville or Ottawa. When I was young, it was a good place to grow up for baseball, but for hockey it was a bad place. I wanted to play pro. Baseball was cheap; all you needed was a pair of cleats and a glove. We didn't have that much money," MacKenzie said. "Nowadays kids have too much money."

Scout Wish Egan of the Detroit Tigers, who signed Hal Newhouser and Al Kaline, would often search for talent at Ontario parks. "Egan would invite the better players to go work out at Briggs Stadium. I remember Reno Bertoia was invited one year," MacKenzie said. But it was the Philadelphia A's, following tryout camps in Chatham, who landed MacKenzie. He was signed in 1950 by scout Joe Boley six years before the A's moved to Kansas City. MacKenzie quit high school and was given a train ticket to Sanford, where the A's staged their minor-league camp. "You didn't ask for bonus money," says MacKenzie. "Everyone who signed thought that they had a shot at making it to the majors. In my day it was easy to get signed, but harder to make it. Now it's hard to get signed and easier to make it. If a player gets signed now, he has a fighting chance."

MacKenzie backs up his theory by pointing out that teams like the New York Yankees and St. Louis had more than 30 farm clubs, while the A's had more than 20. Now, most teams have six farm teams. "That meant me, I had to climb over 40 catchers," he said. "In my day scouts would sign players out of senior ball. They don't do that anymore."

MacKenzie, who grew up listening to Ernie Harwell broadcast Tigers' games, spent 1951 at Class-C Rome, New York, where he hit .133, Class-D Taraboro, North Carolina, where he batted .191, and Class-C Corning, New York, where he hit .223 with nine RBIs. The next year saw him back at Corning, and in 1953 he was at Class-C at St. Hyacinthe, Quebec, batting .223 with three homers and 46 RBIs. In 1954 at Drummondville, Quebec, he hit .265 with two homers and 36 RBIs. "I saw lots of guys with more ability than I had and were home in two weeks," MacKenzie said. "They'd get homesick. Or miss their girlfriends. Or didn't like their jobs. You'd get sent to either Savannah or Macon where it's hot. You'd go to the park every day at 3 p.m., not out until 11 p.m., and you don't like the manager." MacKenzie said in his day most managers were rough-and-tough characters, ruling with the iron hand of a John McGraw or a Leo Durocher. "What I had going for me was the fact I was mentally tough, or maybe I was too bull-headed," MacKenzie said.

The following winter the A's moved to Kansas City from Philadelphia, and in the spring MacKenzie was invited to his first major-league training camp. After his major-league moment, he spent the rest of 1955 at

Class-B Lancaster, Pennsylvania, where he played for manager Hank Biasatti of Windsor, Ontario. In the Piedmont League final, Biasatti's team bussed from Lancaster, through the hills, and caught the ferry to Norfolk, Virginia, arriving at 5 a.m. The manager went to the front desk of the Nelson Hotel, the team hotel, where he was told that the rooms for the Lancaster players would not be available until noon. Replied Biasatti: "Why don't you just line us up and shoot us?"

So, lefty Carl Watson headed for the team bus and brought out some bats and balls. "Carl was from Maryland's eastern shore, but he had an accent like he was from the Carolinas," MacKenzie said. The players trundled to the second floor where there were maybe 50 feet of mirrors on the walls. The first hitter stood with a bat ready to begin a game of pepper, anticipating a lob so he could hit an easy one hopper to the players lined up 20 feet away. "Except Carl didn't toss the ball. He just reared back and fired the ball into the mirror and shattered it. Man, did we take off," MacKenzie said. The pepper players headed for an all-day, all-night movie house, which were plentiful in a Navy town, and didn't return until 3 p.m. when the bus was supposed to leave for the park. "There was Hank waiting, wanting to know who wrecked the mirror. We never told him, but we had to pay for it," MacKenzie said.

Lancaster won the Piedmont League title and the gate receipts were shared between the two teams, with the winners getting the larger shares. "Around Christmas I got a cheque for $9.37," MacKenzie laughed.

MacKenzie was at spring training with the A's again in 1956 and 1957, both times being sent down to Single-A. "I had three big-league spring trainings. Lou Boudreau was very good to me. I don't buy that when I hear Canadian kids don't get a chance," MacKenzie said. "Boudreau gave me a good chance; if I'd have been good enough I'd have been playing there." MacKenzie says his role in the A's system changed as he went from being a prospect to an organizational player. "I played so long that I think they hated to send me home," he said. "As an organizational guy, if they had a hot prospect pitcher, some guy that was wild as hell, they'd send me in to catch him."

MacKenzie's final year was at Double-A Amarillo, where he batted .236 with nine RBIs in 1958. "Amarillo had a stockyard in centre and the prevailing wind was blowing in towards the plate," MacKenzie recalled with a sniff. "The smell was so bad we couldn't play day games." The odor aside, MacKenzie says he wouldn't change a single moment of his minor-league life. "After nine years in pro ball, I'd do it all over again," he said.

MacKenzie isn't the only Canadian who had a taste of major-league baseball only to be sent back to the minors after one game. In all, 14 others had the same date for their major-league debut and their final game, with

Mel Kerr of Souris, Manitoba, called up by the 1925 Chicago Cubs, the only position player without an at-bat. MacKenzie was the only player with a singular at-bat.

Towards the end of MacKenzie's playing days, Leamington had finally got an arena and MacKenzie worked there in the off-season. When he retired from baseball in 1959, he came home, got a full-time job, went back to school for his high school degree and then took courses at the University of Western Ontario in London. Unlike many former pros, MacKenzie didn't become a bitter man after retiring. He had married Gail in 1956 and together they returned to Canada. MacKenzie worked in Leamington parks and recreational from 1959-62, then moved 80 miles down the road to Petrolia, where he worked for 6 1/2 years in the same capacity. And, finally, he took a job in Mooretown, where he worked for 21 years, before retiring in 1989 and turning his attention to the old ball-park in Courtright.

Before MacKenzie, the village of Courtright (pop. 500) was mainly known for its half dozen hotels that served the Michigan residents who would cross the river for whiskey. Now Courtright draws visitors to its beautiful ballpark. MacKenzie, with the help of local resident Bob Barnes, restored the ballpark one item at a time with funds from bingos. They built or added the grass infield, a warning track, the light standards, the scoreboard, the outfield fence, the brick wall behind home plate and the hitter's backdrop. "And in 2004, we put in major-league irrigation and drainage."

MacKenzie's Courtright team was then one of the first of the many Ontario teams to break away from the Ontario Baseball Association, first because of their proximity to Michigan and, second, they wanted to do more for the kids. "We saw what people like Wayne Norton did in British Columbia, getting players off to school," said MacKenzie. "There wasn't anyone in Ontario doing that at the time. There was no place for kids to go." So, the Courtright Seahawks were born in 1992, recruiting players from Windsor, Chatham, Woodstock and London. "Jan Prozorowicz sent a lot of kids on to school at St. Clair Community College," MacKenzie said, talking about the college's assistant coach. "There's not many guys around like Jan. A lot of guys talk a good game, but when it comes to getting their hands dirty they stand back. Jan throws batting practice, hits fungos. He barges right in."

MacKenzie began coaching for Team Canada and manager Bill MacKenzie (no relation) in 1978. Canada had very little time to put a team together for the 1984 Los Angeles Olympics, where baseball was a demonstration sport. Originally, there were going to be five invited countries plus the U.S. Then Cuba pulled out, joining the Soviet boycott, and the tournament was expanded to eight teams, adding Chinese Taipei, Italy and Canada. Bill MacKenzie was running the show for Baseball Canada and he brought 41 players to the University of Windsor for a 10-day evaluation camp so manager Eric MacKenzie could select his team. They headed to The Netherlands for a pre-Olympic tournament, the 13th annual Haarlem Invitational near Amsterdam. Also making the trek was a couple of U.S. college teams, and Chinese Taipei.

"Canada was very popular in Holland because of everything our country had done to liberate The Netherlands during World War II," MacKenzie said. "We drew 10,000 fans to our games, easy." Team Canada flew from Amsterdam, spent a night in Toronto and then it was off to Los Angles. Playing before sellout crowds at Dodger Stadium, Canada blew a lead to lose 4-3 to Nicaragua in 12 innings, lost to South Korea 3-1, and were eliminated despite edging previously unbeaten Japan 4-3. In the final, Japan beat Team USA, which featured future major leaguers Will Clark, Oddibe McDowell, Billy Swift, B.J. Surhoff and Shane Mack.

MacKenzie also coached in the 1978 World Seniors in Bologna, Italy; the 1979 Pan-Ams in San Juan, Puerto Rico; the 1980 Worlds in Tokyo; the 1981 Intercontinental Cup in Edmonton; the 1982 Worlds in Seoul, Korea; the 1983 Worlds in Belgium and the Pan-Ams in Caracas, Venezuela; the 1985 Intercontinental Cup at Edmonton and the 1986 Pacific Cup in Kindersley, Saskatchewan. The best Team Canada members he ever coached? "On the mound it would be Mike Gardiner and Steve Wilson," MacKenzie said. Gardiner pitched five seasons for the Seattle Mariners, the Boston Red Sox, Montreal Expos and Detroit Tigers, appearing in 136 games, making 46 starts. He was 17-27 in his career. Wilson pitched six seasons with the Texas Rangers, Chicago Cubs and Los Angeles Dodgers, working in 205 games. Wilson was 13-18 with six saves.

Our first visit to Courtright was in 1999. So, what has MacKenzie been doing since? When we checked in with him in December 2004, he was taking radiation treatments in London for skin cancer. Aside from that, though, he has been doing what he always did. The Sarnia Indian Reserve, known as Aamjiwnaang, built a new ball field in 1996. Yet, band elders saw more weeds on the diamond than ball players. And so the field sat, decaying. Prozorowicz and MacKenzie began working on the field in 1999. "Right now it's better than Courtright," MacKenzie said. The diamond on the reserve has a grass infield, lights and a warning track. "It has a perfect slope. It has sand underneath the grass. They built it properly, right from the start. They wanted a major-league field and they built one; its 408 to centre and 390 in the gaps, too big for the majors."

While he looked after the parks in Moore Township, MacKenzie lived 30 miles away in Bright's Grove, home of golfer Mike Weir, who won the 2003 Masters. So, is MacKenzie the second most famous resident of Bright's Grove or, given that Weir spends most of his time in Utah, the most famous?

"I am the least famous person in town," said MacKenzie.

The locals would beg to differ.

THE CLOSER

11

He stands alone. He is wearing his sweat-stained lucky hat and his Kareem Abdul-Jabbar goggles and is perched atop an 11-inch high mound in the 18-foot circle in the middle of the diamond. The game doesn't proceed until he wants it to. Other players are at a standstill until he decides to allow things to unfold. It's no different whether he is being watched by 43,065 fans urging him to get the final three outs at Dodger Stadium, or whether he is at SBC Park in San Francisco where 40,232 hooting and hollering fans are hoping he bounces one to the screen.

That is Eric Gagne's lot in life. His chosen profession. The man in the baggy pants stands alone. He doesn't have a double-play partner. He's seldom on second waiting for help from a teammate to drive him home. And he's never the middleman on a tandem relay throw to the plate. But he's okay with that. Gagne, who went 678 days between blown saves for the Dodgers between 2002 and 2004, has been alone before.

Gagne grew up in Mascouche, Quebec, 10 minutes north of Montreal. This small-town guy with the hair on his chinny-chin chin does something no one else has ever been able to do before in Los Angeles Dodger history: He keeps fans in their seats until the end of the game, rather than bolting early to beat the traffic and listen to radio announcer Vin Scully. How good is an 84-consecutive-game string of saves? Well, no one has ever done it before. Gagne is in a class of his own among major-league closers. He went 84-for-84 while compiling a find-it-if-you-can earned run average of 0.82 to win the National League's 2003 Cy Young Award. During the streak, he had more saves than hits allowed (71).

Remember how in Little League or peewee, the eighth-place hitter would step in ever so gently at the outside edge of the batter's box, wanting no part of an inside pitch? The other dugout would yell: "Easy out! Easy out!" That could have been the cry from the Dodger dugout for each hitter during Gagne's streak. Between Aug. 26, 2002, against the Arizona Diamondbacks, and July 5, 2004, again against the Diamondbacks, 31 of Gagne's 84 save opportunities came with none out and a one-run lead in the ninth inning. Not a lot of room for error. Although he allowed home runs during his streak to Barry Bonds, Jason Giambi and Pedro Feliz, Gagne went 31-for-31. The rest of baseball's closers, over that same span, converted 73.4 percent of saves under the same circumstances. Gagne stood alone among big-league closers.

Closer to home, he stood as a testament to Quebec's baseball development program.

Quebec is the most unified province in the country when it comes to getting players to the next level. And Gagne is just the tip of the iceberg. The program has produced several other major-league prospects, including Montreal righty Martin Mainville from the Academie Baseball Canada (ABC), chosen in the second round by the Expos in 1993, and catcher Pierre-Luc "Pete" Laforest of Gatineau, selected in the 16th round of the 1995 draft by the Expos out of Fort Scott Community College in Kansas after playing at the ABC. British Columbia, it can be argued, has had the most success on the national stage in the last 10 years through to 2005, and it has the most high profile players in the majors. Yet many contend Quebec does a better job at developing players. From 2000 through 2004, Quebec was the only province to hit double figures with 10 golds at the Canadian championships in the six age groupings from peewee to senior. On the overall medal count, Ontario (six golds) leads with 22, followed by British Columbia (seven) and Quebec with 21 apiece.

The roots of Quebec's success can be traced to 1987, when the provincial association, under president Richard Belec and technical director Albert Marier, adopted a three-pronged development program. The first step was creation of a six-team midget-AAA league in which the federation hired the coaches and selected the 16-year-olds, and implemented standard coaching and training to prepare the teenagers for Canada's youth team or U.S. colleges. Second, in 1990, the Academie Baseball Canada was established, providing an opportunity for players from Quebec and eastern Canada to train year round. Third, also in 1990, the final and maybe most distinctive piece of the puzzle was added when the first Sport-Études program was established in a Montreal high school.

The Sport-Études schooling concept exists in many countries in various forms. Promising athletes are identified and streamed into schools that combine academics with athletics. In France, for example, the schools are used to develop soccer players, or in Austria the focus is on alpine skiers. In Quebec, where 31 high schools participated in the Sport-Études programs in 2005, there are 2,150 student-athletes training in 32 sports. In baseball, the schools provide aspiring and graduated Midget AAA players a September-to-May program where they train 15 hours per week as part of the school curriculum.

"Athletes start class at 8:30 each morning and are done by noon," said Andre Lachance, who worked with Baseball Quebec and now works with Baseball Canada. Players take transportation to a training facility and work out from 1:30-4:30 p.m. and study in the evening. "The bad thing for elite athletes used to be that they had to go to school all day long and then practice," Lachance said. "They dilute energy and wind up not performing. This frees up evenings to study." Students must maintain a 75 percent average in each class or they won't be delivering fastballs later in the day.

As a result of Quebec's three-pronged development initiatives from 1987 to 1990 (plus the addition in 1999 of a fourth, Les Ailes du Quebec summer program) the player development cycle never ends in Quebec. Fresh arms are always on the way. Hitters never stop training. Some 120 players compete in the Quebec midget league (for players age 16-17). The best of those players move on to Les Ailes for an 85-game schedule, which runs through the summer, pointing toward the Canada Cup or Greg Hamilton's Team Canada. Those programs run from April until August. Then the ABC (for 16-20 year olds) kicks in and operates from September until April.

"When we arrive at a national championship our players know how to play, know how to back up third, know who is going where when the other team bunts, or whatever," said Richard Emond, who has been with Baseball Quebec since 1973. "All the other provinces pick their teams two weeks before. We practice bunt defense, relays, whatever (all year round). We know who can do this and who can do that when we arrive at the nationals because we practice throughout the year." While teams in Ontario fight with Baseball Ontario and other teams for players, and while other provinces have splinter groups breaking away from the provincial bodies, no province is as united as Quebec towards winning national titles and getting players to the next level. "We're by far light years ahead when it comes to organization," Emond said proudly. "The ones who join our program really want to play the game."

The proof of Baseball Quebec's commitment can be seen in the size of its office staff. Other provincial organizations have small staffs, usually two or three people. Baseball Canada has four full-time employees. Baseball Quebec has 12. And the proof of its success can be seen in Eric Gagne.

Growing up, Gagne played hockey, describing himself as a goon, skating with future Montreal Canadiens goalie Jose Theodore. As much as he loved baseball, he believed hockey could also be a career path. "Eric was a bulldog," said Emond. The fork in the road for Gagne started to appear when he was 15 and he had a chance to attend Polyvalente

Edouard Montpetit High School in Montreal, which was part of the province's Sport-Études program. He studied in the morning and pitched in the afternoon. But his years there weren't without turmoil. During his first year, he commuted by bus four hours each day. Then he moved into a basement apartment near the school and had to cope with feelings of loneliness. At home, his father Richard Gagne, a bus driver in Mascouche, and his mother Carole Roux, a waitress, went through a divorce, and Gagne developed an eating disorder. "I had anorexia for about three years," he recalls. "I was sad about my parents getting divorced." With the help of a psychologist, he eventually won his battle, but the war isn't over. "You always have it. The reason I got better was simple—I started eating again," Gagne said. "When I had it, I wasn't throwing hard, didn't have any energy. I'd go through a hard workout and get tired. And I was moody." Baseball was his salvation. "Every day I had baseball to look forward to. As soon as class was over at noon, it was baseball, baseball, baseball."

Gagne went through the Quebec "farm system" just as it was scripted in the Baseball Quebec boardroom. At age 15, he pitched midget for Repentigny at Parc Lafontaine in Montreal, where Dodgers scout Claude Pelletier saw him for the first time in 1991, and followed him to Longueuil and across the province. Gagne was with the ABC for one year. Troy Croft of St. John's, Newfoundland was in his third year when Gagne arrived. "He was still in high school, but you could tell he would do something," Croft said. "He had a live arm, but sometimes had control difficulties. Wherever we went, scouts were there to see him. You never think a guy you played with will win a Cy Young Award, but it happened and good for him."

Throughout these years, Gagne had continued to play hockey, but in 1994 he had to choose between his two sports. The rough and ready-to-rumble defenseman, his knuckles scarred from fights, had to decide between a hockey scholarship from the University of Vermont Catamounts or a baseball scholarship from Seminole State Junior College in Oklahoma. That same year he had been drafted by the Chicago White Sox in the 30th round. Gagne selected baseball and Seminole State. And it was a bit of a culture shock for a French-Canadian from the big city moving to the Oklahoma town of 6,899. He didn't speak English and after the first day he thought to himself: "What in the world am I doing here?"

While Richard Gagne mailed his son tapes of TV shows in French to ease the loneliness, Oklahoma gradually grew on him. By watching TV shows like *Mad About You*, Gagne improved his English. He says he learned his work ethic from Seminole State coach Lloyd Simmons. "Up every morning at 4:30, do weights, go for a jog, have breakfast at 6:30 and be in class at 7:30," Gagne said. "I didn't know how hard I had to work to become a complete player until I went to school."

The White Sox never made him an offer—never even contacted Gagne—despite the fact he was 11-0 with a 1.20 ERA as the third man in the Trojans' rotation. When he wasn't drafted in June of 1995, he accepted an invitation to pitch for Team Canada. Right-hander Jason Birmingham of Sarnia, Ontario was in camp in Windsor and was so impressed with Gagne he phoned his father, Dodger scout Rick Birmingham. The elder Birmingham drove to Windsor and he was impressed, too.

I remember seeing Gagne at Nelson Park in Burlington, Ontario, as Jim Baba's Team Canada senior squad criss-crossed the country, heading for Edmonton and the 1995 Olympic qualifier. Baba had made Gagne his closer. Claude Pelletier, who was working then for the Dodgers, remembers the young Gagne not as a pitcher, but as a thrower. "He was an average young pitcher, a little wild, but I think he found himself with Team Canada as a reliever," said Pelletier. After following Gagne and seeing him improve, Pelletier called scouting director Terry Reynolds to ask for a Dodger cross-checker to fly in for a look at Gagne. Reynolds asked Pelletier a pointed question, the way scouts often ask: "How can you want us to look at a guy who pitched in the U.S. when not one team liked him?" Pelletier remembers taking a deep breath and saying into the phone: "Because I like him." Scout Eddie Bane flew to Calgary to see Gagne pitch and liked what he saw. In fact, his words were "lock him in a room until you get him signed." Gagne signed a contract on July 26, 1995 in Kelowna, British Columbia before the pre-Olympic qualifier began. He was given a $75,000 bonus.

Why baseball over hockey?

"Passion," Gagne said. "I have a passion for baseball and a love of baseball. Pro baseball scouts approached me, so it was a lot more tempting."

Gagne worked 11 games for Canada as the team made its way west for the Olympic qualifier, pitching 12 scoreless innings, striking out 20 and walking four. With the 1996 Olympics in Atlanta, the U.S. didn't have to qualify. Cuba was expected to take one of the two berths, and the other was a jump ball. In the semi-final, Gagne worked the final 3 1/3 innings, allowing three runs as Nicaragua romped to a 12-6 win and the final Olympic berth. Players scattered after the tournament, with Gagne returning to Quebec. When the Dodgers came to Olympic Stadium that September, Pelletier took Gagne to the park. Gagne pitched off the mound and L.A. pitching coach Dave Wallace helped work on Gagne's curve.

Once Gagne reached spring training at Vero Beach, he was placed in a starter's role. Gagne made his debut at Single-A Savannah in 1996, going 7-6 with a 3.28 ERA in 21 starts, walking 43 and striking out 131 in

115 1/3 innings. Then he missed all of 1997 recovering from Tommy John surgery to his right elbow, unable to play catch for six months after the operation. After the lonely life of rehabbing, the Dodgers refused to allow Gagne to use his slider and splitter, so he experimented with pitches. In 1998, he fanned 144 in 139 2/3 innings and walked only 48 with Single-A Vero. In his final seven starts, he was 5-1 with a 1.63 ERA and fanned 65 batters in 49 innings, including 13 in his final outing. For the season, he was 9-7 with a 3.74 ERA in 25 starts.

In 1999, Gagne had a great start at Double-A San Antonio—after he was able to see the plate. He was prescribed eyeglasses and, to say the least, the adjustment was not smooth. In his first game wearing glasses, he threw 18 straight balls. (Scar tissue from a hockey injury prevented him from using contacts.) But he persevered with his made-in-Canada hockey mentality. In the sixth inning of a game on September 2, Gagne's record was 12-4 with a 2.63 ERA. He led the league with 185 strikeouts in 167 2/3 innings, allowing only 122 hits, and had held opposing batters to a .201 average. After the season, he'd be named the Dodgers' minor league and Texas League pitcher of the year. San Antonio was playing Midland that night and Gagne was on a roll in the sixth when pitching coach Mark Brewer came to the mound and told Gagne his work was done. Gagne look puzzled. Brewer said: "You have two choices: Stay and try to strike out four guys for the Texas League record, or catch a flight to join the Dodgers."

Gagne handed him the ball and floated off the mound.

Seven days later, Gagne started against the Florida Marlins at Pro Player Stadium in Miami. The 23-year-old faced Marlins' righty Ryan Dempster of Gibsons, British Columbia in the first all-Canadian National League match-up since July 28, 1973, when Fergie Jenkins of Chatham, Ontario started for the Chicago Cubs against the St. Louis Cardinals and Reggie Cleveland of Swift Current, Saskatchewan. In the years since the first major-league match-up of Canadian starters in 1884, when, according to research by Neil Munro, Bob Emslie of Guelph, Ontario pitched for Baltimore against Cincinnati's Billy Mountjoy of London, Ontario, head-to-head meetings of Canadians have been rare. In the American League, the last all-Canuck match-up was on July 20, 1991, between the Angels' Kirk McCaskill of Kapuskasing, Ontario and the Indians' Denis Boucher of Lachine, Quebec. In Miami, Gagne had a solid debut, throwing six scoreless innings, fanning eight and walking one. He allowed two singles. Of the first six Marlins he faced, Gagne fanned four. It was the best outing by a Dodgers' rookie since Pedro Astacio fanned 10 and pitched a three-hit, complete-game shutout against Philadelphia in 1992. The other Canuck, Dempster, didn't fair badly either. He had seven strikeouts in seven innings, but like Gagne, got a no-decision in Florida's 2-1 win.

Scout Claude Pelletier was in Miami for the Gagne-Dempster matchup. He first scouted the pair in 1994 when the pitchers were roommates with John Harr's Team Canada. While Gagne came out of the weeds—an undrafted free agent making it to the majors—Dempster was high profile from the time he was 17. He was the first Canadian selected in 1995, taken in the third-round by the Texas Rangers and given a $200,000 signing bonus. With the Rangers in a playoff drive in 1997, Dempster was dealt to Florida for veteran John Burkett. By 1999 Pelletier had traded in his Dodgers cap after 13 years to take up a New York Mets radar gun. He may have been paid by the Mets, but that night and any other time Gagne takes the mound, his heart bleeds as much Dodger blue as Tommy Lasorda's. "We made a pact a long time ago," Pelletier said. "I told Eric 'when you make it, I'll be there.'"

Richard Emond, manager of the Team Canada juniors in 1993, schooled both Dempster and Gagne. "I had them both when they were 16," Emond said. "They were so young then; five years later I'm watching them pitch against each other on the TV."

Gagne beat the first-place Houston Astros on Oct. 1 in Houston, 5-1, for his first win. It was also the first time Gagne faced one of his boyhood idols. "Jeff Bagwell, he walked on a 3-2 pitch, walked again on four pitches and then he grounded out hard to second," said Gagne, who worked six scoreless innings, allowing five hits. The next two seasons Gagne struggled, owning and losing the fifth starter's job. He started 2000 at Triple-A Albuquerque and was promoted April 15. He spent 10 games with the Dodgers, was demoted twice and recalled twice. At Triple-A he was 5-1 with a 3.88 ERA, while with the Dodgers he was 4-6 with a 5.15 ERA in 19 starts.

Pelletier lives in Ste. Lessard, Quebec and every year during Christmas week Gagne visits him for dinner. Each spring at Pelletier's other home, in Vero Beach, the scout invites a handful of players over for his wife Frances' internationally famous spaghetti and "some vino." In the spring of 2001, the invitation list included: Dodger minor leaguers Nial Hughes of Cardigan, Prince Edward Island and David Detienne of Dartmouth, Nova Scotia; scout Bob Isabelle of Montreal; Walt Burrows, Canadian director for the Major League Scouting Bureau; and Dodger scout Jim Chapman of Vancouver. Gagne phoned and asked whether he could bring along Dodgers' teammate Luke Prokopec, an Australian.

"The younger guys there looked up to them, asked questions," Pelletier said. "Eric and Luke mixed in well. No one pretended to be anyone that they weren't. They knew that a few years before they were in the shoes of the minor leaguers." Pelletier said he'd read that there were hard feelings between the Canuck and the Aussie as they both battled for a job in the Dodger rotation. "That was silly. They shared a house in L.A. with their girlfriends and shared a hotel room in Vero," Pelletier said. "They were competitors, but it was may-the-best-man win. There weren't hard feelings between them."

Gagne had three stints with L.A. in 2001, when he wasn't at Triple-A Las Vegas, where he went 3-0 with a 1.52 ERA in four starts. He made the opening day roster, started the second game of the season, and had a no-decision against Randy Johnson and the Arizona Diamondbacks. Making the second most starts (24) for the Dodgers, he was 6-7 with a 4.75 ERA. The bat bag had not even been packed at season's end when talk began that the Dodgers were going to trade one of their young starters, either Prokopec or Gagne.

Don Welke, a former Blue Jays' scout then working for the Dodgers, had his sights set on Jays' shortstop Cesar Izturis. To ease their salary burden, Toronto asked the Dodgers to take Paul Quantrill of Port Hope, Ontario, as well. In return, The Jays could have had either Gagne or Prokopec. They chose Prokopec. The Dodgers threw in minor-leaguer Chad Ricketts of Welland, Ontario, and the 2-for-2 swap was completed at the winter meetings in Boston. The trade has left Jays' fans wondering what might have been had Gagne come to Toronto instead of Prokopec, who made 12 starts, was injured and is out of baseball. Asked about the Dodgers offering him to the Jays, Gagne said: "I heard it the other way around. But for two days, I had myself psyched up about going to Toronto and being closer to home. I knew someone was going."

Gagne had a career 11-14 mark with a 4.61 ERA as a starter when manager Jim Tracy had the wisdom to tag him as his closer in April 2002. He has been the Dodgers' unchallenged closer ever since. "Maybe we knew what we were doing when we made him our closer in 1995," said Team Canada manager Jim Baba.

Ferguson Jenkins ranks as the best Canadian pitcher ever. No debate. This isn't a Betty vs. Wilma, or Ginger vs. Mary Anne argument. Jenkins produced, winning at least 20 games for the Chicago Cubs for six consecutive seasons, a run which ended in 1972. In 1971, Jenkins became the first Canadian to win a Cy Young for pitching excellence when he went 24-13 with a 3.96 ERA. He worked 325 innings, pitched 30 complete games and struck out 263. He was elected to the Hall of Fame in Cooperstown in 1991. Still, while it's tough to suggest a closer is better than a starter who won 284 games over his 19 years, an argument is brewing on the hot stove. When Gagne won the 2003 Cy Young award, he took 28 of 32 first-place votes. He was 55-for-55 in save opportunities, breaking Tom Gordon's record for consecutive saves to start a season.

Gagne had a 2-3 won-loss record and a 1.20 ERA with 137 strikeouts, walking only 20 in 82 1/3 innings.

"He was devastating," bullpen mate Paul Quantrill said. "He throws 95 to 100 miles per hour, can put it pretty much where he wants it and his best pitch is his change. That's pretty scary." It was Quantrill who gave Gagne the nickname B.D.A. (Big Dumb Animal) after overhearing Gagne telling reporters how Jesse Orosoco and Quantrill taught him everything he knows.

Gagne earned a relatively low $550,000 in 2003. His worst game of the season was a messy eighth at the all-star game in Chicago, when he gave up a two-run, game-winning homer to Hank Blalock of the Texas Rangers. That didn't cost the Dodgers, but the National League lost home-field advantage for the World Series. Not that it affected the Florida Marlins, who won at Yankee Stadium. In December, Gagne finished second in the voting for the Lou Marsh award as Canada's male athlete of the year to Masters champion Mike Weir. Two months later, Gagne and his agent, Scott Boras, went to arbitration and filed for a salary of $8 million, while the Dodgers countered with a $5-million offer. There isn't a middle ground in salary arbitration. The arbitrator picks one of two numbers and at this hearing he picked the Dodger number. "Going to arbitration is not always fun, but that's the business part of it," Gagne said when he arrived in Vero for spring training. "It's over with now and I'm back to work."

As the streak continued into 2004 unabated, all kinds of words were used to describe Gagne. Consistent. Dominating. Automatic. Intimidating. Overpowering. And even ridiculous. "It is ridiculous, ridiculous anyone could be that good for so long," said Dennis Eckersley, who was inducted into Cooperstown in 2004. Eckersley was dubbed "El Perfecto" for saving 48 of 50 opportunities with the A's in 1990. So, is Gagne *Monsieur Parfait*? Eckersley, a Boston broadcaster, hadn't seen Gagne that much early in the 2004 season. The saves kept rolling in. Then, he went "out of my way to see him." "I didn't realize he threw that hard," Eckersley said. "Watching him, it's an accomplishment for someone to hit a ground ball to second. Some guys have a change or split which they throw out of the zone and hope the hitter swings. Anytime I've seen him throw his change, it's a called strike. Hitters don't have a chance."

Gagne regularly hits 99 m.p.h. and has a devastating curve. "What I don't get is why he didn't get anyone out as a starter," Eckersley said. "The old baseball saying is: 'Let's see how the guy reacts to failure.' Well, when is he going to fail?"

From Rimouski, Quebec to Culver City, California Gagne has worshipers. He also has a detractor in former L.A. reliever Mike Marshall. "A three-run lead, starting the inning with no one on, what's the big deal, anybody should be able to do it," Marshall said. "If I only had to pitch 70 innings (Gagne worked 82), I could have gone home in June. Trying to justify what he did into a Cy Young season and a fabulous accomplishment ... well, it's not." Marshall, critical of closers in general and Gagne in particular, appeared in 106 games and pitched 208 1/3 innings for the 1974 Dodgers, sometimes working three or four innings, as he won the Cy Young.

"Aw, I heard all that crap too when I started working one inning," Eckersley said. "The kid didn't change the rule."

"What's wrong with Marshall?" asked Reds' reliever Danny Graves. "Is he jealous that Gagne is getting all the attention as the all-time best L.A. reliever? Nobody in baseball wants to face Gagne and in Marshall's prime he wouldn't be able to do what Gagne is doing."

What sets Gagne apart from others?

"He has three weapons. Mariano Rivera has two," an NL advance scout said, assessing Gagne and his New York Yankees counterpart. "Some days when the fastball isn't there, and it happens to everyone, Rivera has a cutter and he throws a sinker, but Gagne has three pitches." Gagne throws an overpowering fastball, a multiple-grip changeup and a knee-buckling curve.

Gagne's day on the road begins when he arrives at the park at 3 p.m. for a night game. After a bite to eat, Gagne goes through a 75-minute workout with the weights (one day upper body, one day lower body, one day off). Next is a 45-minute cardio session. Then he watches video of himself. "I always watch the good stuff, never a bad game," said Gagne. Once the game begins, Gagne watches the first five innings from the club-house and tries to guess whether this will be a work night. In the seventh, he heads to the bullpen and mentally prepares for the final three outs. "You would get mentally exhausted if you walked around all day thinking about the ninth," Gagne said. "I try not to think about the ninth until I get to the bullpen."

Some nights the phone rings, some nights it doesn't. When manager Jim Tracy calls for him at Dodger Stadium, Gagne takes a final sip of either Mountain Dew or coffee, the bullpen door opens, "GAME OVER!" flashes on the Jumbotron and the sound system blares *Welcome to the Jungle*, by Guns 'n' Roses. In comes Gagne, with his linebacker thighs, billy goat goatee, oversized uniform pants and his game-over, warm-up-the-bus, this-one-is-in-the-books look in his eye. "I've never been intimidated. I've always challenged hitters," Gagne said. "I don't fear Barry Bonds" (who is 5-for-17with one homer and three RBIs against Gagne)."

Whether instructional league, spring training or in the minors, Gagne has worked with some of the best teachers, like Edwin Correa, Mark Brewer,

Dean Treanor and Hall of Famer Sandy Koufax. "It was awesome working with Koufax in 2001," Gagne said. "He taught me a lot, but the main thing was that he told me to be myself and not try to be someone I wasn't." He learned his changeup from Correa at Savannah, his curve ball at San Antonio and it was Treanor who helped the most with "my make-up."

"I learned from a lot of people along the way," Gagne said. "Everyone knows how to throw a change; I trust it more than a lot of guys."

Dodger scout Don Welke, who signed Blue Jays' Cy Young Award winner Pat Hentgen, and Treanor, who was at Triple-A Albuquerque, were always staunch supporters of Gagne at organizational meetings. "Eric was a good student," Welke said. "He was told the same things every other pitcher was. It took him until 2001 to pick up that curve ball. He struggled with it at the start."

At the July 31 trade deadline in 2004, the Dodgers dealt set-up man Guillermo Mota, catcher Paul Do Loca and Juan Encarnacion to the Marlins for starter Brad Penny and Hee Seop Choi. Trading Mota meant a bigger workload for Gagne. "What you saw over the final two months as we tried to clinch a spot in the post-season was a perfect example of the Canadian mentality," said Logan White, the Dodgers' scouting director. "Eric carrying a bigger load after our trade is the perfect example. Most wouldn't want to throw more, most want to throw less to protect their arm." Gagne was 7-3 with 45 saves as he walked 22 and fanned 114 in 82 2/3 innings. He finished seventh in the Cy Young Award voting. And for the second straight season, he won the NL Rolaids Relief award.

The consecutive-saves streak had come to an end July 6. Gagne, entrusted with a 5-3 lead in the ninth, gave up an RBI double to Arizona pinch-hitter Luis Gonzalez and then Chad Tracy delivered a run-scoring single off an 0-2 changeup. The end of the streak gave everyone a breather to count some significant numbers compiled during the record run. Here's what Gagne did:

• Allowed 61 base runners.

• Watched Dodger opponents blow 28 saves (there were 969 blown saves in the majors).

• Tallied 207 strikeouts, walking only 34, while allowing only 71 hits.

• Held opponents hitless in 60 percent (50-for-84) of his saves and he allowed one or none in 92 percent (77-for-84) of his saves.

• Inherited 23 runners and none scored.

• Recorded 38 saves with a one-run lead, 17 saves with a two-run lead and 29 with a three-run lead.

What kind of reviews did Gagne receive?

"Without exaggerating, I'd put it up there near Joe DiMaggio's 56 consecutive-game hit streak," Tony LaRussa, St. Louis Cardinals manager, said. "It wasn't like he's had a bunch of three-run leads. He's unbelievable. There's so many things that could go wrong and cost you a save. It's really amazing."

Joe Torre, Yankee manager, who has Rivera in his stable, was also impressed. "It was absolutely remarkable for him to do it during a pennant race," Torre said. "It's not like playing every day like Cal Ripken's streak; this was performing every time he was asked. The only streak I can compare it to is DiMaggio's."

Gagne wants to be with the Dodgers forever, but realizes that if Wayne Gretzky can be dealt, so can he. While the Dodgers held the negotiating hammer in 2004, it turned in the favor of Gagne early in 2005. The 29-year-old signed a two-year, $19-million deal, the second richest contract ever earned by a Canadian, behind only Larry Walker. Gagne will get $8 million in 2005 and $10 million in 2006. L.A. has a $12-million option for 2007 with a $1 million buyout. Gagne can void the option and become a free agent, yet if he voids the option, he would receive a buyout of $250,000 to $1 million, depending on games finished the next two years. No matter how you slice it, it's a comfortable financial cushion for Gagne, his wife Valerie Hervieux—whom he wed in 2001 with the vow: "Valerie, I pledge you my heart and my arm"—and their two children, Faye and Maddox.

Gagne has come a long way since he found himself alone at age 15 and living in a Montreal basement apartment so he could pursue his baseball dream. Now when he is alone, it is on a pitcher's mound, where he performs the solitary role of a baseball closer. He is asked which is more difficult, coping as a lonely teenager or facing the clean-up hitter with the tying run on second? But he doesn't pick either. "My first couple of days at Seminole," Gagne said. "It took four or five months at Seminole before I learned English and was able to communicate. Then I started dreaming in English; when you dream in English, that's when you are truly bilingual."

Gagne's life has undergone dramatic change since his days in Mascouche. The would-be hockey goon who turned to baseball but went undrafted is today a multi-millionaire celebrity playing in one of baseball's most glamorous markets. And he is a Baseball Quebec success story, a testament to what can be achieved by streaming talented young players into a well-organized development program. As a teenager, the distance between Polyvalente Edouard Montpetit High School in Montreal and Dodger Stadium must have seemed vast. Today, though, when Gagne looks back, the chasm wouldn't seem so large. What unites the two is the game itself. Or, as Gagne puts it: "I love the smell of grass, the crack of the bat. For me it's an adrenaline rush."

A MAN FOR
ALL SEASONS

12

A first-time visitor knocks on the door of the house in upscale Leaside, a neighborhood in Toronto. The dog sleeping in the hall awakens and charges towards the door like a Brahma bull coming out of chute No. 3 at the Calgary Stampede. He's in full stride, sprinting and yelping as he bounces towards the door to protect the homestead. Seconds behind comes Dr. Ron Taylor, former major league reliever, yelling: "Attack! Attack! Attack!" The visitor backs away before realizing this is just a display of the sense of humor Dr. Ron Taylor cultivated during his three separate lives on the third rock from the sun. On his final "Attack!" call you can see that Taylor has caught the dog and is holding him by his collar.

You move closer to the door, flashing back to 2003 when you shared a car with Dr. Taylor and his wife Rona to a downtown hotel at baseball's winter meetings in New Orleans. All the bags are loaded, the cabbie slips the car out of park and from the front seat you see Taylor's meaty paw reach onto the back of the front seat:

"Driver, driver," Taylor says in almost a frantic manner. The driver brakes and turns around.

"Before we get started ... do you accept cash?" Taylor asks.

Laughter fills the cab. It was so funny one rider left his cell phone in the cab.

Back inside the Leaside house, the visitor pets the dog, which has suddenly become calm.

"So, how old is your dog?"

Seven.

"What's your doggie's name?"

Maude. Named her after my mother.

"What kid of doggie is Maude?"

A Rottweiler.

If the panel from the popular old game show *What's My Line* were quizzing Taylor they'd likely be stumped.

Was Taylor: An athlete? An engineer? A doctor? The answer would be all of the above. Or another appropriate guess might be: "A stand-up comic?" A busy life? Well, yes. Today, Taylor is a family practitioner who also works at a sports injury clinic and does duty as a team doctor with the Toronto Blue Jays. In former lives, he graduated with a degree in engineering and won two World Series rings.

Taylor is as quick with a quip as he was with his fastball on the outside corner. He has a perfect delivery, with the timing of an atomic clock. He's so dry he could work the Sahara Hilton. "I'm the son of Irish pioneers," Taylor said. "My mother went down to the dock to take the boat (pause) to Australia, but she was late (pause) so, she took the next boat (pause) and here I am."

One time, Dr. Taylor, who has a rather large proboscis, had an attractive woman in his office who asked if he could suggest a plastic surgeon. The woman wanted her nose fixed. Taylor has a mug that suggests he may have been a former sparring partner of Mike Tyson's. Taylor didn't think surgery was necessary. Back and forth they went. "I need an operation," the patient said. "No you don't," said the doctor. Finally, he gave up. "OK, if you really need one, I know a real good doctor," Taylor said. "I'll send you to the guy who did my nose."

His humor is self-deprecating, the Canadian way.

"In my early years as a doctor, I was on call in the emergency room," Taylor said. "They bring in an accident victim and I'd examine him. He was dead. I would tell the family the bad news. They would look at me and say (pause): 'We want a second opinion.'" He tells even funnier stories, notices you writing them down and says: "I don't think that would be suitable for a book." They aren't off-color stories, just tales he doesn't think a doctor should be telling.

Yet, underneath the layers of the jock and the talk is a good man who has been known to quickly re-arrange his schedule to see an injured pitcher in his draft year. Throw away the two university degrees and Taylor's story is not uncommon among Canadians who've made it to the major leagues. He starred on a local Toronto diamond (Talbot Park), was guided by an important mentor and coach (Chester Dies and Ron Roncetti) and he clawed his way up the organizational ladder to the majors. Growing up in the 1950s, Taylor followed the New York Yankees, with Hall of Fame outfielder Mickey Mantle, lefty Whitey Ford and right-hander Bob Turley. "Usually there were only a handful of Canadians playing," Taylor said. "The fact that I was a Canadian playing an American game was never a problem. It would have become more evident when I would show up after spring training to join a team." That's because Taylor went to school during his first years in pro ball, so therefore he missed the daily rituals of spring training until he graduated from university.

"When I showed up with a club in the first month it usually meant someone was going to be leaving," Taylor said. "And these guys had been together since spring training began in March."

When Taylor signed in 1955, there were six Canadians in the majors: right-hander Bob Hooper of Leamington, Ontario with the Cincinnati Reds; Reno Bertoia of Windsor with the Detroit Tigers; right-hander Ozzie Van Brabant of Kingsville, Ontario and catcher Eric MacKenzie with the Kansas City A's; right-hander Bob Alexander of Vancouver with the Baltimore Orioles; and outfielder Glen Gorbous of Drumheller, Alberta, with the Philadelphia Phillies. "Most years there were only a handful of Canadians," Taylor remembered. And in 1956 there were only two: Bertoia and Gorbous.

Ron Taylor bucked the odds, as his ancestors had for decades. Walter Taylor, Ron Taylor's grandfather, and his wife Elizabeth were pioneer farmers who settled in Flesherton, Ontario. His grandparents on his mother's side, William and Emily Evans, were from Wales. "They made me look sane," Taylor joked. "They loved to party; usually it was all day Friday." Evans was in the cavalry, fighting for the British Empire in the Boer War, serving under Sir Robert Baden-Powell in the defense of Mafeking at the turn of the century. After that, he was the proprietor of the Red Lion pub in Welshpool, Wales. Walter Taylor eventually moved to Toronto and ran W. Taylor Cash Grocer & Confectioner at the corner of Carlaw and Victor. He had a son named Wes, who worked for Dunlop Tire and Rubber for more than 50 years. He wouldn't leave Dunlop because the company kept him working during the depression. Wes and his wife Maude had two children, Carole and a younger child named Ron, born Dec. 13, 1937.

Ron discovered baseball at Leaside in 1950. He was the second-best pitcher behind Bill Kennedy on the Rotary Club peewees. Although Taylor was a natural lefty, his mother had other plans. "My mother made me use the other arm. They used to say using your left arm was bad for your heart," Taylor said. "If I stuck with the left hand, I'd still be pitching." Kennedy and Taylor threw to catcher Charlie Burns, later of the Boston Bruins. Frank Cronk, Wes Taylor, Phil Stein and Trace Mains, an ex-Leaside mayor, coached.

The peewees won the Ontario title and then Taylor *et al* moved up to the Rumble bantams in 1952. In 1954, Taylor made a lifetime connection, the type every young player seeks, as he joined the Metropolitan Motors club. Ron Roncetti was the coach, winner of eight titles in 12 years. As it turned out, he also became Taylor's mentor. "Ron turned a lot of our lives around," said Taylor. "At a time when we doubted our own self worth, he gave it to us."

Roncetti, who later was inducted into the Canadian Baseball Hall of

Fame, owned a billiard parlor at Yonge and Dundas Streets in Toronto that, Taylor said, helped augment his income "when some New Yorker would think he'd take a few quick bucks from a dumb Canadian." Taylor recalled one night when he was 16 and, upon leaving the billiard hall, someone accidentally broke the door, making it impossible to lock. "I phoned home and said 'Mom, I'm at a sleepover,' and she said, 'That's fine, Ronnie, where are you?' 'I'm at a billiard hall.'" The four players slept on the tables.

Even at a young age, Taylor was multi-tasking. Many summer nights he'd finish work, unloading bunker oil from tankers in Toronto harbor, then head to Maple Leaf Stadium to throw batting practice for 30-to-45 minutes for Triple-A Toronto Maple Leaf hitters, and then head north to Talbot Park to pitch for Roncetti. Today, it is known as the Shrine, in a sarcastic manner, by visiting teams to Talbot Park. Outfielders dodge a light standard, which is in play, as they scamper up a terrace in left. It's 275 feet down the left-field line, while left-handed hitters can pull a ball 400 feet only to see the right fielder standing, waiting. "You have to be part mountain goat to play here," said Howie Birnie, who has been at Leaside six or seven nights a week since 1952. "It was worse before 1988, when two light standards were in play."

For all of its quirks, Talbot Park turned 58 in 2004. Howard Talbot, a former Leaside mayor, donated the land at Bayview and Eglinton—not far from where Taylor lives now—and former pro goalie Phil Stein, who played one game for the 1939-40 Leafs before becoming Leaside's first recreation director, started the Leaside Baseball Association. In the 41 years Leaside has been a member of the Ontario Baseball Association, it has won 18 championships and 46 Metro Toronto titles. Ontario titles went to the 1946 and 1986 peewees, and the 1993 and 1995 midgets.

Roughly 9,000 games have been played on the two fields. Field No. 2 is named in memory of organizers Carmen Bush and Leith Hibbert. Field No. 1, the Shrine, is named after Leaside's most famous alumni—Taylor and Roncetti. Back in 1955, it was just called Field No. 1, and it was where Roncetti, who scouted for the Milwaukee Braves, took his boss, Roland Gladu, for a look at Taylor. Gladu came, saw and was not impressed. "He said I threw across my body and wasn't interested," Taylor said. It was a mere bump in Taylor's road.

Heading into the summer, Taylor joined the Air Force reserve and fueled de Haviland Vampire fighter jets at the Canadian Forces Base at Downsview in north Toronto. His dream was to fly them. The day before Labour Day weekend, Cleveland Indians' scout Chester Dies took Taylor on a train to Cleveland. Dies had been unable to convince his supervisor, Clare Hoose, to come to town for a look. "We checked into the hotel, the next day woke up, had a root beer float and headed over to Municipal Stadium," Taylor remembered. Once in the stadium, it was no walk in the park for either Dies or the teenager. Minor league director Laddie Plazec was not impressed that his scout had shown up with an uninvited guest for a look-see. "They had an open office and I could hear Plazec chewing him out," Taylor said. "I remember thinking 'Gee, this isn't going the way I thought it would.'"

Dies, the scout, and Taylor, the understudy, were told to come back the next day. Plazec would allow Taylor to throw a side session in the bullpen. "Pitching coach Mel Harder came over and had a look," Taylor said. Taylor was told to come back again the next day to throw again in the bullpen. This time manager Al Lopez, later elected to Cooperstown as a manager, caught Taylor.

Taylor was called inside afterwards for a meeting.

"Would you like to sign?" Plazec and Lopez asked.

"Sure, but I want the max," Taylor said.

In 1955, rules regarding bonuses prevented anyone from receiving more than $4,000—anything more and he would have to stay on the major-league roster the next two years. The Indians gave Taylor $4,000, of which $2,900 was spent on tuition to attend the University of Toronto.

Dies' full-time job was as a sheet metal worker for the board of education. His labor of love was being an ivory hunter for the Indians, just as my father was. "Walking into that park with Chester was like a scene out of *The Natural*," Taylor said. "Chester changed my life. His belief in me was overwhelming."

Taylor went to North Toronto Collegiate, told his teacher he was going to play pro ball, then come back and write his exams. The response? "Son, you are making a terrible mistake." In the spring of 1956, Taylor was at spring training. There were 250 players in camp. His number was 247. "I know the letter 'T' is low in the alphabet, but not that low," Taylor said. Another minor leaguer, No. 9, working out with the Indianapolis club, befriended Taylor. His name? Roger Maris.

Then, Taylor was off to Class-D Daytona Beach, earning $250 a month. He went 17-11, throwing 247 innings with an ERA of 3.13. At the end of the season, Taylor told minor-league director Laddie Plazec of his plans. "I want to go back to school and finish Grade 13. I'll play for you, but I'll only play in the summers," Taylor said. "I had them on the hook—I won 17 games."

The Indians suggested he attend Case Institute in Cleveland in the off season. He declined. The response from Plazec? "Son, you are making a terrible mistake." Missing spring training because of school, Taylor showed up at Class-C Fargo, North Dakota, and went 9-7 with a 3.40 ERA in 1957. The next season he was with Class-C Minot, North Dakota, where he was

14-10 with a 2.86 ERA. Again, Taylor arrived after spring training because of school, and players greeted his arrival with "Here comes Canada."

The best three pitchers in the league that year were Gaylord Perry, Bo Belinsky and Taylor. In 1959, he made it to spring training and was 9-9 with a 4.12 ERA at Single-A Reading. The next year he graduated first-class honors from the University of Toronto with an electrical engineering degree. He was 10-10 with a 3.42 ERA at Reading. In 1961, Taylor moved to Triple-A Salt Lake City, where he was 8-9 with a 4.57 ERA. The spring of 1962 saw Taylor at the Indians' camp, wearing No. 66, which was much better than No. 247. Taylor pitched 23 scoreless innings at Tucson to make the staff.

Mel Harder, who was there for Taylor's impromptu walk-on tryout in 1956, was still the pitching coach. Harder suggested the Indians keep Taylor. Taylor showed he wasn't a flower that only blooms in the spring. His first major-league start in 1962, at Boston's Fenway Park, turned into an epic pitching battle with the Bill Monbouquette of the Red Sox. Through the first nine innings, Taylor and Monbouquette held each team scoreless. Then, both Monbouquette and Taylor put up zeros in the 10th and then the 11th. Mombo, who later became a pitching coach in the Jays' minor-league system while Taylor was the team physician, worked a scoreless top of the 12th. Taylor allowed a leadoff liner to centre by Carl Yastrzemski to open the 12th. Indians' centre fielder Ty Cline charged in as the ball sailed over his head for a triple. Tribe manager Mel McGaha instructed Taylor to walk the next two hitters intentionally. Then, Carroll Hardy hit a grand slam to give Boston a 4-0 win. In his first major-league start Taylor's complete-game line was 11 innings, 10 hits, four earned runs, three walks and five strikeouts.

Taylor gained his first major-league win April 24, 6-3 over the California Angels and Dean Chance, but the Indians demoted him May 22 after he appeared in eight games, going 2-2 with a 5.94 ERA, cutting his salary from $6,000 to $5,000. At Jacksonville, Taylor pitched every three days and wound up 12-4 with a 2.63 ERA. Third baseman Mike de la Hoz nicknamed him 'Steely' since he pitched like a man of steel. "Ron was with Jacksonville when I was with Atlanta," catcher Tim McCarver said. "He was lights out that year."

The Indians dealt Taylor and Jack Kubiszyn to the St. Louis Cardinals on December 15. Taylor was pitching winter ball for the San Juan Senators in Puerto Rico. Cards' general manager Bing Devine phoned Taylor, told him he had pitched enough and it was time to shut it down for the winter. Taylor didn't know it until he reached St. Louis, but the Cards' manager Johnny Keane had been to see him pitch. Arriving in camp with the Cards he found his locker was next to future Hall of Famer Stan Musial. "If you want to get your shoes shined put them in my locker, I'm a big tipper," Musial said. At the time, Musial was making $70,000 and didn't mind sending Taylor's shoes out with his and then paying the tip. Taylor was earning $10,000.

Taylor entered a game in the ninth with the bases loaded and one out September 14 against the Milwaukee Braves, saving a 3-2 win for Bob Gibson. Taylor didn't have an easy row, striking out future Hall of Famers Hank Aaron and Eddie Mathews to end the game. In all, Taylor appeared in 54 games, starting nine times. He went 9-7, with a 2.84 ERA, and shared the Cards' lead for saves, 11, with Bobby Shantz.

The 1964 season continued a productive string for Taylor, appearing in 63 games, going 8-4 with 4.62 ERA and two saves. Facing the Giants, Taylor came on with the bases loaded. Willie Mays was striding towards the plate. Out came Keane, the manager, and Taylor remembers the conversation going something like this:

Keane: "The bases are loaded."

Taylor: "I already know that."

Keane: "Willie Mays is coming up."

Taylor: "I had that figured out."

Keane: "Well, don't give him anything to hit, but don't walk him."

Taylor struck out Mays. "I didn't strike him out that often; he got me a few times," Taylor said.

It was a giddy time when the Cards clinched the NL pennant in St. Louis. The clubhouse attendant kept playing a World War II song, *Pass the Biscuits Miranda*, because the Cards had not been to the Series since 1946 and Miranda was a hit at that time. Tim McCarver remembers back-up catcher Bob Uecker dancing naked to the music, side-stepping broken champagne bottles.

"So, naturally we all go to Stan Musial's restaurant to continue the celebration," said McCarver. "We look around and someone says 'Where's Ronnie?' We couldn't find him anywhere." Two clubhouse attendants were dispatched to the Cards' clubhouse. "Here was this soon-to-be-a doctor, this brilliant, analytical mind which earned two degrees, lying in his locker, behind the clothes hanging from above. Only his feet were sticking out."

Asked whether the story was true, Taylor said: "I was relaxing."

Taylor was a fierce competitor for the Cards and that was never more evident than on October 11 at Yankee Stadium, Game 4 of the 1964 Series. The Yankees led the series 2-1 and scored three times in the first inning. Cards' starter Ray Sadecki faced four hitters and retired one man—Phil Linz was erased when catcher McCarver threw him out attempting to steal third. Roger Craig worked the next 4 2/3 innings, allowing two singles, and Carl Warwick led off the sixth with a single, pinch-hitting for Craig. Manager Keane had Taylor throwing in the left-field bullpen between the foul line and the grandstand. "The New York fans were leaning over, heckling the way New York fans do," Taylor said. Curt Flood singled and Dick Groat reached on an error to load the bases. Cards' third baseman Ken Boyer then hit a grand slam off lefty Al Downing for a 4-3 St. Louis lead. Their lead gone, the Yankee chorus turned it up a notch. After the third out, Taylor made his entrance to boos from the 66,312 in attendance.

"Walking in from the bullpen all you could see was the immense crowd, the auxiliary scoreboards, the TV cameras with the red lights on top flicking on and off," Taylor said.

Taylor walked by third baseman Kenny Boyer, who said: "Keep the ball down Ronnie." Taylor said: "Thanks Kenny."

"I did my warm-ups and then all I could see was Tim McCarver's glove. I couldn't hear the crowd," Taylor said. "I just played catch with Tim." Taylor made it look as easy as pitching at Talbot Park. Elston Howard grounded out, Tom Tresh struck out and Joe Pepitone bounced out to end the sixth. Clete Boyer popped to first, Johnny Blanchard flew to centre and Phil Linz grounded out in the seventh. Bobby Richardson grounded out to Taylor's best friend, shortstop Dal Maxvill. Then Taylor got Roger Maris, who had befriended him years before with the Indians. He grounded out, the ball going off Taylor to shortstop Dick Groat, who threw to first for the out. After walking Mickey Mantle, Taylor struck out Howard to end the eighth.

Tresh grounded back to Taylor to open the ninth, Pepitone bounced to first and Clete Boyer grounded to first to give Taylor the save. In four hitless innings, Taylor allowed one base runner—the walk to Mantle—and recorded eight of the 12 outs on ground balls.

"You know, when you talk about the greatest pitching performances of the post season, that is really a game that never got its due," said Mike Shannon, the Cards' right fielder that day and now a St. Louis broadcaster. "Roger gave up two singles in 4 2/3 innings and Ronnie held them hitless for four innings. We shut down that powerful Yankee club. If we don't win that game I don't even know if we're going back to St. Louis; we're down 3-1 with one more game to play at Yankee Stadium."

Fans haven't forgotten the game. It was named the seventh most important game in the history of the franchise, according to the book *Cardinal Nation*.

"We had two guys go out there who weren't expected to pitch the rest of the game and beat them," McCarver, now a Fox analyst, said. "I mean, after all, they were the Yankees. Ron would tell me to set up outside on left-handed hitters and he'd throw his heavy fastball time after time, to the same spot."

Bob Gibson won Game 5 and the Yanks won Game 6 in St. Louis, forcing Game 7 at Sportsman's Park. During batting practice the pitchers always played a game: left-handed hitters, captained by Sadecki, versus the right-handed hitters, captained by Taylor. "Sadecki's team complained that we had batted out of order and went to Bob Uecker, our commissioner, for a ruling." Taylor got rid of the evidence by eating the lineup card. "We were a loose bunch, playing games like that before Game 7." Not to worry, Gibson pitched a complete-game win.

The sweet afterglow of a World Series didn't last long for Taylor. On June 15 the next year, with the Cards in seventh place, Mike Cuellar and Taylor were dealt to the Houston Astros for pitchers Hal Woodeshick and Chuck Taylor.

"I didn't want to play in Houston; it was too hot," Taylor said. "When I got there I told GM Paul Richards it was a bad trade ... for both clubs."

Taylor was 1-5 with a 6.40 ERA and four saves with Houston to finish the 1965 season, and he was 2-3 with a 5.71 ERA in 1966. In 1967, Taylor's contract was sold to the New York Mets, which was considered the end of the major-league line. The Mets were on their way to losing 100 games for the fifth time in their first six seasons. Wes Westrum was the Mets manager and before breaking camp in St. Petersburg he brought in vice-president and former manager Casey Stengel to address the club.

"I want you boys to know that you are the New York Metropolitans," Stengel said. "You have Tom Seaver, who is 22 and in 10 years he will be an all-star. You have Nolan Ryan, who is 20 and in 10 years he'll be on his way to the Hall of Fame. You have Jerry Koosman, who is 24 and in 10 years he'll be one of the best left-handers in the game. And you have Ron Taylor. He's 29, and if he looks after himself, in 10 years he has a chance to be 39."

The Mets went 61-101. Not that things were bad, but as Taylor said: "If we were rained out, half the team would have a victory party." Taylor was the closer with a 4-6 record, a 2.84 ERA and eight saves. In the off-season, he came home to practice engineering.

Gil Hodges, the former Dodger first baseman, took over as manager in 1968. Taylor was 1-5 in 58 games with a 2.70 ERA and 13 saves as the Mets improved to 73-89. Taylor remembers Hodges, the former Dodger first baseman, coming out of the dugout suggesting Taylor walk Hank Aaron intentionally and face Orlando Cepeda because first base was open.

Taylor said: "I'd rather face Aaron."

Hodges: "You what? Well, you better get him out."

Taylor got Aaron to bounce to second and headed into the dugout. Said

Hodges: "You're crazier than I thought."

One day in 1969, Taylor looked as if he'd lost his bearings as he staggered around looking for a ball hit back at the mound by Montreal Expos' Boots Day. "The line drive hit me right in the head. I looked to my left, to my right and then heard a roar and another roar," Taylor said. "I didn't know what happened." Hodges came to the mound and, when Taylor asked what happened, said: "You got a double play off your head; you get an assist." The ball had ricocheted off Taylor's head right to first baseman Ed Kranepool, who stepped on first and threw to second baseman Buddy Harrelson for the 1-(noggin)-3-6 double play. "Nowadays, we'd med-evac a guy to the hospital if that happened," said Taylor.

That September, after a 100-62 season, the Mets went to the National League Championship Series for the first time, as the Miracle Mets. Late in the season, it was our first time in a major-league clubhouse, leading to the first of hundreds of dumb questions we'd ask. "So, can you guys beat the Mets?" I asked Hank Aaron in the visitor's clubhouse at Montreal's Jarry Park. "Well, we played them 12 times and they've beat us eight out of 12, so ..." Aaron said. I quickly learned you were supposed to know those things if you wanted to walk into a clubhouse.

In Game 1, Taylor worked two scoreless innings in relief of Tom Seaver. Taylor got the Game 2 win and the Mets went on to sweep the Braves in the best-of-five series to advance to the World Series against the Baltimore Orioles. After the Orioles had won the opener at Baltimore's Memorial Stadium, Mets' lefty Jerry Koosman took a 2-1 lead into the bottom of the ninth in Game 2 and retired the first two hitters. Then Koosman walked Frank Robinson and Boog Powell. Hodges called on Taylor to face future Hall of Famer Brooks Robinson. "I got to 3-2 on him and they were off and running on the pitch; it was the worst possible situation for me, for us," Taylor said. But Robinson grounded to third baseman Ed Charles, who threw to first for the out to end the game. Four days later, it was all over. The Mets scored twice in the eighth for a 5-3 win at Shea Stadium to take the Series in five games.

"It was bedlam. Fans came running onto the field, tearing up turf, some people stole home plate," Taylor said. "We had the ticker tape parade down the canyon of heroes. The people tore buttons off our blazers and ripped moulding off the sides of our cars."

In all, Taylor worked 10 1/3 scoreless innings in the post-season, allowing three hits, while walking two and striking out nine. That followed a season where he was 9-4 with a 2.72 ERA and 13 saves.

He had two more years in New York before the Montreal Expos purchased Taylor as an insurance policy for the 1972 season. They released him April 20 and he signed the same day with the San Diego Padres. His fourth outing with the Padres was his final one in the majors, a 9-3 loss to the Expos at Jarry Park. Taylor recorded the final two outs of the sixth, then with one out in the seventh he allowed a single to Ron Hunt and back-to-back homers to Mike Jorgensen and Ron Fairly. The final hitter Taylor faced was Ken Singleton, who grounded to first.

What to do now? Taylor decided to go back to school to become a doctor. The idea came to him in 1968, when he toured Guam and Okinawa to meet U.S. troops along with Denny McLain of the Detroit Tigers and Montreal-born Pete Ward of the Chicago White Sox. The next year, after winning the World Series, he traveled into the war zone near Saigon and headed to more hospitals. Two years later, he again toured Guam and the rest of the Pacific theatre. "I got the chance to meet doctors and talk to them about what they were doing," Taylor said. "It was good for soldiers to see people supporting them. It was such a controversial war."

What Taylor the baseball player did as he made the rounds was write down the phone numbers of the soldiers' parents. He then called each and every one when he got home to tell them he'd seen their son, and he was going to be okay. "My wife Rona says of all the things I ever did in life, that was one of the best ever." During his 1969 trip, he learned how special the Mets' Series win was to some troops. "The soldiers who were Mets fans told us how they fired their weapons into the air when they heard that the Mets had won. They told us Charlie didn't know what was going on," Taylor said.

Back home, Taylor began his journey toward becoming a doctor. In speaking with the dean of student affairs at the University of Toronto in 1972, he was told several thousand people apply and only 200 are accepted. "The Dean asked me: 'What have you being doing lately?' I said playing major-league baseball," Taylor said. "I told him I was switching careers because baseball had died a natural death and my training as an electrical engineer was obsolete. He asked if he could look at my transcripts, and when he looked up and asked 'are these yours?' I knew I was in trouble."

Taylor, 35 at the time, was told that rarely is anyone over 30 accepted into medical school. He was to take an honors science course and the school would consider it, with the odds on being accepted 50-50. So he went from a ballplayer's lifestyle to a priest's. From waking at 11 a.m., being at the park by 3 p.m. and leaving at 11 for a bite to eat at bars, Taylor re-arranged his shank of the day. He'd attend class from 8 to 5 p.m., then sleep four hours and study from 9 p.m. until 7 a.m. "There was very little distraction like friends or baseball or football," Taylor said. "That's how I was able to get through and it was very effective."

Taylor's mother had died in 1967, but his father, who had retired and was living alone, supported his new career. "I moved back into my old bedroom. I was single at the time, and didn't really have any responsibilities," Taylor said. "It was like a time warp." That was in 1973. Taylor gained entry into medical school. Before his first class, he spent the summer coaching in Lethbridge, Alberta and took the Alberta entry to the Canadian senior championships in Edmonston, New Brunswick. In September 1973, Ron Taylor, age 36, started the first day of the rest of his life. "First class I showed up for, they thought I was a repairman. They were looking for my tool kit," Taylor said. "On rounds sometimes they thought I was a volunteer patient." He graduated in 1977 and soon after became the Blue Jays' team physician, the beginning of an association that has lasted through four decades.

In 1999, the Mets staged their 30th reunion and the players stayed at the New York Athletic Club. Down the street was an Irish bar. Most of the Mets managed to find it. At closing time, Jerry Koosman, Tug McGraw and Taylor remained. "I said nothing has changed since 1969," Taylor remembers. "Here are the three of us together at closing time."

These days, Taylor's day begins at 6 a.m. "I see a lot of people in my office who aren't happy in their jobs," Taylor said. "I love what I do." What he does, as always, is multi-task. Besides running his own successful family practice, he has two other irons in the fire. As the Blue Jays' physician, along with Dr. Allan Gross, an orthopedic surgeon, Taylor manages the health care of the more than 200 players throughout the Jays' system.

Taylor also runs the S.C. Cooper Sports Medicine Clinic with Dr. Erin Boynton at Toronto's Mount Sinai Hospital. Cooper played second base for Toronto Lizzies and was a prominent civil engineer, working on projects like the St. Lawrence Seaway and Ontario's 400 system of highways, as well as being a sponsor for a team in the Leaside junior league. Taylor and Cooper met when Taylor was attending medical school and became friends. "He's like the second Chester Dies in my life," Taylor says. The clinic opened in 1979 and sees an average of 3,000 injuries a season. That's roughly 75,000 elbows, knees, shoulders ... sports injuries of any kind, except for backs.

Many at the sports clinic don't know they are being attended to by a World Series hero, two times over. It's the same inside the Jays' trainer's room. Taylor may have four World Series rings (he also received rings for the Jays' championships in 1992 and 1993), but he only wears his engineering ring. When Taylor congratulated Jays' reliever Tim Crabtree on his first big-league save in 1996, Crabtree replied: "What a feeling; it's a feeling you'll never comprehend."

"I'm 67 years old. I played in the majors for 11 years. Eleven years is a blip in my life when you think about it," Taylor said. "But I have a lifetime of friends. It's like Vince Lombardi told his Green Bay Packers before big games ... 'Win today and you have brothers for life.' I have two sets of brothers, the Cardinals and the Mets."

On the home front, Taylor has two sons with his wife Rona, whom he met at Mount Sinai Hospital in 1978 when he was a resident and Rona worked as a nurse. Their first date was a Jays' game. They wed Sept. 26, 1981. Matthew Taylor is studying film at Queen's University and Drew Taylor is in his junior year at the University of Michigan. While Drew has his mother's good looks—he wouldn't mind his father's shoulders—he has grown up to be just like dad. In 1997, Drew was named Leaside bantam most valuable player, 45 years after his father won the same award. In the spring of 2003, Drew picked up his first college win, pitching 8 1/3 innings as the Michigan Wolverines beat the Bethune-Cookman Wildcats 7-5 at Jackie Robinson Park in Daytona Beach. Ron Taylor's first win as a pro was 47 years earlier in the same Daytona park.

"When I was really young it was difficult, my father worked a lot, but any time he could come to games he was there," Drew said. "It was more of a big deal pre-high school."

Around the house it is comedy central.

"When Drew first started playing a lot of his teammates wanted to come to the house to meet a major leaguer," Rona said. "It was quiet with the boys when they would come in. Ron likes to think that they were in awe. I prefer to think it was a little traumatic; they came in expecting to see this stud former player and they saw an old man."

Drew has pictures of Bob Uecker, the Hall of Fame broadcaster, David Wells, the only Blue Jay invited to Taylor's house, and his father in his room. On the wall of Matthew's room are autographed pictures of Jerry Koosman, Mickey Mantle and his father. And he has an autographed program from a Joe DiMaggio Hospital fundraiser, signed by the Yankee Clipper himself. DiMaggio did not sign for many people. Once, Yanks catcher Matt Nokes asked him for an autograph on Old Timers Day at Yankee Stadium and DiMaggio told him to see his agent. "We walked over to Joe and I told Matthew not to ask," Taylor said. Matthew stood there program in hand. DiMaggio said "Don't worry about it Matthew, let me sign that for you."

Drew, something of a late bloomer, has shown signs of following in his dad's footsteps. A pitcher, he garnered no interest from U.S. colleges when he graduated from high school, although Terry McKaig of the University of British Columbia Thunderbirds offered him a spot. He was set to head to B.C. in the fall of 2001, but during that summer, on the way to the Connie Mack World Series with the Ontario Blue Jays and coach Danny Bleiwas, Drew's 93 miles-per-hour fastball caught the eye of U.S. college recruiters. The 6-foot-4 lefty turned down a $200,000 signing bonus from the Atlanta Braves and $150,000 from the Toronto Blue Jays, and decided to go to Georgia Tech. After a disappointing rookie season in which he worked only 9 1/3 innings, Taylor transferred to Michigan, where he blossomed, going 9-1 in 14 starts with a 3.97 ERA. In 95 1/3 innings he fanned 51 and struck out 25. He won the Geoff Zahn Award as Michigan's Most Valuable Pitcher and was named Big 10 Pitcher of the Year. The next year, 2004, he made only one start before being sidelined with tendinitis. But that setback hasn't dulled his aspirations. Like his father, Drew has a passion for baseball and for school.

"I'm going to take this as far as it will take me," Drew says. "I'm not saying I'm a superstar, but I set high aspirations. I'm looking toward medicine as well."

In his father's footsteps he strides. From father to son.

THREE ROADS
TO ATHENS

13

The long and winding road to a windswept hill on the shores of the Mediterranean one fateful August evening began on the similarly-windswept but very different northern shore of Lake Erie, in a town known for its migrating birds and its embrace of all things to do with tomatoes. And 200 miles to the northeast, on the fast-flowing banks of the Credit River in the backyard of the Bread and Honey Festival. And another 50 miles to the northeast of that, in a hamlet settled by Pennsylvania Quakers in a heavenly valley on the northern slope of the Oak Ridges Moraine, an environmentally-sensitive area an hour north of Toronto that contains the headwaters of 65 river systems.

Of the 11,099 separate journeys taken to reach Athens and participate in the Games of the XXVIII Olympiad, just a little less than one percent began within the boundaries of Canada's largest province. Of those, only one-third originated in Ontario's major cities. In baseball, perhaps more than most sports, it sometimes seems that small town and rural roots provide the best opportunity of developing the particular blend of physical skills and stubborn perseverance that brings eventual success. Or maybe it's just that in those places there is less to divert a father's attention.

Danny Klassen, the shortstop, best fielder and most experienced major leaguer among the regulars on Canada's 2004 Olympic baseball team, was only 12 hours old when Vic Klassen returned to the hospital after running errands for wife Helen and laid a Wilson A-2000, six-fingered glove beside the incubator. The couple's first child had weighed seven pounds, 15 ounces, but because he was stuck in the birth canal and wasn't breathing when he was born, doctors had him placed in an incubator.

"He gave us some worries for a few days," Helen said.

No need to worry, as it turned out. Klassen grew up to stand six feet and weigh 190 pounds. His is a story of perseverance, of growing up with a dream and riding out the inevitable lows that mark the journey. And although there was a time leading up to the Olympics when he might have been regarded by some as a 'paper' Canadian, a closer look reveals otherwise. Klassen was born in Leamington, a southwestern Ontario town of

26,000 on the shores of Lake Erie, 50 kilometres from Detroit and just a stone's throw from Point Pelee, Canada's most southern point. Deep in farming country, Leamington boasts of being the tomato capital of Canada, and it has the H.J. Heinz plant, the tomato-shaped water tower and the fiberglass tomato information booth in the centre of town to prove it.

A long time ago, in another Ontario town, a television sports announcer named Max Jackson would inevitably set up an important game with a variation of, "Well, all roads lead to the Memorial Centre tonight as the Kingston Frontenacs host the hated Hull-Ottawa Canadiens in playoff action." You had to make four turns to get to the rink, so not all roads actually led directly to the rink. You still had to plot your own personal route.

So it is in baseball. How many roads lead to a professional career? Think of it as an intricate maze of tall green hedgerows that an unsuspecting guest encounters in an English garden. Some players crash into a dead end, as when a single baseball scout sees something he doesn't like. Or at another turn, a lush thicket, in the form of an arm injury, rears up in the path. Others bump into homesickness, or a manager who yells and screams and says "are you from Canada or Candyland?" Only survivors escape the maze.

This is the story of three such survivors, and the particular paths each took to a career in professional baseball. From his arrival on the shores of Lake Erie, Danny Klassen made it all the way to the major leagues. From birth in Mississauga, the suburb immediately to the west of Toronto, and growing up in Georgetown, home to 24,000 not to mention the Bread and Honey Festival, so did Shawn Hill. Hill, who battled odds and micro tears in his right elbow, jumped from Double-A to the Montreal Expos a month before the Olympics, becoming, as events later developed, the last Canadian to start a game for the franchise. He would pitch six solid innings for underdog Canada against Cuba in the Olympic semi-final before handing the lead over to the bullpen, in the person of Chris Begg. Begg, who ran into more hurdles than the others, both on his career path and on that day in Athens, wasn't drafted out of high school, wound up with only nine-plus innings his first year of university, transferred, won conference pitcher of the year honors and still wasn't drafted. He sent out resumes like a graduating university student and landed a job with an independent team, which folded. His contract was purchased by another. And then, suddenly, Begg didn't have to send out any more resumes. His contract was purchased by the San Francisco Giants. Unlike Klassen and Hill, he hadn't tasted the big leagues before Athens. But he was only a couple of correct turns away. All three played integral roles in Canada's

Olympic dream-chasing team, but before their lives and stories converged in Greece, they began, in Leamington (pop. 26,000), in Georgetown (pop. 24,000) and in Uxbridge (pop. 17,000), three small towns in southern Ontario.

Klassen is just the second major leaguer to come from Leamington, following in the distant footsteps of Bob Hooper, who pitched six years in the majors, three with the Philadelphia A's, two with the Cleveland Indians and one with the Cincinnati Reds. His best season was his rookie year of 1950, at age 28. Legendary manager Connie Mack used Hooper as his closer with the A's and he finished 15-10 with five saves. A contemporary of Hooper's growing up in Leamington was Herb Hamm, a fastball player who had seven kids, most of whom became fastball players themselves. Four of them—Vic, Ronnie, Paul and Richard—went on to win championships. Mind you, none could hold a candle to the star of the next generation, the son of Herb's daughter Helen, especially when it came to breaking windows in grandpa's greenhouse.

"If someone broke a pane of glass they were in trouble, but if a baseball broke the glass there were not any repercussions," Vic Klassen, Danny's father, said. "All it meant was the first thing in the morning we were repairing the glass in the greenhouse."

When Klassen was three, he and his parents moved to Port St. Lucie, Florida, because his pop, apparently growing tired of tomatoes, had hatched an idea about growing cucumbers. Not that Leamington was ever really left behind. Some summers, Danny would return to visit grandmothers Mary Hamm and Anna Klassen and spend endless hours on local diamonds.

In Port St. Lucie, Vic bought 10 acres and proceeded to tear down an orange grove to use five acres for cucumber production. The rest of the property was heavily wooded, but not for long. As Danny fell in love with baseball, with Little League age approaching and a second son Bryan now part of the family, Vic began clearing trees to build a baseball diamond. "Well, I'd been there a while, it was rural and it was my property," is the way Vic put it. Pine trees came tumbling down over a two-month period. A bulldozer and a dragline excavator took up residence. Klassen sold the trees to a lumber company. Red clay was imported from Georgia, the same kind you see at a major-league spring training site. From another part of Georgia came 419 Bermuda grass. "We had four 18-yard trucks bring in dirt," Klassen said, guessing 80,000 tons in all was moved. The diamond was leveled with Florida clay and then the red clay went on top. A few years later, when Danny was back up north during the summers playing for Leamington Legion No. 84, he would gain as much attention for his shoes as his playing ability. "Danny would come home to play and the other kids would say 'what's all that red stuff on your cleats?' since most of the diamonds in Ontario were stone dust," Vic recalled.

It took "the better part of the year" to complete the field, and all the excavation had left behind a hole large enough to make a pond, thanks to the state of Florida's natural seepage. The 15-foot deep hole filled with water and Vic stocked it with bass. "We had little gators in the pond and a couple of big ones, but they didn't bother anyone," Klassen said. The sprigs were planted and, like the Klassens in their new neighborhood, took root.

Klassen's field of dreams was located five miles from the New York Mets' spring training complex, east off highway U.S. 1. The locals called it Klassen's Field, and it was soon a destination for Little League games and practices. "I guess I started building it when Danny was seven. He was a year too young to play Little League the first year it was built, but he was able to practice with the team." Initially, insurance wouldn't cover Klassen's Field, but then in the second year the Port St. Lucie Little League paid the bill for the insurance. Every off-season Klassen would re-touch the field, and every spring young Danny would immerse himself in the game. "I think the best thing my parents ever did was steer me away from basketball and football as a youngster," said Danny. "It was baseball, baseball, baseball. It was the best thing they could have done to help me."

When he wasn't playing the game, he was watching it on TV. Vic had bought one of the first satellite dishes on the market, "almost as big as a house," he joked, so he could watch his beloved Detroit Tigers. The dish didn't pick up the sound of the announcers, just the picture. So, Danny would mark down each pitch, as in "Kirk Gibson hit a 2-2 fastball to right field. Alan Trammell singled on a 1-0 pitch, Steve Kemp had an RBI single and Champ Summers hit a fly ball to score Trammell in a 6-5 win over the Milwaukee Brewers June 16." Commercial time was spent with father throwing a ball and son either catching it or chasing it down.

Eventually, Danny figured out how to get the Los Angeles Dodgers' games from the coast on the dish, so he could continue following the team that they watched in person during spring training at Vero Beach's Holman Stadium, where they had season tickets. "I'd be up and out the door at 4:30 each morning, so I'd fall asleep on the couch during the Dodger game," the father said. "The next day Danny would go through the game with me pitch by pitch over breakfast."

Helen Klassen knew her son's dream was to become a major-league player. So she wasn't surprised when he declared as much when asked to write the usual 'what-do-you-want-to-be-when-you-grow-up?' essay for his class at Morningside Christian Academy in Port St. Lucie. When the teacher handed back the papers, across Danny's was written: "This is an unattainable goal. Please re-write." Helen wrote the teacher back. "This is not an unrealistic goal, my son will not be re-writing the essay," Helen recalled writing. "I didn't hear from that teacher again. She was wrong to try and crush a young boy's dream."

When the Tigers reached the 1984 World Series against the San Diego Padres, Vic and Danny couldn't resist the urge to see their heroes in the flesh on the October stage. "We didn't have tickets but we flew up for the game and bought some from scalpers," said Vic, who remembers paying $100 a game for all three games at Tiger Stadium. "The Tigers were our team." Righty Milt Wilcox picked up the win as Detroit won Game 3, 5-2. Right-hander Jack Morris then pitched a complete-game, 10-hitter for a 4-2 win on Saturday to put the Tigers one win away. Kirk Gibson homered into the upper right field deck at Tiger Stadium in the eighth inning off Goose Gossage to ensure an 8-4 win on Sunday and send the whole state of Michigan into frenzy. As the Klassens were exiting the grand old park, the first cars were being overturned—soon to be set on fire— alongside Michigan Avenue in a wild celebration that left an indelible, ugly mark on Detroit's image. "I grabbed Danny by the hand," Vic said, "and got out of there. Since we'd been to Tiger Stadium so often we knew how to get to our private parking spot quickly and get on the road home."

Klassen's baseball education continued at John Carroll High School, where he was an honors student in the classroom and an all-star on the field. In his senior year, he went to the state's all-star game. "It was a big deal that year to go to the Florida High School all-star game; Alex Rodriguez was there," said Danny, who signed a letter of intent to attend Florida State in the fall of 1993, but changed his mind when the Milwaukee Brewers selected him in the second round of the June draft. Brewers' scouts Demmi Maneri and Russ Bovay offered Klassen a signing bonus of $200,000 U.S. to forgo Florida State and, at decision time, the offer was too good.

While Danny had dreamed of being the next Alan Trammell for his favorite team, the Tigers, and while pop thought his son was doing well, he couldn't believe what he saw on one scouting report. "Some scouts showed me their reports when they compared him to Alan Trammell," Vic said. "One guy wrote 'If you want to know what this high schooler is like, just watch the Tigers and Trammell.'" Klassen progressed from rookie ball to Double-A by 1997, leading all Double-A and Triple-A shortstops with a .331 average, plus 14 homers, 81 runs batted in and 112 runs scored. Oh yes, and there were those 50 errors.

With the Tampa Bay Devil Rays and the Arizona Diamondbacks preparing for the expansion draft, the respective brain trusts came around to watch the prospects.

Arizona manager Buck Showalter showed one night and was seated behind home plate. He asked pitcher Steve Woodard, who was doing the charting for El Paso, what the deal was with the left side of the El Paso infield. Third baseman Mike Kinkade would finish the season with 60 errors and Klassen had 50. Woodard suggested Showalter take a look at the infield. After the game, as the winning team shook hands, Showalter walked out to shortstop and kicked around one rock. Another. And another. He saw the uneven playing surface.

And so, when the Diamondbacks were born, Arizona selected Klassen in the second round. He started the 1998 season at Triple-A Tucson before getting called up to the Diamondbacks on July 4. Hitless in his first major-league start, he nevertheless managed three walks and a run scored in a 7-4 win over the Astros at Houston's Astrodome with mom and pop flying in for the game. Six days later, in his Bank One Ballpark debut in Phoenix, Klassen collected his first big-league hit, a single off Brett Tomko in the second inning, and added a two-run home run in the ninth off Danny Graves, finishing 3-for-4 against the Cincinnati Reds. Klassen reached base safely in 13 of his first 14 games with the D-Backs before a 4-for-44 slump had him Tucson-bound. Two games after being sent down, he fractured his left shoulder and was done for the year.

And so it went. In 1999, Klassen underwent arthroscopic surgery on his right knee and appeared in just one game with Arizona and 64 with Tucson. In 2000, he was Arizona's starting third baseman on opening day, subbing for injured Matt Williams. Playing out of position, the career middle infielder made only two errors in 20 starts, then started 10 straight games after Williams got injured again. Then, on July 7, he was rounding second in Oakland and strained the flexor tendon in his big toe and was gone for two months. "That was Danny's lowest ebb," his father said. "He had worked his way back to be the opening day third baseman and then he got hurt again."

Once again, Klassen made the Diamondbacks roster to open the 2001 season but was experiencing pain in his right foot. Bad news again. He had a stress fracture. The aftermath of the surgery, together with the rarity of the injury, meant he would miss the rest of the season, save seven games at Tucson. "They put some pins inside his foot," Vic said. "The operation had only been done twice, once each by two doctors. They were arguing over who would get to perform the surgery." Craig Counsell took over Klassen's spot at second base as the Diamondbacks made it to the World Series against the New York Yankees. Klassen and his parents were in Phoenix for Game 7 as Luis Gonzalez hit a flare over Derek Jeter's head and a drawn-in infield to give Arizona a 3-2 come-from behind win against the game's greatest closer, Mariano Rivera. Despite his absence from the active roster, the club made sure Klassen was in the clubhouse to celebrate its first ever championship. "(Owner) Jerry Colangelo treated us in a first-class manner," the father said. "Danny had his picture taken with the World Series trophy."

Again in 2002, Klassen was with the Diamondbacks when they broke camp. This time he lasted two games before going back on the disabled list with an inflamed right toe. When he returned, it was to split the remainder of the year between Tucson and Double-A El Paso. As a six-year minor-league free agent, Klassen signed with his beloved Tigers' organization in 2003. Playing at Triple-A Toledo allowed him to go home, driving along highway 30 to Leamington for visits to his grandmothers. Recalled to the Tigers in mid-August, he finally got to wear the uniform he had worshipped as a child. "My parents flew in, my pass list was about 20," Klassen said. In 22 games, Klassen batted .247 with one homer and seven RBIs. In 2003 and 2004, he was back at Triple-A, losing his spot in '04 to Carlos Guillen, whom he had beaten out years before for an all-star berth at Double-A. At the 2004 Olympics in Athens, Klassen remained hopeful about his future with the Tigers. But among the scouts at the Olympics was the Cubs' Gary Hughes. In the off-season Klassen signed with the Cubs.

When most people score games they put stars beside stellar defensive plays or circle the outs in their scorebooks. In Italy and Athens, Klassen led Team Canada with 10 fine defensive plays, from the grass, from the hole and behind second base. Second baseman Stubby Clapp had seven and third baseman Peter Orr five. Asked whom Klassen might be compared to, manager Ernie Whitt replied: "He's like Cal Ripken, not real quick, but he's always in the right spot and always makes the play." A few moments later, Whitt revised his remarks: "No, comparing someone to Ripken is unfair. I'd say he's more like Alan Trammell." From watching the dish in Port St. Lucie, to the 1984 World Series and worshipping Trammell, Klassen was now being compared to his favorite player.

"I didn't really appreciate that first year, in 1998, playing second every day," Klassen said. "I didn't realize how hard it was to get that job. The first year I was 22 playing every day and now I'm 29 and I've been unable to win a starting job. Injuries teach you to enjoy life one day at time."

The lessons the game has taught through his fledgling major-league career have been numerous and sometimes painful. One lesson didn't directly pertain to baseball. It came during an encounter with one of his Arizona coaches, Carlos Tosca, and it's the one Klassen remembers best. With the Diamondbacks, manager Buck Showalter, a veterans' manager, would look after the older guys like Jay Bell, Matt Williams or Devon White. Younger players would talk to bench coach Tosca. "I remember vividly one time at Wrigley Field, we were in the batting cage in the right field corner," Danny said. "I was really struggling and had had a bad round. Carlos was there and he'd met my parents earlier. He put his arm around me and said 'no matter what happens, you have a wonderful family.' That kind of put things into perspective, I know how lucky I am."

From son to father. And mother.

And what ever happened to Klassen's Field? Well, when brother Bryan grew up and developed a love of cracker horses, Vic Klassen converted the diamond from a ball field where infielders and outfielders once roamed to a pasture where horses could do the same. "They're quick turning, an agile breed used in rodeos," the father says. "The horses taught Bryan discipline, the horses had to be fed every morning at 6 o'clock."

• • •

Determination has always been part of Shawn Hill's character, a trait that his parents, Heather and Rick, were quick to discover. There is no disguising the pride they have in their son's accomplishments, and representing their country in Athens—as the youngest player on Team Canada, no less—ranks high on the list. But it's not No. 1. Nor is the moment in 2000 when he was drafted by the Montreal Expos, the second high schooler picked in the draft. Or when he walked into Olympic Stadium in an Expo uniform for the first time.

"It had to be when he played with the Shoppers Drug Mart team," said Heather, noting that Shoppers was the sponsor whose name graced her son's uniform way back in house league T-ball. Turns out that Hill, who was in Grade 2 and seven years old at the time, caught his leg between a curb and a car while running bases in his grandmother's yard in Mississauga. He yanked his leg out so hard from where it was wedged that he broke it. Rick told the doctor how important the upcoming T-ball season was to his son. So, Hill played first base with a cast on his leg and was the last hitter, meaning he only ran until the opposing team threw the ball into home plate. Hill ran like peg-leg Pete, progressing as far around the bases as he could until the outfielder threw the ball in. When he slid, he threw up a cloud of dust as if a parks tractor was dragging the field.

"He'd go to the hospital with dew and mud on his cast," said Heather. Shawn went through three casts. "The last time we went in, they just laughed. We had the same people putting on his cast each time," Rick said. "Shawn always had a passion for playing the game."

Hill's dad got to share that passion in the best of ways, co-coaching his son with the Mississauga North Tigers for six summers, until 1995, when the boy was 14 and the family moved to Georgetown. "He was playing triple-A in Mississauga, we moved and he was stuck playing C-ball," Rick recalled. "We fought tooth and nail for them to allow him to play in Mississauga, but it didn't work out." Then, Rick dropped by the house of friend Mike Chapelle, who mentioned the Mickey Mantle (age 16 and under) Ontario Blue Jays, who spent a large part of the summer touring in the U.S. and were coached by legendary sand lot player Bobby Smythe. Smythe liked what he saw and Hill became the Jays' starting shortstop. "I dropped Shawn at the park, drove to work and cried all the way," Heather said of Shawn's first road trip. "My eyes were puffy, my face was red, I was a mess. When I walked in the door people asked 'what happened, what happened?' I said 'I think I just sent my son off to boot camp.'"

After two seasons with the Jays, another turning point was just a few pitches away.

In 1998, Hill attended the Major League Bureau camp staged at the immaculate Connorvale Field in Toronto. Former major-leaguer Tim Harkness, who was scouting for the San Diego Padres, asked Major League Baseball's Canadian scouting director, Walt Burrows, if Hill, a Grade 12 student, could take a turn on the mound. He had the second best velocity in camp. "Where do you pitch?" Burrows asked. "I don't," answered Hill. "Well, you'd best get on a team that allows you to pitch," Burrows said. The next season, Hill was pitching for Smythe's Etobicoke Rangers juniors and Harkness made Hill a 33rd round choice of the San Diego Padres that June. Bothered by a micro tear in his right elbow, Hill returned to Grade 13 at Bishop Reding Catholic Secondary School in Milton, Ontario, which meant he would go back into the draft. Hill "popped," as scouts like to say, at a February 2000 indoor workout in Etobicoke, throwing a "free and easy" 88 miles per hour according to the radar guns. Come June, the Padres were ready to select Hill again, but Expos' scout Alex Agostino beat them to the punch, choosing him in the sixth round and coughing up a $115,000 U.S. bonus. Hill made his professional debut in 2000 in rookie ball, then improved steadily through two seasons in Single-A. But in each of those years, his right elbow would flare up and he would need to spend time on the disabled list.

Hill made two stops in 2003, at Single-A in Brevard, Florida, and Double-A in Harrisburg, Pennsylvania, finishing a combined 12-5 with a 2.69 ERA. He was added to the Expos' 40-man roster in October 2003, the first Canuck homegrown to make the grade since Derek Aucoin of Lachine, Quebec in 1996. Starting 2004 back at Harrisburg, he went 5-6 with a 2.99 ERA in 16 starts, though his heart was occasionally an ocean away. "I'd be wearing my Team Canada hat around the park and my team-mates would say 'take that off,'" Hill said. "And I'd say 'you guys have a nice time in Harrisburg in August.'" Then, on June 21, the kid from Georgetown was told he was being promoted to Montreal. He drove to Harrisburg and flew to Montreal. Heather and Rick, along with grand-parents Marie and Tom Hill, were at Montreal's Olympic Stadium to see

Shawn wear an Expo uniform for the first time. There was speculation that Hill, who has been a starter his whole career, would start against the Jays at SkyDome in the opener of a three-game series June 25-27. "He throws strikes, has a good sinker and slider, and doesn't get excited," said Expos coach Claude Raymond at the time. "He was one of our final cuts in the spring. I don't think he'll be available for the Olympics." The Expos were at SkyDome to play the Blue Jays in front of 16,484 fans—or 16,439, if you don't count the Hill clan. Hill had 45 relatives and fans to see him, including his father's mom Vivian, his grandparents Noreen and Willie and his sister April.

Pitching at SkyDome would have been a perfect homecoming for Hill, who grew up in Mississauga listening to broadcasters Tom Cheek and Jerry Howarth as a Jays fan, but the three-game series would go down in the books with two wins for the Jays and no appearances for Hill. His major-league debut finally came June 29 when he was thrust into a starting role against the Philadelphia Phillies, filling in for right-hander Tony Armas, who was coming off a shoulder injury. Twelve days had passed since his last start with Harrisburg, and the lack of work showed. He worked just 2 2/3 innings, allowing nine runs. The Philly announcers giggled, saying Hill is from "Mrs-rag-a-war-ga, no wait, Mrs-U-ah-gah-ra ... whatever, he's from Canada." The disappointment of that loss only lasted until his next start, July 4, when he worked five innings, allowing a single run against the Jays in Puerto Rico. Then, in his third start, Hill allowed seven runs in 1 1/3 innings and was demoted in mid-July with a 16.00 ERA.

Meanwhile, Team Canada had announced its preliminary Olympic roster July 15, 2004, three days after it had been filed with Games officials. Hill's name wasn't on it because he was still with the Expos. He would have been a lock for the Olympic roster had he been in the minors. He had been instrumental in Canada advancing at the Olympic qualifying tournament in Panama in November 2003—11 2/3 innings, seven strikeouts, six earned runs—and was the only starter who had logged major-league time in 2004. Hill reckoned that his Olympic dream was done, but suddenly, the Minnesota Twins announced they were recalling first baseman Justin Morneau, who had been named to the Olympic team. On July 31, when it became clear that, with the way Morneau was swinging the bat, he would be staying with the Twins, Hill was added in his place. But after all the problems with his elbow, there was still the hurdle of having to be examined by Expos doctor Larry Coughlin. He passed that and two days later he flew back to Harrisburg for an MRI exam. Results were negative and, after a conference call between doctors in Harrisburg and Montreal, he was given the green light for Athens. The only stipulation Expos' farm director Adam Wogan put on Hill was that he start only twice during the Olympics, limiting his outings to five innings or 85-to-90 pitches, whichever came first. Team Canada agreed. Hill hastily headed for Baltimore, where Team Canada was playing Greece at Camden Yards.

The other bit of roster intrigue didn't turn out as well for Team Canada. The team's best pitcher, Jeff Francis, made his Triple-A debut on July 17, after which Colorado Rockies general manager Dan O'Dowd told the *Denver Post* that Francis would start Aug. 6 at Colorado Springs and after his debut at high altitude, would "either be in the big leagues or the Olympics. We won't keep him in the minors, that wouldn't be fair to the kid. Right now, we're 50-50." But somehow that all changed and on Aug. 9, after Francis made his first start at the Springs, the Rockies informed Team Canada that the lefty would start two more games in the minors and be promoted Aug. 25 to start in Atlanta, making him a non-starter for Team Canada. "Obviously we did not make Canadian baseball happy," said O'Dowd at the time. "But honestly, we don't answer to them as it relates to our future. This is a special kid." O'Dowd didn't mention that the Chinese Taipei bullpen for the Olympics boasted Chin-Hui Tsao, like Francis one of the Rockies' top pitching prospects. The Rockies allowed Tsao to attend the Olympics if Chinese Taipei would waive his military commitment, begging the question, would Francis have been available in Athens if Canada had a better armed forces?

At the pre-Olympic tournament in Italy, where Canada was a perfect 4-0, Hill pitched the clinching game, a 2-1 win over Chinese Taipei. He needed only 52 pitches to sail through five innings, striking out five and allowing one run. In Athens, he helped the Canadians get to 3-0, pitching five scoreless innings—allowing three hits—in a 7-0 win over The Netherlands. Four days later, Hill was given the ball against Cuba to decide which team would go to the gold-medal game. He allowed two runs in the first inning and gave up only one hit in the next five innings. He did his job, but the bullpen couldn't hold back the Cuban tide.

From Harrisburg to Montreal to Athens, Hill's season had been a journey with as many or more downs as ups. His parents felt the bumps as much as Hill himself. "Early in 2004 things weren't going well," Heather recalled. "Shawn phoned and he said 'I'm ready to pack it in.' I asked 'What are you going to do if you aren't playing baseball and chasing your dream?' He said 'I haven't figured that out yet.' Within a week everything was back to normal." Two weeks after returning from Athens, Hill finally had his showdown with his oft-injured elbow. "I told them (the Expos) at the exit physical I want the doctor to tell me what is wrong," Hill said. "My elbow was bad in Greece, it was bad with the Expos, it was bad with Harrisburg. Every single year from June on it is bad." As it turned out, the truth hurt even more. At season's end, Hill underwent

Tommy John surgery by orthopedic surgeon Dr. James Andrews. Dr. Andrews removed a bone spur off the back off Hill's right elbow as well as some scar tissue and placed a new ligament in the elbow.

The Expos placed Hill on waivers and he cleared, meaning he'll earn $50,000 for sitting out the 2005 season, rather than the $70,000 he earned for playing in 2004. Still, two decades earlier Hill would have been out of the game. Now his arm will have a new life. Eric Gagne came back from Tommy John surgery to win the Cy Young Award. When Hill returns, his goal won't be to get to Montreal, but rather Washington, D.C., the new home of the Expos ... er ... Nationals.

The young man's future trials seemed a lifetime away one night at a patio table outside the Hellenic Sports Complex in Athens. Mom Heather was a couple of tables away, keeping a reporter-cum-author company. "I thought it might be nice to come over here, sit and have a beer with my son, but he doesn't drink," Heather said. Her mind drifted back a few days to the night of the Olympic opening ceremonies, when she was still at home, before heading to the airport for the long flight. As her son entered the stadium during the parade of nations, he phoned home. "He said, 'Whatever your emotions are, it's 10 times better.' I cried. I cry all the time when he phones. It can be 'okay then, we'll see you in two days,' and I'll still cry."

Tom Hanks had it wrong in the movie *A League of Their Own*. There is too crying in baseball.

●●●

No one would ever say that Chris Begg's baseball career is hanging by a thread. Not when he's on the mound mowing down hitters with work-manlike precision. However, behind the scenes—or shall we say underneath everything—Begg is held together with fabric about the size of blades of grass. More precisely, underwear threads.

Remember seeing the sweat-stained hat of New York Yankees' closer John Wetteland and others in post-seasons gone by? As long as they're going good, the cap stays. Sweat rings and all. Like playoff beards and hair in post-season hockey. Well, Begg has a similar habit, just a little further south of the equator. He wore the same boxers in 2004 as he did in 1995 pitching for the Peterborough Tigers juniors.

Begg's tattered underwear has avoided clubhouse washing machines throughout the Double-A Eastern League and the Triple-A Pacific Coast League, at the 2004 Olympics and with the Grand Canyon Rafters of the Arizona Fall League. "Mostly they're just an elastic band with one side hanging down almost to my ankle," said Begg. "Players talk about my underwear, or rather lack of it." The scene for this revelation is the Olympic Athletes Village in Athens, about as far away from hometown

Uxbridge as these gaunchies have gone in the winding road of Begg's career. Outfielder Jeremy Ware, Begg's teammate on Canada's 2004 Olympic squad, couldn't resist a visual demonstration. Going into the next room, he emerged with a pair of old shorts and ripped them to illustrate how the strand of fabric was still attached to the waistband and dangled more than twice the length of the shorts. "I don't ever want to get near him in the clubhouse. When he pulls out that damn thing, his underwear stinks," Ware said. When Begg is home, his mother Debbie washes the underwear, or what's left of it, in a lingerie bag, or else the few shreds will disappear the way the sock monster steals socks. And when he's on the road? Well, what's left of his undies don't get washed.

"I really don't think this habit will catch on the way the sweat-stained cap has," laughed Begg.

Back in 1994 at his Grade 10 science class at Uxbridge Secondary, the only high school in the town of 17,000 located about 40 kilometres north-east of Toronto, Begg's teacher—Mrs. Orschel, the pitcher remembered— had given out an assignment: Write an essay on what you want to be when you grow up. Begg handed in his assignment. Years later, worries later, doubts later, after the San Francisco Giants had signed the right-hander out of the independent Northern League, Mrs. Orschel entered the office of Dr. Peter Begg, a chiropractor in Uxbridge and Chris' father. Like all teachers, she had a long memory. "I'll never forget how she told me about reading in the paper how Chris had signed and her remembering what Chris had written, how he wanted to be a ball player and in brackets he'd added, 'I really think I can do it,'" the father recounted.

Dr. Begg remembers the first tryout his son attended and the coach saying: "I think we've got ourselves a pitcher here." That was news to the good doctor, who had moved to Canada from Portsmouth, England, when he was eight years old and had no idea what a pitcher was. Dr. Begg's base-ball education, as well as his son's, has come a long way. Father picked up the memorabilia bug and now has induction photos with statistical summaries of over 60 Hall of Famers from his trips to Cooperstown. His prized collectibles are a Yogi Berra rookie card and a signed Barry Bonds game bat. Before coming home from Athens with his Olympic jersey, signed by each player, Chris' most prized possessions, along with his base-ball cards, were an autographed Barry Bonds bat and a baseball signed by Hall of Famer Nolan Ryan. Is that one Bonds-signed bat or two? "It's one," Dr. Begg said. "We'll see whose bat it is when Chris moves out of the house."

Along the way, Dr. Begg came to rely on an old patient, a long-time amateur coach and former associate scout for the Toronto Blue Jays, Greg "Chopper" Minor. Minor ran summer camps for the Jays and liked what he saw when 15-year-old Chris attended in 1994. "They wanted what was best for their son ... I told them he should pitch for Steve Terry, a national team coach," recalled Minor, who also arranged for Begg to take pitching lessons from Remo Cardinale, former national team pitching coach. "I remember Remo saying that Chris had something most kids didn't. Chris had control and he had great location. All he was lacking was strength. I believed that some day he would pop."

Begg's path to the pros was far from conventional, which would be either through the June major-league draft or by attending a four-year U.S. school, then entering the draft after his junior year. After pitching for Terry and the Peterborough Tigers in 1997, Begg, again relying on Minor for input, headed to South Carolina and Winthrop University in the spring of 1998. But Begg pitched barely at all and with a month left in the season, asked coach Joe Hudak what his role would be for the next season. He was told that he needed to change his arm slot, since Begg was throwing directly over the top. He had two choices: Shut things down now and make the changes, or pitch the rest of the season and make the change before next season. "The day after our meeting I went back and told coach I thought it was best to make the change right away," Begg said. "Immediately I was throwing harder and my fastball had more life." In the off-season, Begg called Minor again and, based on some calls the coach made, signed a letter of intent to pitch for Niagara University and coach Jim Mauro. Mike McRae, of Niagara Falls, Ontario had been an assistant at Winthrop and was now Mauro's assistant at Niagara.

The summer of 1999 was pivotal for Begg in another way. He visited Jim Dixon of Achievement Strategies at his Markham office north of Toronto. Dixon conducts Neuro Linguist Programming to help elite athletes visualize successful results in their daily challenges, whether it be bending over a seven-foot putt or concentrating at the free-throw line. Dixon has worked with area pro golfers, dressage coaches, amateur and professional basketball players, as well as baseball players. Hill was his first baseball player. "I figured it would take a long time, but I only needed a few visits," Begg said. "I had had a horrible year at Winthrop. I was starting to question myself: What I was doing playing baseball?"

The neuro in NLP refers to the mind and how it organizes thoughts, the linguist refers to how we talk to ourselves—'why did I do that?' or 'that was stupid'—and the program is how we put things together. "We focused on mental toughness and visualization," Dixon said. "Chris has some exercises he does to this day. It's like driving a car. You don't have to think driving your car downtown, you just drive."

Begg's biggest problem was that he had been repeatedly told by coaches that his fastball would never be more than 83 miles per hour and that his upper body wasn't developed enough to stand up to the daily grind of baseball. "The real key was that he had been programmed (that) he needed to be a certain weight, throw a certain speed," Dixon said. "We established that every time he threw a pitch he tightened up his muscles worrying about velocity. How do you best throw a baseball? Same as you hit it … with loose muscles. Worrying about his velocity affected his other pitches." Begg and Dixon unraveled the problems and the thought process in four sessions. "Who knows what confidence is? You can't put confidence in a wheel barrow and bring it to me," Dixon said. "People talk about confidence, but we started with goal setting. If you say to a golfer 'don't pay attention to that pink dress over there in the gallery,' where does the mind go? It thinks about the pink dress, it has to in order to not think about it. If he wants to throw with more velocity, he has to relax. You give any athlete a trigger that helps their skills and they will improve quickly. I'm fascinated with Chris because he just does it."

Dixon left Begg with a number of visualization techniques. "Mostly, it was on how to get in the zone, stay in the zone, both over the course of a game and a season," Begg said. "That really helped. I'd say that jump-started my pitching. I still use the techniques and plan on going in for a tune-up before spring training." With his arm angle changed and his new visualization techniques in tow, Begg headed to Niagara, where he picked up a slider. Soon, everything clicked; the newcomer jumped right into the rotation. "In college, my focus was far and above anyone else's," said Begg, a statement that comes out of left field considering his usual shy, self-effacing style. "I've been asked what I do and have been asked to talk about it with people. I explain it to teammates. It's a ton of visualization."

Before a game, Begg used to go to a quiet place to think. Now, as a starter in the Giants' system, if he sits in front of his locker, head in his hands, no one bothers him. The starting pitcher is off limits in a clubhouse where barbs and one-line insults flow constantly, notwithstanding where you hit in the order or how much money you make. Reporters aren't allowed to ask a starting pitcher questions until after the game. Usually, the starter carries so much influence on the day he's pitching that he has control of the clubhouse radio or CD player before the game. "It takes about 10 minutes for me to state to myself what my goals are and get myself focused. Then, I go through my pitches, slowly and methodically," Begg says. "Between innings it only takes 15 seconds; I go through all my pitches. I can see myself throwing each pitch on each side of the plate for strikes."

For three springs, Begg was Niagara's ace and in the summer continued to pitch for Peterborough. "I'd see him at tournaments, when I was scouting," Minor said. "It was quite comical. Dr. Begg would show up and all the pitchers would run over to get him to loosen up their arms. Then, the family would sit and watch." In 2001, the rangy right-hander was 8-3, the highest win total in school history, with a 2.63 ERA, and as the June draft approached both the Pittsburgh Pirates and Toronto Blue Jays expressed interest. "Bill Byckowski, who was in charge of scouting Canadians for the Jays, liked his arm action," said Minor, wearing his Jays cap. "But the Toronto scouts who saw him at Niagara didn't like his velocity." The draft came and went. The only phone calls came from friends asking whether he was drafted. There weren't any visits to discuss a signing bonus. Fact was, Begg probably would have signed for a copy of the contract and a team jacket. What to do now? Call Chopper, of course. "Greg got a look at me when I was 15; he saw something in me and we became close over the years. He kept trying to get the Jays to sign me," Begg said. "In the baseball realm he was our go-to guy." Minor told Dr. Begg that Chris would have to "take the long way around; he'd have to get into pro ball through the back door."

Minor got Begg the addresses and fax numbers for all 50 independent teams. Begg went to work with the fax machine, whirring out resumes with his stats. He heard back from five clubs and chose to sign with the Albany-Colonie Diamond Dogs in the Northern League. He was 3-2 with a 2.53 earned run average and one save in 21 games. In September 2002, after Albany folded, the San Diego Padres brought Begg to Chicago for an invite-only workout. The cattle call included 60 independent players and the Padres left an impression that they'd sign him. But once again, Begg was disappointed. Next, his contract was purchased by the St. Paul Saints, also of the Northern League. Independent league teams are a notch below minor league affiliates, but St. Paul is more high profile than some minor-league stops, a favorite destination for former major-leaguers on the comeback trail or first-rounders holding out for more cash. In St. Paul, Begg went 7-0 in eight starts with a 1.50 ERA, stats that would earn him the Northern League rookie of the year award at season's end, even though by that point Begg was long gone. The Giants, on the advice of scout Dick Tidrow, had purchased his contract in July. With the Single-A San Jose Giants, Begg started five games, going 4-1 with a 1.15 ERA, then finished the season by making his final four starts at Double-A Norwich in Connecticut. In all, he won 14 games before taking his visualization techniques and his good-luck underwear, or rather what was left of it, to join Team Canada for its Olympic qualifying tournament in Panama.

The success of his first season with the Giants and in Panama allowed Begg to start the 2004 season at Triple-A Fresno. "He had a career year, a career year and a half, actually," Minor said. "Here was a guy who was never drafted and in his second full season in the minors, he was in

Triple-A. That says a lot to me." Begg struggled with his mechanics at Fresno, finding himself with a 2-5 record and a 6.97 ERA before being returned to Double-A Norwich.

Despite his stumble as a starter in the minors, there were never any doubts about his value to Team Canada, which had been using him out of the bullpen. Canada played 14 games in August 2004 from the first exhibition game in Baltimore to losing the bronze medal game to Japan, winning 10, with Begg appearing in eight games. He pitched 14 innings in total, allowing 14 hits and four earned runs while walking two and striking out seven. He earned plenty of admirers, and not all because of his baseball prowess. "Oh my goodness," said one attractive woman behind home plate, watching as the 6-foot-3 Begg, long and lean and with long locks, strode purposefully to the mound against Greece. "Who is this pitcher? He's so dreamy I could eat him with a spoon." Heading into the semi-final against Cuba, the dreamy hurler had pitched 11 2/3, allowing seven hits and one run (0.71). Taking over in the seventh, he allowed three singles but escaped with a scoreless inning.

Begg allowed a leadoff single to Cuban shortstop Eduardo Paret on the first pitch of the eighth. Then, he got Michel Enriquez to bounce to third baseman Peter Orr on a 1-2 pitch. But Orr's throw sailed into right field. Yulieski Gourriel, Cuba's No. 3 hitter, hit a 1-2 pitch to left to score Paret and tie the game. Begg was gone. Eight hitters and two more Canadian relievers later, Cuba had put up a six spot and held off a late Canadian rally to earn a trip to the gold medal game. Afterwards, Begg shouldered the blame for the loss, though, in stand-up fashion, so did Orr and others on the team. "The thing about the team in Panama and Greece was how quickly we all came together. Paul Spoljaric is the nicest guy on the team," Begg said. "It's like we'd played together for four years. The only guy I ever played with before was Peter Orr."

After the Olympics, Begg returned to Norwich to pick up two more wins, finishing the season with a 9-1 record and a 2.30 ERA. Since his first paycheck, he had forged a 27-10 win-loss record with a 2.83 ERA, plus 175 strikeouts and only 61 walks in 264 innings. Said his dad, describing what anyone from the most respected scouting director to the newest area scout would say is the perfect makeup for a pitcher, "I don't think I have ever seen Chris angry. He might get quiet after a loss, but never angry."

"You meet so many people in this game, good, bad, whatever, but this could not have happened to a nicer guy and a nicer family," Minor said. "You don't reach this level without a strong family background. His goal was to play pro ball and he wasn't getting a chance. People always said he was short (on talent), or not good enough. Well, he's met every challenge they threw at him."

Begg can visualize himself making Triple-A, the next step on the organizational ladder to the majors, and then the show itself. Based on his rapid two-year rise, it's a good bet he'll reach his goal. The only doubt may be whether his underwear will vaporize completely before he gets there.

LIKE FATHER, LIKE SON 14

The 1989 movie *Field of Dreams* was a smash hit, both in baseball-crazed boroughs like Boston and Houston and in Little League towns across North America. Not to mention Sweden and Croatia. The film adaptation of W.P. Kinsella's book, *Shoeless Joe*, will probably be talked about 100 years from now.

"It's not really a story about baseball," actor James Earl Jones told reporters when he visited Cooperstown, New York, and the National Baseball Hall of Fame for a viewing upon the movie's 15th anniversary tribute in 2004. "It's about fathers and sons and the bond they forge through baseball. For many boys the first time they really bond with their father is when pop says 'Let's go out in the backyard and have a catch.'"

Like Ray Kinsella and John Kinsella at the end of *Field of Dreams*, Canada's greatest father/son baseball combination spent plenty of summer evenings playing catch on the front lawn of their house on Old Salmon Arm Road in Enderby, British Columbia, a town of 3,015 souls halfway between Calgary and Vancouver. The game was as natural to Gerry and Kevin Reimer as their magnificent surroundings at the top of the Okanagan Valley. Through the 1970s and 1980s, Enderby was their world, and the two made quite a team: Father Gerry, who had spent 11 seasons playing pro ball, never quite making it to the majors; and son Kevin, who would play 13 years in the pros himself, including four seasons in the big leagues. The passion for the game was effortlessly passed from father to son. Today, Kevin still "gets chills" whenever he watches *Field of Dreams*. Gerry Reimer goes his son one better. In 2002, he had his picture taken walking out of the *Dreams*' cornfield in Dyersville, Iowa. "We were playing old-timers slo-pitch at a tournament in Marion, Iowa, and drove over to see it," Gerry said.

As in *Field of Dreams*, where the son tries to ease the memories of rebelling against his father, the Reimers' is a story not without its hurts, its failures and its what ifs. That's especially so with respect to Kevin, who admits his temper, his pride and his occasional over-indulgence in alcohol got in the way at crucial junctures. Gerry has remained non-judgmental and supportive. "He's a grown man," he said after Kevin walked away from the game two months into the 1998 season, annoyed that the Seattle Mariners had not seen fit to call him up from their Triple-A farm team.

Ten years before turning his back on the game, Kevin's future had seemed limitless. In early September 1988, he was basking in the afterglow of the Tulsa Drillers winning the Double-A Texas League title and drinking champagne, whooping it up the way winners do in the club-house. His manager, Jim Skaalen, had an announcement to make and he wanted the whole team to hear: Lefty Kenny Rogers, lefty Steve Wilson, catcher Chad Kreuter and designated hitter Reimer were being elevated to the Texas Rangers for the remainder of the season. After the congrats were out of the way, Reimer headed for the phone to call his father. "I called home and said 'Dad we made it, we made it to the majors,' I didn't say *I* made it," Kevin Reimer said. "I said *we* on purpose, because I wouldn't have made it without my father. My father helped me all along the way, drove me the half hour to Vernon, from Enderby, took balls between the legs trying to catch me on our front lawn and coached me all those years."

Of the Tulsa four, Rogers pitched in 2004 for the Rangers, his 16th season in the majors; Kreuter was back with the Rangers in 2003, his 16th year in the bigs; Wilson, of Victoria, British Columbia, threw his last pitch in the majors for the Los Angeles Dodgers in 1993, his sixth season, and Reimer had his final major-league at bat in 1993, having played parts of six seasons.

Growing up on the Canadian prairies, in Melville, Saskatchewan, Gerry Reimer had been a track star before turning to baseball, at one time ranking third in the country in the high jump. Using the old scissors kick, he jumped 6-foot-4 7/8 in 1955. For a time, he held the Canadian schoolboy record. Some years Canada would take its top three finishers to the Summer Olympics. For the 1956 Olympics in Melbourne, only one high jumper was chosen and Reimer stayed home. "My father has never had a chip on his shoulder and never felt hard done by or bitter," Kevin said of his father. "I was never as good as he was in track, or in baseball and in a whole lot of sports, he was way better than me. I don't think I was better than him in anything and he played hockey and basketball, too."

The elder Reimer played outfield and first base at Western Washington University in Yakima, Washington in 1958, although he was there on a track scholarship. Once, after a good outing on the road, a scout from the Pittsburgh Pirates approached him. "We talked and he said 'I'm at this hotel, give me a call,'" Gerry recalled. "The thought of me being able to play pro ball? I thought someone was playing a practical joke." Reimer never called, but fortunately for him that wasn't his only chance. Eddie Taylor, a scout from the Philadelphia Phillies, also approached Reimer and this time the youngster thought, "Gee, maybe someone knows something I don't." He signed and was off to rookie ball. Over the next few years, he progressed steadily, from Class-D to Class-B to Double-A. Along the way, he kept running into an opposing pitcher named Pat Gillick. "He used to walk everyone," Gerry said. "And then pick guys off first base. Man, was he sneaky." One night, though, Reimer's team rocked the young left-hander. "The next night we run into him in a bar and Lee Elia (the future major-league manager) tells him why we were able to beat him so badly. Lee told him how his mouth was relaxed, almost smiling, when he threw a curve ball, but it was a straight line as he strained to throw his fastball. How stupid were we? We told him how we were able to pick up his pitches." The next time Reimer saw Gillick, the lefty, "had made the adjustments and beat us."

Next for Reimer was a trip to Triple-A Buffalo in 1962, where he was a teammate of right-hander Ferguson Jenkins for a few games. "I had a great spring at the big-league camp with the Phillies in Clearwater," Gerry said. "They told me 'You should be here right now, but go down, have a good year at Triple-A and we'll see what happens.'" He started well at Buffalo, but, bothered by an off-season hockey injury to his leg, needed time off. "If I'd had a complete year, who knows what would have happened," Reimer recalled, "but I kept re-tearing the muscle in my leg." The Buffalo Bison website sums up the 1962 season like this: "Home runs were dime-a-dozen. Frank Herrera, back from the Phillies, hit 32 and had 108 RBIs, leading the league in the first category and tying for first in the second. Ex-Michigan football player John Herrnstein hit 23 homers; catcher Bob Lipski added 19 and Lee Elia and Jim Frey each had 16. Gerry Reimer hit 11 and led the league in throwing bats."

After his contract was sold to the Cincinnati Reds, Reimer spent three seasons in Double-A, another back in Buffalo and finished up with two seasons back home, or close to it, patrolling left field for the Triple-A Vancouver Mounties, where his teammates included future major leaguers Sal Bando, Joe Rudi, Tony LaRussa, Steve Boros, Joe Nossek and Marcel and Rene Lachemann. In 1967, he batted .260 with four homers and 74 RBIs. The next season he hit .249 with 16 homers and 63 RBIs. And then, 11 years after it had begun, it was over. Reimer had finished up with a career .300 batting average, plus the best catch of all, Gloria, who he'd met while playing in Macon, Georgia in 1963.

It was also in Macon that the father-and son story began. On June 28, 1964, the public address announcer boomed, "Now batting ... Gerry Reimer ... Gerry's wife, Gloria, just had a little baby boy today." As the applause drifted down from the grandstand, Lynchburg catcher Duane Josephson whispered to Reimer: "Nothing but fastballs ... that's what you get." Not that it helped. "I still struck out," Reimer laughed. "My head was so much in the clouds over being a father for the first time."

After retiring from baseball, Gerry returned to Enderby, where his mom and dad had moved, to help run Reimer's Department Store, which sold men's and women's clothing and school supplies. And tutor his son in the finer points of the game. "I wanted to follow in my father's footsteps for as long as I can remember" Kevin said. "My father was a lifetime .300 hitter and that includes those four years at Triple-A when there were only 20 teams. Look at what he accomplished. He was a much better hitter than I was and I'm not being biased." Told of the son's assessment, the father scoffs: "Oh, baloney. The only thing I could do better than Kevin was run faster. Neither one of us were that good defensively, but I saw Kevin play first base one spring—I played first base better than him." Asked about that .300 average, the former rabbit is quick with an answer: "I hit .100, but I ran .200 to get to .300."

Kevin's earliest baseball memory is when he was four years old and his father was an outfielder-first baseman for the Mounties at Capilano Stadium in Vancouver. Most nights, scenic Capilano was his playpen. It was his world and the Mounties and their fans were living in it as he bounced from section to section during the game. Before the game he'd be on the field or in the umpire's room sitting on the lap of Mountie short-stop Ozzie Chavarria and bugging him for candy. And during batting practice Kevin never failed to tell Mounties' manager Mickey Vernon how good he was. One night the young sprite put on a show. "It was after infield and the umps weren't out on the field yet," Kevin remembered. His father gave him a fungo bat and grabbed a bag full of balls. "I was a cocky little kid, all the time saying 'you should see me hit!' They thought I wasn't any good," Kevin said. "The first couple of pitches, I pulled right into the Vancouver dugout. I had all these big adults scrambling to get out of the way and yelling 'turn the other way.'" Kevin hit all the balls, but when pop said "pick 'em up," he was too embarrassed to venture onto the green grass of the infield.

He grew up in the Okanagan Valley, full of orchards and sunshine, playing hockey and baseball. Kevin loves recalling a particular evening when he was eight or nine years old and he and his dad were playing catch on the front lawn. "I was catching Kevin, using (Mountie catcher and later Seattle Mariners' manager) Rene Lachemann's glove," Gerry remembered. "When he got tired, he dropped to his knees and a couple of pitches later ... Kevin's pitch short-hopped me and hit me square between the legs." Baseball pointers and pain, from father to son. "Fathers and sons are supposed to play catch with one other," Kevin laughed. "I don't think it's written anywhere that the father is supposed to get drilled in the 'noids."

Gerry says he didn't push his son, and the example he gives is the time he wanted to make Kevin into a switch hitter. "Every time we'd try it, Kevin would say 'oh no it hurts my wrist'; he was real young. I wanted to call him a wimp, but I just let it go; he hit left-handed," Gerry said. Kevin was recruited by junior hockey teams, who were intrigued by the defenseman with the booming shot, but his parents refused to let him leave home for hockey. So he concentrated on baseball. At age 14, the younger Reimer was the batboy for his father's senior team, the Enderby Legionnaires, but then he "started getting as big as the players," recalled Gerry. "Kevin became tired of being a flunky, 'go get my hat, go get my helmet,' so he asked if he could play." The playing manager Reimer approached the others on the team before the 1980 season and told them: "I'll step down for one year as a player, run the club and Kevin will play." The Legionnaires won the senior provincials and represented British Columbia in the western Canadian championship in Glenboro, Manitoba. Playing at an advanced level at a tender age prepared Reimer for the stiffer competition ahead. "We didn't just show up for games; everybody came to practice," Reimer said. "For a young guy, playing with older guys you had to show you were mature enough to play at that level. You had to bear down."

After playing for the B.C. Selects, Reimer played for the 1981 Team Canada team which traveled to Newark, Ohio, for the first world youth friendship series. Brockville's Brian McRobie managed the team and, according to Reimer, "he was tough." In the end, "I'm not sure they wanted to keep me," recalled Reimer, "but we had an older coach who was really in my corner from day one. They called him The Bear." The Bear was also known as Harry Moore of Sarnia, Ontario.

Gerry Reimer wanted his son to attend a school in either Minnesota or North Dakota to play both hockey and baseball. Kevin thought he would be behind players south of the border and wanted to concentrate on one sport. So, Gerry phoned Wayne Norton, a former Mountie teammate, British Columbia baseball guru and dedicated Team Canada coach, for help. Norton sent along information on colleges and universities offering baseball. The Reimers wrote seven letters to coaches in California, explaining Gerry's background, how the family was making a trip to Anaheim and Disneyland, and asked whether they'd be interested in looking at Kevin. Gerry received four return letters and one phone call from Orange Coast College coach Chuck Mayne in Costa Mesa. "Kevin took batting practice and pulled everything into the right field bleachers. They wanted him," Gerry remembered. "I said yes on one condition? I don't want him sitting on the bench. They assured me Kevin would play." Reimer led Orange Coast in home runs and swung a hot bat for Team Canada from the first pitch when he arrived at the national team's training camp in Windsor in 1983. Manager Eric MacKenzie, who coached or managed Team Canada from 1978 until 1986, calls Reimer "the best pure hitter" he ever coached. Team Canada went to Belgium, beat Cuba in a tournament, and then headed to the 1983 Pan-Am Games in Venezuela. Reimer excelled, and Baseball Canada named him its player of the year.

After his second season at Orange Coast, several major-league teams wanted Reimer to sign. "Teams were talking, wining and dining me, but when the New York Yankees called, everyone backed off," Reimer said. "I wanted $75,000. The Yankees were offering $50,000. I said I knew I could go back to school for my senior year and come out the next year and get $100,000." Then came an invite from MacKenzie to play for Team Canada in the 1984 Olympics. Brian McRobie was back as a coach. Now, 6-foot-2 and 225 pounds, Reimer had bulked up since he'd last seen McRobie, as a bench warmer three years earlier. "I got off the plane, said hello and gestured to McRobie. Things had changed, I was a little cocky. I couldn't wait to say 'check me out now,'" Reimer said. After a 10-day camp at the University of Windsor, Team Canada flew to The Netherlands for a pre-Olympic tournament. In 1981, Reimer had been given a Team Canada jacket, which he passed on to his dad as a gift. For the pre-Olympic trip, he asked Gerry if he could borrow it back. "My father had said 'Okay, but take extra care and don't trade it,'" Reimer said. In Holland, the boys headed off to a dance club, where Reimer told other players to watch his jacket. When he came back to the table, the jacket was gone. Upset over losing a family treasure, Reimer returned to the dorm where the team was staying and "I punched a wall, like a dumb ass; I always called it my hockey mentality. That was the first Team Canada jacket I'd ever had. Plus, it wasn't mine any more. I had lost my father's jacket."

Turned out, the jacket wasn't lost or stolen. Reimer's giggling teammates were too scared to say anything that night, but the next day one of them told him that the jacket had been checked at the coat check. Kevin went back to the club and recovered his jacket. "I felt even worse, they felt even worse," said Reimer. "That just crushed me. I don't hold it against those guys. It was a practical joke, that's what we do on the road. My problem was that I went all snapper head." Reimer's wardrobe was now intact, but the fourth and fifth metacarpal bones in his right hand were not. Canada won the Haarlem tournament and headed to L.A., where Reimer visited with a Canadian Olympic team doctor, who took one look at the X-rays and asked: "Do you have a good job?" Reimer replied: "No, I'm going to school and playing baseball. Are you trying to tell me I'll never play again?" The doctor nodded yes. "How bad was that? Shouldn't you try to be positive until you have to cut the thing off?" Reimer said 20 years later. He then flew to Vancouver to have surgery performed on his hand. Pins had to be installed from the top of his knuckles to his wrist.

After a so-so season with Cal-State Fullerton, Reimer went back into the draft for 1985 and was an 11th round choice of the Texas Rangers. When Texas scout John Young offered him a $15,000 signing bonus—$35,000 less than he'd turned down from the Yankees the year before—he signed. He broke in slowly but then came his breakthrough year of 1988, when he hit .302 with 21 homers and 76 RBIs for Tulsa, won the Double-A Texas League title and was promoted to the Rangers, appearing in 12 September games. On Sept. 27 at Comiskey Park, Reimer clubbed his first major-league home run, a solo shot off Chicago's Shawn Hillegas. On the final day of the season, Kevin arranged for Gerry to fly on the team charter from Seattle to Dallas since Kevin was off to winter ball and wouldn't be able to drive his old Ford Fury, the one he'd bought from his grandmother, home to Enderby. "That was my one taste of big-league baseball," Gerry said. "Guys were doing business on their laptops. Each player got a seat and a half on the plane." Oh yes, and he met the biggest Ranger of them all:

Kevin, to a teammate: "Nolie, I want you to meet my father, Gerry."

Nolan Ryan: "Hey, real glad to meet you Mr. Reimer."

Gerry: "When you talk to me, please call me either Gerry or 'Reims.'"

Ryan: "Nope, you're older, so it's Mr. Reimer."

Reimer gives a lot of credit for his success to his Tulsa manager, Jim Skaalen; the two got along well, which wasn't always the case. "Managers either loved me or hated me. They didn't get my sense of humor and I had a bit of a temper," Reimer said. "It was the same in basketball, or hockey; coaches and I didn't always get along. But Jim, he had managed me from Port Charlotte all the way up to Triple-A. That's why we won in the minors—there was a good respect and a rapport with the players."

Reimer spent 1989 and the first couple of months of 1990 back at Triple-A Oklahoma City, before being promoted to the Rangers June 2. Under manager Bobby Valentine, he played 64 games and hit .260 with two homers and 16 RBIs. Father joined son in Port Charlotte, Florida for spring training in 1991. Then the two headed off to Arlington, Texas, where the Rangers opened the season against the Milwaukee Brewers. President George H. Bush threw out the ceremonial first pitch, since his son George W. Bush., was one of the co-owners of the Rangers. In the bottom of the second inning, "Kevin hit one out," recalled Gerry, remembering the cheers of the 40,560 in attendance as if it were yesterday. "It was a very exciting, heart-warming moment. Then we noticed people in the seats turning and pointing to us saying 'that's his parents.'"

Reimer looked to have arrived in 1991, with 20 homers, 69 RBIs and a .269 average in 136 games. With that, he joined a select group of Canadians with 20-homer seasons, a list that includes Jeff Heath, Pete Ward, George Selkirk Larry Walker, Corey Koskie, and, now, Jason Bay.

"I'm really proud of being a Canadian and I never let anyone forget that," Reimer said in 1992. "A lot of the guys never let me forget it either." Fellow Ranger Jack Daugherty pointed to Reimer in the SkyDome dugout in 1992 and said: "There he is, eh, the hoser." The Canuck's batting practice attire consisted of a 'Canada' T-shirt, complete with cartoon Mounties. That season, Reimer had a .267 average with 16 homers and 58 RBIs in 148 games and was prominent enough to earn the nickname Kevin Reimer (Reason) from ESPN's Chris Berman.

As the Rangers headed into the off-season, major-league teams compiled protected lists to get ready for the expansion draft, which would stock the Florida Marlins and Colorado Rockies rosters. Outfielder Nigel Wilson of Ajax, Ontario, from the Jays, went second over-all to the Marlins. Seven picks later, Reimer went to the Rockies. But as soon as the draft was done, Colorado general manager Bob Gebhard dealt Reimer to the Milwaukee Brewers. In Milwaukee, all general manager Sal Bando, who had been one of Gerry's teammates in Vancouver, wanted Reimer to do was replace local icon Paul Molitor, who had declared free agency and signed with the Jays to supplant Dave Winfield. Bando explained that Reimer was "more of a long-term player than Molitor." Molitor retired after the 1998 season with 3,319 career hits. Reimer would hit .268 with 13 homers and 60 RBIs in 125 games in his only season in Milwaukee; he never saw the majors again.

In the winter of 1993, Reimer signed a two-year deal to play for the Fukuoka Daiei Hawks in Japan to "set his family up for life." Wife Christine and daughter Shelby went east as well.

"The first year was tougher on my family than me; they were left on their own a lot," Reimer said. Playing with former Chicago White Sox reliever Bobby Thigpen, Reimer hit .296 with 26 homers and 97 RBIs under manager Rikuo Nemoto. He was voted a member of the league's Best Nine. In 1995, playing under Japan's all-time home run king, Sadaharu Oh, Reimer ran into his old issue with managers. "He had a high leg kick and I had a high leg kick, so that wasn't a problem," Reimer said. The real problem was that the Canadian had signed to be a designated hitter but in his second season an older Japanese player decided he wanted to DH, and Oh agreed. That put Reimer in the outfield, where he immediately drew criticism for his fielding. "I busted my butt out there, but when I signed, it wasn't as outfielder. I told him (Oh) through the translator 'you can't teach an old dog new tricks,'" Reimer said.

The ill will between player and manager came to a head when Reimer was struggling at the plate. He'd hit two balls on the nose at the left fielder, both for outs. He went out to the field in the top of the ninth only to look up and see a defensive replacement come trotting out. "To be removed in the middle of the inning, that's the biggest insult in the game," Reimer said. "Plus we were only down two runs. The translator said 'Oh wanted to get this right-handed hitter ready for the next game, since a lefty was going to start.' I said 'well, there's a right-hander throwing tonight.'" Reimer stomped off and booted the medical kit, sending tongue depressors flying. The translator told Reimer to shower and go home. He was fined $10,000. "Thigpen and I were always looking at hunting and fishing magazines," Reimer said. "I was thinking how much hunting and fishing gear could I have bought with that." The next day, the Hawks owner came in for a meeting and Reimer stated his case: "You guys are paying me a lot of money, you guys talk about playing with pride, that's all I was doing." The owner asked Reimer if he had $100 in his wallet. Reimer paid up. Fine reduced by $9,900. He finished the season hitting .254 with 10 homers and 52 RBIs in 103 games, but it was time to head home. Reimer didn't think he'd have any trouble finding major-league employment, but it turned out that the only offer was from the Minnesota Twins to play with their Triple-A affiliate in Salt Lake. After splitting the 1996 season between Salt Lake and Tacoma, Seattle's top farm club, Reimer was hitting .345 with three homers and 21 RBIs in June 1997, when he decided he didn't want to be a minor-leaguer anymore.

Today, he describes it as walking away on his terms. "My nose was out of joint, maybe I should have sucked it up and played for a couple of years," Reimer said. "Was (walking out) the right thing to do? Probably not. I knew I could still play, I just don't know if anyone else knew." Besides, he was tired of the 4 a.m. wake-up calls in the minors, though he didn't mind getting up that early to fish or hunt.

In his big-league career, Reimer logged three years and 150 days' service time, playing 488 major-league games with 52 homers and 204 RBIs. Christine and Kevin Reimer's daughter, Shelby, was about to start school and Kevin wanted to spend more time with his family, which also includes a younger daughter, Tea. They returned to Enderby, which is Christine's hometown as well. "Nothing against American girls, but I guarantee if I had married an American girl I probably would be divorced by now," Reimer said.

In 1985, when Reimer signed, there were four Canadians in the majors: Terry Puhl, from Gerry Reimer's hometown of Melville, Saskatchewan, with the Houston Astros; Doug Frobel of Ottawa, who graduated from Art Neilsen's Ottawa-Nepean Canadians and was with the Pittsburgh

Pirates; Kirk McCaskill of Kapuskasing, Ontario, with the Anaheim Angels, and Edmonton's Dave Shipanoff, with the Philadelphia Phillies. At the end of the 2004 season, there were 20 Canadians in the majors. "One reason," says Reimer, "is that both scouts and other kids saw Larry Walker, Steve Wilson and myself playing in the majors. The three of us brought attention to Canadians. The Blue Jays winning back-to-back World Series really brought a lot of attention to baseball. Everyone in Canada is a hockey player until they turn 15 or so, but there's another sport you can make a living at. You can be 22 and still be coming into your own in baseball. Canadian players are making great leaps and bounds with their progress, thanks to the exposure south of the border and the coaching."

Ultimately, neither half of the best father/son duo in Canadian baseball history has any regrets about the two decades each spent chasing his baseball dream. These days, Gerry still plays slo pitch ("the ball comes in a lot slower, but it goes out quicker"), for a team in his winter home in Apache Junction, Arizona that recently won the world over-65 championships. He doesn't look back and think about how close he came to making the majors. "I was happy to do what I did and happy to see what he (Kevin) did," said the proud papa and husband of 41 years. "Our son brought a lot of excitement into our lives, following him around."

As for the son, "Deep down, honestly, if I had it to do all over again, I think that I wouldn't drink. That was my biggest downfall. I think it affected my game. I don't mean going to the bars, but if there were people to visit with in the clubhouse, I'd be there, whether it was talking hitting and pitching with Brian Downing, Goose Gossage or Nolan Ryan." As of December 2004, Reimer hadn't had a drink in three years. "Maybe if I hadn't drank I wouldn't have pissed so many people off, but I don't have any regrets about anything," Reimer said. "What irks me is that it's a chemical dependency."

These days, Reimer sells archery equipment and runs a taxidermy shop out of his Enderby house. He has stuffed deer heads, life-sized bears and bear rugs. He says taxidermy is really an art form. Reimer says if either of his daughters has a school recital, he'll shut things down early. He goes skiing when he wants to, and helps coach volleyball at school. He and the whole family are into competitive archery and, once in a while, he'll still strap on the blades for a game of old-timers' hockey.

"Some people I meet aren't happy in life, they never find their niche in life," he said.

"My dream came true to be a ball player. This is a second dream come true. I almost feel guilty."

GO WEST, YOUNG MAN

15

If a pickpocket attended any of the Canadian national baseball championships, the perfect place for him to work would be behind the row of spectators gazing at the board listing the tournament draw. There, coaches and players stand transfixed, almost in a trance. Hmmmm, they think in provincial fashion, wheels grinding in the hot sun ... now, if we win this game and they lose this one ... then we could. ... The games are listed by provincial abbreviations and they are the same whether it is the midget championship in Melville, Saskatchewan, the peewee final at Summerside, Prince Edward Island, or the senior championships in Edmonston, New Brunswick.

B.C. vs. N.B. - 2 p.m.; Que. vs. N.S. - 4 p.m.; Man. vs. B.C. - 8 p.m.

Finally, someone with the innocence of Macaulay Culkin in *Home Alone* will ask: "What does B.C. stand for?" And with Chris Rock's timing, another player/executive/parent will reply: "B.C.? I think it stands for Best in Canada."

You could call it boasting. Or you could say that the west coast of Canada is merely a northern extension of California. Yet, if the tag fits, wear it. Best in Canada? It's British Columbia. It ain't bragging if you can back it up, the saying goes. And B.C. can back it up. From 1995 through 2004, of the 62 available national baseball championships at the peewee, bantam, midget, Canada Cup, junior and senior level competitions, British Columbia won 18. Quebec, with almost twice the population of B.C., ranked second with 16 golds, while Ontario, with almost three times as many people, was third with 15. Alberta (five), New Brunswick (four), Nova Scotia (three) and Saskatchewan (one) rounded out the leader board.

Since Canadians first became eligible for the major-league June draft in 1985, Ontario leads with 215 players selected, followed by B.C. with 144 and Quebec with 90. But in the past decade, the momentum has clearly swung west. In 2004, 17 of the 38 Canadians chosen hailed from B.C. Ontario was next with 12. Moreover, in the history of the major-league draft, only five Canadians have been drafted in the first round: Of those, three—Adam Loewen of Surrey, who went fourth over-all (out of 1,050 high schoolers and collegians selected) to the Baltimore Orioles in 2002; Jeff Francis of North Delta, who went ninth over-all the same year to the Colorado Rockies, and Kevin Nicholson of Surrey, who went 27th over-all to the San Diego Padres in 1997—hail from the left coast; (the other two, by the way, are Dave Wainhouse of Scarborough, Ontario, who went 19th over-all to Montreal in 1988 and Scott Thorman of Cambridge, Ontario, who went No. 30 to Atlanta in 2000). You want more? Of the 17 Canadians selected in the first 100 picks of the draft since 1985, seven are from British Columbia, five from Ontario, three call Quebec home and two hail from Alberta. Not that the B.C. stories end in the early rounds of the draft. Jason Bay of Trail was the 645th player selected in the 2000 draft, picked by the Montreal Expos. In 2004, he became the first Canadian to earn rookie of the year honors, with the National League's Pittsburgh Pirates.

The reasons you hear for B.C.'s dominance are several and varied. Some say it's because the province's weather is most conducive to the game. Some trumpet the impact of the Premier League for 16-, 17- and 18-year-olds, acclaimed by others from coast to coast as the best development model in the land. Others cite the presence of coach Terry McKaig's highly regarded baseball program at the University of British Columbia, the only four-year Canadian university that participates in the U.S. college ranks. And many say that the uniformly high level of coaching has been the most important ingredient in home-growing prime time players.

The Premier League, started in 1995 and composed of 13 teams, is unique in that while other provinces field three different sets of teams in the 16-18 age group, B.C. places all its best players on the same diamonds together. "The Premier League has good coaching and kids don't play other sports," said McKaig. "Counting practices, the league runs from February to October. This is the first generation of players to make baseball a year-round sport."

The league is blessed with talented coaches like Bill Green, who now coaches the Coquitlam Reds and tutored Larry Walker a lifetime ago, as well as minor leaguers Matt Rogelstad and Shawn Bowman; Doug Mathieson, of the Langley Blaze, who has produced minor leaguers in his son Scott Mathieson and Adam Parliament; Dave Empey of North Shore, who mentored Chris Mears and Simon Pond, and John Harr, who now runs the North Shore Twins after coaching big-leaguers Matt Stairs, Rob Butler, Paul Spoljaric, Denis Boucher and Corey Koskie at the now-defunct National Baseball Institute, which drew players from across the country. And then there are Ari Mellios and Dennis Springenatic.

Mellios, coach of the North Delta Blue Jays since 1995, differs from most coaches in Canada and 98 percent of those in the U.S. in that he can flip on the television almost any summer night and catch one of his former players in action. Justin Morneau and Jeff Francis were North Delta teammates who took different routes to the majors, although both played in the Premier League and for Team Canada. The Twins chose Morneau as the top Canuck in the 1999 draft out of high school; Francis headed to McKaig's program at UBC and came out a more polished pitcher. "To think that five years ago these guys were playing for me in high school ..." said Mellios, his voice trailing off in amazement.

Eight kilometres removed from Mellios' home base, Springenatic of the Fraser Valley Chiefs keeps producing talent as if he has a cookie-cutter machine behind a batting cage, next to the one with the portable pitching mound. The team changed its name from the Whalley Chiefs to Fraser Valley heading into the 2003 season as Springenatic began recruiting players from all over the Lower Mainland, not just Surrey. And if he needs an extra chip in the recruiting sweepstakes, you can imagine the impact of his being able to tote up the signing bonuses of his kids and arrive at a number nudging $6 million.

"In 2002, when Loewen and Francis came out, and Morneau was on his way, people asked why?" Springenatic said. "A lot of these players' parents were good athletes. Now, you have people coaching who were good players, but not quite good enough to make it. They're coaching and teaching. Plus, there are more indoor facilities (four). When I played in the mid 1980s there weren't any."

In those years, respect wasn't available in abundance when Canadians traveled south of the border. Springenatic was an outfielder with Team Canada when the team journeyed to Dayton, Ohio, to play Team USA in a four-game series. "From the moment you walked into the park, you felt from the crowd and people around we weren't given much respect, even (by) their coach, Ron Fraser," Springenatic said. "They didn't give our coaches much respect. (Then) we beat them three out of four. We had Rheal Cormier, Denis Boucher and Matt Stairs as our 160-pound shortstop. They were surprised that we had guys better than their guys. You could hear them saying 'this guy's from Canada?'" Going on two decades later, it's a very different story. "Now, you go down there you are respected as soon as you walk in the park," said Springenatic. "We go to Seattle or Oregon, you see their best pitcher. Now, they know about Jeff Francis and Adam Loewen."

Springenatic first saw Loewen play for Kennedy-Surrey, which went to the Little League World Series in 1996, then again when he pitched junior Little League and again when he was 15. He tried to recruit him, as did most teams in the Premier League. But Springenatic had an edge. Al Loewen, Adam's father, was friends with Ken Myette, whose son Aaron had pitched for Springenatic's father, Orest. Loewen came to The Dugout indoor facility, run by Marty Lehn and Brent Crowther, to train at an early age and Myette, a former minor-leaguer, was instructing. "He threw about 85 to 87 miles per hour in Grade 10, but he was wild," Springenatic said. "One time we went south to play (a team) coached by Bill Caudill, the former Jay. Julio Cruz and Adam hooked up in a good one. That was the first time Adam hit 90 miles per hour. Adam was like 'Hey, I hit 90 miles per hour.'" Springenatic remembers driving to Seattle for another game in which Loewen, in Grade 11 at the time, threw a no-hitter. "They didn't know what hit them, it was over in an hour and an half," he said. "I'll tell you how impressive it was ... the plate umpire asked if he'd sign his lineup card after the game."

Loewen came out of the Premier League a power pitcher—one scout has compared him with Hall of Famer Steve Carlton. "Adam plays with ease and possesses the unique ability to elevate his game as the level of competition increases," said Greg Hamilton, coach of Team Canada's national junior team. "He is the most talented player I've ever seen. With us, he was like a man among boys." Leading up to the 2002 major-league draft, the Loewen family was receiving 10 calls nightly from scouts and agents. Loewen answered questions such as: "Will you sign or are you going to school?" hundreds of times. Some requests were a little more unusual than others. "One scout asked how big my hand was and then traced my hand on a piece of paper," he said.

In Loewen's final game before the draft, he left the mound after reading his pitch count (95-to-100), sat down on the bench and cried. "Adam had been under the microscope for two years," Springenatic said. "Scouts would watch how he walked. He'd been taking phone calls and inter-viewing representatives. He was upset that was the last game he was going to play for the Chiefs." The scene was caught on TV. What wasn't caught was Springenatic walking up to Loewen and tapping him on the shoulder. "You okay, Big?" the coach asked, invoking the nickname for his 6-foot-6 star. "If you're able, you're third up." Loewen walked but did not score, leaving the game tied 2-2.

The Baltimore Orioles made Loewen the fourth over-all pick, by far the highest any Canadian had been drafted. Five picks later, the Rockies took Francis, meaning that Canada had two players taken before the great state of Texas had two players taken. Florida and California, all traditional powerhouses for No. 1 picks, also had two picks each in the top nine. Unable to reach an agreement—Baltimore offered a $2.5 million signing bonus in the summer, while Loewen's representatives were reported to have asked for a $3.9 million—Loewen opted instead to attend a junior college, Chipola College, in Marianna, Florida, thus keeping open his option of signing with the Orioles until a week before the 2003 draft. Five minutes before the deadline, Loewen's representative, Michael Moye, agreed to a deal while the lefty toiled away on a Tiger Woods golf video game. Loewen signed a multi-year, major-league deal worth $4.02 million, which included a $3.2-million signing bonus. In 2003, he saw some duty in Class-A Aberdeen, and, in 2004, Loewen was shut down in August with a partially torn labrum in his left shoulder.

For three other British Columbians, 2004 was also a season to remember.

Justin Morneau's breakthrough season was as hectic as they come, and July the busiest month of all. In the week of July 11, 2004, he played in the Futures Game for top minor league prospects on Sunday in Houston as part of the major-league all-star festivities, was in Pawtucket, Rhode Island, Monday as a Triple-A all-star for the home run derby, played in the Triple-A all-star game Wednesday, returned to his team in Rochester on Thursday, then was on a plane to Kansas City Friday morning to hit clean-up for the American League Central Division champion Minnesota Twins.

Morneau, selected 87th over-all in the 1999 draft and signed by Twins scout Howie Norsetter, led all Canadians in the minors with 22 homers at Rochester in 2004, then hit 19 more with the Twins in 280 at-bats, not even half a season. "Morneau is as still as John Olerud when he swings," said one National League scout, "but with much more power."

Ari Mellios recruited the New Westminster native for the B.C. Selects at the national championship in Red Deer, Alberta in 1997 and in his first season, as a Grade 11 student, Morneau hit 40 homers, batting .512 with 120 RBIs. Mellios says Morneau hit one homer in a small park, tiny Penticton. All the rest were legitimate home runs. Most power hitters have problems going the other way. Not Morneau, who absolutely punished the ball when it was thrown down and away or on the outside corner. Of his 40 homers that year, 26 were on pitches away. "What he had to learn was to hit legitimate fastballs in on his hands," Mellios said. "He had to keep his hands in and turn on balls. He always had legitimate power away. Justin could flat out hit; he showed power like no other player I've ever seen before or since. I've never come across a player like him. You see hitters who once in a while can do what Justin does, no one is even close on a consistent basis." The most memorable homer Mellios ever saw Morneau hit wasn't one of his 2004 blasts with the Twins, but rather six years earlier at the midget nationals at Red Deer. "It was the longest I've ever seen in my life and that includes big league games," the coach said. "One of our parents paced it off. The ball traveled 475 feet. He was using a minus-5 aluminum bat. People underestimate how good a hitter he is. He will hit for average; he won't be a .260 hitter, he doesn't swing at bad pitches."

Morneau made his major-league debut as the Twins' designated hitter on June 10, 2003. Had it been June 12, he would have retained his eligibility for the 2004 Rookie of the Year Award and would have had an excellent shot at beating out Bobby Crosby of the Oakland A's, thereby joining Jason Bay and making Canada two-for-two in the major-league rookie awards. In his first at-bat, Morneau received a standing ovation when he hit a foul ball off a Metrodome speaker with his first full swing. On the night, he had two of the Twins' three hits in a 5-0 loss to the Colorado Rockies. After the game, coach Al Newman made the 6-foot-4, 230-pound Morneau move his news conference to the middle of the clubhouse and reliever LaTroy Hawkins planted a towel full of shaving cream into Morneau's face. Welcome to the big leagues, kiddo.

In 2004, Morneau batted ahead of fellow Canuck Corey Koskie, who in the off-season would move on to the Toronto Blue Jays, and played against the one player he idolized growing up, Colorado's Larry Walker. "That's pretty cool, three former goalies," said Morneau, whose idol growing up was National Hockey League goalie Andy Moog but who gave up puck-stopping after Grade 11. Ever proud of his roots, Morneau displays a red maple leaf tattoo on his left shoulder. Twins' manager Ron Gardenhire said he had two reasons for having the Canucks hit back to back in the lineup. One was because of their power. The other, he explained, was so "they can talk Canadian in the on-deck circle."

When the Twins visited Safeco Field in Seattle in August 2004, Mellios was on hand. "It really hit me (then) … to see his name on the scoreboard in giant letters and then the announcer said 'now batting … Justin Morneau'," sighed Morneau's old coach. So, for the rest of the year, was there a special name for a 5-3 groundout on the scorecard, Koskie at the hot corner throwing to Morneau at first … like, maybe, the Canadian Club? "Naw," said Morneau, "it's just a case of one bad goalie throwing it across the diamond to another bad goalie."

Informed of Morneau's analogy, Koskie shook his head and declared: "*He* might have been a bad goalie … *I* was a good goalie."

Jeff Francis never played goal, but he was nicknamed 'Boomer' by his grandfather, in honor not of lefty pitcher David Wells, but rather erstwhile Montreal Canadiens' great Bernie "Boom-Boom" Geoffrion.

Francis blazed through the minors in 2004 before being called up Aug. 25 by the Colorado Rockies, a decision that was steeped in controversy in that the 23-year-old pitcher was prevented from pitching for Team Canada at the Olympics. With the Rockies, he had a 3-2 record with a 5.15 ERA in seven starts. In moving from Double-A Tulsa to Triple-A Colorado Springs, Francis led all Canadian minor-leaguers with 16 wins in the minors, going 16-4 with a 2.21 ERA. In all, he threw 155 innings, averaging 11.4 strikeouts per nine innings. For his season to remember, Francis was named minor league player of the year by highly respected *Baseball America*, the first time a Canadian has won the honor in the 24-year history of the award.

Francis pitched for North Delta for three years before joining the University of B.C., where he blossomed under Terry McKaig, leading to his ninth over-all selection in the 2002 draft. "I saw 18 pitchers and he was the best one, hands down," said future Hall of Famer Tony Gwynn after the 2004 Futures game, a part of baseball's all-star festivities. Francis was a late bloomer as a pitcher, but only in terms of velocity. Mellios remembers him going 19-0 in 1999 and 18-1 in 1998, mostly on the strength of the outstanding movement rather than the speed he had on the ball. "When Jeff graduated high school, the reality was his velocity wasn't there," Mellios said. "That made Jeff a better pitcher; he learned how to pitch and to locate pitches. He was the best I've ever had in making adjustments and one of the smartest. He was a sponge."

With an SAT score of 1210 and a 4.0 grade point average, Francis was pursued by San Diego State, Oregon State and Villanova among other big U.S. schools before finally deciding to stay home and attend UBC. In his first start against highly-regarded Lewis-Clark State Warriors at Lewiston, Idaho, he worked four innings, allowing 10 hits and 11 runs on two, three-run homers and one two-run homer—all on curve balls. Remembered McKaig, "It was the first time ever he'd been lit up. I had a little talk with him afterwards and the first thing he asked was 'When is my next start against them?'" When the return match came three weeks later, Francis was outstanding, working eight innings, allowing only six hits, striking out 13 and leaving with the score deadlocked 3-3. "That gave you an indication of how special he was," McKaig said. "He got lit up, wanted to face them again and made enough adjustments to get 13 strikeouts. He was so far beyond his years on a mental level. The way he learned things was unseen at the collegiate level."

After showing up at UBC with a 79-mile per hour fastball, Francis steadily improved his velocity. "Towards the end of his freshman spring he was at about 84 miles per hour and the next fall as a sophomore, he was at 88," McKaig said. "That's almost 10 miles per hour in a year." McKaig has his own explanation for the dramatic jump in performance. "One of the worst things about playing summer ball is that kids pitch one day and play a position the next," McKaig said. "Francis used to play first when he wasn't pitching. He'd pitch and then the next day be out there throwing to bases in infield practices. Rest increases velocity. Coaches phone and ask how we bumped Francis' velocity. We didn't give him any special mechanics; we asked him to follow our long-toss and strength and conditioning programs."

McKaig concedes that B.C. has a natural advantage over the other provinces because of the weather and thinks the growth will continue because of the Jeff Francis Factor. "We go to Little League camps now and kids will say 'I know who Jeff Francis is, I want to go to UBC,'" said McKaig, who expects his next ace to be Jonathan Forest of St. Hubert, Quebec, the first Quebec player to enroll at UBC to play baseball. After pitching at Chipola College in Marianna, Florida, Forest turned down an offer at the University of Tennessee and headed for the west coast. Why? "Jeff Francis pitched here," Forest told McKaig. "Three years ago, if you talked to the best players in the country, they'd pay you lip service," McKaig said. "Now we're in the mix with the top NCAA Division I schools when it comes to recruiting. It's all because of Jeff Francis."

And yet, as exceptional as Morneau's and Francis' 2004 seasons were, both had to take a back seat to the year enjoyed by a kid from the mining town of Trail, nestled in the mountains of southeastern British Columbia. Despite playing in just 120 games for the Pittsburgh Pirates, Jason Bay became the first Canadian to win a major-league rookie of the year award, as well as the first Pirate to win the award since it was instituted in 1947. The left fielder hit .282 with 26 home runs and 82 RBIs to earn the National League Rookie of the Year honor. Given a $20,000 grant for winning the latter by the Major League Baseball Players Association, Bay donated the money to the Ronald McDonald House, a facility that allows parents to stay free of charge while their children are patients at Pittsburgh Children's Hospital.

When a player is with four organizations in four years, it usually means he has some warts on his game. But in the case of Bay, in the years following his 645th over-all selection by the Montreal Expos out of Gonzaga University in the June 2000 major-league draft, it was more the case that he was a player highly sought after by other teams in deals. After spending spring training of 2001 with the Expos, Bay was dealt March 27 to the New York Mets for Lou Collier. Three months later, he was traded to the San Diego Padres for Steve Reed. Finally, in August 2003, the Pirates came calling and landed him in a package for Brian Giles.

A shoulder injury suffered during the last week of the 2003 season led to arthroscopic surgery, causing Bay to remain behind in Bradenton, Florida, when the Pirates broke camp and ultimately miss the first month of 2004. Upon joining the Pirates in early May, he quickly made up for lost time. "I came into the season just wanting to establish myself as a regular," he said after earning the rookie nod, taking 25 of 32 first-place votes to easily out-distance San Diego shortstop Khalil Greene. "There was a certain amount of expectation (because) I had done well after coming over from San Diego the season before. But I'd like to do better. I'm not going to get comfortable off one good season." Noted Pittsburgh manager Lloyd McClendon, "He does a lot of things well. I don't think anyone thought he would be this good this fast, though."

As Bay was enjoying his breakthrough season, his sister Lauren, 23, was pitching for Team Canada women's softball team in Athens. Turns out that the Bays have athletic genes; their uncle Gerry Moro, now a winemaker in California, was a two-time Olympian in the decathlon.

It will be difficult for Bay to match the thrills he experienced after his rookie season. He had a brief chat with Canadian Prime Minister Paul Martin while appearing as a guest on a radio talk show in Vancouver. "We're very patriotic people in Canada, so speaking with the prime minister was a very big deal," Bay said.

Intriguingly, if not for the those pivotal extra two days Morneau spent on the Twins' roster in June 2003, British Columbia would have been gunning to go two-for-two in major-league rookie awards in 2004. Morneau's 19 home runs, 58 RBIs and .271 average in just 280 at bats with the Twins compared awfully favorably to the 22-homer, 64-RBI, .239 season of Oakland A's shortstop Bobby Crosby, who enjoyed 265 more at bats and received 27 of 28 first-place votes in the balloting.

Mind you, it's probably a good thing for the rest of Canada it didn't happen. There would be no living with the Best in Canada boys after that.

16

C'MON BABY, LIGHT A FIRE

Baseball, the game itself, is not about one moment, but rather a collection of moments, moments alternatively dramatic, exciting, embarrassing, heartbreaking or funny. Baseball is all about memories, good and bad, and laughs, chuckles and, maybe especially, belly laughs. We remember watching the Blue Jays on spring mornings in Dunedin. Players would do their sprints, then go through their exercises down the right-field line under the watchful eye of the strength and conditioning coach. Meanwhile, manager Cito Gaston, his coaches and the minor-league instructors would gather and for half an hour tell stories and laugh so hard they were dropping their fungo bats.

We asked some coaches to recount tales and were always told, "half of them aren't printable, they're just memories ... good stories."

Whether the diamond is on the west coast, down east or somewhere in between, there is the same flow of stories when baseball people gather. The stories in this chapter didn't take place on the same day, or even in the same millennium, but what they have in common is their roots—their Canadian roots. They all either took place in Canada or involved a Canadian player. As such, they are designed to permit the reader to piece together his or her own sense of what it is that makes Canadians who play baseball, and the way they play the game, something distinct. Part of that may be the slightly skewed, uniquely Canadian sense of humor that underpins many of the stories. And part of it may just be an inner voice that keeps insisting that, hey, we're different, eh?

• • •

Mike Kelly, bench coach of the North Delta Blue Jays, was sitting quietly in the dugout on a visit to Husky Stadium at Seattle in 2004. The Jays were playing Wilkinson Academy. The plate ump was not, shall we say, having a real good day on balls and strikes. The usual crowd was watching the Connie Mack league game on the University of Washington campus: Parents, grandparents, girlfriends and down the line a man walking his dog had stopped to watch. Kelly went to the mound to talk to his pitcher Ryan Omerod. He stood on the mound and stood and stood.

Finally, the plate ump took off his mask and approached the mound. "You making a flip?" the umpire asked, inquiring whether Kelly wanted to make a change. "You see the guy in the stands down there with his dog?" Kelly said. "I'll take those two and put them behind the plate, because they can see better than you." Kelly was gone and in came reliever Brent Lavallee.

• • •

Andy Lawrence played six years in the New York Mets' and Montreal Expos' systems. He was a teammate of Larry Walker at Double-A Jacksonville. He certainly deserved better than this. But 10-year-olds who ask, "If Yankee Stadium is the name where the Yankees play, what is the name of Fenway Park where the Red Sox play?" have little sense of history. In 1998, Lawrence was running his Ontario Youth Baseball camp in Mississauga, Ontario. He was also scouting Ontario for the Mets and was decked out in his orange and blue Mets' uniform. Noticing Lawrence's stylized "NY" cap, a child approached and asked in an innocent manner: "Mr. Lawrence ... uh ... do you work for New York Fries?"

• • •

Martin Mainville was pitching for the Academie Baseball Canada, drawing both crowds and scouts in 1993. Start time for the ABC was always TBA, because the games couldn't start until after the Montreal Expos, the primary Olympic Stadium tenant, had finished playing their games and the mound was repaired. At the time, Tom Valcke was the Canadian director of scouting for the Major League Baseball Scouting Bureau. It was his job to keep the scouts supplied with information. One night in Montreal there was a long delay starting the ABC game and the concessions were closed, so Valcke placed an order for St. Hubert chicken to make a delivery. A week later he tried to do the same thing for 40 scouts. "Deliver it to the guys behind home plate," Valcke said into the phone. Some time later, with a hitter at the plate and Mainville beginning his wind-up, someone from the ABC dugout along the first-base side shouted "Time!" Mainville stumbled out of his delivery. Then, emerging from the dugout headed to home plate was the St. Hubert delivery man, carrying so much food that he couldn't see over what he was carrying as he headed toward the catcher and the umpire ... you know, the guys behind the plate. The umpire kindly re-directed him to the scouts sitting in the seats.

• • •

Wes Lillie was playing third base for the Galt, Ontario juveniles in the 1940s and his club had the bases loaded and no one out. After the first couple of pitches Lillie noticed that the runner on third had been taking an extra long lead off. Before the next pitch he jogged to the mound and chatted briefly to the pitcher, and also sneaked the ball from the pitcher's glove and told him to stay off the rubber to eliminate a balk call. After returning to his position he moved behind third and stuck the ball in his back pocket. When the runner led off, Lillie yelled to the base ump he had the ball and was running toward the runner, by now a sitting duck. So far so good, except, Lillie couldn't quite yank the ball from his tight flannel baseball pants. The runner took off and scored while Lillie still fought a losing battle with his back pocket. Shortstop Bill Wylie frantically wrestled Lillie to the ground and attempted to pry the ball loose, to no avail. By time they succeeded, two more runners had crossed the plate. Talk about a new twist on the old hidden ball trick.

● ● ●

Howie Birnie of Leaside umped the plate in 1984 at the annual Pearson Cup game between the Montreal Expos and the Blue Jays, which was played to benefit amateur baseball. At the time, Pete Rose was with the Expos. Lefty Bryan Clark was facing Rose and for one of the few times in his umping career Birnie, who had worked international competitions and thousands of amateur games, felt nervous. Rose had a way of taking a pitch and turning to look the ball into the glove. On the 2-2 pitch, before Birnie could say "ball," Rose announced "inside." On the 3-2 pitch in an exhibition game, Birnie figured Clark would throw a fastball. The pitch came in looking good; Rose dropped his bat and raced to first as he normally did. Birnie pumped his arm, "Strike three." One small problem … it wasn't a fastball, but rather a breaking ball, which broke down and out of the strike zone. Birnie walked briskly towards third, noticing the Expos' Andre Dawson on the bench howling. After the game, Birnie was walking off with umpire Dick Willis and asked "Was that pitch to Rose low?" Without breaking stride, Willis turned, looked at Birnie and said, "Before or after it bounced?"

● ● ●

Greg Mullens of Saskatoon came to the plate with two out in the final inning of the gold medal game of the Canadian senior championships between Team Saskatchewan and Team Quebec at Riverside Park in Windsor, Ontario in 2003. Saskatchewan trailed by a run, but with two out had the tying run on second. The count on Mullens went to 2-2 and the pitch came in. Mullens thought it was low and let it go. Just then, he heard the ump call "Steerike, yer out." As Quebec players celebrated winning the national title, some Saskatchewan players argued. Tension was high. Fans were screaming. Mullens strode toward the dugout, full of angry indignation. Off the front of the dugout near the stairs stood a solitary metal bucket that looked inviting. With one mighty kick Mullens, quite out of character, booted it, sending it flying. Except the bucket wasn't empty, it was loaded, but not with baseballs or water. A groundskeeper had left a half-filled bucket of white lining paint in the wrong spot. The bucket soared through the air splattering paint all over the ceiling, the back wall and his teammates' gear. One Saskatchewan player began to laugh, a couple more joined in, and then a few more after that, until finally everyone on the field was roaring. Finally, Mullens broke out laughing, too. The tension of moments before was completely gone.

• • •

Jake Cole was the playing-manager for the Goulbourn Royals in 1975 in the Senior Interprovincial League in the Ottawa area. They were playing their season opener against the Renfrew Red Sox, who had runners on first and second with none out. The batter popped up to shortstop. "INFIELD FLY, INFIELD FLY!" base ump Merv Bonney yelled. Easier said than done. The shortstop on this windy day had trouble tracking the ball and then it disappeared into the sun. The runner at second had a better angle on the ball than the shortstop, broke for third and slid in safely. As soon as time was called a blue streak could be spotted from behind the plate. It was Cole, eyes bulging, headed for the base ump screaming, "He didn't tag! He didn't tag! He didn't ..." The bearded Cole was stopped in mid-sentence as the clips on his shin guards caught, locked and suddenly he was running like a one-legged man as he went down head first on the back of the dusty mound. Bonney walked over to dryly observe: "He didn't have to tag since your shortstop wasn't able to catch the ball."

• • •

Tim Harkness of Montreal was as green as the grass of the Shibe Park infield in Philadelphia when he arrived for his first major-league workout in 1955 at age 17. Harkness took batting practice before the Philadelphia Phillies played the Milwaukee Braves. While watching infield from the dugout, Phils' manager Mayo Smith told Harkness to go to first base. "It was easy, compared to what I was used to, every throw was right there, right in my face," Harkness remembered. Then, Smith pointed to short-stop Granny Hamner and motioned down. Hamner began to throw balls in the dirt. Known for his soft hands, Harkness was able to scoop most of the throws until one got away. The ball bounced near the Braves dugout where future Hall of Famer Warren Spahn and teammate Bob Buhl sat toweling off after their bullpen sessions. "Hey kid," growled Buhl, a World War II veteran of the Battle of the Bulge. "One more ball comes over here I'm coming out there to kick your ass." Harkness fielded flawlessly the rest of the workout.

• • •

Ryan Hornblower was manning his position in right field and minding his own business in the top of the first inning. Stratford was hosting St. Thomas in junior Intercounty play on a spring night in 1995. Stratford had one out and a man on first when all of a sudden Stratford players noticed Hornblower on the ground writhing in pain. Catcher Damon Topolie guessed that Hornblower's appendix had burst. When Stratford players arrived at Hornblower's side, he pulled up his shirt to show circular red welt just below his ribs. "Hornblower, what happened?" Topolie asked. "I got hit with one," Hornblower said. Some wondered whether he'd been shot. Finally, the outfielder was able to explain that he'd been struck by a golf ball from the neighboring course. Golfers often tried to cut the corner just outside the outfield fence on the par-four hole. Play resumed when the laughter died down.

• • •

George Brice needed one out for a no-hitter as his Kelowna Labatts hosted the Vernon Luckies in an Okanagan Mainline Baseball League game in 1964 at Elks Stadium in Kelowna, British Columbia. Gord Nuyens, a Pete Rose-type hitter, slapped a hard two-bouncer at Brice. The ball deflected off the glove of the 6-foot-2, 155-pounder and disappeared into his pants. George wasn't sure whether his fly might have been open or if the ball entered his pants through his belt area because he was wearing oversized pants. He had just moved to town from Victoria and they were the only pair of pants the club could find for him. The ball was so difficult to retrieve that Nuyens hustled to second on the play. It was ruled a double, although the error argument was dutifully made. After a delay of five minutes, George Brice struck out John Kashuba swinging.

• • •

Rob Butler, who won a World Series ring with the Toronto Blue Jays in 1993, remembers playing for Triple-A Scranton. Their catcher, Rick Wrona, was in the midst of a terrible slump, angry at the world. Butler said Wrona could never be taken seriously because he was the type of guy who at 5:30 a.m. at the start of another plane flight would come out of the bathroom with toilet paper stuck to his shoe and pretend he didn't know it was there. On this night, the slumping Wrona struck out for a third time in the game on a pitch that didn't make it to the plate. After the catcher blocked the ball, Wrona picked it up, tagged himself for the out and threw the ball down to third. Butler remembered it was so crazy and funny that teammates didn't even fine him in kangaroo court.

• • •

Dave Roberts was pitching for the North Delta Blue Jays against Cowichan Valley in the B.C. Premier League in 1996. The Jays' bench thought that the plate ump's strike zone was roughly the size of a golf ball. Coach Mike Kelly went to the mound. When the ump asked if he was going to make a change, Kelly said: "I'm gonna make your day. I'm going to bring in someone who throws hard, so you can hear the strikes, because you sure as hell can't see them."

On came Dave Lee to pop the glove.

• • •

Jess Bechard knew what to do in a bunt situation when he was playing first base. It's just that he'd never done this before. Guelph had its leadoff hitter on first after a walk late in an Intercounty midget game against Brantford at Hastings Park in 1994 in Guelph, Ontario. The next hitter, as expected, bunted down the first-base line. With the runner off for second, Bechard fielded the ball and tagged the batter. While the Brantford shortstop covered second, the third baseman had charged on the bunt and remained in front of the plate, leaving third base uncovered. The runner took off for third and so did Bechard. He raced across the infield and tagged the sliding runner out to record both ends of the double play, unassisted.

• • •

Mike Griffin was at the plate for the Ottawa-Nepean Canadians juniors with the bases loaded on a trip to Trois Rivieres in 1981. Coaching third, I realized we had to score here, because we were trailing 4-2, and the bottom end of the order was up in the top of the seventh. Griffin turned on a 2-2 pitch and pulled it down the line. I took a few steps towards left for a better view when the ball hit the chalk, the white lime spraying four feet in the air, near the warning track of the old Double-A Eastern League park. I waved all three runners home. Griffin had given us a 5-4 lead and we had a fresh closer. Suddenly we saw the base umpire, standing behind the mound motioning foul ball. Out I went. After about two minutes of me talking and him staring I remembered going over the ground rules at home plate—this ump had not said a word. Perhaps he didn't speak English and my Grade 10 French was useless. Griffin, completely bilingual, was called over from second, and the following conversation ensued:

"Michael, ask this gentleman politely *en français* why he called the ball foul?"

"Bobby, he said he called it foul because it was a foul."

"Michael, ask him if it was a foul ball how come the chalk went four feet high in the air?"

"Bobby, he says it was foul."

"Michael, ask him about the chalk."

"Bobby, he says he saw the ball hit the line ... but I don't know how I am going to tell you this ... now be calm ... he says the ball hit the left-field line, but it hit the foul side of the line."

"Michael, the guy did not take one step from behind the mound to get an angle and he can see where the ball landed from 275 feet away, but he can't see chalk in the air? Well, you tell him he's the second worst ump I've ever seen, the worst does games at the CNIB and he is a no good $!#)% ."

"Oh Bobby, I'm not telling him that."

Griffin returned to the batter's box and promptly bounced back to the pitcher. Time to warm up the bus.

● ● ●

Darcy Blommaert of Yorkton, Saskatchewan, came on to pitch in relief for the Saskatchewan Selects in a game against the Manitoba Selects at St. Boniface as a tune-up for the Canada Cup in Stonewall, Manitoba. Blommaert did not look comfortable throwing his warm-up pitches and after he faced the first hitter, manager Todd Plaxton realized he was in trouble. Plaxton called the ump over and asked whether he could go to the mound to find out what the problem was without using one of his trips. The ump thought it was okay, as he'd seen Blommaert struggling as well, apparently trying to adjust his cup. When Plaxton reached the mound, he asked his pitcher what the trouble was. Replied Blommaert, "my ovaries are sore." Plaxton asked him to repeat what he said and in a serious voice, Blommaert replied, "my ovaries were sore." Plaxton, who eventually guessed Blommaert had one of his testicles caught in the cup, giving him a sore stomach, told him he'd be okay once he was adjusted. The umpire laughed hysterically and shook his head all the way to the plate.

● ● ●

David Krug of Oakville, Ontario was on the mound for Team Canada in the 1990 world senior championships in Edmonton. And Krug was in trouble with the bases loaded and none out against The Netherlands. The Dutch hitter lined a ball back through the box, which hit off the heel of an off-balance Krug. The ball went to shortstop John Leonard of Oakville, who flipped to second baseman Barry Petrachenko of Welland. He stepped on second and fired to first baseman Gary Van Tol of Pincher Creek, Alberta. Double play? Van Tol then threw across the diamond to third and eventually the runner who had begun the play on second was erased in a rundown, while the runner from third scored. Triple play, right? Players on both teams were puzzled. Then, when Krug reached the dugout he told coaches Bernie Beckman and Jim Ridley that the ball had hit his foot and never touched the ground. So, three were out and The Netherlands was taking the field, with a run in the books. Ridley argued that the ball had never touched the ground, so it was one out after the ball hit Krug and went to Leonard; a second when Petrachenko stepped on second, and a third when Van Tol caught the ball at first. The rundown was a waste of time. But did the runner on third tag up after the line drive was caught? The Canadians took the field, appealed at third and the umps ruled that the runner had not tagged. To erase the run, Canada had to get a fourth out and prevailed 7-6.

• • •

Chris Harber was at his St. Francis practice in the Connie Mack league at Ottawa's LaRoche Park in 1965. Coach Moe Lasalle had some athletic notables such as Dwight Fowler, who later played tight end at Bridgeport University and was head coach of the University of Ottawa Gee-Gees in 1976; speedy Jake Cole and righty Bob Game, who later was signed by Detroit Tigers' scout Bobby Prentice. Before practice, Lasalle tossed his car keys to Stan Daley and asked to him to fetch the equipment from the trunk of his old Chevy, which had a standard transmission. Unknown to everyone, Daley did not have a driver's license and he proceeded to drive the car from the parking lot, down a steep hill and onto the field. Daley used the Chevy to play "El Matador" with LaSalle identified as the bull, chasing Lasalle around the diamond with the car. The inexperienced Daley was unable to control his speed. Eventually Lasalle jumped onto the hood and was subsequently speared in the butt by the hood ornament. When the dust settled, Lasalle cancelled practice.

• • •

Lionel Ruhr of Regina was coaching first base for Team Canada in the 1988 World Youth championships in Windsor, Ontario. Now Ruhr, everyone says, is one of the most mild-mannered people in baseball. Yet, as he watched a Canadian runner called out at first on a bang-bang play by umpire Jim Cressman, Ruhr lost his temper and was in Cressman's face arguing and yelling. Out sprinted Canada manager Jim Ridley to get in between Cressman and Ruhr. "Did you get that play right? DID YOU GET THAT PLAY RIGHT?" Ridley demanded of Cressman. When Cressman said, "Yes," he had it right, Ridley replied in a loud voice "Well, what the hell am I doing here?" The manager quickly spun and returned to the dugout as players and fans roared with laughter.

• • •

Larry Haggitt was one of the better hitters ever to grace Labatt Park in London. A powerful left-handed hitter with Popeye-style forearms for the London Majors who had played in the Tigers' system, he would drive in for games from Leamington. On Friday nights his wife would accompany him, drop him off at the park and go shopping. One night about the third inning, Haggitt crushed a long home run over the fence and even over the brown wooden fence surrounding the park. It was at least 450 feet and smashed through the windshield of a car on Riverside Drive. The car turned out to be Haggitt's own, with his wife driving.

• • •

Mel Oswald of the Canadian Thunderbirds has coached baseball for years, yet his funniest memory happened on a mushball diamond. It qualifies here only because Oswald saw it on his way to his car following a base-ball doubleheader at Bernie Arbour Stadium in Hamilton. Seeing that the team in the field led by one run, two were out, the stands were full and two runners were aboard, Oswald paused to stand outside the left-field fence of Mohawk Sports Park to see the outcome. The hitter hit a towering shot on a 1-1 pitch to deep left centre field not far from where Oswald was leaning against the frost fence. The left fielder, who had been playing rather shallow, ran in the direction the ball was traveling, but somehow got turned around and his pants fell to his ankles, causing him to fall back-wards. The ball came down right into the glove of the now prostrate and pantless player for the final out. Upon making the catch, the player imme-diately rose to his feet to show the ump he had made the catch while his pants remained at his ankles. Both dugouts filled with laughter.

• • •

Remo Cardinale, former Blue Jays' farmhand, remembers playing centre field in an exhibition game with the Oakville A's to prepare for the over-45 masters nationals in 2002. Dick Hames, the new reliever, took the mound. "I look in and he's throwing underhand, like a softball pitcher, I figured ah, he's just warming up," Cardinale said. "The hitter stepped in and he still threw underhanded. I turned to the guy in right and said 'What's going on?'" Hames, of London, pitched for Richmond Hill Dynes, the 1972 world championship softball team. And he got people out in masters baseball throwing from down below. "In baseball a curve breaks down, a changeup tails down," Cardinale said. "Throwing a fastball underhanded, you can make the ball rise. Hitters had a lot of trouble with him. Holding on guys was difficult."

• • •

Satchel Paige and Sal "The Barber" Maglie, both former major leaguers, were at Cockshutt Park in Brantford, Ontario in the late 1960s. The Brantford Red Sox of the Intercounty League brought in the Buffalo Simon Pures for the annual Shriners Game, a charity event. Paige and Maglie were going to pitch two innings each, Paige for Brantford and Maglie for Buffalo. Roger "Oyster" McGowan, the Sox catcher, warmed up Paige while the Shriners band was tuning up down the left field foul line. McGowan accidentally threw the ball over Paige's head and it was swallowed up by the tuba. In the first inning, Brantford's Al Dostal laid down a bunt on the aging Maglie and beat it out easily. That didn't sit well with Maglie, who earned his nickname by pitching high and tight, the ultimate 'close shave' barber. Although scheduled to pitch only two innings, Maglie stayed in the game for the third. When Dostal came to the plate, The Barber knocked him down not once, but twice, on pitches right under the hair on his chinny-chin chin.

•••

Dennis"Birdman" Bradley worked a walk leading off an inning for the Brantford Red Sox against the Hamilton Cardinals at Brantford's Cockshutt Park in 1977. A converted fastball player, Bradley did not know all the nuances of the game. One out later, with a 2-1 count on the next hitter, Sox manager Terry Clark gave the hit-and-run sign. Larry Weimers hit the ball on a line to left centre. It looked like extra bases. However, speedy Cardinal outfielder Larry Fisher got a great jump and made a remarkable catch in left centre. Bradley was approaching third, only to see and hear Clark waving his arms and yelling, "Get back, get back." Bradley put on the brakes and retreated. Realizing he wasn't going to make it back to first if he re-traced his steps, he cut across the infield grass, over the mound and slid into first base, ahead of the throw. Bradley stood on first, brushing off dust from his head-long slide, when the ump yelled, "Yer out for not retouching second." Bradley's response was, "What do ya mean out? I beat the ball." Players in the Sox dugout were in tears with laughter. Asked about it later, Dennis said with a straight face, "I thought it was the quickest way back."

•••

Greg Cranker was coaching his Erindale Cardinals team at the Ontario senior eliminations in 1996 at Windsor. After a bad call, Cranker approached the home plate ump. "Am I getting paid?" Cranker said in a quiet, even-mannered voice. The ump said he didn't think so. "How many of my kids are getting paid?" Cranker asked. The ump guessed none. "What about the other team, do you think they are getting paid to play or that their coaches are getting paid?" The umpire said no. "Well, how come you—the only guy getting paid—is making all the mistakes and screwing it up for everyone else who is playing for fun?" Not surprisingly, the manager didn't manage to get in another question before his ejection.

•••

Larry Oakley played shortstop for the Peterborough Tigers in 1974. They played the Keene Expos, coached by Roger Neilson, the long-time National Hockey League coach, in the Ontario junior playdowns. Peterborough had the tying run on third. After a mound conference, all hell broke loose. "We had Fred Garvey on third, Dave Clements was catching and he threw what looked like the ball into left," Oakley remembered. "Garvey came home and was tagged out!"

Clements had thrown a peeled apple wide of third while keeping the ball inside his chest protector.

•••

Tim Harkness, originally from Lachine, Quebec, often carried with him an Upper Deck card of Jimmy Piersall crossing home plate while running backward in 1963. "That's me, the on-deck hitter with my hand out ready to shake his hand and he's backing into me," Harkness said of his New York Mets' teammate. "Duke Snider had hit his 400th homer shortly before and there wasn't much fuss in the papers. So Piersall said 'I've got 99, wait 'til you see my 100th." Piersall went deep, ran his routine way to first, turned and back-pedaled the rest of the way around the bases. When Piersall crossed the plate, ump Tom Gorman gave the safe sign and ejected Piersall for "making a mockery of the game."

• • •

Peter Schaeffer of Hamilton and former Negro League player Jimmy Wilkes of Brantford were recognized as two of the Intercounty's best umpires in 1975. They were assigned to work a Guelph C-JOYs-London Majors game at London's Labatt Park. Schaeffer missed a call, according to the Majors fans, and as so often happens a couple of hits followed. At the end of the inning, the public address announcer intoned: "And for Guelph in that half inning, three runs on two hits, one London error and one gigantic boo-boo by the ump." Schaeffer promptly booted the announcer out of the park.

• • •

Arty Leeman began his pre-game bullpen session for the Kingston Centennials down the right field line on a sunny Saturday afternoon to pitch against the Kendal Frank Real Estate at Bowmanville's Soper Creek Park in 1968. It didn't last long. Leeman hurt his arm after about 10 pitches. Usually baseball doesn't get nerve-wracking until the late innings. It's not supposed to be that way just 20 minutes before the first pitch. But suddenly, there was panic on the Kingston bench. We only had one pitcher on the trip since the others had commitments. Traveling with one pitcher was no big deal. Kendal was not a strong team, even though John Quantrill, the father of future major leaguer Paul, was in the bullpen. Cliffy Earl, who took over running the team when my father got sick, surveyed the situation and asked Bucky Davis, a strong-armed, back-up outfielder, to warm up. Davis was the excitable type but he was willing to run through a wall or through Soper Creek. Leeman began his crash course by instructing him how to stand on the rubber. Finally, Leeman suggested maybe he should throw a few pitches from the stretch because "there was a small chance he'd be making a few pitches with a base runner or two aboard." Davis took the mound in the bottom of the first. He looked in for catcher Billy Kyle's signal, although Davis only had one pitch—a fastball. He started his motion and came to the set position, gazed out of the corner of his eye at first and threw home.

The ball had just popped Kyle's glove when we remember Leeman calling time and racing to the mound. He asked Davis why he was throwing from the stretch without anyone on base. This was years before major-league relievers often worked from the stretch with no one on base. "Well," growled Davis, "you can't be too careful." Davis went seven innings and Elwyn Watts the final two in a 7-1 win.

•••

Gerry "Doc" Wager, coach of the Kingston Ponies, regarded the situation with a worried look on his face. The remaining teams at the 1973 Ontario Baseball Association senior eliminations were battling each other and the elements. Rain had washed out most of Saturday morning's action, wood chips had been placed on the Megaffin Stadium infield, gasoline has been dumped and the field had been raked ... only to have it rain again. Now, hours later, chips had been laid and the gas was being poured again. Wager looked first at the skies and then at the field. This would be the final attempt as the stores had been closed. Along about then came Kingston right fielder Clyde "Camel" Harris, who said: "Well, Doc, I guess the chips are really down."

•••

Bob Yanus had all his pitches working one night in June of 1977 for the Ottawa-Nepean Canadians. Yanus, a 33-year-old native of Poughkeepsie, New York, hadn't given up a hit against the Hull Beavers and was pitching in the fourth when, all of a sudden, the power went out, putting the field in darkness. He was ahead 4-0 after three full innings. The game would be completed five weeks later on the Canadians' next trip to Hull. No way could we let anyone else pitch. The well-rested Yanus took the mound and worked the rest of the way without allowing a hit, catching a pop-up for the final out in a 9-0 victory, thanks to catcher Billy Courchaine putting down the right fingers and three hits by Brian Burns. Yanus walked three and struck out six, getting nine ground-ball outs. The team retired to centre fielder Mark Gryba's house to discuss matters and celebrate. Around 4:30 a.m. someone thought it would be a good idea to phone Yanus' high school coach with the news. The coach, Willard Coon, was sleeping, strangely enough, at home in Dover Plains, New York. "Do you remember Bobby Yanus?" we asked. "Sure, what happened to him?" asked the coach sleepily. "He just pitched a complete game no-hitter, the final pitch was four hours ago and the first pitch was five weeks ago."

•••

Conrad Young was a two-way performer; he could hit home runs and he could pitch complete games. The Ottawa-Nepean Canadians were playing the Etobicoke Indians, managed by Bob Smyth, at Iroquois Park at a 1979 tournament in Whitby. Our Canadians were down 2-0 in the fourth when Young hit a solo homer. Coaching at third, I watched the ball clear the fence, then looked to second, expecting to see Conrad in his customary home run trot. No Conrad. I looked to the batter's box to see if he had watched it, which was a no-no. Again no Conrad. There, 15 feet past first base down the right-field line was Conrad, face down, being attended to by first base coach Ronnie Thompson. Turned out that everyone was watching the ball except one player on the bench. He said that as Conrad reached first, he pumped his left hand hard in excitement just as he stepped on the bag and had injured himself in the groin. Conrad was a talent, but handling pain was not his strength. Now what, I thought, as I walked over. As the other bench began to argue, I approached one of the umps heading to huddle with the other one. "Look, you guys better get this right. This is a book rule—any player injured after hitting a home run has six minutes to make it around the bases," we told them, making up the rule on the spot. Conrad needed one player on each side to lean on as he hobbled the rest of the way around the bases. The run didn't matter anyway. We got beat 5-1, despite one of the longest tours of the bases ever. Needless to say, Young was embarrassed and didn't want to ever see Etobicoke again. Still, he retired the final 13 hitters in order in a complete-game, 2-1 win over the Indians at the Ontario eliminations six weeks later in Sudbury.

•••

Jeff Bond was working on fumes after errors extended him in the sixth inning. Finally he got out of the inning and the Erin Mills Eagles took a 10-9 lead into the top of the seventh against Caledonia at Ireland Park in the Burlington juvenile tournament in 2000. John O'Donnell had hard-throwing Tom Malyk warmed up and ready to close the game. As the second hitter, Malyk disagreed with a strike call and was ejected. So, out went Bond to the mound for the bottom of the inning. This had a chance to be over real quick. The leadoff hitter doubled off the top of the fence on the first pitch. The next hitter bunted down the first base line. It was fair, it was foul and it came back fair as first baseman Mike Lukajic picked it up. Seeing the Caledonia runner had turned the corner at third and shortstop Stuart Kingston had snuck in behind him, he threw across the diamond for the first out. So one out, a man on first. The next hitter doubled off the top of the fence in left again. The ball came in quickly, the runner was waved, Kingston's relay was a one-hopper which catcher Ben Chisholm caught and the runner slid into his mitt. Chisholm looked up to see the batter jogging out by the shortstop and threw to third baseman Justin Pollard. He walked over to the runner, who said: "Why are you tagging me? There are three out." Pollard said, "Well, you're wrong," applied the tag to his shoulder and added, "but you're right now." And that was the game. Bond got a 1-2-3 inning, a runner thrown out at the plate and two thrown out heading to third.

• • •

Tony Batista was claimed on waivers from the Toronto Blue Jays by the Baltimore Orioles and the phones were ringing. It was June 25, 2001. That afternoon I wrote how the Jays had saved $11.95 million by moving their third baseman halfway through the second year of his four-year deal. That evening, I was helping coach Dave Pilkington's Erin Mills Eagles bantams, which were playing the Forest Glen Twins. Watching the top of the first, Erin Mills scored six times on four walks, an error and a couple of hits. I asked starter Andrew Laverty: "What do you think of the ump so far?" He said not good. I told him he could expect the same strike zone, but unlike the Forest Glen starter he had a good lead, so "he could throw it down the pipe." Some 10 minutes later our lead was 6-3, two runners were aboard and only one out when Laverty appeared frustrated. I headed to the mound.

Laverty had his head down, kicking at the rubber. He finally looked up to say: "You told me not to be bothered, but I've thrown more strikes that were called balls than the strikes he called strikes." I told Laverty, "You're a great control pitcher, you can handle this." As Laverty began to take in the words, the cell phone in my pocket rang and I made a quick exit. On the phone was former Jays manager Jim Fregosi, asking why the Jays didn't pull Batista off waivers. I asked if we could call him back. Laverty got a pop-up and a strikeout to escape the jam. After the lopsided win, I compiled a few notes, sort of like a script, punched in Fregosi's phone number and gave the phone to Laverty, who said: "Hello Mr. Fregosi, this is Andrew Laverty. I am 13 years old. I'd just like to ask you not to disturb me on the mound in future, when I am in a difficult situation and I am getting advice from a learned expert, whom we call Mississauga's Mel Queen." Fregosi, who had Queen as his pitching coach, replied: "Andrew, I phoned because I knew you needed help when I heard that you were talking to that dumb pitching coach. I'm surprised he even found the mound and didn't walk around in right field looking for it for 10 minutes." Fregosi laughed and laughed when Laverty passed me the phone. "That was cute," Fregosi said. "But you still don't know anything about pitching." As usual, the man had a point.

• • •

Pitcher Dan Reardon of the St. John's Capitals wasn't on the mound on a steamy August day in 1976 at jammed Jubilee Field in Corner Brook, Newfoundland. The Corner Brook Barons were hosting their rivals in the eighth inning of the seventh game of the senior provincials. It was a tense time in the St. John's dugout, for the Capitals trailed by three runs. Reardon, a right-hander and a member of the Newfoundland baseball

Hall of Fame, writes what happened next as he watched from the dugout:

"Our coach, Pat Hurley, knew all too well that we were down to six outs. He paced and he paced. His face reddened by the ceaseless sun and his Irish fury. A Mickey Mantle worshipper, he was more Ruthian in shape, giving way to that bulging middle atop spindly legs. He was as volatile as the Bambino too and as ravenous of appetite. The leadoff batter for Corner Brook singled to left. The next guy, with no bunt in mind, slapped another to right. Pat's pace quickened. His face scarlet, from his mouth, sudden and raw, like searing lava, came a gush of profanity that would have made the venerable Babe blush. Seated next to me was our manager, Edgar Hartery, a rather corpulent fellow himself. He sat in silence, his stony face hardened by worry and frozen in fear of Pat's simmering wrath. Doubt had left our bench now and crept onto the field. It seemed to slacken their shoulders and make heavy their steps. Two men on base. Nobody out. Pat alone moved now. We all sat, rendered lifeless, faint prayers offered to the summer sun. 'Jesus!' jumped from that panicked mouth. 'We've got to light a fire under these guys!'

"Pat was close to a coronary. Whether it was Pat's invocation of spiritual aid or the tread of deviousness that I was blessed with at birth, something sparked within me. Without a word, I hastily gathered the swirl of paper candy wrappers and debris that add an odd aura to any dugout. Edgar watched in muted curiosity. The dugouts in Corner Brook are truly dug out. Some four feet below field level, they have a cement canopy overhead. Everyone, besides Edgar, was unaware of my paper collecting. Pat still paced, still swore, eyes devouring each pitch. A large, dented garbage can squat half full in the corner of the dugout. I quickly helped it find its capacity. When in hushed tones I asked Edgar for his lighter, the first hint of understanding and disbelief crossed his face. 'What are you doin'?' 'Pat said to light a fire under these guys, so I'm lightin' a fire.' As the first flames licked the dugout walls and a choking smoke mushroomed onto the field, I doubt if any of the old-timers who had perched for so many bright summers in the worn bleachers that ringed the diamond had ever witnessed the like.

"The flames continued to flick and the smoke belched and everything and everyone stopped, caught in the strangeness of the moment. As the inferno subsided, shock turned to laughter. I sat there, as dumbstruck as the rest, never revealing my guilt. In a moment it was over and the game resumed. Two men aboard. But then something happened. A line drive out. A strikeout. A fly to left. Zero runs. Into the smoke-stained dugout they raced, ready to fight back and fight back we did. In the gleeful unpredictability of sports we scored four runs and went on to win.

"Had our boys needed something to shake their lethargy? Had the strange humor of the moment relaxed those tense muscles? Had some fire-hungry deity been appeased that splendid afternoon? Had the tongues of flame rhymed some sacred chant, lifting our battered spirits and filling them with the fire of hope, the impassioned heat of promise? The promise that we could win. The promise that baseball always gives, even if it does tempt and tease. The promise so clearly held within its definite white lines, the promise of summer, the promise of youth, the promise that will always lead us home."

From coast to coast in Canada, they are playing baseball.
And they are telling stories.

AU REVOIR, WHICH
MEANS GOOD BYE

17

On Sept. 29, 2004, Claude Raymond arrived at Olympic Stadium just before 11 a.m. for an organizational meeting to discuss the 2005 season. The meeting didn't end until 3:15 p.m. About 15 minutes later, Expo president Tony Tavares entered the clubhouse and announced that the Expos, owned by Major League Baseball, would play the 2005 season in Washington, D.C.

"Players were happy, 81 home games in one place, less travel, they didn't have to go through customs and immigration—everyone in the room was happy but me," Raymond said. "I put my head down, waited and waited. Then I went in front of my locker and put my head down again."

And so it was that the fifth consecutive final September for baseball in Montreal turned out to be the real one.

"It's like having a sick friend for three years and knowing he's going to die," Sebastien Rivest, 24, of Baseball Quebec said. "But when it does happen, it's still a shock. I'm going to remember my father taking me to the Big O for the first time ... a lot of memories are going away."

While Tavares talked about how it was a good business decision for the franchise to leave Montreal, we looked around at the long-time employees and thought about the team that was brand new when we were 18. We thought of our father, of driving from Kingston to Jarry Park. He would have one eye on the approaching storm clouds, as the whole car worried whether the game would be cancelled, and one eye on the road. That was scary, because dad lost his left eye playing football at Queen's. We once had a string of three straight rain outs: drive to Montreal, await the news, eat at a brasserie and head home. Who would have thought that 10 years later we'd be sitting in seat No. 13 in the first row of the press box covering the Expos?

We covered the Expos from 1979 until 1986, an era when writers traveled on charter flights and had more access. It was a different time. No one made $15 million a season. Players told stories and jokes. We thought of friendships. Like Bob Dunn, Ian MacDonald and Michael Farber, and the laughs we had. And especially Serge Touchette of *Le Journal de Montreal*. Lefty Neal Heaton, who had allowed 39 homers in two years, was dealt to the Pittsburgh Pirates in the spring of 1989. A writer told Heaton he wold pitch better with the Bucs, since they had such an outfield with Barry Bonds, Andy Van Slyke and Bobby Bonilla. Asked Serge: "Where are they going to play? The 14th row?" On the Expos' final day in Montreal, we thought of friendships, of father and memories, and we cried at our seat in the press box. One of the best franchises in the game in the 1980s was about to become a footnote.

Peter Loyello grew up in Dollard Des Ormeaux, Quebec. He worked with the Expos and is now a vice-president with the Florida Marlins. His father Jim would take him and his brother Perry to games, first at Jarry Park and then at Olympic Stadium. "My dad would buy bleacher seats for my brother and me," Loyello said. "We would ask him questions during the game and he'd explain the game to us. You can't do that in a movie theatre. He made sacrifices to bring us to the 1981 post-season games against the Philadelphia Phillies." Loyello turned the tables for the final game, treating his mom, Madeleine, to the final home game. He met his buddies by the "oom-paa-paa" band, which used to rock in the 1980s. Like old times. In 1981, Jim took his sons to the Montreal Children's Hospital Celebrity Sports Gala and the brothers Loyello had their picture taken with outfielder Tim Raines. In 2001, Loyello had Raines autograph that picture. The last game Peter, his father Jim, and grandfather Jim went to was a 22-inning game in 1989, in which Rick Dempsey of the Los Angeles Dodgers homered to beat the Expos. Grandpa complained when they took him home after the 19th. Loyello was working for Triple-A Ottawa when he was hired by the Expos two days before the start of spring training in 1995. His parents were out of the country, so he clipped the note announcing his hiring from the *Montreal Gazette* and left it on the fridge. His parents phoned West Palm and "boy, was the old man ever pleased." Jim Loyello lost his battle to cancer in 1996 and Peter says: "I never really had the chance to thank him enough." Funny how fathers usually know just the same.

Fern Barette, 87, former press box custodian who took in Mack Jones, Warren Cromartie and Larry Parrish as boarders, was there at the final home game, saying: "Here for the first, here for the last." He walked down press row, saying goodbye to everyone a final time, and watching him, we cried all the way. Cheering and following the Expos was a love affair. Take Ari Mellios of the North Delta Blue Jays, who coached Justin Morneau and Jeff Francis. Those names are worth talking about, but when we mentioned the Expos, his former players were left in the dust. "You covered the Expos? You were there in 1981 when Rick Monday homered off Steve Rogers with the Expos a win away from the World Series?" he says excitedly from the west coast. Mellios grew up in Park Extension near Jarry Park and went to bed when the Expos were at home, with his window open, listening to P.A. man Claude Mouton announce: "John Boc-A-Bell-AH."

The Olympic Stadium was a haven for beer, smoked meat and hot dogs. With the Expos gone, a fan paid $2,605 for what is widely believed to be the last surviving hot dog of the Montreal era in Major League Baseball. Guy Laliberte, founder of the Cirque du Soleil, bid roughly 700 times the stadium price to win an online charity auction for the steamed wiener on a bun. The bun has been dried, varnished and placed with the replica wiener in the original Styrofoam container atop a trophy. And so, too, was the Expos franchise stuffed and mounted, anchored forever in baseball history with a career record of 2,755-2,943, for a .484 winning percentage.

Compared to Barette and Claude Raymond, Rivest, Loyello, and Mellios were Johnny-come-latelys to following the Expos. Raymond's background with the Expos goes back farther than Aug. 19, 1969, the first day he pitched in an Expo uniform. His Expo roots go all the way back to when he was asking fans to buy season tickets for a team which had not played a game. So, from before the first pitch to after the very last, Raymond, in succession a pitchman, a pitcher, a broadcaster and a coach, never stopped working for the Expos.

"In a few years if you say, 'I pitched for the Expos,' and people will say, 'You pitched for the what?' To hear that would break my heart," Raymond said. "What about guys like Steve Rogers, who played their whole career here? The Washington Senators moved to Texas. The St. Louis Browns moved to Baltimore. Nothing is left of their history. That's sad." The first French-Canadian, and maybe the proudest player, to ever wear an Expos uniform hopes no one takes whiteout to the history books for his team. "I was proud watching Rusty Staub, Gary Carter, Andre Dawson, Tim Wallach, Tim Raines, Dennis Martinez and Vladimir Guerrero, who might have been the best player in the world when he left," Raymond said. "I've been proud of my team and my city all along, except for the last few years when (owners) Claude Brochu and Jeffrey Loria took the team into the dumper."

Raymond, who still remembered, as a 10-year-old, watching Jackie Robinson break in with the old Montreal Royals at Delormier Downs, also recalled that every time "we had some good players, we lost them or sold them. The city of Montreal and the province of Quebec has good ball fans, but they became frustrated with ownership."

For die-hard Expos fans, following their fortunes was pure rollercoaster, akin to dating a woman who dumps you and keeps coming back to dump you again. Like being eliminated on the final day of the 1979 season, like being eliminated the next-to-last day of the 1980 season, like losing a berth in the World Series in 1981 on Monday's home run, or like being six games up on the Atlanta Braves on Aug. 12, 1994, when the players went on strike and Brochu was amongst the hardliners who didn't mind cancelling the entire post-season and, of course, the World Series. Legendary Montreal writer J.P. Sarault equated rooting for the Expos to being stuck in a room in a burning building with the air supply nearing an end. "You run to the first window, no luck, it's jammed," Sarault would say. "You go to the next window and you can't get that open either, it's just been painted. Finally, you head to the last window and you open it, you stick your head out the window and you are taking deep breaths, filling your lungs with deep breaths of fresh air ... and all of a sudden the window slams down on the back of your neck. That's what it is like to cheer for the Expos."

Expos broadcaster Dave Van Horne, like Raymond, was connected with the team from the beginning, welcoming listeners via television and radio with his customary "Glad to have you aboard." He's now working for the Florida Marlins, but the Expos memories run deep and he dug into them to come up his personal list of Top 10 memorable Expo moments:

10. The production of the Expos' farm system in the early years, with the arrival of homegrowns like Gary Carter, Andre Dawson, Tim Raines, Larry Parrish and Steve Rogers.

9. Vladimir Guerrero's 1999 season. Guerrero hit 42 homers and knocked in 131 runs. He finished the season with a .600 slugging percentage.

8. Mike Schmidt's two-run homer off Stan Bahnsen in 1980 with one out in the top of the 11th inning which gave the Philadelphia Phillies a 6-4 win and eliminated the Expos from the race before 50,794 at Olympic Stadium. The Expos had been leading 4-3 in the ninth inning when Bob Boone blooped a two-out single to centre off Woody Fryman to tie the game.

7. Pedro Martinez's 1997 season in which he won the Cy Young Award as he went 17-8 in 31 starts with a microscopic ERA of 1.90. Martinez fanned 305 in 241 1/3 innings to take 25 of the 28 first-place votes.

6. The 1994 Expos, which had a 74-40 record and sat six games up on the Atlanta Braves on Aug. 12 when contract talks stalled, the players went on strike and management refused to negotiate.

5. Bill Stoneman tossing a no-hitter against the Philadelphia Phillies April 17, 1969 at Connie Mack Stadium in Philadelphia before 6,496 fans. Deron Johnson bounced to shortstop Maury Wills for the final out

of the game, which was fitting as Stoneman retired 10 outs on ground balls. Rusty Staub's three-run homer in the fourth off Jerry Johnson was all Stoneman needed as the Expos climbed to 4-5 on the season.

4. Dennis "El Presidente" Martinez was perfect heading into the ninth inning, holding a 2-0 lead July 28, 1991 at Dodger Stadium. Martinez got Mike Scioscia to fly out to left and struck out Stan Javier. One to go. Martinez got pinch-hitter Chris Gwynn to fly out to Marquis Grissom in centre and as the ball came down Van Horne, working the game with Ken Singleton on TSN, declared, "El Presidente, El Perfecto."

3. The Expos' first game at Jarry Park, April 14, 1969 as Montreal edged the St. Louis Cardinals 8-7 before 29,184. Dan McGinn, who homered in the season opener, worked 5 1/3 innings of relief for the win. Mack Jones knocked in five runs, with a three-run homer in the first off Nelson Briles, and hit a two-run triple in the second. A star was born and so was Jonesville in the left-field bleachers. Yet, the 5-0 lead evaporated with a seven-run St. Louis fourth and it was 7-7 in the seventh when Coco Laboy doubled and scored on a McGinn single.

2. Right-hander Steve Rogers blanked Steve Carlton and the Philadelphia Phillies 3-0 in the deciding game of the National League division series Oct. 11, 1981 to move them into the National League Championship Series against the Los Angeles Dodgers. Rogers pitched a complete game, walking one, striking out two and knocking in two runs himself.

And Van Horne's No. 1 highlight in Expo history ...

1. The Expos' very first game, at Shea Stadium on April 8, 1969. Up 11-6, heading into announcer Russ Taylor's first nervy ninth. The Mets scored four times, as Duffy Dyer homered off Bob Shaw, before Gene Mauch brought in reliever Carroll Sembera. He allowed an infield single to Amos Otis and walked Tommy Agee before striking out Rod Gaspar to end the game. Shaw picked up the win and Cal Koonce took the loss. Coco Laboy hit a homer off Mets' reliever Ron Taylor of Toronto.

Fittingly, Van Horne, was on hand for the last home game, too, as the Expos' opposition on that fateful late September evening was the Florida Marlins, the team for which Van Horne now calls the play-by-play. The Marlins trounced the Expos 9-1 before 31,395 mourners, and when it was over the players gathered around as a video of the highlights of 36 years played on the scoreboard. When the clips were done, the players gathered around Raymond as he began to speak, in French, into the microphone. "I thanked them for the 36 years that they spent backing us," Raymond said. Some fans were crying, thinking of memories of years gone by. Others held infants in their arms; sure that one day they would tell them about this, the day baseball died in Montreal. "I thanked them for all the respect they showed me and the team over the years," Raymond said of his speech. "Finally I told them, maybe a miracle will happen."

And then Raymond, a man who never showed his emotions, stood on the Olympic Stadium carpet and cried. He turned to give the microphone to Brad Wilkerson, in his fourth season with the Expos, but Wilkerson was too upset to speak. "Wilkerson saw me crying and put his arm around me and he wound up in tears," Raymond said. "He tried to console me. First thing I knew I had to console him, he was so upset." Since Wilkerson was a no-go, Raymond gave the microphone to Jamey Carroll, in his third year. Carroll finished speaking, handed the mike to Livan Hernandez, and headed to hug Raymond. Hernandez, who played two seasons in Montreal, spoke in Spanish, gave the mike to Joey Eischen and then he too headed to wrap his burly arms around Raymond. Eischen did the same. Then another Expo, and another.

Finally, Raymond saw Tim Raines, promoted to the Expos as a coach in September, standing nearby and motioned for him to go next. Raines grew up an Expo, breaking in in 1979 and staying until 1990. Raines spoke from the heart—and touched his heart—of good times and bad times and fun times in Montreal. Of the five speakers, one spoke Spanish, three spoke English and one spoke French. It was difficult to hear upstairs in the press box. Maybe it was the sound system. Maybe it was that your ears don't function when you are weeping.

Raines wrapped his arms around Raymond. "When Raines finished I couldn't help but cry," Raymond said. "For all those players, those who spoke and those who didn't, that was the ultimate compliment for me. That they could make to an old man like me cry."

More and more players came to say that they were sorry Raymond had lost his team.

When he finally became disentangled from the grasp of players, he did some interviews and looked around. None of the fans wanted to leave. Neither did Raymond. He walked around some more, did more interviews and then instead of being 67, he felt 17 again. Baseball, it has often been said, is an unyielding, powerful mistress, with sorceress-like powers. Raymond headed to the mound "just to see what it feels like one last time." He looked up and there were 15 cameras between him and the mound.

Bob Natal, an Expo coach, found a ball for Raymond. Now, Raymond didn't have a catcher. A cameraman volunteered. And then Claude Raymond—not Marlins reliever Rudy Seanez, who got Terrmel Sledge to pop up to third baseman Mike Mordecai for the final out of the game, as the box score will show—reared back and threw the final pitch at Olympic Stadium

"I said to myself I don't want to leave this place, it might be the last time I am ever in here," Raymond said. He wandered around some more after that, not aimlessly, but thinking of the torrent of memories he'd had in an Expo uniform. Like in 1970, when he saved 23 games as the Expos went from 59 wins to 69 wins. Like Wallace Johnson's pinch-hit triple off Neil Allen at Shea Stadium in 1981 to clinch the second-half of the strike-marred season and win the National League East title. Raymond's son Claude-Marc, 33, arrived on the field. Claude-Marc was crying. His father started crying again. Raymond looked up to see his wife Rita crying in the seats. He went into the tunnel and into the clubhouse for a few minutes. He later emerged to see Rita outside the clubhouse and she said: "You're not dressed yet?" "Nope," Raymond said. "I'm going to drive home to St. Jean with my uniform on. If I take it off, I might lose it."

After the funeral, the Expos headed to New York, the same place where it all began 35 summers before, for the wake. They had three games remaining against the Mets. The final day was going to be another rough one, taking off the uniform for the last time. Bags had to be downstairs by 10 o'clock Sunday morning. Rita and Claude had sent them to the lobby of the New York Hilton with the bellman. The bus was at 10:30. It was a few minutes before they were going to leave when the phone called them back. "The phone rang as we headed toward the door and it was my daughter Natalie," Raymond said. Natalie, 34, had something to tell her father: "I know this is going to be a hard day for you, but I want to tell you that I am pregnant." Raymond said he went through the 162nd game of the Expos' final season, and the 5,698th and final game in franchise history "like it was any other game" since he was thinking of his next grandchild. Except that his mind kept drifting to moments and memories from thje past.

Like how pitching inside bothered Willie Mays and Roberto Clemente and got them off their game, but it didn't bother Willie McCovey and only got Hank Aaron angry. Like becoming the first French-Canadian to win a game in Montreal, with the Milwaukee Braves in a 7-5 win, May 16, 1969. Like how executives John McHale and Paul Richards helped to steer him on his path through the majors.

There were not a lot of role models for Raymond, or any Canadian chasing a big-league dream, when he signed in 1954 at the age of 17. At that point, there were four Canadians, all from Ontario, in the majors: right-hander Ozzie Van Brabant of Kingsville with the Philadelphia A's; outfielder Tom Burgess of London with the St. Louis Cardinals; right-hander Bob Hooper of Leamington with the Cleveland Indians, and Detroit Tigers infielder Reno Bertoia, who was raised in Windsor. Romeo Pilon, a scout with the Brooklyn Dodgers, signed Raymond after his dominating performances in junior play. The righty was invited to Delormier Downs, home of the Dodgers' Triple-A team, the Montreal Royals, for all the pomp and ceremony involved with signing a local player. "I signed, but I was still going to school," Raymond said. "The Dodgers were supposed to get permission from George Troutman of the commissioner's office and they didn't." The commissioner's office ruled that Raymond was a free agent and could sign with any team—except the Dodgers—after Feb. 1. Now, the chase was on. The Pittsburgh Pirates, the Cleveland Indians, the New York Giants and the Milwaukee Braves all wanted to sign Raymond. Since the Pirates had a franchise in the Class-C Provincial League, the St. Jean Canadians, they thought they had an edge. Rolland Raymond came home from work as a textile superintendent after his son Claude had visited the offices of the St. Jean club to talk with Pirates officials. That night, scout Roland Gladu of the Braves showed up at the Raymond house with his sales pitch. Later, the father said to his son: "Do you want to play for St. Jean or play ball and move up? Sign with the Braves if you want to move up."

As Raymond recalls, "I signed for two-fifty."

"You mean $250,000?" he is asked.

"No, $250; all I wanted was a chance," Raymond said.

The Braves and Pirates' offers were the same, but Milwaukee said they'd give him another $250 if he was still on the roster June 1 and $500 if he was on the roster Aug. 1. Rolland was not an athlete as he was injured in a farm accident, but Raymond's uncle, Gaston Raymond, was a solid hockey player—skating with Maurice Richard and Butch Bouchard with the Verdun juniors—and played baseball too. He taught Raymond "a lot about the game." He made his debut at Class-D West Palm Beach, progressed to Triple-A Wichita and then, in 1959, was selected by the Chicago White Sox in the Rule V draft. On Opening Day, April 10, he was at Tiger Stadium. "They called my name 'No. 28, Claude Ray-MAND' and I jogged out of the first base dugout. They sang the anthem and I thought to myself, 'Well, I made it to the big leagues, it was my dream ... once I got to Triple-A.'"

He returned to the majors with the Braves in 1961, playing part of that season and the next before going to the Houston Colt 45s in the expansion draft. Reacquired by the Braves, who had by now relocated to Atlanta, midway through the 1967 season, Raymond was with the club in Cincinnati in 1968 when they were about to announce the National League's two new expansion franchises. "I was so proud when Montreal got the team in 1968," Raymond said. "The Braves were in Cincinnati, staying at the Gibson Hotel. There wasn't any ESPN, so we watched the five minutes of sports and the broadcaster said: 'The expansion teams will be announced at midnight and it looks as if San Diego and Buffalo will get franchises.'" The next morning Raymond walked across the street and bought a paper to read Montreal and San Diego were granted franchises. "I told everyone what a great city Montreal was," Raymond said. That off-season, former Dodger Jean-Pierre Roy of Montreal, Verdun's Ron Piche of the Chicago Cubs and Raymond, now under contract to the Cubs, helped sell Expos season tickets for the expansion franchise, working the phones for their hometown team, trying to drum up business.

On May 16, 1969, with the Braves visiting Montreal and the score tied 5-5 in the 11th, manager Luman Harris called on Raymond. Intoned Jarry Park announcer Claude Mouton, "Coming in to pitch for the Braves ... No. 36 ... from St. Jean, Quebec ..." "I don't think the people even heard my name or whether it was even announced, the noise was so great and lasted so long," Raymond said. "It was very emotional. Normally, as a player I didn't let my emotions show." Raymond warmed up, admitting "I couldn't do anything ... the ball kept rolling out of my hand." Catcher Bob Tillman and first baseman Tito Francona came to the mound to settle down Raymond. "Hey, Frenchie," Francona said. "You've been telling us all along how great these fans were and how you wanted to pitch here. Now, kick yourself in the butt and let's go."

Gary Sutherland flew out to centre, then John Bateman singled and Manny Mota grounded into an inning-ending double play. Francona then hit a two-run homer off Elroy Face in the top of the 12th. Raymond set down the Expos, getting Don Bosch to ground to second. Maury Wills singled to centre, but Rusty Staub lined to left and Mack Jones bounced to short, making Raymond the first Canadian reliever to win a game in his home province in the majors. Three months later, on Aug. 19, Expos general manager John McHale, who had been Raymond's boss with the Braves, purchased the righthander's contract. He made his Expo debut the same day at Jarry Park, pitching a scoreless inning in a 5-4 loss to the San Diego Padres before 14,250 fans.

Raymond became manager Gene Mauch's closer in 1970, saving 23 games, good for fourth in the National League. But after struggling through 1971—1-7 with a 4.70 ERA—the reliever retired to the broadcast booth, where he toiled for 30 years as a French language broadcaster for the team, 18 years on television, 12 on radio, before Expo manager Frank Robinson hired him to coach in 2002. That's how he came to still be wearing that uniform at the end.

Looking to the future, Raymond wonders; "I think of senior citizens who used to listen to all the games on radio or watch the games on TV. This summer will be kind of boring." Asked about his favorite Expo memories, he picks that final home game in 2004; picking up the win for the Braves in 1969 at Jarry Park; beating the New York Mets in 1981, and then adds a stunner. Tim Raines, infielder Bryan Little, Raymond and Expos mascot Youppi made an off-season visit to St. Justin's Hospital in Montreal as part of the annual Expo caravan. Raymond was walking behind the group as they moved down the hall.

"I looked in a room and saw a little boy trying to move his TV," said Raymond, who went in to help. "First, he didn't talk. I asked if he had seen Raines, Little and Youppi. He had, so I told him we were going to the other wing and coming back to the play area where the two wings meet. I told him he should come, but he said he wanted to watch TV." The nurse told Raymond he'd taken on a difficult assignment. The boy, who had each leg in a cast, had not been out of his room in more than a year. The Expo group returned to the play area and there they saw the youngster coming down the hall, moving slowly on his crutches. "That was better than a win or a save," Raymond said. Such was the hold the Expos once had on the city of Montreal, and its hearts.

The old pitcher called his final three years as a coach in Montreal his best in the game. "Never in those three years did I not want to get to the park early," Raymond said. Robinson treated him with respect, after Expo vice-president Claude Delorme had suggested his name as a coach, and even spoke to Raymond about joining him in Washington, until it developed that the Nationals' new general manager, Jim Bowden, "wanted his own people."

Still, Raymond planned to head for the Nationals' spring training camp in Melbourne, Florida, just the same. Old habits die hard.

"So, I'll watch them work out and walk on the beach," said the ultimate Expo.

THE NORTHERN GAME

18

My best weekend ever in baseball—from playing second in the Kingscourt Little League, to being the batboy for father's Kingston Dunbricks, to coaching peewee and senior teams for 35 years, to covering major-league baseball across the continent—was the final weekend of July, 1999, when I got to hob-nob with some of the game's all-time greats at Cooperstown, New York. As the crow flies, Cooperstown is only about 130 miles from Kingston. But, really, for a kid who spent dreamy Saturday mornings in Bert Vince's Smoke Shop on Princess Street, we're talking about traveling to the moon.

As president of the Baseball Writers of America Association—no big deal, it rotates city by city on a yearly basis—I was invited to speak ... er, mumble ... at the National Baseball Hall of Fame induction ceremonies. It was a banner year, with Robin Yount, Nolan Ryan, George Brett and Orlando Cepeda leading the list of the seven inductees. Thankfully, due to the large cast of inductees, my scheduled five-minute speech was reduced to just a few opening remarks. All I had to do was welcome the crowd and present Bob Stephens of the *San Francisco Chronicle* with the 1998 J.G. Taylor Spink Award for meritorious contributions to baseball writing. Oh, and I should mention that I'd be standing in front of a future American president, a live audience of 50,000 at Cooperstown, and a North American television audience. It was a long way from the Cricket Field where I spent so many happy childhood hours with father but, then again, not so far at all. What to say to such an audience? What would father say? Easy. I told them I was proud to be Canadian ... and that baseball is the best game of them all.

Okay, so that might be heresy in many parts of Canada. After all, way back in 1859, the government of the day anointed lacrosse as "Canada's National Game". In 1994, an amendment, in the form of a private members' bill, C-212, was introduced into parliament. Canada's "National Sport Act", which subsequently passed unanimously, received royal assent and became law, states that the country wished officially: "To recognize Hockey as Canada's National Winter Sport and Lacrosse as Canada's

National Summer Sport."

But based on its long history, on its timeless character, on the distinct
way we have approached it and on our growing prominence in the major
leagues and internationally, you can make a pretty good argument that our
northern brand of baseball ought to be recognized, too, as something
distinct and special.

The chapters in this book are, we hope, a testament to that, though
they only really scratch the surface. Putting aside the minor pro leagues
and semi-pro leagues and amateur leagues and youth leagues, not to
mention the international game, Canada's contribution to major-league
baseball is in itself substantial. There are, of course, the 218 players. But as
well, there are so many others—owners, managers, coaches, executives,
umpires—who have each tread a unique path to a place in the game. Take
Milwaukee Brewers' general manager Doug Melvin, one of only four
Canadians to hold the GM post at the highest level (the others being Gord
Ash with the Toronto Blue Jays, Murray Cook with the Montreal Expos
and Cincinnati Reds, and George Selkirk with the old Washington
Senators).

Melvin, a Chatham native, was signed in 1971 for $1,000 by Ken
Beardslee of the Pirates after attending camps in Midland, Michigan for
three summers. "I didn't negotiate," said Melvin, a pitcher. "As a Canadian
all you were looking for in those days was an opportunity." Cook was the
Pirates' farm director at the time, but that was no help to Melvin when he
was released in 1973 after two years in Single-A. Looking for work, Melvin
headed to Florida and hooked up with Pat Gillick, the New York Yankees'
farm director, and Cloyd Boyer, the pitching coach. They gave him a
10-day contract, "you know, 'stay if you want,'" Melvin said. He stuck
around for six years, pitching in Single-A and Double-A, before asking
Jack Butterfield, the farm director, for a meeting.

Melvin: "Am I still a prospect?"

Butterfield: "No, you aren't."

Melvin: "I guess you don't want to have a conference call with all your
scouts and talk it over?"

Home he came to Chatham, not knowing what to do. He was home a
month when Butterfield called. With an older coaching staff of Yogi Berra,
Mike Hegan and Mickey Vernon, the Yankees needed help throwing
batting practice. The job paid $10,000. Melvin said yes and, before he'd
thrown his first pitch, got a $2,000 raise when the Yanks asked him to take
on the additional chore of charting games and being their eye in the sky.
Owner George Steinbrenner wanted him to help position new outfielders
Dave Winfield and Jerry Mumphrey, who'd come over from the National
League. In the off-season Melvin would return to Chatham, working as a

security guard or driving a furniture truck. Three seasons later, Melvin suddenly found himself promoted to Yankees' scouting director. When Cook failed to protect righty Tim Belcher from the Rule V draft, and he was taken by the Oakland A's, Steinbrenner fired one Canadian, Cook, and promoted another, Melvin, into his job.

Canadians are also owners—and we don't just mean ex-owners like J.J. Lannin of the Red Sox, Charles Bronfman of the Expos or R. Howard Webster of the Blue Jays—but current executives like Victoria native Jeff Mallett, one of the majority owners of the San Francisco Giants, Toronto's Jeffrey Royer, one of the four co-owners of the Arizona Diamondbacks, and Toronto's Ted Rogers with the Blue Jays. And they have been league executives. After leaving his post as president of the Blue Jays in 1997, Paul Beeston, of Welland, Ontario was hired as president of Major League Baseball, a post he held until 2002. At one point he was being touted by many owners as the logical successor to commissioner Bud Selig.

Canadians have also made their mark as coaches and instructors. To name a few, Dave MacKay of Vancouver, a St. Louis Cardinals' coach; Rob Thomson, of Coruna, Ontario, Team Canada catcher at the 1984 Olympics, who is now the Yankees' vice-president of player development and runs spring training for Joe Torre's team; Orv Franchuk of Lac La Biche, Alberta, a former Team Canada coach who is the minor-league hitting instructor for the Boston Red Sox; and Bobby McCullough of Toronto, a Team Canada grad (1981-85) who works on the grounds crew at Atlanta's Turner Field to make sure that there aren't any bad bounces for third baseman Chipper Jones.

Canadians have also made a mark as umpires. Jim McKean of Montreal, who played seven years with the Canadian Football League's Montreal Alouettes and Saskatchewan Roughriders, worked in the majors for 28 years and is now a supervisor of umpires. Paul Runge, of St. Catharines, umpired 25 seasons. Internationally, Don Gilbert of Windsor was named the International Amateur Baseball Federation umpire of the year in 2004. And then there is Shanna Kook of Toronto, the fifth female umpire to work in the minors. She was hired to work the Rookie-Class Pioneer league in 2003 and was there again in 2004. A second-year music student at McGill University in 2001, she was studying the viola when the sweeter strains of baseball beckoned. "I come from a very traditional Korean family," Kook said. "My father said no. My mother thought it would be best if I finished school first. I can always go back to school; I won't always be able to umpire."

And then there is a long list of poor souls who opted to forsake the baseball diamond altogether for the hockey rink. We're talking about two-sport stars who showed great potential in baseball but felt more comfortable on blades than cleats. Clark Gillies and Bob Bourne were signed by the Houston Astros before they went on to win Stanley Cups with the New York Islanders. Jason Woolley, Curtis Brown, Paul Ysebaert, and Yvon Corriveau all had to choose between baseball and hockey. For another of Canada's current sporting superstars, the choice wasn't between baseball and hockey. Bob Burrows remembers coaching a cat-like shortstop at Lambrick Park in Victoria, British Columbia, who, many said, was the best player in the province until he quit playing when he got to Grade 11. Turned out, mind you, that Steve Nash had something of a future ahead of him in the National Basketball Association.

Succeeding in baseball as a Canadian is all about perseverance. And that can come in many forms. There are players who are forever working hard on the fundamentals, but that is not always enough. Sometimes even the brightest prospect needs something more. Lise Devey, a teacher from Lachute, Quebec, was attending a conference where she met a baseball coach from the University of Southeastern Louisiana. Back home, she gave the coach's phone number to her son, Phil, a pitcher. "I must have spent $300 in long-distance phoning the coach to give me a chance," Phil Devey said. "Finally, the coach said, 'Okay, come down and you can walk on.'" Devey was drafted in the fifth round by the Los Angeles Dodgers in 1999 and pitched six scoreless innings against Australia in the Athens Olympics.

Scott Thorman had loved baseball all his life. When he was 12, he came across a contest in which the top prize was a week at the Ernie Whitt Baseball Academy. To enter, he had to write a letter to explain why he wanted to attend the camp. A month earlier, Scott's father had passed away. On May 28, 1994, his letter was published in the *Toronto Sun*. Here's some of what it said:

I am 12 years old and one day I hope everybody will recognize the name Scott Thorman, ace Blue Jay pitcher and rookie sensation. I've been playing ball since I was four. During the winter I play on a Triple-A hockey team, mostly to stay in shape for ball season.

Ever since I was five years old I have dreamed of playing baseball for the Jays. Baseball is easy for me, since I practice every day, but it's getting harder, because most of my friends refuse to catch for me. My fastball has been clocked at 68 miles per hour and is pretty accurate, but it hurts the catcher's hand. Sometimes other places (if I miss).

My mom is my biggest fan, always standing by me, even if I have a bad game. My mom knows I want to play pro ball someday and supports me, but tells me that when the game stops being fun, it is time to walk away. Up until now, my dad has been a coach on my team every year since T-ball. Sometimes this was hard. Now it is even harder. My father died of skin cancer April 23 (last week). I've been to a few practices since then

*and it sure seems different that he isn't there too. I know that he would
want me to keep doing what I love to do, but I really miss him.*

*I still want to be a Jay someday, so I'll keep practicing. I've lost my
favorite coach, as well as my dad, so I know how hard this will be.
Maybe time at baseball school will help.*

*My dad can't coach me anymore, so I'll need help from somebody else
who knows baseball.*

Scott Thorman, 12

Thorman's letter from the heart earned him a week at the camp. He
attended more and more of Whitt's camps over the years, honing his
hitting skills under instructor Rick Johnston and his pitching mechanics
under Remo Cardinale. Six years later he became the first Canadian high
schooler ever selected in the first round as an infielder, by the Atlanta
Braves. Some clubs had him projected to go in the second round as a
pitcher. In 2003, he was with manager Ernie Whitt when Team Canada
qualified for the Olympics. Small world.

It's all about perseverance. Who knows, for some it can pay off in the
ultimate tribute to a ball player, an induction ceremony in Cooperstown.
So far, only one Canadian, pitcher Ferguson Jenkins, has made it. But you
have to think that if he plays a few more seasons, Larry Walker would have
a pretty decent shot. And, down the road a bit, how about Eric Gagne?

As for me, one induction speaking engagement was enough to last a
lifetime. That 1999 weekend began on the Friday night at the Otesaga
Hotel in Cooperstown at a cocktail party where the first guy I bumped
into was George Brett, who reminded me of a trip I'd made to Kansas City
in 1988. Kevin Boland, a former newspaper writer in Toronto, had asked
me to deliver an audiotape to Brett. I found Brett in the K.C. clubhouse
and gave it to him. The next night, during batting practice he came over,
blue eyes bugging beneath the bill of his blue helmet. "Know what was on
that tape?" Brett asked. I said no. "It was a lengthy interview with Charlie
Lau explaining his hitting theories."

Lau had been Brett's mentor and died in 1984. Brett was fired up. He
said he'd been up until 4 a.m. and had listened to the tape four times,
calling it a wonderful refresher course. "What do you think, three hits
tonight?" I asked. He replied: "Three line drives for sure." He had four
hits.

My son had joined me for the trek to Cooperstown. When I was young,
I'd spent countless hours with my dad and his pals as they talked baseball.
Now, Bob Jr. was at my side as we spoke to Hall of Famers Jim Palmer,
Nolan Ryan, Bobby Doerr and Enos "Country" Slaughter. We bumped
into Pete Rose at a restaurant on Sunday. On the Saturday tour of the Hall
we ran into Texas Governor George W. Bush. When we first encountered

Bush, he ran the Texas Rangers. He was the son of the President, George Bush, back then, and he'd shoot the breeze with writers behind the batting cage at Arlington Stadium. Sometimes he'd point out a secret service man who'd be standing in the shade of the second-deck overhang, hiding from the 100-degree heat instead of keeping close tabs on Bush. "Watch this," Bush would say, and then he'd clap his hands loudly. The secret service man would recoil as the noise crackled in his earpiece.

In Cooperstown, we reminded the future President what a difficult interview he'd been when we sat with him for five innings in Port Charlotte, Florida in 1991, as the Jays played his Rangers. He was shocked and asked why. The problem, I said, was that he was seated to my right in the box seats along the first-base line. It's common practise to look interview subjects in the eye, but that would have been potentially suicidal this day because, as I explained to Bush, with a grunting Nolan Ryan firing heat, the Jays' right-handed hitters, failing to get around on Ryan's fastball, kept fouling pitches our way. Etiquette suggested I should be looking at my conversation partner, but survival dictated I keep an eye on the ball. With that, I got my son away from Bush before he could ask the presidential candidate if he thought he actually could beat wrassler Hulk Hogan, who was thinking of running for U.S. president.

The next day the people on the dais met behind the stage in the lobby of a hockey rink, where I ran into former Jays president Paul Beeston, then the CEO of Major League Baseball and a man who knew my deep-seated aversion to public speaking. Better that I could have stuck my hand into a rattlesnake's nest. "THERE ARE 50,000 PEOPLE OUT THERE, IT'S ON ESPN, IT'S ON TSN, DON'T SCREW IT UP!" Beeston yelled. "IF YOU FOUL UP YOU WILL EMBARRASS OUR WHOLE COUNTRY!"

Just what my nerves needed. We headed elsewhere, walking aimlessly amongst the Hall of Famers, when all of a sudden we heard: "Hey you, over here." It was Willie Mays, he was talking to me. "You and me are going to talk baseball, let's go ..." Mays said. Surely he was not a *Toronto Sun* reader. I asked why and he said, "start talking and eventually you'll know why." Me? Talking ball with Willie Mays? Not even the best stories from Harv Milne's Bicycle Repair Shop all those years before had an ending like this.

"Okay, I got one," I told the best player in the room. The Jays had been at Yankee Stadium that April as the Yankees paid tribute to the legend Joe DiMaggio, who had died during spring training. DiMaggio always insisted upon being introduced at banquets as the "greatest living ball player." It didn't matter where he was, or whether Ted Williams, Hank Aaron or Mays was also there. The previous month we were in Montreal and asked Expo manager Felipe Alou who he thought was the greatest living player. Starting in 1958, Alou played six years in right field alongside center fielder Mays with the San Francisco Giants. Traded to the Milwaukee Braves in 1963, he spent six years in center alongside right fielder Henry Aaron.

"Who did Felipe pick? Who did he pick?" said Mays, who was sloped over the way a lot of 68-year-olds are. When I told him that Alou had picked him, Mays stood as erect as a West Point cadet. Alou reasoned that he had played with Mays in winter ball, in Japan and in the majors and he'd "never seen anyone as intense. He is the one player I tell my children that I played with. He was a slugger with speed, ran headlong into fences and never got hurt."

During my story I'd noticed Governor Bush to Mays' left and New York Governor George Pataki to his right. Mays would rather talk to a dopey ball writer than a politician.

Then it was show time, and Cincinnati Reds broadcaster George Grande gave out way too many compliments when he introduced me. I got through my opening remarks okay, said how indeed I was proud to be from Canada, "like Ferguson Jenkins to my left and Paul Beeston to my right and like Larry Walker. At the risk of not being allowed back into the country by immigration, I'm here to say that baseball is the best game of them all."

They told me later some people cheered. A couple of other comments and I'd be done, save for reading the inscription on the Spink plaque. This was going to be a snap. Why had I even worried? Four graphs down, one to go ... and I tripped over the word "accurate." Not once, not twice, but three times. Listeners heard "act-U-lat, act-EUR-Lat, and act-Uh-ler-ate." Finally, I said, "aw, I just write it, I can't pronounce it."

After pictures were taken, on the way to my seat Hall of Famer Brooks Robinson motioned me over. I was expecting a good-natured shot. He stuck out his hand. "Good job, son, you did fine." Whispered Bob Feller, the Cleveland Indians' Hall of Famer seated beside me: "One good thing, you kept it damn short."

Ted Williams, confined to a wheelchair, left part way through the ceremony and was given a standing ovation. Williams was my father's favorite player and I thought somewhere from above the hills outside Cooperstown, my father must be watching it all unfold. There was a commercial break with George Brett on deck to speak, so we headed to the arena and the washroom. Governor Bush, having heard Nolan Ryan speak, was getting into his van to make a flight home. Bush got out of the van and we shook hands. I moved quickly with my right hand to put it up to my mouth to whisper something to him, but the words never came. Instead, implanted in my chest with a thud, was the sharp elbow of a Texas

Ranger—not the ballplayer kind, but the pistol-packing kind.

"He's okay," Bush said. "What were you going to say?" I could only reply that I lost my train of thought when the elbow landed.

Growing up in Kingston, former players often dropped by my father's house. One night Harold Buck arrived about 15 minutes before we left for a peewee game. (I played for the Tigers and a patient coach named Jimmy McLaughlin.) Buck was called "Hair Pin." I asked father why and he said it was becasue Buck was wound a bit too tight and was prone to do things that were unexpected, like a woman's hair pin flying loose.

On the way to the game, Buck began telling stories. Like the one about how, when he played the infield, he'd ask a runner to step off the bag so he could straighten it and then, with the ball in his hand, tag him out. Or, when someone slid in on a bang-bang play, he'd tell the runner it was a foul ball. The guy would retreat to first and he'd throw him out. They were great stories for a 12-year-old, but did things like that really happen? When one of the umps failed to show for the game, Buck volunteered to work the bases. Walking onto the field he winked at me and the light bulb went on. Sure enough, the first time a guy stole second, he was safe. Holding the ball, I asked him to step off the base so I could straighten the bag. He did, was tagged and Buck screamed: "Yer out!"

From father to father's former player to father's son.

Two innings later a guy slid in safely on a bang-bang play and I said, "foul ball." Up he got and trudged to first. I threw to first and—perhaps this is the reason I became a writer—the throw sailed wide and he arrived safe. Driving to the park that evening I already had a deep love of baseball, formed while reading *The Sporting News* on the bottom rung of the news-stand at Bert Vince's Smoke Shop in Kingston. When the opposing coach complained to Buck about my trickery, my heart beat faster. What would happen now? Buck returned to his position and gave me another wink. With that, my love affair with baseball was crystallized.

Over the years, ballpark memories have been made thousands of times with thousands of youngsters in hundreds of towns across this country. For many, they would be moments to treasure or to share later when getting together with old friends. For others, they would be moments that launched college and pro careers leading to the minors, the majors, and even around the world, playing for Team Canada.

That's the magic of the game, a made-in-Canada magic. These days it is clearly spreading, taking more Canadians to the forefront of the sport than ever before. The northern game is entering a new, golden era.

I meant what I had said in Cooperstown. Baseball really is the best game of all.

Appendix A

CANADA'S MAJOR LEAGUERS

Below are career statistical summaries through the 2004 season for the 218 Canadians who have played at least one game since 1871 in the major leagues, divided into separate lists for 121 batters and 100 pitchers. Three batters who also have pitching records—Joe Knight, Tip O'Neill and Fred Osborne—are on both lists. In instances where a player was foreign-born but raised in Canada (four Americans, two Italians, one Irishman), he has been included here. Also included is Kirk McCaskill, born in Kapuskasing, Ontario but raised in the United States. As well, the five Canadian managers from the major leagues are listed.

Each player entry comprises three lines of information:

• The first line provides basic biographical data, including date and place of birth and, when applicable, death date.

• The second line lists the player's most common position, his batting/throwing preference (left or right, or both), the years he played in the majors and his teams.

• The third line lists his career statistical totals in 10 categories for batters and 11 for pitchers.

In baseball's early years statistics were not kept for runs batted in and stolen bases, and when a total is stated as "—" it indicates the statistic is not known.

The statistics and biographical information are courtesy of *Total Baseball: The Ultimate Baseball Encyclopedia*, with assists from research by Larry Humber and The Society for American Baseball Research (SABR).

Dating back to 1871, seven leagues are widely recognized as being "major leagues."

The leagues are abbreviated here as follows:

National League (-N)   American League (-A)
National Association (-n)   American Association (-a)
Union Association (-u)   Players League (-P)
Federal League (-F)

Teams are abbreviated as follows:

Anaheim-Ana; Arizona-Ari; Altoona-Alt; Atlanta-Atl; Baltimore-Bal;
Boston-Bos; Brooklyn-Bro; Brooklyn Atlantics-BroA; Brooklyn
Eckfords-BroE; Buffalo-Buf; California-Cal; Chicago-Chi; Cincinnati-Cin;
Cleveland-Cle; Colorado-Col; Columbus-Clb; Detroit-Det; Florida-Fla;
Houston-Hou; Indiana-Ind; Kansas City-KC; Los Angeles-LA;
Louisville-Lou; Milwaukee-Mil; Minnesota-Min; Montreal-Mon;
New York-NY; Oakland-Oak; Philadelphia-Phi; Pittsburgh-Pit;
Providence-Pro; Rochester-Roc; San Diego-SD; San Francisco-SF;
Seattle-Sea; St. Louis-Stl; St.Paul-Stp; Tampa Bay-TB; Texas-Tex;
Toronto-Tor; Troy-Tro; Washington-Was; Worchester-Wor.

The key to the statistical columns is as follows:

Batting—Games Played–G, At-bats–AB; Runs–R; Hits–H; Doubles–2B;
Triples–3B; Home Runs–HR; Runs Batted In–RBI; Stolen Bases–SB;
Batting Average–Avg.

Pitching—Wins–W; Losses–L; Winning Percentage–PCT; Games
Played–G; Game Starts–GS; Complete Games–CG; Shutouts–SH;
Saves–SV; Innings Pitched–IP; Strikeouts–SO; Earned Run Average–ERA.

Managing—Years–Yrs; Games Managed–G; Wins–W; Losses–L; Winning
Percentage–PCT.

BATTERS

G	AB	R	H	2B	3B	HR	RBI	SB	Avg.

ANDRUS, WIMAN: b:10/14/1858, Orono, ON, d:6/17/1935
3B, B-/T-, 1885 Pro-N

| 1 | 4 | 0 | 0 | 0 | 0 | 0 | 0 | — | .000 |

ARCHER, JIMMY: b:5/13/1883, Dublin, Ireland (raised in Toronto, ON), d:3/29/1958
C, BR/TR, 1904-18 Pit-N, Det-A, Chi-N, Bro-N, Cin-N

| 847 | 2646 | 246 | 660 | 106 | 34 | 16 | 296 | 36 | .249 |

BALAZ, JOHN: b:11/24/1950, Toronto, ON
OF, BR/TR, 1974-75 Cal-A

| 59 | 162 | 14 | 39 | 8 | 1 | 2 | 15 | 0 | .241 |

BARTON, VINCE: b:2/1/1908, Edmonton, AB, d:9/13/1973
OF, BL/TR, 1931-32 Chi-N

| 102 | 373 | 64 | 87 | 12 | 4 | 16 | 65 | 1 | .233 |

BAY, JASON: b:9/20/1978, Trail, BC
OF, BR/TR, 2003-04 SD-N, Pit-N

| 150 | 498 | 76 | 141 | 31 | 5 | 30 | 96 | 7 | .283 |

BERTOIA, RENO: b:1/8/1935, St. Vito Udine, Italy (raised in Windsor, ON)
3B, BR/TR, 1953-62 Det-A, Was-A, KC-A, Min-A

| 612 | 1745 | 204 | 425 | 60 | 10 | 27 | 171 | 16 | .244 |

BIASATTI, HANK: b:1/14/1922, Beano, Italy (raised in Windsor, ON), d:4/20/1996
1B, BL/TL, 1949 Phi-A

| 21 | 24 | 6 | 2 | 2 | 0 | 0 | 2 | 0 | .083 |

BRANNOCK, MIKE: b:10/25/1851, Douglas, MA (raised in Guelph, ON)
3B, B-/T-, 1871-75 Chi-n

| 5 | 23 | 4 | 2 | 0 | 0 | 0 | 0 | 2 | .087 |

BURGESS, TOM: b:9/1/1927, London, ON
1B, BL/TL, 1954-62 Stl-N, LA-A

| 104 | 164 | 19 | 29 | 8 | 1 | 2 | 14 | 2 | .177 |

G	AB	R	H	2B	3B	HR	RBI	SB	Avg.

BUTLER, RICH: b:5/1/1973, Toronto, ON
OF, BL/TR, 1997-99 Tor-A, TB-A

| 86 | 251 | 30 | 56 | 5 | 3 | 7 | 22 | 4 | .223 |

BUTLER, ROB: b:4/10/1970, Toronto, ON
OF, BL/TL, 1993-99 Tor-A, Phi-N

| 109 | 218 | 32 | 53 | 13 | 2 | 0 | 21 | 3 | .243 |

CAMERON, JACK: b:9/22/1884, Sydney, NS, d:7/12/1963
OF, B-/TR, 1906 Bos-N

| 18 | 61 | 3 | 11 | 0 | 0 | 0 | 4 | 0 | .180 |

CASEY, BOB: b:1/26/1859, Adolphustown, ON, d:11/28/1936
3B, B-/T-, 1882 Det-N

| 9 | 39 | 5 | 9 | 2 | 1 | 1 | 7 | — | .231 |

CLAPP, STUBBY: b:2/24/1973, Windsor, ON
2B, BB/TR, 2001 Stl-N

| 23 | 25 | 0 | 5 | 2 | 0 | 0 | 1 | 0 | .200 |

CLARKE, NIG: b:12/15/1882, Amherstburg, ON, d:6/15/1949
C, BL/TR, 1905-20 Cle-A, Det-A, Stl-A, Phi-N, Pit-N

| 506 | 1536 | 157 | 390 | 64 | 20 | 6 | 127 | 16 | .254 |

COCKMAN, JIM: b:4/26/1873, Guelph, ON, d:9/28/1947
3B, BR/TR, 1905 NY-A

| 13 | 38 | 5 | 4 | 0 | 0 | 0 | 2 | 2 | .105 |

COLLINS, CHUB: b:10/12/1857, Dundas, ON, d:5/20/1914
2B, BB/TR, 1884-85 Buf-N, Ind-a, Det-N

| 97 | 362 | 50 | 71 | 9 | 3 | 0 | 26 | — | .196 |

COLMAN, FRANK: b:3/2/1918, London, ON, d:2/19/1983
OF, BL/TL, 1942-47 Pit-N, NY-A

| 271 | 571 | 66 | 130 | 25 | 8 | 15 | 106 | 0 | .228 |

CONGALTON, BUNK: b:1/24/1875, Guelph, ON, d:8/19/1937
OF, BL/TL, 1902-7 Chi-N, Cle-A, Bos-A

| 309 | 1172 | 117 | 342 | 27 | 13 | 6 | 131 | 32 | .292 |

DALY, TOM: b:12/12/1891, St. John, NB, d:11/7/1946
C, BR/TR, 1913-21 Chi-A, Cle-A, Chi-N

| 244 | 540 | 49 | 129 | 17 | 3 | 0 | 55 | 5 | .239 |

DEE, SHORTY: b:10/4/1889, Halifax, NS, d:8/12/1971
SS, BR/TR, 1915 Stl-A

| 1 | 3 | 1 | 0 | 0 | 0 | 0 | 0 | 0 | .000 |

DORSEY, JERRY: b:-/-/1854, d:11/3/1938
OF, BL/T-, 1884 Bal-U

| 1 | 0 | 0 | 0 | 0 | 0 | — | — | .000 |

DUCEY, ROB: b:5/24/1965, Toronto, ON
OF, BL/TR, 1987-2001 Tor-A, Cal-A, Tex-A, Sea-A, Phi-N, Mon-N

| 703 | 1279 | 190 | 309 | 78 | 13 | 31 | 146 | 22 | .242 |

DUGAS, GUS: b:3/24/1907, St. Jean de Matha, QC, d:4/14/1997
OF, BL/TL, 1930-34 Pit-N, Phi-N, Was-A

| 125 | 218 | 27 | 45 | 9 | 3 | 3 | 23 | 0 | .206 |

DUNN, STEVE: b:12/21/1858, London, ON, d:5/5/1933
1B, BL/T-, 1884 Stp-U

| 9 | 32 | 8 | 2 | 0 | 0 | — | — | .250 |

ERAUTT, JOE: b:9/1/1921, Vibank, SK, d:10/6/1976
C, BR/TR, 1950-51 Chi-A

| 32 | 43 | 3 | 8 | 1 | 0 | 0 | 1 | 0 | .186 |

FROBEL, DOUG: b:6/6/1959, Ottawa, ON
OF, BL/TR, 1982-87 Pit-N, Mon-N, Cle-A

| 268 | 542 | 70 | 109 | 21 | 4 | 20 | 58 | 13 | .201 |

GARDNER, ALEX: b:4/28/1861, Toronto, ON, d:6/18/1926
C, BR/T-, 1884 Was-a

| 1 | 3 | 0 | 0 | 0 | 0 | 0 | 0 | — | .000 |

GIBSON, GEORGE: b:7/22/1880, London, ON, d:1/25/1967
C, BR/TR, 1905-18 Pit-N, NY-N

| 1213 | 3776 | 295 | 893 | 142 | 49 | 15 | 345 | 40 | .236 |

G	AB	R	H	2B	3B	HR	RBI	SB	Avg.

GILLESPIE, JIM: b: Ontario
OF, BL/TR, 1890 Buf-P

G	AB	R	H	2B	3B	HR	RBI	SB	Avg.
1	3	0	0	0	0	0	0	0	.000

GLADU, ROLAND: b:5/10/1911, Montreal, QC, d:7/26/1994
3B, BL/TR, 1944 Bos-N

21	66	5	16	2	1	1	7	0	.242

GORBOUS, GLEN: b:7/8/1930, Drumheller, AB, d:6/12/1990
OF, BL/TR, 1955-57 Cin-N, Phi-N

117	277	29	66	13	1	4	29	0	.238

GRANEY, JACK: b:6/10/1886, St. Thomas, ON, d:4/20/1978
OF, BL/TL, 1908-22 Cle-A

1402	4705	706	1178	219	79	18	420	148	.250

GUIEL, AARON: b:10/5/1972, Vancouver, BC
OF, BL/TR, 2002-04 KC-A

211	729	108	175	47	0	24	103	5	.240

HANNIFAN, PAT: b:4/20/1866, Halifax, NS, d:11/5/1908
OF, BB/TL, 1897 Bro-N

10	20	4	5	0	0	0	2	4	.250

HARKNESS, TIM: b:12/23/1937, Lachine, QC
1B, BL/TL, 1961-64 LA-N, NY-N

259	562	59	132	18	4	14	61	7	.235

HEATH, JEFF: b:4/1/1915, Fort William, ON, d:12/9/1975
OF, BL/TR, 1936-49 Cle-A, Stl-A, Was-A, Bos-N

1383	4937	777	1447	279	102	194	887	56	.293

HODGSON, PAUL: b:4/14/1960, Montreal, QC
OF, BR/TR, 1980 Tor-A

20	41	5	9	0	1	1	5	0	.220

HUMPHRIES, JOHN: b:11/12/1861, North Gower, ON, d:11/29/1933
C, BL/TL, 1883-84 NY-N, Was-a

98	364	34	52	3	0	0	6	—	.143

HUNTER, BILL: b:-/-/1855, St. Thomas, ON
C, BR/T-, 1884 Lou-a

2	7	1	1	0	0	0	0	—	.143

HYNDMAN, JIM: b:7/9/1866, Hamilton, ON, d:1/16/1934
OF, B-/T-, 1886 Phi-a

1	4	0	0	0	0	0	0	0	.000

IRWIN, ARTHUR: b:2/14/1858, Toronto, ON, d:7/16/1921
SS, BL/TR, 1880-94 Wor-N, Pro-N, Phi-N, Was-N, Bos-P, Bos-a

1010	3919	552	982	141	45	5	396	93	.251

IRWIN, JOHN: b:7/21/1861, Toronto, ON, d:2/28/1934
3B, BL/TR, 1882-91 Wor-N, Bos-U Phi-a, Was-N, Buf-P, Bos-a, Lou-a

322	1272	222	315	55	19	3	93	56	.248

JOHNSON, ABBIE: b:01/19/1874, London, ON, d:11/28/1960
2B, B-/T-, 1896-97 Lou-N

73	252	26	60	8	2	0	37	2	.238

JOHNSON, SPUD: b:-/-/1860
OF, BL/TL, 1889-91 Clb-a, Cle-N

331	1324	246	400	45	31	4	238	93	.302

JONES, BILL: b:4/8/1887, Hartland, NB, d:10/10/1946
OF, BL/TR, 1911-12 Bos-N

27	53	6	12	2	1	0	5	1	.226

KERR, MEL: b:5/22/1903, Souris, MB, d:8/9/1980
BL/TL, 1925 Chi-N

1	0	1	0	0	0	0	0	0	—

KLASSEN, DANNY: b:9/22/1975, Leamington, ON
3B, BR/TR, 1998-2003 Ari-N, Det-A

85	261	34	59	8	2	6	23	2	.226

KNIGHT, JONAH: b:9/28/1859, Port Stanley, ON, d:10/16/1938
OF, BL/TL, 1884-90 Phi-N, Cin-N

133	505	69	156	29	8	4	69	17	.309

G	AB	R	H	2B	3B	HR	RBI	SB	Avg.

KNOWLES, JIMMY: b:9/5/1856, Toronto, ON, d:2/11/1912
3B, BR/T-, 1884-92 Bro-a, Pit-a, Was-N, NY-a, Roc-a, NY-N

| 357 | 1389 | 185 | 335 | 40 | 28 | 9 | 132 | 83 | .241 |

KOSKIE, COREY: b:6/28/1973, Anola, MB
3B, BL/TR, 1998-2004 Min-A

| 816 | 2788 | 438 | 781 | 180 | 13 | 101 | 437 | 66 | .280 |

KYLE, ANDY: b:10/29/1889, Toronto, ON, d:9/6/1971
OF, BL/TL, 1912 Cin-N

| 9 | 21 | 3 | 7 | 1 | 0 | 0 | 4 | 0 | .333 |

LAFOREST, PETE: b:1/27/1978, Hull, QC
DH, BL/TR, 2003 TB-A

| 19 | 48 | 0 | 8 | 2 | 0 | 0 | 6 | 0 | .167 |

LAFOREST, TY: b:4/18/1917, Edmundston, NB, d:5/5/1947
3B, BR/TR, 1945 Bos-A

| 52 | 204 | 25 | 51 | 7 | 4 | 2 | 16 | 4 | .250 |

LAKE, FRED: b:10/16/1866, Cornwallis, NS, d:11/24/1931
C, BR/TR, 1891-1910 Bos-N, Lou-N, Pit-N

| 48 | 125 | 12 | 29 | 6 | 0 | 1 | 16 | 4 | .232 |

LAROQUE, SAM: b:2/26/1863, St. Mathias, QC, d:6/5/1933
2B, B-/TR, 1888-91 Det-N, Pit-N, Lou-a

| 124 | 482 | 66 | 120 | 22 | 5 | 2 | 50 | 28 | .249 |

LAWRENCE, JIM: b:2/12/1939, Hamilton, ON
C, BL/TR, 1963 Cle-A

| 2 | 0 | 0 | 0 | 0 | 0 | 0 | 0 | 0 | .000 |

LEPINE, PETE: b:9/5/1876, Montreal, QC, d:12/3/1949
OF, BL/TL, 1902 Det-A

| 30 | 96 | 8 | 20 | 3 | 2 | 1 | 19 | 1 | .208 |

LISI, RICK: b:3/17/1956, Halifax, NS
OF, BR/TR, 1981 Tex-A

| 9 | 16 | 6 | 5 | 0 | 0 | 0 | 1 | 0 | .312 |

LYONS, PAT: b:3/-/1860, Belleville, ON, d:1/20/1914
2B, BR/TR, 1890 Cle-N

| 11 | 38 | 2 | 2 | 1 | 0 | 0 | 1 | 0 | .053 |

MACKENZIE, ERIC: b:8/29/1932, Glendon, AB
C, BL/TR, 1955 KC-A

| 1 | 1 | 0 | 0 | 0 | 0 | 0 | 0 | 0 | .000 |

MCGOVERN, ART: b:2/27/1882, St. John, NB, d:11/14/1915
C, BR/TR, 1905 Bos-A

| 15 | 44 | 1 | 5 | 1 | 0 | 0 | 1 | 0 | .114 |

MCKAY, CODY: b:1/11/1974, Vancouver, BC
C, BL/TR, 2002, 2004 Oak-A, Stl-N

| 37 | 77 | 7 | 19 | 2 | 0 | 0 | 8 | 0 | .287 |

MCKAY, DAVE: b:3/14/1950, Vancouver, BC
2B, BB/TR, 1975-82 Min-A, Tor-A, Oak-A

| 645 | 1928 | 191 | 441 | 70 | 15 | 21 | 170 | 20 | .229 |

MCKEEVER, JIM: b:4/19/1861, St. John, NB, d:8/19/1897
C, BR/T-, 1884 Bos-U

| 16 | 66 | 13 | 9 | 0 | 0 | 0 | — | — | .136 |

MCLEAN, LARRY: b:7/18/1881, Fredericton, NB, d:3/24/1921
C, BR/TR, 1901-15 Bos-A, Chi-N, Stl-N, Cin-N, NY-N

| 862 | 2647 | 183 | 694 | 90 | 26 | 6 | 298 | 20 | .262 |

MCMILLAN, GEORGE: b:9/1/1863, Ontario, d:4/18/1920
OF, B-/T-, 1890 NY-N

| 10 | 35 | 4 | 5 | 0 | 0 | 0 | 1 | 1 | .143 |

MEAD, CHARLIE: b:4/9/1921, Vermillion, AB
OF, BL/TR, 1943-45 NY-N

| 87 | 261 | 18 | 64 | 8 | 1 | 3 | 27 | 3 | .245 |

MILLER, DOC: b:2/4/1883, Chatham, ON, d:7/31/1938
OF, BL/TL, 1910-14 Bos-N, Chi-N, Phi-N, Cin-N

| 557 | 1717 | 184 | 507 | 96 | 15 | 12 | 235 | 64 | .295 |

G	AB	R	H	2B	3B	HR	RBI	SB	Avg.

MOORE, JERRIE: b: Windsor, ON, d:9/26/1855
C, BL/T-, 1884-85 Alt-U Cle-N, Det-N

| 35 | 133 | 13 | 35 | 4 | 1 | 1 | 10 | — | .263 |

MORNEAU, JUSTIN: b:5/15/1981, New Westminster, BC
DH, BL/TR, 2003-04 Min-A

| 114 | 386 | 53 | 100 | 21 | 0 | 23 | 74 | 0 | .259 |

MORRISON, JON: b:-/-/1859, London, ON
OF, BL/T-, 1884-87 Ind-a, NY-a

| 53 | 222 | 33 | 58 | 6 | 8 | 1 | 3 | 0 | .261 |

MULLIN, HENRY: b:4/17/1862, St. John, NB, d:11/8/1937
OF, BR/T-, 1884 Bos-U Was-A

| 36 | 128 | 14 | 17 | 3 | 1 | 0 | 0 | — | .133 |

MURPHY, LARRY: b:3/17/1857, d:10/6/1911
OF, BL/T-, 1891 Was-a

| 101 | 400 | 73 | 106 | 15 | 3 | 1 | 35 | 29 | .265 |

NICHOLSON, KEVIN: b:3/29/1976, Vancouver, BC
SS, BB/TR, 2000 SD-N

| 37 | 97 | 7 | 21 | 6 | 1 | 1 | 8 | 1 | .216 |

O'BRIEN, JOHN: b:7/14/1870, St. John, NB, d:5/13/1913
2B, BL/TR, 1891-99 Bro-N, Chi-N, Lou-N, Was-N, Bal-N, Pit-N

| 501 | 1910 | 246 | 486 | 47 | 17 | 12 | 229 | 45 | .254 |

O'CONNOR, DAN: b:8/11/1868, Guelph, ON, d:3/3/1942
1B, BL/TR, 1890 Lou-a

| 6 | 26 | 3 | 12 | 1 | 1 | 0 | 5 | 5 | .462 |

O'HALLORAN, GREG: b:5/21/1968, Toronto, ON
C, BL/TR, 1994 Fla-N

| 12 | 11 | 1 | 2 | 0 | 0 | 0 | 1 | 0 | .182 |

O'HARA, BILL: b:8/14/1883, Toronto, ON, d:6/13/1931
OF, BL/TR, 1909-10 NY-N, Stl-N

| 124 | 380 | 49 | 88 | 9 | 3 | 1 | 32 | 31 | .232 |

O'NEILL, BILL: b:1/22/1880, St. John, NB, d:7/20/1920
OF, BB/TR, 1904-6 Bos-A, Was-A, Chi-A

| 206 | 746 | 77 | 181 | 15 | 2 | 2 | 42 | 41 | .243 |

O'NEILL, FRED: b:-/-/1865, London, ON, d:3/7/1892
OF, BR/T-, 1887 NY-a

| 6 | 27 | 4 | 9 | 1 | 1 | 0 | 3 | 3 | .333 |

O'NEILL, TIP: b:5/25/1858, Woodstock, ON, d:12/31/1915
OF, BR/TR, 1883-92 NY-N, Stl-a, Chi-P, Cin-N

| 1052 | 4298 | 879 | 1435 | 222 | 92 | 52 | 757 | 161 | .334 |

O'ROURKE, FRANK: b:11/28/1894, Hamilton, ON, d:5/14/1986
3B, BR/TR, 1912-31 Bos-N, Bro-N, Was-A, Bos-A, Det-A, Stl-A

| 1131 | 4069 | 547 | 1032 | 196 | 42 | 15 | 430 | 100 | .254 |

OSBORNE, FRED: b:5/-/1865, Alberta
OF, BL/TL, 1890 Pit-N

| 41 | 168 | 24 | 40 | 8 | 3 | 1 | 14 | 0 | .238 |

OSTROSSER, BRIAN: b:6/17/1949, Hamilton, ON
SS, BL/TR, 1973 NY-N

| 4 | 5 | 0 | 0 | 0 | 0 | 0 | 0 | 0 | .000 |

OWENS, FRANK: b:1/26/1886, Toronto, ON, d:7/2/1958
C, BR/TR, 1905-15 Bos-A, Chi-A, Bro-F, Bal-F

| 222 | 694 | 59 | 170 | 25 | 11 | 5 | 65 | 9 | .245 |

OXLEY, HENRY: b:1/4/1858, Covehead, PEI, d:10/12/1945
C, BR/T-, 1884 NY-N, NY-a

| 3 | 7 | 0 | 0 | 0 | 0 | 0 | 0 | — | .000 |

PHILLIPS, BILL: b:-/-/1857, Saint John, NB, d:10/7/1900
1B, BR/TR, 1879-88 Cle-N, Bro-a, KC-a

| 1038 | 4300 | 562 | 1175 | 214 | 98 | 17 | 534 | 39 | .273 |

PIRIE, JIM: b:3/31/1853, Ontario, d:6/2/1934
SS, BB/T-, 1883 Phi-N

| 5 | 19 | 1 | 3 | 0 | 0 | 0 | 0 | — | .158 |

G	AB	R	H	2B	3B	HR	RBI	SB	Avg.

POND, SIMON: b:10/27/1797, North Vancouver, BC
OF/DH, BL/TR, 2004 Tor-A

G	AB	R	H	2B	3B	HR	RBI	SB	Avg.
16	49	4	8	2	3	1	6	0	.163

PUHL, TERRY: b:7/8/1956, Melville, SK
OF, BL/TR, 1977-91 Hou-N, KC-A

G	AB	R	H	2B	3B	HR	RBI	SB	Avg.
1531	4855	676	1361	226	56	62	435	217	.280

RADMANOVICH, RYAN: b:8/9/1971, Calgary, AB
OF, BL/TR, 1998 Sea-A

G	AB	R	H	2B	3B	HR	RBI	SB	Avg.
25	69	5	15	4	0	2	10	1	.217

RANDALL, NEWT: b:2/3/1880, New Lowell, ON, d:5/3/1955
OF, BR/TR, 1907 Bos-N, Chi-N

G	AB	R	H	2B	3B	HR	RBI	SB	Avg.
97	336	22	71	10	5	0	19	6	.211

REID, BILLY: b:5/17/1857, London, ON, d:6/26/1940
2B, BL/TR, 1883-84 Bal-a, Pit-a

G	AB	R	H	2B	3B	HR	RBI	SB	Avg.
43	167	25	44	5	0	0	0	—	.263

REIMER, KEVIN: b:6/28/1964, Macon, GA (raised in Enderby, BC)
OF, BL/TR, 1988-93 Tex-A, Mil-A

G	AB	R	H	2B	3B	HR	RBI	SB	Avg.
488	1455	162	376	85	4	52	204	7	.258

RILEY, JIM: b:5/25/1895, Bayfield, NB, d:5/25/1969
2B, BL/TR, 1921-23 Stl-A, Was-A

G	AB	R	H	2B	3B	HR	RBI	SB	Avg.
6	14	1	0	0	0	0	0	0	.000

ROBERTSON, SHERRY: b:1/1/1919, Montreal, QC, d:10/23/1970
OF, BL/TR, 1940-52 Was-A, Phi-A

G	AB	R	H	2B	3B	HR	RBI	SB	Avg.
597	1507	200	346	55	18	26	151	32	.230

ROSEN, GOODY: b:8/28/1912, Toronto, ON, d:4/6/1994
OF, BL/TL, 1937-46 Bro-N, NY-N

G	AB	R	H	2B	3B	HR	RBI	SB	Avg.
551	1916	310	557	71	34	22	197	12	.291

ROWAN, DAVE: b:12/6/1882, Elora, ON, d:7/30/1955
1B, BL/TL, 1911 Stl-A

G	AB	R	H	2B	3B	HR	RBI	SB	Avg.
18	65	7	25	1	1	0	11	0	.385

SCANLON, PATRICK: b:3/25/1861, Halifax, NS, d:7/17/1913
OF, BL/T-, 1884 Bos-U

G	AB	R	H	2B	3B	HR	RBI	SB	Avg.
6	24	2	7	1	0	0	—	—	.292

SELKIRK, GEORGE: b:1/4/1908, Huntsville, ON, d:1/19/1987
OF, BL/TR, 1934-42 NY-A

G	AB	R	H	2B	3B	HR	RBI	SB	Avg.
846	2790	503	810	131	41	108	576	49	.290

SIDDALL, JOE: b:10/25/1967, Windsor, ON
C, BL/TR, 1993-98 Mon-N, Fla-N, Det-A

G	AB	R	H	2B	3B	HR	RBI	SB	Avg.
73	142	7	24	5	0	1	11	0	.169

SKETCHLEY, BUD: b:3/30/1919, Virden, MB, d:12/19/1979
OF, BL/TL, 1942 Chi-A

G	AB	R	H	2B	3B	HR	RBI	SB	Avg.
13	36	1	7	1	0	0	3	0	.194

SMITH, FRANK: b:11/24/1857, Fonthill, ON, d:10/11/1928
C, BR/T-, 1884 Pit-a

G	AB	R	H	2B	3B	HR	RBI	SB	Avg.
10	36	3	9	0	1	0	0	—	.250

SMITH, POP: b:10/12/1856, Digby, NS, d:4/18/1927
2B, BR/TR, 1880-91 Cin-N, Buf-N, Cle-N, Wor-N, Lou-a, Phi-a, Clb-a, Pit-a, Pit-N, Bos-N, Was-a

G	AB	R	H	2B	3B	HR	RBI	SB	Avg.
1112	4268	643	971	141	87	24	358	169	.228

SMITH, TOM: b:-/-/1851, Guelph, ON, d:3/28/1889
2B, BR/T-, 1875 BroA-n

G	AB	R	H	2B	3B	HR	RBI	SB	Avg.
3	13	0	1	0	0	0	1	0	.077

SNYDER, COONEY: b: Toronto, ON, d:3/9/1917
C, B-/T-, 1898 Lou-N

G	AB	R	H	2B	3B	HR	RBI	SB	Avg.
17	61	4	10	0	0	0	6	0	.164

STAIRS, MATT: b:2/27/1968, Fredericton, NB
OF, BL/TR, 1992-2004 Mon-N, Bos-A, Oak-A, Chi-N, Mil-N, Pit-N, KC-A

G	AB	R	H	2B	3B	HR	RBI	SB	Avg.
1172	3499	536	930	196	10	194	634	24	.266

STEWART, ANDY: b:12/5/1970, Oshawa, ON
C, BR/TR, 1997 KC-A

G	AB	R	H	2B	3B	HR	RBI	SB	Avg.
5	8	1	2	1	0	0	0	0	.250

G	AB	R	H	2B	3B	HR	RBI	SB	Avg.

SUMMERS, KID: b:1868, Toronto, ON, d:10/16/1895
C, BR/TR, 1893 Stl-N

| 2 | 1 | 1 | 0 | 0 | 0 | 0 | 0 | 0 | .000 |

THOMPSON, TUG: b:9/5/1856, London, ON, d:9/1/1938
OF, BL/TR, 1882-84 Cin-a, Ind-a

| 25 | 102 | 10 | 21 | 3 | 0 | 0 | 0 | — | .206 |

VADEBONCOEUR, GENE: b:7/15/1858, Louiseville, QC, d:10/16/1935
C, BR/TR, 1884 Phi-N

| 4 | 14 | 1 | 3 | 0 | 0 | 0 | 3 | — | .214 |

WALKER, LARRY: b:12/1/1966, Maple Ridge, BC
OF, BL/TR, 1989-2004 Mon-N, Col-N, Stl-N

| 1888 | 6592 | 1289 | 2069 | 451 | 61 | 368 | 1259 | 228 | .314 |

WARD, PETE: b:7/26/1939, Montreal, QC
3B, BL/TR, 1962-70 Bal-A, Chi-A, NY-A

| 973 | 3060 | 345 | 776 | 136 | 17 | 98 | 427 | 20 | .254 |

WATKINS, BILL: b:5/5/1858, Brantford, ON, d:6/9/1937
3B, BR/T-, 1884 Ind-a

| 34 | 127 | 16 | 26 | 4 | 0 | 0 | 0 | — | .205 |

WEBER, JOE: b:2/15/1862, Hamilton, ON, d:12/15/1921
OF, B-/T-, 1884 Det-N

| 2 | 8 | 0 | 0 | 0 | 0 | 0 | 0 | — | .000 |

WHITEHEAD, MILT: b:-/-/1862, Toronto, ON d:8/15/1901
SS, BB/TR, 1884 KC-U Stl-U

| 104 | 415 | 63 | 86 | 15 | 1 | 1 | — | — | .207 |

WILSON, NIGEL: b:1/12/1970, Oshawa, ON
OF, BL/TL, 1993-96 Fla-N, Cin-N, Cle-A

| 22 | 35 | 2 | 3 | 0 | 0 | 2 | 5 | 0 | .086 |

WINGO, ED: b:10/8/1895, Ste. Anne de Bellevue, QC, d:12/5/1964
C, BR/TR, 1920 Phi-A

| 1 | 4 | 0 | 1 | 0 | 0 | 0 | 1 | 0 | .250 |

WOOD, FRED: b:7/21/1865, Dundas, ON, d:8/23/1933
C, BR/T-, 1884-85 Det-N, Buf-N

| 13 | 46 | 4 | 3 | 0 | 0 | 0 | 1 | — | .065 |

WOOD, JIMMY: b:12/1/1844, Canada, d:11/30/1886
2B, B-/TR, 1871-73 Chi-n, BroE-n, Tro-n, Phi-n

| 102 | 487 | 162 | 162 | 33 | 12 | 3 | 83 | 30 | .333 |

PITCHERS

W	L	PCT	G	GS	CG	SH	SV	IP	SO	ERA

ALEXANDER, BOB: b:8/7/1922, Vancouver, BC, d:4/7/1993
BR/TR, 1955-57 Bal-A, Cle-A

| 1 | 1 | .500 | 9 | 0 | 0 | 0 | 0 | 11 | 2 | 10.64 |

ATKINSON, BILL: b:10/4/1954, Chatham, ON
BL/TR, 1976-79 Mon-N

| 11 | 4 | .733 | 98 | 0 | 0 | 0 | 11 | 147.1 | 99 | 3.42 |

AUCOIN, DEREK: b:3/27/1970, Lachine, QC
BR/TR, 1996 Mon-N

| 0 | 1 | .000 | 2 | 0 | 0 | 0 | 0 | 2.2 | 1 | 3.38 |

BAHR, ED: b:10/16/1919, Rouleau, SK
BR/TR, 1946-47 Pit-N

| 11 | 11 | .500 | 46 | 25 | 8 | 0 | 0 | 219 | 69 | 3.37 |

BEDARD, ERIK: b:3/5/1979, Navan, ON
BL/TL, 2002, 2004 Bal-A

| 6 | 10 | .375 | 29 | 26 | 0 | 0 | 0 | 170.1 | 122 | 4.63 |

BOUCHER, DENIS: b:3/7/1968, Montreal, QC
BR/TL, 1991-94 Cle-A, Tor-A, Mon-N

| 6 | 11 | .353 | 35 | 26 | 0 | 0 | 0 | 146 | 77 | 5.42 |

BOWSFIELD, TED: b:1/10/1935, Vernon, BC
BR/TL, 1958-64 Bos-A, Cle-A, LA-A, KC-A

| 37 | 39 | .487 | 215 | 86 | 12 | 4 | 6 | 662.1 | 326 | 4.35 |

W	L	PCT	G	GS	CG	SH	SV	IP	SO	ERA

BURNSIDE, SHELDON: b:12/22/1954, South Bend, IN
BR/TL, 1978-80 Det-A, Cin-N

W	L	PCT	G	GS	CG	SH	SV	IP	SO	ERA
2	1	.667	19	0	0	0	0	30	18	6.00

BUXTON, RALPH: b:6/7/1911, Weyburn, SK, d:1/6/1988
BR/TR, 1938-49 Phi-A, NY-A

0	2	.000	19	0	0	0	2	36	23	4.25

CALVERT, PAUL: b:10/6/1917, Montreal, QC, d:2/1/1999
BR/TR, 1942-51 Cle-A, Was-A, Det-A

9	22	.290	109	27	5	0	5	301.2	102	5.31

CLEVELAND, REGGIE: b:5/23/1948, Swift Current, SK
BR/TR, 1969-81 Stl-N, Bos-A, Tex-A, Mil-A

105	106	.498	428	203	57	12	25	1809	930	4.01

COOK, EARL: b:12/10/1908, Stouffville, ON, d:11/21/1996
BR/TR, 1941 Det-A

0	0	.000	1	0	0	0	0	2	1	4.50

CORMIER, RHEAL: b:4/23/1967, Moncton, NB
BL/TL, 1991-2004 Stl-N, Bos-A, Mon-N, Phi-N

65	59	.524	556	108	7	1	2	1123.1	706	4.01

CORT, BARRY: b:4/15/1956, Toronto, ON
BR/TR, 1977 Mil-A

1	1	.500	7	3	1	0	0	24.1	17	3.33

CRAIG, PETE: b:7/10/1940, LaSalle, ON
BL/TR, 1964-66 Was-A

0	3	.000	6	4	0	0	0	18	3	11.50

CRAIN, JESSE: b:7/5/1981, Toronto ON
BR/TR, 2004 Min-A

3	0	1.000	22	0	0	0	0	27	14	2.00

CROSBY, KEN: b:12/15/1947, New Denver, BC
BR/TR, 1975-76 Chi-N

1	0	1.000	16	1	0	0	0	20.1	11	8.41

CURRIE, CLARENCE: b:12/30/1878, Glencoe, ON, d:7/15/1941
BR/TR, 1902-03 Cin-N, Stl-N, Chi-N

15	23	.395	53	38	31	4	2	371.1	111	3.39

CYR, ERIC: b:2/11/1979, Montreal, QC
BR/TL, 2002 SD-N

0	1	.000	5	0	0	0	0	6	4	10.50

DAVIAULT, RAY: b:5/27/1934, Montreal, QC
BR/TR, 1962 NY-N

1	5	.167	36	3	0	0	0	81	51	6.22

DEMARAIS, FRED: b:11/1/1866, Montreal, QC, d:3/6/1919
B-/TR, 1890 Chi-N

0	0	.000	1	0	0	0	0	2	1	.00

DEMPSTER, RYAN: b:5/3/1977, Sechelt, BC
BR/TR, 1998-2004 Fla-N, Cin-N, Chi-N

51	56	.477	184	156	8	2	2	984.2	796	4.99

DICKSON, JASON: b:3/30/1973, London, ON
BL/TR, 1996-2000 Cal-A, Ana-A

26	25	.510	73	63	2	1	0	397	214	4.99

DOYLE, JOHN: b:-/-/1858, Halifax, NS, d:12/24/1915
B-/T-, 1882 Stl-a

0	3	.000	3	3	3	0	0	24	5	2.62

EMSLIE, BOB: b:1/27/1859, Guelph, ON, d:4/26/1943
BR/TR, 1883-85 Bal-a, Phi-a

44	44	.500	91	90	85	5	0	792.1	362	3.19

FISHER, HARRY: b:1/3/1926, Newbury, ON, d:9/20/1981
BL/TR, 1952 Pit-N

1	2	.333	8	3	0	0	0	18.1	5	6.87

FORD, GENE: b:4/16/1881, Milton, NS, d:8/23/1973
BR/TR, 1905 Det-A

0	1	.000	7	1	1	0	0	35	20	5.66

W	L	PCT	G	GS	CG	SH	SV	IP	SO	ERA

FORD, RUSS: b:4/25/1883, Brandon, MB, d:1/24/1960
BR/TR, 1909-15 NY-A, Buf-F

W	L	PCT	G	GS	CG	SH	SV	IP	SO	ERA
99	71	.582	199	170	126	15	9	1487.1	710	2.59

FOWLER, DICK: b:3/30/1921, Toronto, ON, d:5/22/1972
BR/TR, 1941-52 Phi-A

| 66 | 79 | .455 | 221 | 170 | 75 | 11 | 4 | 1303 | 382 | 4.11 |

FRANCIS, JEFF: b:1/8/1981, Vancouver, BC
BL/TL, 2004 Col-N

| 3 | 2 | .600 | 7 | 7 | 0 | 0 | 0 | 36.2 | 32 | 5.15 |

GAGNE, ERIC: b:1/7/1976, Mascouche, QC
BR/TR, 1999-2004 LA-N

| 24 | 21 | .533 | 282 | 48 | 0 | 0 | 152 | 530 | 604 | 3.29 |

GARDINER, MIKE: b:10/19/1965, Sarnia, ON
BB/TR, 1990-95 Sea-A, Bos-A, Det-A, Mon-N

| 17 | 27 | .386 | 136 | 46 | 0 | 0 | 5 | 393.2 | 239 | 5.21 |

GREEN, JASON: b:6/5/1975, Port Hope, ON
BR/TR, 2000 Hou-N

| 1 | 1 | .500 | 14 | 0 | 0 | 0 | 0 | 17.2 | 19 | 6.62 |

GREEN, STEVE: b:1/26/1978, Greenfield Park, QC
BR/TR, 2001 Ana-A

| 0 | 0 | .000 | 1 | 1 | 0 | 0 | 0 | 6 | 4 | 3.00 |

HANDRAHAN, VERN: b:11/27/1938, Charlottetown, PE
BL/TR, 1964-66 KC-A

| 0 | 2 | .000 | 34 | 2 | 0 | 0 | 1 | 61 | 36 | 5.31 |

HARDEN, RICH: b:11/30/1981, Victoria, BC
BL/TR, 2003-4 Oak-A

| 16 | 11 | .593 | 44 | 44 | 0 | 0 | 0 | 264.1 | 234 | 4.12 |

HARDY, ALEX: b:9/29/1877, Toronto, ON, d:4/22/1940
BR/TL, 1902-03 Chi-N

| 3 | 3 | .500 | 7 | 7 | 5 | 1 | 0 | 47.2 | 16 | 4.34 |

HARRIS, BILL: b:12/3/1931, Duguayville, NB
BL/TR, 1957-59 Bro-N, LA-N

| 0 | 1 | .000 | 2 | 1 | 0 | 0 | 0 | 8.2 | 3 | 3.12 |

HARRISON, TOM: b:1/18/1945, Trail, BC
BR/TR, 1965 KC-A

| 0 | 0 | .000 | 1 | 0 | 0 | 0 | 0 | 1 | 0 | 9.00 |

HILLER, JOHN: b:4/8/1943, Toronto, ON
BR/TL, 1965-80 Det-A

| 87 | 76 | .534 | 545 | 43 | 13 | 6 | 125 | 1242 | 1036 | 2.83 |

HILL, SHAWN: Mississauga, ON 2004 Mtl-N
BR/TR, 2004 Mtl-N

| 1 | 2 | .333 | 3 | 3 | 0 | 0 | 0 | 9.0 | 10 | 16.00 |

HOOPER, BOB: b:5/30/1922, Leamington, ON, d:3/17/1980
BR/TR, 1950-55 Phi-A, Cle-A, Cin-N

| 40 | 41 | .494 | 194 | 57 | 16 | 0 | 25 | 620.2 | 196 | 4.80 |

HORSMAN, VINCE: b:3/9/1967, Halifax, NS
BR/TL, 1991-95 Tor-A, Oak-A, Min-A

| 4 | 2 | .667 | 141 | 0 | 0 | 0 | 1 | 110.2 | 61 | 4.07 |

HOY, PETER: b:6/29/1966, Brockville, ON
BL/TR, 1992 Bos-A

| 0 | 0 | .000 | 5 | 0 | 0 | 0 | 0 | 3.2 | 2 | 7.36 |

JENKINS, FERGIE: b:12/13/1942, Chatham, ON
BR/TR, 1965-83 Phi-N, Chi-N, Tex-A, Bos-A

| 284 | 226 | .557 | 664 | 594 | 267 | 49 | 7 | 4500.2 | 3192 | 3.34 |

JOHNSON, MIKE: b:10/3/1975, Edmonton, AB
BL/TR, 1997-2001 Bal-A, Mon-N

| 7 | 14 | .333 | 81 | 32 | 0 | 0 | 2 | 218 | 147 | 6.85 |

JONES, MIKE: b:7/6/1865, Hamilton, ON, d:3/24/1894
BL/TL, 1890 Lou-a

| 2 | 0 | 1.000 | 3 | 3 | 2 | 0 | 0 | 22 | 6 | 3.27 |

W	L	PCT	G	GS	CG	SH	SV	IP	SO	ERA

JUDD, OSCAR: b:2/14/1908, London, ON, d:12/27/1995
BL/TL, 1941-48 Bos-A, Phi-N

| 40 | 51 | .440 | 161 | 99 | 43 | 4 | 7 | 771.1 | 304 | 3.90 |

KELLUM, WIN: b:4/11/1876, Waterford, ON, d:8/10/1951
BB/TL, 1901-05 Bos-A, Cin-N, Stl-N

| 20 | 16 | .556 | 48 | 37 | 32 | 2 | 2 | 346.2 | 97 | 3.19 |

KILKENNY, MIKE: b:4/11/1945, Bradford, ON
BR/TL, 1969-73 Det-A, Cle-A, Oak-A, SD-N

| 23 | 18 | .561 | 139 | 54 | 12 | 4 | 4 | 410 | 301 | 4.43 |

KNIGHT, JOE: b:9/28/1859, Port Stanley, ON, d:10/16/1938
BL/TL, 1884 Phi-N, Cin-N

| 2 | 4 | .333 | 6 | 6 | 6 | 0 | 0 | 51 | 8 | 5.47 |

KORINCE, GEORGE: b:1/10/1946, Ottawa, ON
BR/TR, 1966-67 Det-A

| 1 | 0 | 1.000 | 11 | 0 | 0 | 0 | 0 | 17 | 13 | 4.24 |

KRAKAUSKAS, JOE: b:3/28/1915, Montreal, QC, d:7/8/1960
BL/TL, 1937-46 Was-A, Cle-A

| 26 | 36 | .419 | 149 | 63 | 22 | 1 | 4 | 583.2 | 347 | 4.53 |

LANDRETH, LARRY: b:3/11/1955, Stratford, ON
BR/TR, 1976-77 Mon-N

| 1 | 4 | .200 | 7 | 4 | 0 | 0 | 0 | 20.1 | 12 | 6.64 |

LAW, RON: b:3/14/1946, Hamilton, ON
BR/TR, 1969 Cle-A

| 3 | 4 | .429 | 35 | 1 | 0 | 0 | 1 | 52.1 | 29 | 4.99 |

LINES, DICK: b:8/17/1938, Montreal, QC
BR/TL, 1966-67 Was-A

| 7 | 7 | .500 | 107 | 0 | 0 | 0 | 6 | 168.2 | 103 | 2.83 |

LONG, RED: b:9/28/1876, Burlington, ON, d:8/11/1929
BR/TR, 1902 Bos-N

| 0 | 0 | .000 | 1 | 1 | 1 | 0 | 0 | 8 | 5 | 1.12 |

MACKENZIE, KEN: b:3/10/1934, Gore Bay, ON
BR/TL, 1960-65 Mil-N, NY-N, Stl-N, SF-N, Hou-N

| 8 | 10 | .444 | 129 | 1 | 0 | 0 | 5 | 208.1 | 142 | 4.80 |

MAGEE, BILL: b:-/-/1875, New Brunswick
BR/TR, 1897-1902 Lou-N, Phi-N, Was-N, NY-N, Stl-N

| 29 | 51 | .362 | 107 | 89 | 69 | 5 | 0 | 743.2 | 161 | 4.93 |

MARANDA, GEORGES: b:1/15/1932, Levis, QC, d:7/14/2000
BR/TR, 1960-62 SF-N, Min-A

| 2 | 7 | .222 | 49 | 8 | 0 | 0 | 0 | 123.1 | 64 | 4.52 |

MARCHILDON, PHIL: b:10/25/1913, Penetanguishene, ON, d:1/10/1997
BR/TR, 1940-50 Phi-A, Bos-A

| 68 | 75 | .476 | 185 | 162 | 82 | 6 | 2 | 1214.1 | 481 | 3.93 |

MAYSEY, MATT: b:1/8/1967, Hamilton, ON
BR/TR, 1992-93 Mon-N, Mil-A

| 1 | 2 | .333 | 25 | 0 | 0 | 0 | 1 | 24.1 | 11 | 5.55 |

MCCABE, RALPH: b:10/21/1918, Napanee, ON, d:5/3/1974
BR/TR, 1946 Cle-A

| 0 | 1 | .000 | 1 | 1 | 0 | 0 | 0 | 4 | 3 | 11.25 |

MCCASKILL, KIRK: b:4/9/1961, Kapuskasing, ON
BR/TR, 1985-96 Cal-A, Chi-A

| 106 | 108 | .495 | 380 | 242 | 30 | 11 | 7 | 1729 | 1003 | 4.12 |

MEARS, CHRIS: b:1/20/1978, Ottawa, ON
BR/TR, 2003 Det-A

| 1 | 3 | .250 | 29 | 3 | 0 | 0 | 5 | 41.1 | 21 | 5.44 |

MOUNTJOY, BILL: b:12/11/1858, London, ON, d:5/19/1894
BL/TL, 1883-85 Cin-a, Bal-a

| 31 | 24 | .564 | 57 | 57 | 56 | 5 | 0 | 503.2 | 164 | 3.25 |

MYETTE, AARON: b:9/26/1977, New Westminster, BC
BR/TR, 1999-2004 Chi-A, Tex-A, Cle-A, Cin-N

| 6 | 12 | .333 | 47 | 30 | 0 | 0 | 0 | 154.1 | 134 | 8.16 |

W	L	PCT	G	GS	CG	SH	SV	IP	SO	ERA

O'NEILL, HARRY: b:11/20/1892, Lindsay, ON, d:9/5/1969
BR/TR, 1922-23 Phi-A

W	L	PCT	G	GS	CG	SH	SV	IP	SO	ERA
0	0	.000	4	0	0	0	0	5	2	1.80

O'NEILL, TIP: b:5/25/1858, Woodstock, ON, d:12/31/1915
BR/TR, 1883-84 NY-N, Stl-a, Chi-P, Cin-N

| 16 | 16 | .500 | 36 | 33 | 29 | 0 | 0 | 289 | 91 | 3.39 |

OSBORNE, FRED: b:5/-/1865
B-/TL, 1890 Pit-N

| 0 | 5 | .000 | 8 | 5 | 5 | 0 | 0 | 58 | 14 | 8.38 |

PAGAN, DAVE: b:9/15/1949, Nipawin, SK
BR/TR, 1973-77 NY-A, Bal-A, Pit-N, Sea-A

| 4 | 9 | .308 | 85 | 18 | 3 | 1 | 4 | 232.1 | 147 | 4.96 |

PAYNE, HARLEY: b:1/9/1868, Windsor, ON, d:12/29/1935
BB/TL, 1896-99 Bro-N, Pit-N

| 30 | 36 | .455 | 80 | 72 | 57 | 3 | 0 | 557 | 148 | 4.04 |

PFANN, BILL: b:6/-/1863, Hamilton, ON, d:6/3/1904
B-/TR, 1894 Cin-N

| 0 | 1 | .000 | 1 | 1 | 0 | 0 | 0 | 3 | 0 | 27.00 |

PICHE, RON: b:5/22/1935, Verdun, QC
BR/TR, 1960-66 Mil-N, Cal-A, Stl-N

| 10 | 16 | .385 | 134 | 11 | 3 | 0 | 12 | 221.1 | 157 | 4.19 |

PINNANCE, ED: b:10/22/1879, Walpole Island, ON, d:12/12/1944
BL/TR, 1903 Phi-A

| 0 | 0 | .000 | 2 | 1 | 0 | 0 | 1 | 7 | 2 | 2.57 |

PLADSON, GORDIE: b:7/31/1956, New Westminster, BC
BR/TR, 1979-82 Hou-N

| 0 | 4 | .000 | 20 | 6 | 0 | 0 | 0 | 50.2 | 18 | 6.04 |

QUANTRILL, PAUL: b:11/3/1968, London, ON
BL/TR, 1992-2004 Bos-A, Phi-N, Tor-A, LA-N, NY-A

| 66 | 76 | .465 | 791 | 64 | 1 | 1 | 21 | 1186.2 | 689 | 3.74 |

RAYMOND, CLAUDE: b:5/7/1937, St. Jean, QC
BR/TR, 1959-71 Chi-A, Mil-N, Hou-N, Atl-N, Mon-N

| 46 | 53 | .465 | 449 | 7 | 2 | 0 | 83 | 721 | 497 | 3.66 |

REITSMA, CHRIS: b:12/31/1977, Minneapolis, MN (raised in Calgary, AB)
BR/TR, 2001-04 Cin-N, Atl-N

| 28 | 36 | .437 | 209 | 53 | 1 | 1 | 14 | 484 | 293 | 4.44 |

ROSS, ERNIE: b:3/31/1880, Toronto, ON, d:3/28/1950
BL/TL, 1902 Bal-A

| 1 | 1 | .500 | 2 | 2 | 2 | 0 | 0 | 17 | 2 | 7.41 |

ROY, JEAN-PIERRE: b:6/26/1920, Montreal, QC
BB/TR, 1946 Bro-N

| 0 | 0 | .000 | 3 | 1 | 0 | 0 | 0 | 6.1 | 6 | 9.95 |

RUTHERFORD, JOHNNY: b:5/5/1925, Belleville, ON
BL/TR, 1952 Bro-N

| 7 | 7 | .500 | 22 | 11 | 4 | 0 | 2 | 97.1 | 29 | 4.25 |

SHANK, HARVEY: b:7/29/1946, Toronto, ON
BR/TR, 1970 Cal-A

| 0 | 0 | .000 | 1 | 0 | 0 | 0 | 0 | 3 | 1 | .00 |

SHIELDS, VINCE: b:11/18/1900, Fredericton, NB, d:10/17/1952
BL/TR, 1924 Stl-N

| 1 | 1 | .500 | 2 | 1 | 0 | 0 | 0 | 12 | 4 | 3.00 |

SHIPANOFF, DAVE: b:11/13/1959, Edmonton, AB
BR/TR, 1985 Phi-N

| 1 | 2 | .333 | 26 | 0 | 0 | 0 | 3 | 36.1 | 26 | 3.22 |

SINCLAIR, STEVE: b:8/2/1971, Victoria, BC
BL/TL, 1998-99 Tor-A, Sea-A

| 0 | 3 | .000 | 45 | 0 | 0 | 0 | 0 | 34.1 | 26 | 5.24 |

SINCOCK, BERT: b:9/8/1887, Barkerville, BC, d:8/1/1946
BL/TL, 1908 Cin-N

| 0 | 0 | .000 | 1 | 0 | 0 | 0 | 0 | 4.2 | 1 | 3.86 |

W	L	PCT	G	GS	CG	SH	SV	IP	SO	ERA

SPOLJARIC, PAUL: b:9/24/1970, Kelowna, BC
BR/TL, 1994-2000 Tor-A, Sea-A, Phi-N, KC-A

| 8 | 17 | .320 | 195 | 12 | 0 | 0 | 4 | 277.1 | 278 | 5.52 |

STEELE, BOB: b:1/5/1894, Cassburn, ON, d:1/27/1962
BB/TL, 1916-19 Stl-N, Pit-N, NY-N

| 16 | 38 | .296 | 91 | 57 | 28 | 4 | 3 | 487.2 | 217 | 3.05 |

TAYLOR, RON: b:12/13/1937, Toronto, ON
BR/TR, 1962-72 Cle-A, Stl-N, Hou-N, NY-N, SD-N

| 45 | 43 | .511 | 491 | 17 | 3 | 0 | 72 | 800 | 464 | 3.93 |

UPHAM, JOHN: b:12/29/1941, Windsor, ON
BL/TL, 1967-68 Chi-N

| 0 | 1 | .000 | 7 | 0 | 0 | 0 | 0 | 8.1 | 4 | 5.40 |

VAN BRABANT, OZZIE: b:9/28/1926, Kingsville, ON
BR/TR, 1954-55 Phi-A, KC-A

| 0 | 2 | .000 | 11 | 2 | 0 | 0 | 0 | 28.2 | 11 | 7.85 |

VICKERS, RUBE: b:5/17/1878, St. Marys, ON, d:12/9/1958
BL/TR, 1902-09 Cin-N, Bro-N, Phi-A

| 22 | 27 | .449 | 88 | 45 | 29 | 7 | 2 | 458 | 213 | 2.93 |

WAINHOUSE, DAVE: b:11/7/1967, Toronto, ON
BL/TR, 1991-2000 Mon-N, Sea-A, Pit-N, Col-N, Stl-N

| 2 | 3 | .400 | 85 | 0 | 0 | 0 | 0 | 105 | 66 | 7.37 |

WALKER, GEORGE: b:-/-/1863, Hamilton, ON
B-/TR, 1888 Bal-a

| 1 | 3 | .250 | 4 | 4 | 4 | 1 | 0 | 35 | 18 | 5.91 |

WILKIE, LEFTY: b:10/30/1914, Zealandia, SK, d:8/5/1992
BL/TL, 1941-46 Pit-N

| 8 | 11 | .421 | 68 | 12 | 5 | 1 | 3 | 194 | 37 | 4.59 |

WILSON, STEVE: b:12/13/1964, Victoria, BC
BL/TL, 1988-93 Tex-A, Chi-N, LA-N

| 13 | 18 | .419 | 205 | 23 | 1 | 0 | 6 | 345.1 | 252 | 4.40 |

WOOD, PETE: b:2/1/1867, Dundas, ON, d:3/15/1923
B-/TR, 1885-89 Buf-N, Phi-N

| 9 | 16 | .360 | 27 | 24 | 23 | 0 | 0 | 217.2 | 46 | 4.51 |

ZIMMERMAN, JEFF: b:8/9/1972, Kelowna, BC
BR/TR, 1999-2001, 2004 Tex-A

| 17 | 12 | .586 | 196 | 0 | 0 | 0 | 32 | 228.2 | 213 | 3.27 |

ZIMMERMAN, JORDAN: b:4/28/1975, Kelowna, BC
BR/TL, 1999 Sea-A

| 0 | 0 | .000 | 12 | 0 | 0 | 0 | 0 | 8 | 3 | 7.88 |

MANAGERS

Yrs	G	W	L	PCT

GIBSON, GEORGE: b:7/22/1880, London, ON
1920-22 Pit-N, 1925-Chi-N, 1932-33 Pit-N

| 7 | 759 | 413 | 344 | .546 |

IRWIN, ARTHUR: b:2/14/1858, Toronto, ON
1889 Was-N, 1891 Bos-a, 1892 Was-N, 1894-95 Pit-N, 1896 NY-N, 1898-99 Was-N

| 8 | 863 | 416 | 427 | .493 |

LAKE, FRED: b:10/16/1868, Cornwallis, ON
1908-09 Bos-A, 1910 Bos-N

| 3 | 349 | 163 | 180 | .475 |

WATKINS, BILL: b:5/5/1858, Brantford, ON
1884 Ind-a, 1885-88 Det-N, 1888-89 KC-a, 1893 Stl-N, 1898-99 Pit-N

| 9 | 914 | 452 | 444 | .504 |

WOOD, JIMMY: b:12/1/1843, Canada
1871 Chi-n, 1872-Tro-n, 1874-75 BroE

| 4 | 154 | 76 | 76 | .500 |

Appendix B

CANADA'S ALL-TIME MAJOR-LEAGUE LEADERS

BATTERS

GAMES PLAYED
Larry Walker *	1888
Terry Puhl	1531
Jack Graney	1402
Jeff Heath	1383
George Gibson	1213
Matt Stairs *	1172
Frank O'Rouke	1131
Pop Smith	1112
Tip O'Neill	1052
Bill Phillips	1038

AT-BATS
Larry Walker *	6592
Jeff Heath	4937
Terry Puhl	4855
Jack Graney	4705
Bill Phillips	4300
Tip O'Neill	4298
Pop Smith	4268
Frank O'Rouke	4069
Arthur Irwin	3919
George Gibson	3776

RUNS
Larry Walker *	1289
Tip O'Neill	879
Jeff Heath	777
Jack Graney	706
Terry Puhl	676
Pop Smith	643
Bill Phillips	562
Arthur Irwin	552
Frank O'Rouke	547
Matt Stairs *	536

HITS
Larry Walker *	2069
Jeff Heath	1447
Terry Puhl	1435
Jack Graney	1361
Bill Phillips	1178
Tip O'Neill	1175
Pop Smith	1032
Frank O'Rouke	982
Arthur Irwin	971
Matt Stairs *	930

DOUBLES
Larry Walker *	451
Jeff Heath	279
Terry Puhl	226
Jack Graney	222
Bill Phillips	219
Tip O'Neill	214
Pop Smith	196
Matt Stairs *	196
Corey Koskie *	180
Frank O'Rouke	175

TRIPLES
Jeff Heath	102
Bill Phillips	98
Tip O'Neill	92
Pop Smith	87
Jack Graney	79
Larry Walker *	61
Terry Puhl	56
George Gibson	49
Arthur Irwin	45
Frank O'Rouke	42

HOME RUNS
Larry Walker *	368
Jeff Heath	194
Matt Stairs *	194
George Selkirk	108
Corey Koskie *	101
Pete Ward	98
Terry Puhl	62
Tip O'Neill	52
Kevin Reimer	52
Rob Ducey	31

RBIs
Larry Walker *	1259
Jeff Heath	887
Tip O'Neill	757
Matt Stairs *	634
George Selkirk	576
Bill Phillips	534
Corey Koskie *	437
Terry Puhl	435
Frank O'Rouke	430
Pete Ward	427

STOLEN BASES
Larry Walker *	228
Terry Puhl	217
Pop Smith	169
Tip O'Neill	161
Jack Graney	148
Frank O'Rouke	100
Arthur Irwin	93
Spud Johnson	93
Jimmy Knowles	83
Corey Koskie *	66

AVERAGE
(minimum 400 at-bats)
Tip O'Neill	.334
Larry Walker *	.314
Jonah Knight	.309
Spud Johnson	.302
Doc Miller	.295
Jeff Heath	.293
Bunk Congalton	.292
Goody Rosen	.291
George Selkirk	.290
Jason Bay *	.283

* Still active

232

PITCHERS

WINS

Fergie Jenkins	284
Kirk McCaskill	106
Reggie Cleveland	105
Russ Ford	99
John Hiller	87
Phil Marchildon	68
Dick Fowler	66
Paul Quantrill *	66
Rheal Cormier *	65
Ryan Dempster *	51

LOSSES

Fergie Jenkins	226
Kirk McCaskill	108
Reggie Cleveland	106
Dick Fowler	79
John Hiller	76
Paul Quantrill *	76
Phil Marchildon	75
Russ Ford	71
Rheal Cormier *	59
Ryan Dempster *	56

PERCENTAGE
(minimum 200 innings pitched)

Rich Harden *	.593
Jeff Zimmerman *	.586
Russ Ford	.582
Bill Mountjoy	.564
Mike Kilkenny	.561
Fergie Jenkins	.557
Win Kellum	.556
John Hiller	.534
Eric Gagne *	.533
Rheal Cormier *	.524

GAMES

Paul Quantrill *	791
Fergie Jenkins	664
Rheal Cormier *	556
John Hiller	545
Ron Taylor	491
Claude Raymond	449
Reggie Cleveland	428
Kirk McCaskill	380
Eric Gagne *	282
Dick Fowler	221

GAMES STARTED

Fergie Jenkins	594
Kirk McCaskill	242
Reggie Cleveland	203
Dick Fowler	170
Russ Ford	170
Phil Marchildon	162
Ryan Dempster *	156
Rheal Cormier *	108
Oscar Judd	99
Bob Emslie	90

COMPLETE GAMES

Fergie Jenkins	267
Russ Ford	126
Bob Emslie	85
Phil Marchildon	82
Dick Fowler	75
Bill Magee	69
Reggie Cleveland	57
Harley Payne	57
Bill Mountjoy	56
Oscar Judd	43

SHUTOUTS

Fergie Jenkins	49
Russ Ford	15
Reggie Cleveland	12
Dick Fowler	11
Kirk McCaskill	11
Rube Vickers	7
Phil Marchildon	6
John Hiller	6
Bob Emslie	5
Bill Magee	5
Bill Mountjoy	5

SAVES

Eric Gagne *	152
John Hiller	125
Claude Raymond	83
Ron Taylor	72
Jeff Zimmerman *	32
Reggie Cleveland	25
Bob Hooper	25
Paul Quantrill *	21
Chris Reitsma *	14
Ron Piche	12

INNINGS PITCHED

Fergie Jenkins	4500.2
Reggie Cleveland	1809.0
Kirk McCaskill	1729.0
Russ Ford	1487.1
Dick Fowler	1303.0
John Hiller	1242.0
Phil Marchildon	1214.1
Paul Quantrill *	1186.2
Rheal Cormier *	1123.1
Ryan Dempster *	984.2

STRIKEOUTS

Fergie Jenkins	3192
John Hiller	1036
Kirk McCaskill	1003
Reggie Cleveland	930
Ryan Dempster *	796
Russ Ford	710
Rheal Cormier *	706
Paul Quantrill *	689
Eric Gagne *	604
Claude Raymond	497

EARNED RUN AVERAGE
(minimum 200 innings pitched)

Russ Ford	2.59
John Hiller	2.83
Rube Vickers	2.93
Bos Steele	3.05
Win Kellum	3.19
Bob Emslie	3.19
Bill Mountjoy	3.25
Jeff Zimmerman *	3.27
Fergie Jenkins	3.34
Eric Gagne *	3.29

* Still active

Appendix C

CANADA'S ALL-STARS
EXPERTS SELECT DREAM TEAMS

What would a book about Canadian baseball be without targeting the best players in each province?

We asked veteran observers from each province to pick their best from their province. And then we asked renowned STATs Inc. researcher Neil Munro of North Bay, Ontario, to pick the all-time, all-Canadian team.

Our 12 experts have seen a ground ball or two, averaging 48.7 years of involvement in baseball. There really isn't a wrong answer from anyone, just a good place to start a baseball debate.

And away we go ... start your arguments:

BRITISH COLUMBIA
C – Larry Kissock, Trail
1B – Justin Morneau, New Westminster
2B – Jim Chapman, Vancouver
3B – Shawn Bowman, Coquitlam
SS – Kevin Nicholson, Surrey
OF – Larry Walker, Jr., Maple Ridge; Jason Bay, Trail; Gerry Reimer, Enderby
DH – Larry Walker, Sr., Maple Ridge
RHP – Ryan Dempster, Gibsons
LHP – Jeff Francis, North Delta
RP – Jeff Zimmerman, Kelowna
Manager – John Harr, Vancouver
● Selected by Bill Green, of Vancouver, who has been involved in amateur baseball since 1962 as a player, coach, provincial high performance evaluator, worked for the MLB Scouting Bureau and served as a Premier League board member.

ALBERTA
C – Al Price, Calgary
1B – Greg Duce, Lethbridge and Lorne Niven, Barrhead
2B – Dwayne Lalor, Red Deer
3B – Randy Gregg, Edmonton
SS – Terry Hendley, Red Deer
OF – Gord Gerlach, St. Albert; Doug MacPhail, Two Hills; Jim Kotkas, Lethbridge
RHP – Dan Berger, Provost
LHP – Keith Van de Keere, Barrhead and Harold Northcott, Rocky Mountain House
DH – Dave Muhlethaler, Edmonton
Manager – Peter Duncan, Red Deer
● Selected by Harold Northcott of Rocky Mountain House, who has been involved in baseball since 1970 as a pitcher, coach,

manager, technical chairman for the Alberta Amateur Baseball Council and vice president of Baseball Alberta, as well as coaching with the Canadian Youth team for three years and the National Senior team for four years.

SASKATCHEWAN
C – Erwin Doerksen, Moose Jaw
1B – Roy Dean, North Battleford
2B – Rich Eilser, Regina
3B – W. Earle Saunders, Traynor
SS – Pete Prediger, Neilburg
OF – Terry Puhl, Melville; Ken Nelson, North Battleford; Max Bentley, Delisle
DH – Max Bentley, Delilse
RHP – Reggie Cleveland, Swift Current
LHP – Ross "Lefty" Arnold, Fielding
RP – Ron Conklin, Eston
Coach/Manager – Joe Zeman, Saskatoon; Emile "The Cat" Francis, North Battleford
● Selected by Dave Shury of Battleford, who has been involved in baseball across Canada since 1956 as a coach, manager and executive. He is the founder of the Saskatchewan Baseball Hall of Fame and Museum located in Battleford.

MANITOBA
C – Almer McKerlie, Miami; Cliff Seafoot, Souris
1B – Bill Carpenter, Winnipeg
2B – Lloyd Brown, Brandon
3B – Ian Lowe, Bradwardine
SS – Bill "Snake" Siddle, Winnipeg
OF – Gerry MacKay, Brandon; Ken Little, St. Boniface; Mark Fisher, Riverside; Gord Ledochowski, Riverton
DH – Corey Koskie, Anola
RHP – Glennis Scott McConnell, Don "Pete" Rettie, Charleswood
LHP – Gerry Falk, Carman
RP – Orville Minish, Swan River
Manager – Terry Hind, Winnipeg
● Selected by the Manitoba Baseball Hall of Fame committee of Gladwyn Scott, Carberry, Sam Tascona, Winnipeg, and Gerry MacKay, Brandon, who have all been involved as players, coaches and umpires since 1949.

ONTARIO
C – Frank "Blackie" O'Rourke, Hamilton
1B – Hank Biasatti, Windsor
2B – Bobby Prentice, Toronto

234

3B – Reno Bertoia, Windsor
SS – Arthur Irwin, Toronto
OF – Tip O'Neill, Woodstock; Jeff Heath, Port
    Arthur; George "Twinkletoes" Selkirk,
    Huntsville
DH – Goody Rosen, Toronto
RHP – Fergie Jenkins, Chatham
LHP – Ron Stead, Toronto
RPs – Paul Quantrill, Port Hope and John
    Hiller, Scarborough
Manager – George "Moon" Gibson, London
● Selected by Howie Birnie, Toronto, who has
been involved as player, coach, administrator
and executive since 1952.

QUEBEC
C – Pete Laforest, Gatineau
1B – Tim Harkness, Lachine
2B – Jean-Pierre Gauthier, Montreal
3B – Dominic Therrien, Trois-Rivieres
SS – Steve Oleschuk, Montreal
OF – Chuck Este, Verdun; Gilles St. Onge,
    Lachine; Marc Griffin, Ste. Foy
DH – Jacques Monette, Montreal
RHP – Claude Raymond, St. Jean
LHP – Denis Boucher, Lachine
RP – Eric Gagne, Mascouche
Manager – Marcel Racine, Montreal
● Selected by Richard Emond, Montreal, who
has been involved as coach with Baseball
Quebec, Les Ailes Du Quebec, Academie Du
Baseball Quebec and Team Canada since 1955.

NEW BRUNSWICK
C – Richard "Cuffy" McLaughlin, Chatham
1B – Art Leggatt, Chatham
2B – Michael Dunnett, Newcastle
3B – Scott Harvey, Fredericton
SS – Phil Doiron, Moncton
OF – Matt Stairs, Fredericton; Bill Donovan,
    Saint John; Bill Daley, Chatham
DH – John Cann, Newcastle
RHP – Jason Dickson, Chatham
LHP – Rheal Cormier, Cape Pele
RP – Matt Jenkins, Chatham
Manager – Gene "Foggy" Boudreau, Moncton
● Selected by Greg Morris of Miramichi, who
has been involved as player, coach since 1958.

NOVA SCOTIA
C – Frank O'Rourke, Springhill
1B – Peter Goucher, Kentville
2B – Lawson Fowler, Springhill
3B – Jim Pelham, Halifax
SS – Vince Ferguson, Halifax
OF – Danny Seaman, Liverpool, Johnny Clark,
    Westville; William "Buddy" Condy, Springhill
DH – Darren Doucette, Dartmouth
RHP – Wilson Parsons, Halifax
LHP – Vince Horsman, Dartmouth
RP – Jason Bailey, Dartmouth
Manager – Eddie Gillis, New Waterford and
    Danny Seaman, Liverpool
● Selected by Burton Russell of Kentville, who
has written nine books on the history of sport
in Nova Scotia, including *A Century of
Baseball Heroics* and *Baseball Memories: A
History of the Nova Scotia Senior Baseball*

League, 1977-2003. Russell has followed
baseball in the Maritimes since 1946.

PRINCE EDWARD ISLAND
C – Boone Larkin, St. Peter's
1B – Bill Connolly, Morell; Mike Kelly,
    Morrell
2B – Don "Duck" MacLeod, Charlottetown
3B – Fred "Fiddler" MacDonald, Charlottetown
SS – Buck Whitlock, Charlottetown;
    Hubert "Sock" MacDonald, Charlottetown
OF – Marty Koughan, Stratford; Mike Puiia,
    Charlottetown; Wayne MacDonald,
    Charlottetown; Tic Williams, Charlottetown
DH – Albert Roche, Cardigan
RHP – Vern Handrahan, Charlottetown
LHP – Mike Kelly, Morell
RP – George Dunn, Charlottetown;
    Don "Duck" MacLeod, Charlottetown
Manager – Tom MacFarlane, Charlottetown,
    Charlie Ryan, Charlottetown; Jimmy
    "Fiddler" MacDonald, Charlottetown
● Selected by Fred MacDonald, of
Charlottetown, whose family has been
involved in baseball since 1930. MacDonald
writes for the *Guardian Patriot* and picked the
team, save for third base, where Walter
Bradley of Morell pinch-hit. Bradley has been
involved in baseball since 1958 as player,
coach and administrator.

NEWFOUNDLAND
C – Gerry Basha, Corner Brook
1B – Sean O'Leary, Corner Brook
2B – Ray Colbourne, Corner Brook
3B – Gordon Breen, St. John's
SS – Brian Colbourne, Corner Brook
OF – Gary Gulliver, St. John's; Dick Duder,
    Grand Falls; Mickey Walsh, Corner Brook
DH – Terry Ryan, Grand Falls
RHP – Tom Humber, Corner Brook
LHP – Frank Humber, Corner Brook
RP – Bill Hudson, St. John's
Manager – Charlie Riddle, St. John's
● Selected by Ken Dawe of Mount Pearl, who
has been involved in amateur baseball since
1965 as a player, coach and provincial
baseball executive director.

ALL-CANADIAN TEAM
C – George Gibson, London, ON
1B – Bill Phillips, St. John, NB
2B – Pop Smith, Digby, NS
3B – Corey Koskie, Anola, MB
SS – Frank O'Rourke, Hamilton, ON
OF – Larry Walker, Maple Ridge, BC;
    Jeff Heath, Fort William, ON;
    Terry Puhl, Melville, SK
DH – Tip O'Neill, Woodstock, ON
RHP – Ferguson Jenkins, Chatham, ON
LHP – John Hiller, Toronto, ON
RP – Eric Gagne, Mascouche, QC
Manager – Arthur Irwin, Toronto, ON
● Selected by Neil Munro of North Bay, ON,
who has worked for STATS Inc. and followed
baseball since 1953, as a fan, researcher,
SABR member and author, writing the
Canadian Players Encyclopedia.

Appendix D

CANADIAN INTERNATIONALS

All-time list of players who have represented Canada internationally, compiled from Team Canada final rosters:

Adlem, Todd, LHP, Vancouver, BC: 1989 PC

Alexander, Jordy, LHP, Burnaby, BC: 2000 WS; 2001 WC; 2003 WS; 2005 WCQ

Allen, John, LHP, Nanaimo, BC: 1987 WJ

Anderson, Shawn, 2B, Vancouver, BC: 1997 WJ

Andrade, Derek, RHP, Mississauga, ON: 2002 WSG

Andreopoulos, Alex, C, Toronto, ON: 1990 WJ; 1991 PAG; 1993 WSG; 1993 WS

Andrulis, Henry, OF, Etobicoke, ON: 1984 OG

Andrychuk, Jim, INF, Hazlet, SK: 1986 PAC; 1990 WS; 1991 PAG

Angus, Rob, C, Surrey, BC: 1985 IC; 1986 PAC

Anholt, Ryan, OF-INF, Moose Jaw, SK: 1994 WJ; 1998 WS; 2000 WS

Arishenkoff, Tyson, INF, Cranbrook, BC: 2003 WS

Armstrong, Cole, C, Surrey, BC: 1999 WJ; 2000 WJ; 2001 WJ

Arneson, Dean, LHP, Britannia Beach, BC: 1986 WJ

Ashman, Brad, LHP, Westbank, BC: 2004 WSG

Aucoin, Derek, RHP, Brisbriand, QC: 1988 WJ

Avery, James, RHP, Moose Jaw, SK: 2002 WJ

Axford, John, RHP, Port Dover, ON: 2001 WJ; 2003 WS

Bachiu, Larry, 3B, Regina, SK: 1967 PAG

Bailey, Curtis, OF, Red Deer, AB: 1992 WJ

Bailey, Evan, RHP, Kamloops, BC: 2003 WJ

Bailey, Jim, SS, Nanaimo, BC: 1996 WJ

Bailey, Scott, RHP, Waterloo, ON: 1978 WS; 1980 WS

Baldin, Jim, RHP, Niagara Falls, ON: 1983 WS

Ballance, Peter, RHP, Cumberland, BC: 1984 WJ

Barber, Rob, C, Calgary, AB: 1993 WSG; 1993 IC

Barr, Dave, OF, Fredericton, NB: 2004 WSG

Bay, Jason, OF, Trail, BC: 1996 WJ; 2001 WS

Beaubry, Michael, 1B, Joliette, QC: 1971 WS; 1971 PAG; 1974 WS

Beaulieu, François-Alexandre, RHP, Levis, QC: 2003 WJ

Bechard, Jess, INF, Brantford, ON: 1995 WJ; 2000 WS; 2003 WS

Beck, Jeremy, RHP, Brampton, ON: 1996 PAG Jr

Becker, Grant, SS, Red Deer, AB: 1977 WC

Begg, Chris, RHP, Uxbridge, ON: 2003 OQ; 2004 OG

Bell, Brian, C, Stratford, ON: 1971 PAG

Bell-Irving, Steve, C, Burnaby, BC: 2002 WJ

Bender, Dave, OF, Brandon, MB: 1971 WS

Bennett, Ian, RHP, St. John's, NL: 1988 WJ

Bennett, Mike, RHP, Burlington, ON: 1993 WSG; 1993 WS; 1994 WS; 1995 OQ

Bernier, Eric, OF, Laval, QC: 1999 WJ; 2000 WJ

Bertrand, Dominic, OF, Montreal, QC: 1993 PAG Jr

Betts, Brian, SS, Edmonton, AB: 1973 WS; 1973 IC

Betts, Todd, INF, Scarborough, ON: 1991 WJ; 1999 PAG; 2001 WS; 2003 OQ; 2004 OG

Biasucci, Joey, RHP, Toronto, ON: 1988 WJ

Bieniasz, Dererk, RHP, Toronto, ON: 1992 WJ

Birmingham, Jason, RHP, Sarnia, ON: 1990 WJ; 1991 WJ; 1993 WSG; 1993 WS; 1994 WS; 1995 OQ

Bishop, Trevor, RHP, Assiniboia, SK: 1994 WJ

Bisson, Chris, 1B-3B, Toronto, ON: 1995 OQ

Bissonnette Dustin, INF, Prince George, BC: 2004 WSG

Blanchard, Yves, Montreal, QC: 1970 WS

Bland, Robert, RHP, North Bay, ON: 2002 WJ

Blasko, Bob, RHP, Welland, ON: 1974 WS

Bleau, Nicholas, OF-LHP, Mercier, QC: 2003 WJ; 2004 WJ

Blouin, Gary, RHP, Surrey, BC: 1983 WJ; 1984 WJ

Boehm, Andy, C, Portage la Prairie, MB: 1979 WJ

Boguski, Ryan, LHP, Sifton, MB: 1994 WJ

Boisjoly, Eric, INF, Boucherhille, QC: 1993 WJ; 1994 WJ

Boleska, Tom, RHP, Burlington, ON: 2004 WJ

Boniferro, Carlo, OF, Windsor, ON: 1984 WJ

Bonneville, Marc, OF, Bois-des-Fillions, QC: 1998 WJ

Boomer, Brad, C, Cambridge, ON: 1986 WJ

Borghese, Jason, OF, Guelph, ON: 2000 WS
Bouchard, David, LHP-OF, St. Hubert, QC:
1993 PAG Jr
Boucher, Denis, LHP, Lachine, QC: 1986 WJ;
1987 PAG; 2000 WS
Bourgouin, David, RHP, Laval, QC: 1993 WJ
Bousquet, Benoit 2B, St. Hubert, QC:
1993 PAG Jr
Bowman, Shawn, INF-RHP, Coquitlam, BC:
2001 WJ; 2002 WJ
Brabant, Daniel, RHP, Longueuil, QC: 1991 WJ
Brandow, Derek, RHP, London, ON: 1988 WJ;
1989 WS
Bray, Jamie, RHP, Niagara Falls, ON: 1980 WJ
Brewer, Jeff, RHP, Bathurst, NB: 2005 WCQ
Briand, Kevin, LHP, St. Hubert, QC: 1989 WJ;
1989 PC
Brice, George, RHP, Victoria, BC: 1971 PAG;
1973 IC
Brice, Les, INF, Victoria, BC: 1970 WS
Bridges, Bob, LHP, Burnaby, BC: 1977 WC;
1978 WS; 1979 PAG; 1988 WS; 1988 OG
Bridgett, Ted, RHP, Virden, MB: 1971 WS
Brinjak, Peter, RHP, Etobicoke, ON: 1996 WJ
Brnardic, Ryan, RHP, Lasalle, ON: 1999 WJ
Brohman, Mark, INF, Guelph, ON: 2002 WSG
Brook, Greg, 2B, Victoria, BC: 1993 WJ
Brown, Bob, INF, Saskatoon, SK: 1973 WS
Brown, Curtis, INF-C, Moose Jaw, SK: 1994 WJ
Brown, Jody, SS, Windsor, ON: 1989 WJ;
1992 WS; 1993 WSG; 1993 WS; 1994 WS;
1995 OQ
Brown, Paul, OF, Chatham, ON: 1995 WJ
Brown, Winston, SS-OF, Truro, NS: 1984 WJ;
1985 WJ
Brunen, Kyle, OF, Delisle, SK: 1996 WJ;
1998 WS
Buckle, Matt, RHP, Surrey, BC: 2000 WS
Bulach, Rob, OF, Kelowna, BC: 1979 WJ;
1980 WJ
Bultitide, Rick, 3B, Vancouver, BC: 1977 WC;
1982 WS; 1983 WS; 1983 PAG
Bunyan, Lorne, C, Victoria, BC: 1970 WS
Burton, T.J., RHP, Ottawa, ON: 2001 WJ
Butler, Alan, LHP-1B, Toronto, ON: 1985 WJ
Butler, Craig, LHP, St. John's, NL: 1980 WJ
Butler, Rich, OF, East York, ON: 1990 WJ;
2001 WS; 2003 WS
Butler, Rob, OF, East York, ON: 1988 WJ;
1988 WS; 1988 OG; 1989 PC; 1989 WS;
2003 WS; 2005 WCQ
Butschler, Mike, C, Richmond, BC: 1981 IC;
1982 WS
Byckowski, Bill, 1B, Brampton, ON: 1986 PAC;
1987 PAG; 1987 IC; 1988 WS; 1988 OG
Byers, Kevin, LHP, Peace River, AB: 1981 IC

Caig, Norm, C, Surrey, BC: 1971 WS;
1971 PAG; 1972 WS; 1973 IC
Calcagni, Matt, INF, Brampton, ON: 2004 WSG
Call, Ryan, RHP, Kamloops, BC: 1994 WJ
Callaghan, Dave, LHP, Surrey, BC: 1981 WJ
Campbell, Adam, OF, Surrey, BC: 2004 WSG
Campbell, Mark, LHP, St. John's, NL: 1982 WJ
Campeau, Dominic, C, St. Leonard, QC:
1994 WS; 1995 OQ; 1998 WS
Cann, John, 1B, Newcastle, NB: 1992 WS;
1993 WSG; 1993 WS; 1994 WS; 1995 OQ

Cantin, Christian, C, Charlesbourg, QC:
1984 WJ
Capone, Mark, INF, Etobicoke, ON: 2004 WSG
Card, Lee, RHP, Williams Lake, BC: 1998 WS
Cardwell, Fred, RHP, Red Deer, AB: 1965 WJ;
1971 WS; 1971 PAG; 1972 WS; 1973 WS;
1973 IC; 1974 WS; 1975 IC
Carle, Michel, RHP-1B, Montreal, QC:
1984 WJ; 1985 WJ
Carlin, Luke, C-SS, Aylmer, QC: 1998 WJ
Carlisle, Morgan, LHP, Summerside, PEI:
2004 WJ
Carnegie, Mike, RHP, Toronto, ON: 1981 IC;
1983 WS; 1983 PAG; 1984 OG
Caron, David, RHP, Trail, BC: 1996 WJ
Cart, Michael, 3B-1B, King City, ON: 2003 WJ
Carter, Leon, OF, St. Peter's, NB: 1990 WJ;
1993 WSG; 1993 WS; 1994 WS; 1995 OQ
Carter, Steve, RHP, Tecumseh, ON: 1998 WJ
Casaubon, Martin, 3B, Quebec City, QC:
1980 WJ
Cattrysse, Alan, SS, Chatham, ON: 2001 WJ
Cecile, Rob, OF, Windsor, ON: 1989 WS
Chahley, Bill, RHP, Edmonton, AB: 1971 PAG
Changnon, Stephane, RHP, Longueuil, QC:
1989 WJ
Charbonneau, Marc-Andre, OF, Quebec City,
QC: 2004 WSG
Chavarria, David, RHP, Burnaby, BC: 1990 WJ
Chenard, Ryan, RHP, Port Alberni, BC: 1999 WJ
Chlebus, Dan, RHP, Sault Ste. Marie, ON:
1991 PAG
Cho, Hyung, INF, Scarborough, ON: 1999 WJ;
2003 WS
Chong, Yen, INF, Toronto, ON: 1987 WJ
Chubb, Marty, SS, Mannheim, ON: 1995 OQ
Clapp, Stubby, INF, Windsor, ON: 1991 WJ;
1994 WS; 1999 PAG; 2003 OQ; 2004 OG;
2005 WCQ
Clark, David, RHP, Toronto, ON: 2004 WJ
Clarke, Gordie, 2B, Saint John, NB: 1971 PAG
Clarke, Tim, RHP, Vancouver, BC: 1979 WJ;
1980 WS
Cleeve, Mark, 2B, Chatham, ON: 1979 WJ
Clements, Steve, OF-LHP, Vancouver, BC:
1980 WJ; 1981 WJ
Cloutier, Martin, RHP, Gatineau, QC: 1993 PAG Jr
Coates, Steve, OF, Guelph, ON: 2004 WSG
Colbourne, Larry, 3B, Corner Brook, NL:
1980 WJ
Colbourne, Ray, INF, Corner Brook, NL:
1965 WJ
Collins, Joel, C, Richmond Hill, ON: 2003 WJ;
2004 WJ
Collins, Josh, LHP-INF, Fredericton, NB:
2004 WSG
Collins, Kevin, OF, Nepean, ON: 1991 WJ
Collison, Danny, 1B, Brockville, ON: 1980 WJ
Commodore, Wayne, OF, Lethbridge, AB:
1973 WS
Conahan, Preston, PEI: 1982 WJ
Cooper, Dave, 1B, Belle River, ON: 1991 PAG
Cooper, Devon, RHP, Brockville, ON: 2002 WSG
Corbeil, Henry, LHP, LaSalle,QC: 1971 PAG
Corlett, Josh, OF, Chatham, NB: 1982 WJ
Cormier, Rheal, LHP, Cape Pele, NB: 1985 WJ;
1986 WJ; 1987 PAG; 1987 IC; 1988 WS;
1988 OG

Corrigale, Jason, SS, Brampton, ON: 1998 WS
Corriveau, Ivan, RHP-SS, Welland, ON: 1984 WJ
Corriveau, Ricky, C, Welland, ON: 1987 WJ
Cory, Gene, 3B-OF, Wawanesa, MB: 1967 PAG
Cote, Marc-Andre, LHP, Victoriaville, QC:
    1993 PAG Jr
Cote, Jean Robert, RHP, Robichaud Office,
    NB: 1985 WJ; 1989 WS
Cote, Jean Robert, 1B, La Pairie, QC:
    1989 PC; 1989 WS
Cote, Mathieu, LHP, St.Romuald, QC: 1993 PAG Jr
Coughlan, Warren, OF, Burnaby, BC: 1977 WC
Coulombe, Joel, 2B, Montreal, QC: 1982 WJ;
    1983 WJ
Cox, Brian, C, St. Stephen, NB: 1973 WS;
    1973 IC; 1974 WS; 1975 IC
Cox, Kris, OF, Kelowna, BC: 2000 WS;
    2003 WS; 2005 WCQ
Crabb, Dave, OF, NS: 1965 WJ
Craig, Darryl, INF-LHP, Trail, BC: 1993 WJ
Creelman, Blair, LHP, Summerside, PEI: 1982 WJ
Cripps, Bobby, C, Powell River, BC: 1995 WJ
Croft, Troy, OF, St. John's, NL: 1991 WJ
Crowther, Brent, RHP, North Vancouver, BC:
    1998 WS; 2000 WS; 2003 WS; 2003 WS;
    2005 WCQ
Croy, Dean, C, Coaldale, AB: 1989 PC;
    1989 WS; 1990 GG; 1990 WS; 1991 PAG
Cruize, Rick, SS, Pilot Mound, MB: 1973 WS
Curran, Randy, OF, Kitchener, ON: 1987 PAG;
    1987 IC; 1988 WS; 1988 OG; 1989 WS
Curtis, Jim, C, Windsor, ON: 1991 WJ
Cusson, Vincent, RHP, St.Laurent, QC: 1993 WJ
Cust, Rick, 1B, Waskatenau, AB: 1989 WS
Cyr, Eric, LHP, Montreal, QC: 1996 WJ;
    1997 WJ; 2004 OG

Dabrowiecki, Kris, RHP, Toronto, ON:
    2003 WJ; 2004 WJ
Daly, Bill, OF, Chatham, NB: 1973 WS
D'Aoust, Patrick, C, Riviere Beaudette, QC:
    2004 WJ
Darichuk, Ron, 3B, Oakville, ON: 1979 WJ
Darling, Don, 2B, St. Albert, AB: 1973 IC
Da Silva, Fernando, RHP, Brossard, QC:
    1991 PAG
Davidson, David, LHP, Thorold, ON: 2001 WJ;
    2002 WJ
Davis, Joe, RHP, Thunder Bay, ON: 1988 WJ
Davis, John, OF, Corunna, ON: 1978 WS
Davis, Monty, OF, Vernon, BC: 1994 WJ; 1995 WJ
Dawson, Dwayne, RHP, Wheatley, ON: 1989 WS
Debray, Adam, RHP, Richmond, BC: 1995 OQ
de la Sablonniere, Michel, RHP, Montreal, QC:
    1972 WS
Delfino, Lee, SS, Pickering, ON: 1996 PAG Jr;
    1997 WJ; 1999 PAG; 2000 WS; 2001 WS;
    2005 WCQ
Dell Tim, RHP, Tsawwassen, BC: 1986 PAC;
    1987 PAG
Demchuck, Dan, 2B-SS, Trail, BC: 1984 WJ
Demchuck, Terry, 2B, Trail, BC: 1980 WJ;
    1981 WJ
Dempster, Ryan, RHP, Gibsons, BC: 1993 WJ;
    1994 WJ
Dennis, Tim, RHP, Windsor, ON: 1979 WJ
Deschenes, Patrick, RHP, Beauport, QC:
    1996 WJ; 2003 WS

Desgagne, Daniel, RHP, Jonquiere, QC: 1984 WJ
Despres, Danny, 2B, Trois Rivieres, QC: 1985 WJ
Detienne, David, 3B, Dartmouth, NS: 1997 WJ
Devey, Phil, LHP, Lachute, QC: 2001 WS;
    2003 WS; 2003 OQ; 2004 OG
Devlin, Dennis, RHP, Vancouver, BC: 1981 IC
Dickie, Chris, OF, Kitchener, ON: 1996 PAG Jr
Dickinson, Colin, SS, Vancouver, BC: 1986 PAC
Dickinson, Tim, LHP, Chatham, ON: 1983 WJ
Dickson, Jason, RHP-OF, Chatham, NB:
    1991 WJ; 2003 OQ; 2004 OG
Didier, Mike, RHP, Mississauga, ON: 2002 WSG
Dimitrijevic, Rick, OF-C, Windsor, ON: 1983 WJ
Dimitroff, Jim, C-INF, Windsor, ON: 1989 WJ
Dixon, Colin, SS-1B, Vancouver, BC: 1985 WJ;
    1986 WJ; 1998 WSQ; 1998 WS; 1999 PAG
Doerksen, Erwin, C-1B, Eston, SK: 1967 PAG
Doherty, Steve, SS, Richmond, BC: 1992 WJ
Doiron, Phil, OF, Moncton, NB: 1967 PAG
Dorrington, Mike, RHP, Saint John, NB:
    1984 WJ; 1985 WJ; 1986 WJ
Doucette, Len, C, Mt. Stewart, PEI: 1982 WJ
Douris, John, RHP-OF, Scarborough, ON:
    1986 WJ; 1987 WJ; 1987 WS; 1989 WS
Downes, Larry, C, Niagara-on-the-Lake, ON:
    1979 WJ; 1981 IC; 1982 WS; 1983 WS;
    1983 PAG; 1984 OG; 1985 IC; 1987 PAG;
    1987 IC
Doyle, Joe, INF, NS: 1982 WJ
Drew, Brad, LHP, Waterloo, ON: 1995 WJ;
    1996 WJ; 1997 WJ
Dubein, Damien, LHP, Milton, ON: 1992 WS;
    1993 WSG; 1993 WS; 1995 OQ
Dubuc, Charles, LHP, Iberville, QC: 1997 WJ;
    1998 WJ
Duce, Greg, 3B, Lethbridge, AB: 1983 WJ;
    1985 IC; 1987 PAG; 1987 IC; 1988 WS;
    1988 OG
Ducey, Rob, OF, Cambridge, ON: 2003 WS;
    2003 OQ; 2004 OG
Duda, Jeff, RHP, Surrey, BC: 2003 WJ
Duffy, Ryan, LHP, Sombra, ON: 1992 WS;
    1993 WSG; 1993 WS; 1994 WS
Duhamel, Chris, RHP, Hamner, ON: 1996 PAG Jr
Dumouchelle, Pat, OF, Windsor, ON:
    1979 PAG; 1980 WS
Dupere, Marc, OF, Chicoutimi, QC: 1982 WJ
Dupuis, Patrick, RHP, Laval, QC: 1989 WJ;
    1990 WJ
Durette, Jimmy, LHP-OF, Matane, QC: 2003 WJ

Eckstein, Corey, RHP-INF, Abbotsford, BC:
    2003 WJ
Elder, Jake, C, Delta, BC: 2000 WJ; 2001 WJ;
    2004 WSG
Elias, John, LHP, Cote St. Luc, QC: 1967 PAG
Elias, Lenny, OF, Mississauga, ON: 1996 PAG Jr
Elick, John, INF, Calgary, AB: 1972 WS
Eliopolis, Jim, C, Toronto, ON: 1984 OG
Ellins, Larry, INF, Brantford, ON: 1979 PAG
Ellis, Barry, C, Charlottetown, PEI: 1965 WJ
Emanuele, Chris, OF, Mississauga, ON:
    2001 WJ; 2002 WJ
Emard, Jean-François, Montreal, QC: 1998 WJ
Emberley, Dustin, RHP, Weyburn, SK:
    1996 PAG Jr; 1996 WJ; 1997 WJ; 1998 WJ
Emond, Benoit, OF, Farnham, QC: 1994 WJ;
    2005 WCQ

Eng, Chris, SS, Langley, BC: 1998 WJ
Engevik, Glen, 1B, Surrey, BC: 1983 WJ
Erasmus, Tom, RHP, Edmonton, AB:
1979 PAG; 1980 WS
Ertel, Chad, RHP, St. Clements, ON: 1996 PAG Jr
Eskildsen, Mile, 3B, Maple Ridge, BC: 1997 WJ
Eudes, Benoit, LHP, Laval, QC: 1992 WJ;
1994 WS; 1995 OQ
Evans, Jamie, RHP, Burlington, ON: 1987 WJ;
1988 WJ
Evans, John, OF, Windsor, ON: 1989 WJ
Everard, Grant, RHP, Wawanesa, MB:
1971 WS; 1972 WS
Ewasiuk, Ken, LHP-1B, Edmonton, AB:
1967 PAG

Falardeau, Jeff, LHP, Welland, ON: 1993 WJ
Falk, Gerry, LHP, Gretna, MB: 1977 WC
Farina, Justin, LHP, Sarnia, ON: 2005 WCQ
Fellerdeau, Larry RHP, Richmond, BC: 1974 WS
Fera, Aaron, OF, Sault Ste. Marie, ON: 2003 WS
Ferby, Ryan, SS, Lethbridge, AB: 1993 WSG;
1993 WS; 1994 WS
Finlayson, Mike, RHP, Victoria, BC: 1973 WS;
1973 IC; 1974 WS
Fluet, Keith, OF, Saskatoon, SK: 1992 WS;
1993 WSG; 1993 WS; 1994 WS
Foley, Steve, OF, Toronto, ON: 2000 WS;
2005 WCQ
Foran, Matt, LHP, Surrey, BC: 1994 WS
Forest, Jonathan, RHP, St. Hubert, QC:
2001 WJ; 2002 WJ
Fortin, Blaine, C, Lundar, MB: 1994 WJ
Fortin, Troy, C-3B, Lundar, MB: 1992 WJ;
1999 PAG
Fournier, Marc, OF, LaSalle, QC: 1993 WJ
Fournier, Roger, RHP, Montreal, QC: 1970 WS
Francis, Jeff, LHP, North Delta, BC: 1999 WJ
Franchuk, Dale, INF, Wandering River, AB:
1979 WJ
Franklin, Don, 3B, Regina, SK: 1981 WJ
Fraser, Mark, RHP, Sudbury, ON: 1991 WJ
Freeborn, Geoff, LHP, Calgary, AB: 1999 WJ
Frey, Kevin, LHP, Saskatoon, SK: 1986 PAC
Frigon, Patrick, RHP, Laval, QC: 1998 WJ
Frostad, Emerson, 3B, Calgary, AB: 2001 WJ
Fuller, George, SS, Victoria, BC: 1970 WS
Fulton, Jesse, RHP, Toronto, ON: 2004 WSG
Funk, Conrad, OF, Waldeck, SK: 1999 WJ

Gage-Cole, Murray, RHP, Vancouver, BC:
1970 WS
Gagne, Eric, RHP, Mascouche, QC: 1993 WJ;
1994 WJ; 1995 OQ
Gagne, Jacques, OF, Laval, QC: 1965 WJ
Gallow, Rick, RHP, Hamilton, ON: 1982 WJ
Gamble, Mike, LHP, Regina, SK: 1996 WJ
Gamlin, Len, 1B, Vancouver, BC: 1973 IC;
1974 WS
Gardiner, Mike, RHP-C, Sarnia, ON: 1983 WJ;
1984 OG; 1985 IC
Gardner, Scott, C-3B, Hamilton, ON: 1979 WJ;
1980 WJ
Gaudreau, Patrick, OF-INF, Cap-Rouge, QC:
1998 WJ
Gauthier, Derek, 2B, Toronto, ON: 1990 WJ;
1992 WS; 1993 WSG; 1993 WS; 1994 WS;
1995 OQ

Gazzola, Rick, RHP, Thorold, ON: 1980 WS;
1981 IC
Gerk, Jordan, LHP, Kelowna, BC: 1997 WJ
Gervais, David, 1B-3B, Trois Rivieres, QC:
1992 WJ
Gervais, Pat, SS, Trois Rivieres, QC: 1986 PAC
Gervais, Yvon, RHP, Laval, QC: 1971 WS
Gerveatt, Phil, SS, Charlottetown, PEI: 1982 WJ
Girard, David, 3B, Windsor, ON: 1985 WJ
Glatt, Javier, OF, Calgary, AB: 1999 WJ
Gonzalez, Issael, OF-INF, Montreal, QC: 2004 WJ
Gooding, Jason, LHP, Kitchener, ON:
1991 WJ; 1992 WJ; 1993 WSG; 1993 WS;
1995 OQ; 1999 PAG
Goreham, Rob, RHP, Clarks Harbour, NS:
1985 WJ; 1986 WJ
Gosselin, Patrick, RHP, Sherbrooke, QC: 1990 WJ
Goulding, Bob, INF, Corner Brook, NL: 1982 WJ
Goulet, Jean-Guy, RHP, QC: 1980 WJ
Gourley, John, C, Peterborough, ON: 1979 PAG
Grant, Tim, RHP, Vancouver, BC: 2000 WJ
Grantham, Ryan, RHP, Burlington, ON:
1996 PAG Jr
Grass, David, INF, Victoria, BC: 1973 WS;
1975 IC
Gray, Brett, RHP, Wyoming, ON: 2001 WS;
2003 OQ
Gray, Jeff, SS, Yarmouth County, NS: 1979 WJ
Green, Jason, RHP, Port Hope, ON: 1999 PAG
Green, Steve, RHP, Longueil, QC: 1996 WJ;
1999 PAG
Grenier, Jean, LHP-1B, Sherbrooke, QC: 1979 WJ
Griffin, Marc, OF, Ste. Foy, QC: 1986 WJ;
1987 PAG; 1987 IC; 1988 WS; 1988 OG
Griffin, Mike, INF-OF, Nanaimo, BC: 2003 WJ
Grimes, Sean, LHP, London, ON: 1999 WJ;
2000 WJ
Gronnotti, Tom, INF, Vancouver, BC: 1979 WJ
Groulx, Wayne, SS-OF, Welland, ON: 1983 WJ
Guay, Vincent, 1B, Coaticooke, QC: 1990 WJ
Guiel, Aaron, OF, Langley, BC: 1999 PAG;
2001 WS
Guiel, Jeff OF, Langley, BC: 1995 OQ;
2003 OQ; 2004 OG
Guillemette, Jimmy, C, St. Eustache, QC:
1993 PAG Jr
Guimond, Jean-François, RHP, Montreal, QC:
1993 PAG Jr
Gulbranson, Jim, CF, Vancouver, BC:
1971 WS; 1971 PAG
Gullett, Bruce, OF, Edmonton, AB: 1972 WS

Hagedorn, Brad, LHP, Kitchener, ON: 1987 WJ
Haidy, Sam, RHP, Windsor, ON: 1982 WJ
Hallett, Brent, OF, Fredericton, NB: 1974 WS;
1975 IC
Halpenny, Andy, C, Selkirk, MB: 1989 WJ;
1990 WJ
Hanagami, Brian, LHP, Christian Lake, BC:
1973 WS
Hannigan, Jason, RHP, Stoney Creek, ON:
1987 WJ
Harrison, Jesse, 2B, Toronto, ON: 1998 WJ
Hartsburgh, Corey, RHP, Zurich, ON: 1991 PAG
Harvey, Barry, 1B, Victoria, BC: 1970 WS
Harvey, Ian, RHP, Oakville, ON: 2001 WS
Harvey, Scott, Jr., INF-RHP, Marysville, NB:
1965 WJ

Harvie, Brad, 2B, Lethbridge, AB: 1981 WJ;
    1985 IC; 1986 PAC; 1987 PAG; 1987 IC
Haughton, Rick, OF, Surrey, BC: 1974 WS
Havens, Jeff, RHP, Windsor, ON: 1995 WJ
Hawken, Dale, 3B, Provost, AB: 1980 WJ
Hawkes, Ed, LHP, Chatham, NB: 1982 WJ
Hayes, Rex, OF, Vancouver, BC: 1989 PC;
    1990 WS
Hayward, Todd, INF, Courtright, ON: 1992 WS
Hazell, Dick, LHP, Edmonton, AB: 1973 WS
Heeney, Joe, SS, Toronto, ON: 1981 WJ;
    1983 PAG; 1983 IC; 1983 PAG; 1984 OG;
    1985 IC; 1991 PAG
Hegen, John, RHP, NB: 1965 WJ
Heisler, Rod, LHP, Moose Jaw, SK: 1978 WS;
    1979 PAG; 1980 WS; 1981 IC; 1982 WS;
    1983 WS; 1983 PAG; 1984 OG; 1985 IC;
    1986 PAC; 1987 PAG; 1987 IC; 1988 WS;
    1988 OG
Henderson, Jim, OF-RHP, Calgary, AB:
    1999 WJ
Henrichon, Robert, RHP, Montreal, QC:
    1980 WS; 1981 IC
Herauf, Jermey, RHP, Regina, SK: 2003 WS
Herman, Tyler, 1B, Maple Ridge, BC: 1996 WJ
Hill, Doug, OF, Victoria, BC: 1970 WS
Hill, Kyle, RHP, Mississauga, ON: 2004 WSG
Hill, Shawn, RHP, Georgetown, ON: 2003 OQ;
    2004 OG
Hillman, Darren, C, Kitchener, ON: 1987 WJ
Hillman, Stewart, RHP, Windsor, ON: 1988 WS;
    1988 OG
Hodge, Jamie, INF-OF, Aurora, ON: 1979 PAG
Hodges, Steve, RHP-2B, Sidney, BC: 1984 WJ
Hodgson, Brian, LHP, Brandon, MB:
    1967 PAG; 1971 WS
Hodgson, Craig, OF-RHP, Brandon, MB: 1992 WJ
Hoffman, Glen, RHP, Regina, SK: 1990 WJ;
    1992 WS; 1993 WSG; 1993 WS
Holgate, Mike, RHP, Windsor, ON: 1982 WS;
    1983 WS
Hollet, Gerald, OF, Montrose, BC: 1983 WS;
    1983 PAG
Holmes, Russ, OF, Victoria, BC: 1970 WS
Hood, Larry, LHP, Stellarton, NS: 1982 WJ;
    1986 PAC
Hook, Mike, OF, Brampton, ON: 1996 WJ
Hornostaj, Aaron, OF-INF, Waterloo, ON:
    1999 WJ; 2000 WJ; 2001 WJ
Hornostaj, Steve, SS, Waterloo, ON: 2004 WJ
Horsman, Vince, LHP, Dartmouth, NS: 2000 WS
Horsman, Wally, C, Dartmouth, NS: 1987 PAG;
    1987 IC
Horswell, Craig, C, Prince George, BC:
    1993 WSG; 1993 WS; 1994 WS; 1995 OQ
Hosford, Clinton, RHP, North Vancouver, BC:
    1998 WJ
Houde, Benoit, LHP-OF, St. Eustache, QC:
    1980 WJ
Houghton, Rick, OF, Vancouver, BC: 1971 WS;
    1971 PAG
Hoy, Peter, RHP, Cardinal, ON: 1988 WS;
    1988 OG
Hrapchak, Dale, RHP, Saskatoon, SK:
    1992 WJ; 1993 WJ
Hubbel, Travis, RHP, Edmonton, AB: 2001 WS;
    2003 WS
Hull, John, OF, East York, ON: 1996 PAG Jr

Humber, Frank, LHP, Corner Brook, NL:
    1987 PAG; 1987 IC; 1988 WS; 1988 OG
Hunter, Bob, LHP, Winnipeg, MB: 1967 PAG
Huntingford, Matt, OF, Bowen Island, BC:
    1996 WJ; 1997 WJ
Hurst, Cam, OF, Winnipeg, MB: 1967 PAG

Ianuzzi, Joe, OF, Stoney Creek, ON: 1989 WS;
    1991 PAG
Ingham, Daryl, RHP, Winnipeg, MB: 1985 WJ
Ircandia Vince, INF, Calgary, AB: 2004 WSG
Irvine, Joel, C, Dartmouth, NS: 1994 WS
Ivan, John, 3B, Windsor, ON: 1982 WS;
    1983 WS; 1983 PAG; 1984 OG; 1992 WS
Izumi, John, LHP-OF, Toronto, ON: 1986 WJ

Jablonski, David, RHP, Calgary, AB: 1999 WJ
Jackson, Lane, OF, Kindersley, SK: 1967 PAG
Jalbert, Brad, OF, Saskatoon, SK: 2000 WJ
Jamieson, Sam, SS, McAuley, MB: 1972 WS
Janz, Wayne, INF, Winnipeg, MB: 1965 WJ
Jeffrey, Paul, OF, Bridgewater, NS: 1980 WJ
Johnson, Gordie, RHP, Burnaby, BC:
    1978 WS; 1979 PAG
Johnson, Harold, 1B, Calgary, AB: 1980 WS
Johnson, Mike, RHP, Edmonton, AB: 2003 OQ;
    2004 OG
Johnson, Travis, C-1B, Vancouver, BC: 1990 WJ
Johnston, Kevin, RHP, Surrey, BC: 2000 WJ
Johnston, Rick, OF, Peterborough, ON: 1985
    IC; 1987 PAG; 1987 IC; 1988 WS; 1988 OG;
    1989 PC; 1989 WS; 1990 WS; 1991 PAG
Jones, Dean, SS, Montreal, QC: 1981 WJ
Jones, Jeff, RHP, Windsor, ON: 1998 WS
Jones, Paul, 2B, Edmonton, AB: 1998 WJ
Jones, Sean, RHP, Hamilton, ON: 2001 WS;
    2003 WS
Jutras, Serge, SS, Trois Rivieres, QC: 1974 WS

Kangas, Ben, C, Cambridge, ON: 2002 WSG
Karch, Gord, OF, Calgary, AB: 1965 WJ
Kashuba, Michael, RHP, Vernon, BC: 1998 WJ
Kasperski, Dan RHP-OF, Weyburn, SK:
    1986 WJ; 1987 WJ; 1989 WS
Keenan, Mike, RHP, Saint John, NB: 1989 PC;
    1990 WS
Keith, Kevin, OF, Thorold, ON: 1975 WC;
    1975 PAG; 1977 WC
Kelly, Mike, LHP, Morell, PEI: 1965 WJ
Kelly, Scott, RHP, Belleville, ON: 2001 WJ
Kelm, Brian, SS, Barrheard, AB: 1980 WJ
Kemp, Roy, OF, Saskatoon, SK: 1978 WS
Kennedy, Ken, LHP, Vancouver, BC: 1981 WJ
Kenning, Ryan, OF-1B, North Vancouver, BC:
    1998 WJ
Ketchen, Doug, RHP, Calgary, AB: 1989 WS
Kierstead, Mike, RHP, Musquash, NB:
    1999 WJ; 2001 WS
Kingston, Steve, LHP, Saint John, NB: 1980 WJ
Kinley, Bill, INF, Winnipeg, MB: 1980 WS
Kitsch, Trent, 1B-C, Kelowna, BC: 1997 WJ
Klaehn, Bruce, RHP, Kitchener, ON: 1971 WS
Klassen, Danny, SS, Leamington, ON: 2004 OG
Kondro, Brett, LHP, Fort Saskatchewan, AB:
    1995 WJ; 1998 WS
Kotkas, Jim, OF, Lethbridge, AB: 1981 WJ;
    1985 IC; 1986 PAC; 1987 IC; 1987 PAG;
    1988 WS; 1988 OG; 1989 PC; 1989 WS;
    1990 GG; 1990 WS; 1991 PAG

Kroeker, Tim, INF, Saskatoon, SK: 1993 WSG; 1993 WS; 1994 WS; 1995 OQ

Krug, David, RHP, Oakville, ON: 1989 PC; 1989 WS; 1990 GG; 1990 WS; 1991 PAG

Krywionek, Josh, RHP, Hamilton, ON: 2002 WSG; 2004 WSG

Kuhn, Brad, SS, Leduc, AB: 1996 WJ

Kusiewicz, Mike, Nepean, ON: 1994 WJ; 2003 OQ; 2004 OG; 2005 WCQ

Kuzminski, Barry, RHP, Waskatenau, AB: 1980 WS; 1981 IC; 1983 WS; 1983 PAG; 1984 OG; 1985 IC

Labiak, Mike, RHP, Windsor, ON: 1981 WJ

Laboissiere, Gord, C, Brandon, MB: 1978 WS; 1980 WS

Labute, Bernard, C, Windsor, ON: 1982 WJ

Lachance, Alain, INF, Sherbrooke, QC: 1989 WJ

Lachane, Louis, OF, Sherbrooke, QC: 1989 WJ

Lachapelle, Yan, RHP, St.Laurent, QC: 1999 PAG

Laflamme, Martin 3B, Repentigny, QC: 1993 PAG Jr

Laforest, Pierre-Luc "Pete", Gatineau, QC: 1996 WJ; 2003 OQ; 2004 OG

Lafreniere, Martin, LHP, Trois Rivieres, QC: 1998 WS

Lagrandeur, Yan, RHP, Granby, QC: 1995 OQ

Lakovic, Greg, C, Coquitlam, BC: 1993 WJ

Lalor, Dwayne, OF, Red Deer, AB: 1985 IC; 1986 PAC

Lalumiere, Yves, 2B-SS, Montreal, QC: 1979 WJ

Lampitt, Neil, 1B, North Battleford, SK: 1974 WS

Lane, Cam, C-OF, Welland, ON: 1983 WJ; 1984 WJ

Langley, Paul, RHP North Vancouver, BC: 1988 WJ

Lansdell, Daryn, RHP-INF, Victoria, BC: 1983 WJ; 1983 WS

LaPlante, Michel, RHP, Val d'Or, QC: 1991 PAG

Laplante, Reggie, RHP, Beauport, QC: 1997 WJ

Larkin, Matt, C, Kitchener, ON: 1987 WJ

Lauzon, Jacques-Pierre, INF, QC: 1965 WJ

Laveay, Blaise, C, Kamloops, BC: 1991 WJ

Lavigne, Martin, LHP, Loretteville, QC: 1989 WJ

Lawson, Jim, RHP, Richmond, BC: 1986 PAC

Lawson, Russ, INF-OF, Richmond, BC: 1986 WJ

Leavitt, Dale, RHP, St. Stephen, NB: 1982 WJ

Leduchowski, Gord, 3B, Riverton, MB: 1977 WC; 1980 WS

Lee, Jason, SS, Edmonton, AB: 1991 WJ; 1992 WS

Lennerton, Jordan, 1B, Langley, BC: 2004 WJ

Leon, Kyle, OF, Guelph, ON: 2005 WCQ

Leonard, John, SS, Oakville, ON: 1989 WS; 1989 PC; 1990 WS

Lepage, Phil, LHP, Fredericton, NB: 1973 WS; 1973 IC

Lepine, Julien, SS, Charlesbourg, QC: 1999 PAG

Lepine, Olivier, C, Charlesbourg, QC: 1996 WJ; 2003 WS; 2005 WCQ

Leroux, Chris, C, Mississauga, ON; 2001 WJ; 2002 WJ

Lessard, Carl, RHP, Trois Rivieres, QC: 1979 WJ

Leswick, Nick, OF, Calgary, AB: 1997 WJ

Letourneau, Rey, SS, Montmagny, QC: 1991 PAG

Levack, Ron, SS, Windsor, ON: 1979 WJ

Lindsay, Greg, LHP, Burnaby, BC: 1973 WS; 1974 WS; 1975 IC; 1975 PAG

Lindstard, Denis, LHP-1B, Camrose, AB: 1975 IC

Lisowski, Les, LHP, Winnipeg, MB: 1970 WS

Lister, Gerry, OF, Pelly, SK: 1970 WS

Lockwood, Jon, RHP, Toronto, ON: 2003 WS

Loewen, Adam, LHP, Surrey, BC: 2000 WJ; 2001 WJ; 2002 WJ

Logan, Andy, C, Regina, SK: 1971 WS; 1973 WC; 1977 WC; 1979 PAG

Logan, Matt, 1B, Brampton, ON: 1999 PAG; 2001 WS; 2003 OQ

Lonpre, Nicolas, SS-2B, Laval, QC: 1999 WJ

Lorenz, Rob, C-3B, Delta, BC: 1983 WJ

Loye, Corey, RHP, Dartmouth, NS: 1996 PAG Jr

Loyns, Lynn, INF, Naicam, SK: 1999 WJ

Luther, Garry, OF, Don Mills, ON: 1987 WJ

Lychak, Perry, LHP, Edmonton, AB: 1979 WS; 1979 PAG; 1980 WS; 1981 IC

Lynn, Shawn, RHP, North York, ON: 1996 PAG Jr

Mabee, Bob, RHP, Victoria, BC: 1970 WS

MacArthur, Brad, RHP, White Rock, BC: 1975 IC; 1975 PAG; 1977 WC; 1978 WS

MacDonald, Andrew, RHP, Charlottetown, PEI: 2004 WJ

MacDonald, Bruce, RHP, Provost, AB: 1980 WJ

MacDonald, Fred, OF, Charlottetown, PEI: 1965 WJ

MacDonald, Jeff, RHP, Lacombe, AB: 1999 WJ

MacDougall, Dave, 3B-RHP, Charlottetown, PEI: 1980 WJ

Mace, Kyle, OF-INF, Nelson, BC: 2004 WSG

MacFarlane, Charlie, OF, Lantzville, BC: 2001 WJ

MacIssac, Dave, INF, Charlottetown, PEI: 1981 WJ

MacKay, Rod, RHP, Vancouver, BC: 1977 WC

MacKay, Kent, 3B, Charlottetown, PEI: 1980 WJ

MacLeod, Kevin, LHP, Sydney, NS: 1985 WS; 1985 IC

Mainville, Martin, RHP, Montreal, QC: 1992 WJ

Majcher, Mike, LHP, Brandon, MB: 1979 PAG

Malo, Jonathan, SS, St. Roch de l'Achigan, QC: 2001 WJ

Mandryk, Jason, RHP, Langton, ON: 1997 WJ; 1998 WJ

Mann, Larry, RHP, Vancouver, BC: 1975 PAG

Mann, Scott, OF, Oshawa, ON: 1980 WJ; 1981 IC; 1982 WS; 1983 WS; 1983 PAG; 1984 OG

Marcoux, François, OF, Laval, QC: 1993 PAG Jr

Mark, Rick, OF, North Vancouver, BC: 1975 PAG

Martel, Jerome, RHP, Charlesbourg, QC: 1993 PAG Jr

Martel, Jim, RHP, Cambridge, ON: 1982 WS

Martin, Russ, INF, Montreal, QC: 1999 WJ; 2000 WJ; 2001 WJ; 2003 OQ

Martin, Wayne, 1B, New Westminster, BC: 1972 WS; 1973 WS; 1973 IC; 1975 PAG

Martindale, David, SS, Mississauga, ON: 1996 PAG Jr

Mason, Matt, C, Sparwood, BC: 1995 WJ

Matsubara, Fred, RHP, Winnipeg, MB: 1990 WS

Mauthe, Allan, INF, Vancouver, BC: 1985 IC; 1986 PAC; 1987 PAG, 1987 IC; 1988 WS; 1988 OG

Maxwell, Marty, INF, Lethbridge, AB: 1973 WS; 1975 IC; 1975 PAG

Maxwell, Scott, OF, Lethbridge, AB: 1984 OG

Mazzocca, Loris, OF, Laval, QC: 1984 WJ

McAusland, Brian, C, Armstrong, BC: 1979 PAG

McCallum, Geoff, SS, London, ON: 2000 WS; 2003 WS; 2005 WCQ

McConachy, Brock, OF, Winnipeg, MB: 1973 WS

McCullough, Bob, SS, Toronto, ON: 1981 IC; 1982 WS; 1983 WS; 1983 PAG; 1984 OG; 1985 IC

McDonald, Barry, RHP, Vancouver, BC: 1979 PAG

McDonald, Bob, OF, Vancouver, BC: 1990 WJ

McDonald, Mark, RHP, Burlington, ON: 2001 WJ

McElrea, Mike, RHP: 1988 WJ

McGillvary, Scott, RHP, Summerland, BC: 1995 WJ

McGovern, Ryan, LHP, Abbotsford, BC: 2002 WJ

McGraw, Matthew, C, Burlington, ON: 2004 WSG

McIntrye, Don: 1974 WS

McIntyre, Spencer, LHP, Calgary, AB: 1992 WS; 1993 WSG; 1993 WS

McIvor, Rod, OF, Eston, SK: 1972 WS; 1974 WS

McKaig, Terry, OF, Vernon, BC: 1995 OQ

McKay, Cody, 3B-C, Vancouver, BC: 1995 OQ

McKay, Dave, INF, Vancouver, BC: 1970 WS

McKee, Russ, RHP, Vancouver, BC: 1971 WS; 1974 WS

McKenzie, Tommy, SS, Kitchener, ON: 1967 PAG; 1970 WS; 1971 WS; 1971 PAG; 1979 PAG

McKillop, Bob, C, Cambridge, ON: 1967 PAG

McKinlay, Mike, RHP, Duncan, BC: 1991 WJ; 1992 WJ

McKinnon, Ryan, INF, Hamilton, ON: 2002 WSG

McNab, Dereck, RHP, Niagara Falls, ON: 1980 WJ

McNabb, Andy, OF, Dundas, ON: 1993 WSG; 1993 WS

McPhail, Doug, OF, Two Hills, AB: 1977 WC; 1981 IC; 1982 WS; 1983 WS; 1983 PAG; 1984 OG; 1985 IC

McPherson, Stu, OF, Tsawwassen, BC: 1979 WJ; 1980 WJ

Mears, Chris, RHP, Victoria, BC: 1995 WJ; 1999 PAG; 2001 WS; 2003 OQ; 2004 OG

Meier, Jason, OF, Waterloo, ON: 1992 WJ

Meilleur, Rob, RHP, Winnipeg, MB: 1983 WJ

Mejholm, Karl, RHP, Nanaimo, BC: 2002 WJ

Merritt, Graig, C, Pitt Meadows, BC: 1996 WJ

Messier, Alex, RHP, St. Hyacinthe, QC: 1990 WJ

Meyer, Jay, RHP, Brampton, ON: 1994 WJ

Meyers, Mike, RHP, Tillsonburg, ON: 1995 WJ; 1999 PAG; 2003 OQ

Mills, Roy, OF, NS: 1980 WJ

Milo, Richard, OF, Montreal, QC: 1975 IC

Mimeault, Marc-Olivier, C-1B, St. Constant, QC: 2004 WJ

Mitchell, Greg, 1B-3B, Maple Ridge, BC: 1998 WS

Mitchell, Jeffrey, LHP, Riverview, NB: 1990 WJ; 1993 WSG; 1993 WS

Mitchell, Nick, RHP, Vancouver, BC: 1973 IC; 1975 PAG

Mitzell, Glenn, INF, Vancouver, BC: 1989 PC

Mobberley, Steve, SS, Barrhead, AB: 1979 PAG

Moffat, Lyle, OF, Calgary, AB: 1965 WJ

Moniz, Carl, INF, Laval, QC: 2004 WJ

Montaneri, Dave, OF, Windsor, ON: 1979 PAG; 1980 WS; 1981 IC

Moore, Tim, RHP, Saint John, NB: 1995 WJ

Morisseau, François, INF, Montreal, QC: 1980 WJ

Morneau, Justin, 1B, New Westminster, BC: 2001 WS; 2003 OQ

Morris, Kerry, LHP, New Westminster, BC: 1978 WS

Morrison, Greg, 1B, Medicine Hat, AB: 1993 WJ; 1994 WJ; 1999 PAG; 2000 WS; 2003 WS; 2005 WCQ

Mosher, Craig, LHP, Richmond, BC: 1997 WJ; 1998 WS; 2001 WS

Muhlethaler, David, RHP, Edmonton, AB: 1979 WJ; 1983 WS

Muir, Harry, RHP, London, ON: 1990 WJ

Mullens, Greg, RHP, Saskatoon, SK: 2003 WJ

Munch, Randy, SS, Saskatoon, SK: 1971 WS

Munoz, Mike, RHP, Surrey, BC: 1979 WJ

Musselman, Ron, OF, Stratford, ON: 1982 WS

Murray, Steve, LHP, Ennismore, ON: 1996 PAG Jr; 2005 WCQ

Murray, Zach, LHP, Edmonton, AB: 2003 WS

Myers, Darell, LHP, Delta, BC: 1985 WJ

Myette, Aaron, RHP, Surrey, BC: 1995 WJ; 2004 OG

Naccarata, Ivan, 2B-SS, Longueuil, QC: 2000 WJ; 2003 WS

Nailer, Pat, INF, Toronto, ON: 1999 WJ

Nauth, Daniel, RHP, Brampton, ON: 2004 WSG

Nelson, Steve, RHP, Dartmouth, NS: 1999 WJ

Nelson, Tim, 3B, Calgary, AB: 1998 WS

Nelson, Tom, INF, Windsor, ON: 1981 IC; 1982 WS; 1983 WS; 1983 PAG; 1984 OG; 1985 IC; 1987 WS; 1987 IC; 1988 WS; 1988 OG

Neveu, Frederic, C, Laval, QC: 1992 WJ

Neville, Garth, RHP, Binscairth, MB: 1972 WS; 1973 IC; 1975 PAG; 1977 WC

Nicholson, Kevin, SS, Surrey, BC: 1995 OQ; 2003 OQ; 2004 OG

Nicholson, Robert, OF, Calgary, AB: 1991 WJ

Nissen, Steve, RHP, Fredericton, NB: 1983 WJ

Niven, Lorne, DH, Edmonton, AB: 1980 WS; 1981 IC

Noel, Alain, C, Trois Rivieres, QC: 1986 PAC

Northcott, Harold, LHP-1B, Rocky Mountain House, AB: 1980 WJ; 1985 IC; 1986 PAC; 1987 PAG; 1987 IC

Noton, Bill, RHP, BC: 1979 WJ

Oaks, Maurice, INF, Gladstone, MB: 1967 PAG

O'Connor, Shawn, RHP, Pakenham, ON: 1991 PAG; 1992 WS; 1993 WS; 1994 WS; 1995 OQ

Ogiltree, John, RHP, Mississauga, ON: 2000 WS; 2003 OQ; 2004 OG

O'Halloran, Greg, C-OF, Mississauga, ON: 1985 WJ; 1986 WJ; 1988 WS; 1988 OG

Ohrn, Les, P, Dapp, AB: 1973 IC

O'Krane, Dillon, C, Langley, BC: 2003 WJ

Ornest, Maury, 1B, Vancouver, BC: 1978 WS; 1979 PAG

Orr, Peter, INF, Newmarket, ON: 2001 WS; 2003 OQ; 2004 OG

Osberg, Brian, LHP, Lethbridge, AB: 1981 WJ

Osborne, John, 2B-RHP, Toronto, ON: 1973 WS; 1975 IC; 1975 PAG; 1977 WC

Ouellette, Julien, RHP, Montreal, QC: 1965 WJ

Ouellette, Marc-Andre, RHP, QC: 1970 WS

Owen, John, RHP, London, ON: 1979 PAG

Owen, Nick, 1B, Barrie, ON: 1971 WS

Paiement, Ray, RHP, Falher, AB: 1977 WC; 1978 WS; 1979 PAG
Painter, Shawn, OF, Beaconsfield, QC: 1993 WJ
Paisley, Jim, INF, Regina, SK: 1965 WJ
Parisotto, Barry, RHP, Trail, BC: 1987 PAG; 1987 IC; 1988 WS; 1988 OG
Parker, David, RHP, Winnipeg, MB: 2001 WJ
Patenaude, Alain, RHP, Trois Rivieres, QC: 1984 OG
Paul, Kalam, RHP, Winnipeg, MB: 1990 WJ; 2000 WS
Payne, Alfie, SS, Thornhill, ON: 1975 IC; 1975 PAG
Payne, Brad, Thornhill, ON: 1995 WJ
Paz, Jeff, INF, Surrey, BC; 2003 WJ
Pearson, Shawn, OF, Guelph, ON: 1995 WJ
Peley, Josue, INF, Montreal, QC: 2004 WJ
Pelletier, Curties, INF-OF, Nanaimo, BC: 1998 WJ
Pentland, Cam, RHP, Calgary, AB: 1993 WJ
Periard, Alexandre, RHP, St. Eustache, QC: 2004 WJ
Perrone, Rob, RHP, Windsor, ON: 1989 WJ
Petrachenko, Barry, INF, Welland, ON: 1984 WJ; 1989 PC; 1990 WJ; 1990 GG; 1990 WS; 1991 PAG
Picard, Alain, C, Ste. Foy, QC: 1999 WJ
Picard, Jean-Francois, C, Trois Rivieres, QC: 1993 PAG Jr
Picco, John, LHP, Lasalle, QC: 2000 WJ; 2001 WJ; 2001 WS
Picone, Gary, OF, Barrhead, AB: 1973 WS; 1974 WS; 1978 WS; 1979 PAG; 1980 WS
Pietrasko, Jamie, C, Kitchener, ON: 1998 WS
Pimpare, Stephane, LHP, Reptinginy, QC: 1992 WS
Pineau, Rob, OF, Etobicoke, ON: 2002 WSG
Podruzny, Alex, INF, Two Hills, AB: 1981 IC
Pogue, Jamie, C, Guelph, ON: 2001 WS; 2003 WS; 2005 WCQ
Pond, Simon, INF, North Vancouver, BC: 2000 WS; 2004 OG
Poulin, Max, INF, St. Eustache, QC: 2001 WS; 2005 WCQ
Powell, Tony, OF, Port Alberni, BC: 1979 WJ; 1980 WS; 1981 IC
Power, Ken, RHP, Halifax, NS: 1980 WJ
Pranger, Rylan, LHP, Guelph, ON: 2004 WSG
Prata, Danny, LHP, Repentigny, QC: 1993 PAG Jr; 1996 WJ; 2003 WS
Price, Al, C, Barrhead, AB: 1977 WC; 1980 WS
Prophet, Donald, RHP, Gatineau, QC: 1993 PAG Jr

Quinn, Jeff, RHP, Saint John, NB: 1982 WJ
Quintal, Simon, OF, Longueuil, QC: 1993 PAG Jr

Racine, Philippe, SS-2B, La Prairie, QC: 2003 WJ
Radmanovich, Ryan, OF, Calgary, AB: 1993 WSG; 1993 WS; 1999 PAG; 2001 WS; 2003 OQ; 2004 OG
Ralph, Brett, SS-2B, Raymond, AB: 2000 WJ
Ramos, Jeff, C, Toronto, ON: 1993 WJ
Ramsey, Dale, INF, Vancouver, BC: 1975 WS; 1978 WS
Randall, Mark, RHP, Edmonton, AB: 1998 WS; 1999 PAG; 2000 WS; 2001 WS

Rasmussen, Randy, 2B, St. Paul, AB: 1979 WS; 1979 PAG; 1980 WS; 1981 IC; 1982 WS; 1983 WS; 1983 PAG
Raymond, Pascal, RHP, Laval, QC: 1987 WJ
Reeves, Jeff, RHP, Peterborough, ON: 1999 WJ
Reid, Mike, C, ON: 1980 WJ
Reid, Tom, OF, Fredriction, NB: 1973 IC
Reily, Wayne, C, NS: 1965 WJ
Reimer, Kevin, 3B-OF, Enderby, BC: 1981 WJ; 1983 WS; 1983 PAG; 1984 OG
Renigar, Greg, SS-OF, St. Albert, AB: 1980 WJ
Reitsma, Chris, RHP, Calgary, AB: 1995 WJ
Rempel, Andy, OF, Abbotsford, BC: 1999 WJ
Renigar, Greg, INF, Red Deer, AB: 1980 WJ
Rhynes, Cass, C, Cornwall, PEI: 2001 WJ
Rich, Jason, C, Delta, BC: 1997 WJ
Richardson, Brian "BJ", OF, Windsor, ON: 1991 WJ; 1992 WJ
Richmind, Jamie, RHP, Mississauga, ON: 2004 WJ
Ricketts, Chad, RHP, Waterloo, ON: 1999 PAG; 2003 WS
Rivard, Reggie, RHP, Bonnyville, AB: 2005 WCQ
Robertson, Al, 2B, Hamiota, MB: 1967 PAG; 1971 PAG
Robertson, Jeff, 1B-OF, Hamioata, MB: 1983 WJ
Robichaud, Gilles, INF, Montreal, QC: 1971 WS
Robinson, Brad, INF, Coquitlam, BC: 1989 WJ
Robinson, Chris, C, Dorchester, ON: 2002 WJ; 2003 WS
Robinson Scott, RHP, Ajax, ON: 2004 WSG
Robitaille, Martin, OF, Ste. Foy, QC: 1983 WJ; 1984 WJ; 1986 PAC
Rodgers, Wayne, SS, Vancouver, BC: 1974 WS
Rogelstad, Matt, INF, Coquitlam, BC: 1999 WJ; 2000 WJ
Rogers, Brad, RHP, Nanaimo, BC: 2003 WS; 2005 WCQ
Rogers, Ken, 2B-SS, Toronto, ON: 1992 WJ
Romak, Jamie, 3B-1B, London, ON: 2002 WJ
Rose, Ian, 1B-OF, Fredericton, NB: 1981 WJ; 1982 WJ
Rosenlund, Bill, RHP, Vancouver, BC: 1979 WJ
Ross, Bob, INF, Victoria, BC: 1987 WJ
Ross, David, LHP, St. Albert, AB: 1986 WJ; 1998 WS; 2000 WS
Ross, Mike, RHP, Calgary, AB: 1987 PAG; 1987 IC; 1989 PC; 1989 WS; 1990 WS; 1990 GG; 1991 PAG; 1992 WS; 1999 PAG
Roth, Greg, 3B, Pincher Creek, AB: 1983 WJ; 1987 PAG; 1987 IC; 1988 WS; 1988 OG
Rothwell, Derek, RHP-3B, Cambridge, ON: 1985 WJ; 1986 WJ
Rouleau, Guy, RHP, Montreal, QC: 1982 WJ
Rouleau, Mario, RHP, Montreal, QC: 1989 WJ
Rowley, Darryl, LHP, North Battleford, SK: 1984 WJ; 1986 PAC
Rowley, Roy, 3B-RHP, Moose Jaw, SK: 1970 WS; 1971 PAG; 1973 IC
Roy, Alain, OF, Laval, QC: 1992 WS; 1993 WSG; 1993 WS
Roy, Angus, RHP, Mississauga, ON: 1996 WJ
Roy, Jean-Philippe, SS, Cap-Rouge, QC: 1993 PAG Jr
Roy, Robin, RHP, Blainville, QC: 1987 WJ; 1989 PC; 1989 WS
Ruhr, David, OF, Calgary, AB: 1998 WS
Rutherford, James C, Toronto, ON: 2002 WSG

Rypien, Dave, C, Calgary, AB: 1983 WS;
1983 PAG; 1988 WS; 1988 OG; 1989 PC;
1989 WS; 1990 GG; 1990 WS; 1991 PAG

Salhani, Ted, OF, London, ON: 1998 WS
Saulnier, Shawn, RHP, Yarmouth, NS: 1982 WJ
Saunders, Mike, INF-RHP, Victoria, BC:
2003 WJ
Sawa, Randy, LHP, Regina, SK: 1972 WS
Sawicki, Darryl, RHP, Vancouver, BC: 1989 PC
Sawkiw, Warren, INF, Weston, ON: 1985 WJ;
1986 WJ; 1998 WS; 1988 OG
Scalabrini, Patrick, Waterville, QC: 2003 WS
Schell, Todd, OF, Oakville, ON: 1991 WJ
Schlosser, Mark, INF-OF, Medicine Hat, AB:
1992 WJ
Schlosser, Paul, C, Medicine Hat, AB: 2000 WS
Schmor, Brent, RHP, Mission, BC: 1992 WJ
Schroer, Dustin OF-RHP, Langley, BC: 2000 WJ
Schwab, Dave, 2B, Burnaby, BC: 1975 PAG;
1977 WC
Schwabe, Jason, OF, Winnipeg, MB: 1990 WJ
Schwartz, Randy, INF-RHP, Kleinburg, ON:
2003 WJ
Scott, Glennis, RHP, Miami, MB: 1967 PAG;
1970 WS; 1971 WS; 1972 WS
Sgrignoli, Marc, OF, Guelph, ON: 2002 WSG
Shallow, Doug, OF, Gander, NL: 1982 WJ
Shantz, Tyler, INF-OF, Stratford, ON:
1993 WSG; 1993 WS
Sharp, Syd, C, Surrey, BC: 1973 WS
Shuh, Jeremy, RHP, Brockville, ON: 2002 WSG
Siddall, Joe, C, Windsor, ON: 1985 WJ
Sidhu, Arman, SS, Mississauga, ON: 2002 WJ
Simard, Michel, RHP, Charlesbourg, QC:
2001 WS
Simmonds, Keith, INF, Corner Brook, NL: 1982 WJ
Simon, Doug, OF, Regina, SK: 1971 WS;
1973 WS; 1973 IC; 1974 WS; 1975 IC;
1975 PAG; 1977 WC; 1978 WS; 1979 PAG
Siriveau, Nom, Vancouver, BC: 1998 WJ
Smeeton, Chris, RHP, Windsor, ON: 1989 PC;
1989 WS; 1990 GG; 1990 WS; 1991 PAG
Smith, Barry, OF, Toronto, ON: 1975 IC
Smith, Brian, OF, Oakner, MB: 1971 PAG
Smith, Donnie, RHP, Winnipeg, MB: 2000 WS
Smith, Lee, 2B, Moose Jaw, SK: 1997 WJ
Smith, Mel, OF, Hamiota, MB: 1965 WJ
Smith, Ron, INF, Kitchener, ON: 1967 PAG
Smith, Scott, C, Sarnia, ON: 2002 WSG
Smith, Steve, RHP, Mahone Bay, NS:
1992 WS; 1993 WSG; 1993 WS
Smith, Tim, OF, Toronto, ON: 2003 WJ; 2004 WJ
Smith, Wayne, OF, Toronto, ON: 1975 PAG
Smithson, Russell, SS-2B, Port Coquitlam, BC:
2002 WJ
Sokalaski, Steve, RHP, North Vancouver, BC:
1985 WS
Soloman, Ray, RHP, Windsor, ON: 1989 WJ;
1989 PC
Somers, Henry, SS, Vancouver, BC: 1977 WC
Sonntag, Galen, RHP, Brandon, MB: 1984 WJ;
1986 PAC
Sowden, Shane, RHP, Moose Jaw, SK: 1997 WJ
Speller, Roger, OF, Thornhill, ON: 1979 WJ;
1980 WS; 1981 IC
Spoljaric, Paul, LHP, Kelowna, BC: 1987 WJ;
1988 WJ; 1989 WS; 2003 WS; 2004 OG

Springenatic, Dennis, OF, Surrey, BC:
1986 WS; 1987 PAG
Springenatic, Ted, C-3B, Surrey, BC:
1973 WS; 1974 WS; 1975 IC; 1975 PAG;
1977 WC; 1978 WS
St. Pierre, Pascual, 2B, Sherbrooke, QC:
1988 WJ; 1989 WJ
Stairs, Matt, SS-OF, Fredericton, NB:
1986 WJ; 1987 IC; 1988 WS; 1988 OG
Stead, Ron, LHP, Chatham, ON: 1967 PAG
Steffler, Dave, RHP, Keene, ON: 1998 WS;
2000 WS
Stephens, Al, OF, Ajax, ON: 1996 PAG Jr;
1998 WJ
Stern, Adam, OF, London, ON: 2003 OQ;
2004 OG
Stewardson, William, RHP, London, ON: 2000 WJ
Stewart, Andy, C, Oshawa, ON: 1988 WJ;
1999 PAG; 2000 WS; 2004 OG
Stewart, Ryan, INF, Toronto, ON: 2002 WSG
Stezycki, Matt, INF, Tecumseh, ON: 2002 WSG
Stocco, Mark, OF, Milton, ON: 1993 WSG;
1993 WS
Stokke, Dale, INF, Crooked Creek, AB:
1971 WS; 1971 PAG
Stokke Strandlund, Charlie, RHP-INF, Victoria,
BC: 2004 WSG
Strecker, Stefan, RHP, Dundas, ON: 2002 WSG
Stockman, Matt, C, Scarborough, ON:
1998 WS; 1999 PAG
Stockman, Nathan, C, Scarborough, ON:
1996 PAG Jr; 1998 WJ
Stone, Ross, LHP, Nipawan, SK: 1967 PAG;
1971 PAG
Strongman, George, OF, Victoria, BC: 1970 WS
Sweeney, Mike, 3B-SS, St. Stephen, NB:
1979 WJ; 1980 WJ
Szeryk, Neil, 1B-OF, London, ON: 1988 WJ

Tait, Byron, INF-OF, Courtenay, BC: 1983 WJ
Tanaka, Rob, OF, Burlington, ON: 1987 WJ;
1988 WJ; 1992 WS
Tanguay, Dominic, RHP, St. Jean Chrysostime,
QC: 1999 WJ
Tanguay, Martin, 2B, Asbestos, QC: 1997 WJ
Tanton, Calvin, C, Strathmore, AB: 1994 WJ
Tasiaux, Charles, RHP, Quebec City, QC:
2004 WSG
Tayles, Brad, INF, Windsor, ON: 1987 WJ;
1988 WJ
Taylor, Rod: 1973 WS; 1973 IC
Teague, Gamin, 2B, Brampton, ON: 1996 PAG Jr
Teahan, Mike, C, Barrhead, AB: 1973 WS; 1973
WS; 1974 WS; 1975 PAG; 1978 WS; 1979 PAG
Tecklenburg, Daren, 3B-RHP Vancouver, BC:
1989 WS
Tessier, Yves, INF, Drummonville, QC: 1985 WJ
Therien, Dominic, OF, Cap-de-la-Madeleine,
QC: 1989 WJ; 1990 WJ
Thiessen, Pete, RHP, Vancouver, BC: 1975 WS
Thomas, Jim, SS, West Vancouver, BC:
1975 IC; 1975 PAG
Thompson, Bob, RHP-OF, Oak Lake, MB:
1971 WS; 1971 PAG; 1975 IC; 1975 PAG
Thompson, Todd, INF, Trail, BC: 1994 WJ;
1995 WJ
Thomson, Rob, C, Corunna, ON: 1981 WJ;
1984 OG

Thomson, Jeff, RHP, Grande Pointe, MB: 2004 WJ

Thorman, Scott, INF-RHP, Cambridge, ON: 2000 WJ; 2001 WS; 2003 OQ

Thorn, Todd, LHP, Stratford, ON: 1994 WJ

Tilleman, Dale, OF, Taber, AB: 1978 WS; 1979 PAG; 1979 WS

Tobin, Jeff, Pickering, ON: 2004 WSG

Tolson, Ray, OF, Windsor, ON: 1981 WJ

Toneguzzi, Chris, RHP, Thunder Bay, ON; 2001 WJ

Torrance, Ken, OF, Surrey, BC: 1991 WJ

Tosoni, Matt, LHP, Whitby, ON: 2002 WJ

Tosoni, Rene, OF-INF, Port Coquitlam, BC: 2003 WJ

Totenson, Ron, SS, Kelowna, BC: 1979 WJ; 1980 WS

Tremblay, Dominic, RHP, Chicoutimi, QC: 1993 PAG Jr

Tronchin, David, INF, Windsor, ON: 1985 WJ; 1986 WJ

Tucker, Julien, RHP, Lasalle, QC: 2003 WS

Unrah, Brian, LHP, Surrey, BC: 1982 WS

Unrat, Chris, C, Beaconsfield, QC: 2001 WS

Uzelman, Quinn, INF, Kindersley, SK: 1995 WJ

Valiquette, Philippe-Alexandre, LHP, St. Laurent, QC: 2003 WJ; 2004 WJ

Vandecaveye, Doug, 3B, Tilbury, ON: 1996 PAG Jr; 1997 WJ

Van de Keere, Keith, LHP, Barrhead, AB: 1974 WS; 1977 WC; 1978 WS; 1979 PAG; 1980 WS; 1981 IC

Vanderwel, Bill, RHP, Sarnia, ON: 1983 WJ; 1984 WJ

Van Gaalen, Aric, LHP, Edmonton, AB: 2005 WCQ

Van Iderstine, Ben, OF, Regina, SK: 2003 WS

Van Tol, Gary, INF, Pincher Creek, AB: 1989 PC; 1989 WS; 1990 GG; 1990 WS; 1991 PAG

Veinot, Ryan, 2B, Halifax, NS: 1999 WJ

Vendette, Sebastien, RHP, Laval, QC: 2004 WJ

Vetor, Chris, OF-C, Windsor, ON: 1989 WJ

Vickers, Wayne, C, Nanaimo, BC: 1998 WJ

Vienneau, Jacques, OF, Beloeil, QC: 1993 PAG Jr; 1996 WJ

Wainhouse, David, RHP, Scarborough, ON: 1988 WS; 1988 OG

Walcott, Richard, OF, Sydney, NS: 1988 WJ

Walker, Cam, RHP, Souris, MB: 1981 IC

Walker, Darcy, 1B, Campbell River, BC: 1981 IC

Walker, Larry, OF, Maple Ridge, BC: 1984 WJ

Wamback, Trevor, RHP, Lower Sackville, NS: 2001 WS

Ward, Mike, INF, Fredericton, NB: 1980 WJ

Ware, Jeremy, OF, Guelph, ON: 1999 PAG; 2001 WS; 2003 OQ; 2004 OG

Watamaniuk, Ron, SS, St. Albert, AB: 1973 IC

Watson, Al, C, Vancouver, BC: 1975 IC

Watson, Tanner, RHP, Arnprior, ON: 1999 WJ; 2000 WJ

Weatherbie, Bill, RHP, Charlottetown, PEI: 1965 WJ

Webster, Larry, LHP, Vancouver, BC: 1970 WS

Webster, Lorne, C: 1970 WS

Weglarz, Nick, 1B-OF, Stevensville, ON: 2004 WJ

Weibe, Ken, INF, Aberdeen, SK: 1978 WS; 1979 PAG

Westgard, Chuck, RHP, Surrey, BC: 1980 WJ; 1982 WS

White, Jarrett, C, Windsor, ON: 1986 WJ

White, Mark, C, Stratford, ON: 1988 WJ

Wiebe, Ken, 3B, Aberdeen, AB: 1978 WS; 1979 WS

Wiley, Dustin, C, Windsor, ON: 1996 PAG Jr

Williams, Tyler, OF, Delta, BC: 2002 WJ

Wllson, Craig, INF, Sarnia, ON: 1984 OG

Wilson, Larry, OF, Hamilton, ON: 1967 PAG

Wilson, Mark, RHP, Peterborough, ON: 2004 WJ

Wilson, Tom, OF-1B, Laval, QC: 1981 WJ

Wilson, Nigel, OF, Ajax, ON: 1987 WJ

Wilson, Steve, LHP, Vancouver, BC: 1983 WS; 1983 PAG; 1984 OG

Wiltshire, Cory, OF-LHP, Bowen Island, BC: 2003 WJ; 2004 WJ

Woelders, Dan, RHP, Langley, BC: 2000 WJ

Wolfe, Eric, 1B, Willowdale, ON: 2002 WJ

Wood, Joey, C, Cornwall, PEI: 1999 WJ

Wooden, Mark, RHP, Windsor, ON: 1983 WS; 1983 PAG; 1984 OG; 1985 IC

Woolley, Jason, INF, North York, ON: 1987 WJ

Young, Joe, RHP, Fort McMurray, AB: 1991 WJ

Ysebaert, Paul, SS, Sarnia, ON: 1986 PAC

Zebnik, Joey, RHP, Lasalle, QC: 1981 WJ; 1982 WJ

Zehr, Dan, LHP, Guelph, ON: 2004 WJ

Zimmerman, Jeff, RHP, Kelowna, BC: 1993 WSG; 1993 WS; 1994 WS; 1995 OQ

Zimmerman, Jordan, LHP, Kelowna, BC: 1992 WJ; 1993 WJ; 2001 WS

Zynnk, Mike, LHP, Windsor, ON: 1982 WJ

COACHING STAFF

Agostino, Alex, coach, St. Bruno, QC: 1994 WJ; 2003 WS

Arnold, Rob, Vancouver, BC, coach: 1980 WJ

Baba, Jim, coach/manager, Ottawa, ON: 1991 PAG; 1992 WS; 1993 WSG; 1993 WS; 1994 WS; 1995 OQ; 1998 WS; 2003 WS

Baron, Patrick, coach, Quebec City, QC: 2002 WSG; 2004 WSG

Beckman, Bernie, coach/manager, Ottawa, ON: 1987 IC; 1988 OG; 1989 PC; 1993 WSG; 1993 WS

Boehm, Andy, coach, Portage la Prairie, MB: 2001 WJ; 2002 WJ

Boucher, Denis, coach, Montreal, QC: 2003 OQ; 2004 OG

Burgess, Tom, coach, Lambeth, ON: 1999 WJ; 2000 WJ; 2000 WS; 2001 WS; 2003 WS

Cardinale, Remo, coach, Mississauga, ON: 1996 WJ; 1997 WJ; 1998 WS; 2000 WJ; 2004 WS; 2005 WCQ

Chapman, Jim, coach, Vancouver, BC: 1980 WJ

Chavarria, Ossie, coach, Burnaby, BC: 1987 PAG

Clark, Mark, coach, Fredericton, NB: 2004 WSG

Cuthill, Roy, coach, Weldwyn, SK: 1972 WS

Davidson, Bob, coach, Peterborough, ON: 1996 PAG Jr

Desjardins, Andre, coach, Ste. Therese, QC:
1981 WJ
Despres, Danny, coach, Montreal, QC: 1993 WJ
Dunlop, Cameron, coach, Mississauga, ON:
2002 WSG
Emond, Richard, coach/manager, Montreal,
QC: 1989 WJ; 1990 WJ; 1993 WJ; 1994 WS;
1995 OQ
Erasmus, Tom, coach, Edmonton, AB:
1981 WJ; 1983 WJ; 1984 WJ
Fink, Jim, coach, Regina, SK: 1995 WJ
Flood, Tony, coach, Mt. Pearl, NL: 1991 WJ;
1992 WJ
Fournier, Serge, coach, Beloeil, QC: 1987 PAG
Franchuk, Orv, coach, St. Albert, AB:
1977 WC; 1981 IC
Gamlin, Len, coach, Vancouver, BC: 1989 PC;
1992 WJ
Gelinas, Marc, coach, Laval, QC: 1983 WJ;
1984 WJ; 1985 WJ
Gerlach, Gord, coach, St. Albert, AB:
1998 WS; 1999 PAG; 2000 WS; 2001 WJ;
2001 WS; 2003 WS; 2005 WCQ
Graves, Don, manager, Hamilton, ON: 2002 WSG
Green, Bill, coach, Vancouver, BC: 1995 WJ
Groch, Dick, coach, Marysville, MI: 1982 WS;
1983 WS; 1983 PAG; 1984 OG; 1985 IC;
1986 PAC
Hamilton, Greg, coach/manager, Ottawa, ON:
1993 WSG; 1993 WS; 1994 WS; 1995 OQ;
1996 WJ; 1997 WJ; 1999 WJ; 2000 WJ;
2001 WJ; 2002 WJ; 2003 WJ; 2004 WJ;
2004 OG
Handrahan, Vern, coach, Charlottetown, PEI:
1975 IC
Harr, John, manager/coach, Burnaby, BC: 1975
IC; 1975 PAG; 1977 WC; 1987 PAG; 1987 IC;
1989 PC; 1991 WJ; 1992 WJ; 1994 WJ
Jenkins, Ferguson, coach, Chatham, ON:
1987 PAG
Johnston, Rick, coach/manager, Peterborough,
ON: 1996 WJ; 1997 WJ; 1998 WJ; 2005 WCQ
Keith, Kevin, Thorold, ON: 1990 WJ
King, Tom, coach, Saint John, NB: 1982 WJ
Lachance, Andre, Quebec City, QC:
1993 PAG Jr
Lacoursiere, Bob, coach, Saskatoon, SK:
1967 PAG
Laforest, Eric, Boucherville, QC: 1993 PAG Jr
Lalor, Dwayne, coach/manager, Red Deer, AB:
1994 WJ; 1995 WJ
Landry, Joel, coach, Pointe aus Trembles, QC:
2002 WJ; 2003 WJ; 2004 WJ;
Lapp, Jay, coach, London, ON: 1998 WJ
Leduchowski, Gord, Riverton, MB: 1990 WJ;
1991 WJ
Lehn, Marty, coach/manager, Burnaby, BC:
1993 WJ; 1994 WS; 1995 OQ; 1999 PAG;
2000 WS; 2001 WS; 2003 OQ
Leiper, Tim, coach, Ottawa, ON: 2003 OQ;
2004 OG
Lounsbury, Jeff, coach, Niagara Falls, ON:
2004 WSG
Lumley, Bob, coach, Victoria, BC: 1970 WS
Lynd, Terry, coach, Moosomin, SK: 1997 WJ
Mace, Ron, coach, Nelson, BC: 1989 WS
MacKay, Gerry, manager, Kenton, MB:
1967 PAG; 1971 PAG; 1972 WS

MacKenzie, Eric, coach/manager, Mooretown,
ON: 1978 WS; 1979 PAG; 1980 WS; 1981
IC; 1982 WS; 1983 WS; PAG; 1984 OG;
1985 IC; 1986 PAC
MacKenzie, Bill, manager, Ottawa, ON: 1978 WS;
1979 PAG; 1980 WJ; 1983 WS; 1983 PAG
McArthur, Brad, coach, Vancouver, BC: 1989 WS
McKaig Terry, manager, Vernon, BC: 2004 WSG
McKenzie, Tommy, Kitchener, ON: 1971 WS
McLaren, John, coach, Sweetwater, TX: 1977 WC
McRae, Mike, coach, Niagara Falls, ON: 1998 WJ
McRobie, Brian, coach/manager, Brockville,
ON: 1981 WJ; 1982 WJ; 1983 WS;
1983 PAG; 1984 OG; 1985 IC; 1986 PAC
McTavish, Les, coach, Lethbridge, AB: 2004 WJ
Messier, Alex, coach, St. Hyacinthe, QC:
1999 WJ; 2001 WJ; 2002 WJ
Moore, Harry, coach, Sarnia, ON: 1979 PAG;
1981 WJ
Morris, Greg, coach, Chatham, NB: 1978 WS
Myette, Ken, coach, Delta, BC: 1978 WS
Northcott, Harold, coach, Rocky Mountain
House, AB: 1992 WJ; 1993 WJ; 1994 WJ;
2000 WS; 2001 WS
Norton, Wayne, coach/manager, Port Moody,
BC: 1973 WS, 1973 IC; 1974 WS; 1975 IC;
1975 PAG
Payne, Alf, coach, Agincourt, ON: 1982 WJ;
1984 OG; 1985 WJ
Picard, Marc, manager, Pickering, ON:
1996 PAG Jr
Picone, Gary, coach/manager Trail, BC:
1981 WJ; 1981 IC; 1991 WJ
Plaxton, Todd, coach, Saskatoon, SK:
2003 WJ 2003 WS; 2004 WJ
Pratte, Andre, coach, Montreal, QC: 1973 WS;
1973 IC
Randall, Mark, coach, Sherwood Park, AB:
2003 WJ; 2004 WJ
Rasmussen, Randy, coach, St. Paul, AB:
1984 WJ
Ridley, Jim, manager, Milton, ON: 1983 WJ;
1984 WJ; 1985 WJ; 1986 WJ; 1987 WJ;
1988 WJ; 1988 OG; 1989 PC; 1989 WSG;
1989 WS; 1991 PAG
Robertson, Jeff, coach, Birtle, MB: 1995 WJ;
1996 WJ
Robb, David, coach, Lac La Biche, AB: 1999 WJ
Ross, Bruce, coach, Kentville, NS: 1982 WJ
Ruhr, Lionel, coach, Regina, SK: 1987 WJ;
1989 WJ; 1991 PAG
Rypien, Tim, coach, Calgary, AB: 1989 WJ
Sage, John, trainer, Newmarket ON: 2003 WJ
Scott, Gladwyn, coach, Minnesoda, MB:
1967 PAG; 1987 WJ; 1988 WJ; 1989 WJ
Scott, Glennis, playing manager, Miami, MB:
1971 WS; 1972 WS
Seeman, Garneau, coach, Fredericton, NB:
1975 IC
Senechal, Martin, Laval, QC: 1993 PAG Jr
Terry, Steve, Peterborough, ON: 1993 WSG;
1993 WS; 1998 WJ; 1989 WS
Tinnish, Andrew, coach, Burlington, ON:
2002 WSG
Upham, John, coach/manager, Windsor, ON:
1987 WJ; 1988 OG; 1988 WJ; 1989 WJ;
1990 WJ; 1991 PAG
Venerus, Sil, coach, Windsor, ON: 1996 PAG Jr

Whitt, Ernie, manager, Clinton Township, MI: 1999 PAG; 2003 OQ; 2004 OG

Wilson, Rod, coach, St. Stephen, NB: 1987 WJ

SUPPORT STAFF

Ager, Steve, public relations, Sherbrooke, QC: 2001 WJ

Agostino, Alex, business manager, St. Bruno, QC: 1993 PAG Jr

Apa, Phil, trainer, Pierrefonds, QC: 1999 WJ; 2000 WJ; 2000 WS; 2001 WS

Baba, Jim, director general, Ottawa, ON: 2000-05

Bailie, Harvey, team leader, London, ON: 1987 PAG; 1989 PC; 1989 WS; 1991 PAG; 1993 WSG; 1993 WS

Beckman, Bernie, technical director/general manager, Ottawa, ON: 1986-93

Belec, Richard, president Baseball Canada, Montreal, QC: 1994-96

Berard, Earl, team leader, Kindersley, SK: 1990 WJ; 1991 WJ

Briand, Kevin, team leader/manager baseball operations, Gloucester, ON: 1997 WJ; 1998 WS

Burchett, Chris, P.R. coordinator, Ottawa, ON: 1995 OQ; 1999 PAG

Bush, Rod, equipment, Ottawa, ON: 1996 WJ

Byrne, Brendan, business manager, Ottawa, ON: 2001 WJ; 2002 WJ; 2003 WJ

Caron, François, public relations, Ottawa, ON: 1996 WJ

Carter, Ray, president Baseball Canada, Tsawwassen, BC: 2000-05

Charbonneau, Matt, P.R. co-ordinator: 1998 WS; 2004 OG

Cote, Jean-François, public relations, Ottawa, ON: 2002 WJ

Dunlop, Cameron, team leader, Mississauga, ON: 2002 WSG; 2004 WSG

Elliott, Al, business manager, Richmond, BC: 1975 IC; 1975 PAG; president Baseball Canada, 1990-92

Elliott, Kevin, trainer, Saint John, NB: 1995 WJ

Footz, Wally, business manager, Edmonton, AB: 1994 WJ; 1995 WJ

Grant, Duncan, director general, Ottawa, ON: 1993-2000

Halfyard, Bill, president Baseball Canada, St. John's, NL: 1986-90

Hamilton, Greg, general manager, Ottawa, ON: 2000 WS; 2001 WS; 2003 WS; 2003 OQ; 2004 OG

Hamilton, John, director general, Ottawa, ON: 1985-91

Harvey, Scott, business manager, Marysville, NB: 1979 PAG; 1983 WS; 1983 PAG

Hass, Curly, general manager, Winnipeg, MB: 1970 WS

Hays, Mike, trainer, Ottawa, ON: 1998 WJ

Inglis, Brent, Greenfield Park, QC: 1997 WJ

Jones, Gordon, president Baseball Canada, Sackville, NS: 1985-86

Korol, Lorne, technical director/general manager: 1994-95

Lacoursiere, Bob, executive, North Battleford, SK: 1967 PAG; president Baseball Canada, 1967-73

Lavis, Greg, equipment manager, Oakbank, MB: 1998 WJ; 1999 PAG

Lawson, Tom, Toronto, ON; 1996 PAG Jr; 2004 WS

Levigne, Paul, director general, Ottawa, ON: 1979-85

MacKenzie, Bill, technical director, Ottawa, ON: 1981 WJ

Martin, Bill, director general, Ottawa, ON: 1991-93

McKeachie, John, press liason, Victoria, BC: 1970 WS

McLeod, Scott, trainer, Winnipeg, MB: 2002 WSG; 2004 WSG

Mungrue, Reg, trainer, Thorold, ON: 2001 WJ

Murphy, Joey, business manager, Richmond, ON: 1998 WJ

Nolet, Jean-Robert, president Baseball Canada, QC: 1973-74

Olsen, Dave, president Baseball Canada, Winnipeg, MB: 1992-94

Pielak, Cas, president Baseball Canada, Regina, SK: 1974-86

Prest, David, public relations, Ottawa, ON: 2000 WJ

Rice, Ron, president Baseball Canada, Charlottetown, PEI: 1996-2000

Sage, John, trainer, Oakville, ON; 2002 WJ; 2004 WJ

Sanford, Keith, equipment manager, Windsor, ON: 2000 WS; 2001 WS; 2003 WS; 2003 OQ; 2004 OG

Scott, Gladwyn, chef de mission, Warren, MB: 1987 WJ; 1988 WJ; 1989 WJ

Scott, Glennis, manager, Brandon, MB: 1971 PAG

Seymour, Andrew, public relations, Kanata, ON: 1999 PAG

Shannon, Scott, trainer, Toronto, ON: 2003 OQ; 2004 OG

Shury, Dave, executive, Battleford, SK: 1967 PAG

Soulliere, Bernie, business manager, Windsor, ON: 1994 WS; 1995 OQ; 1996 WJ; 1998 WS; 1999 PAG; 2000 WS; 2001 WS; 2003 WS; 2003 OQ; 2004 WJ; 2004 OG

Stecyk, Shane, trainer, Vegreville, AB: 1994 WJ; 1995 WJ; 1996 WJ; 1997 WJ; 1998 WS

Summer, Don, statistics, Brandon, MB: 1967 PAG

Tucker, Mike, media relations, St. Catharines, ON: 2004 WSG

Valcke, Tom, director general, Ottawa, ON: 1988-90

Vendittola, Dr. Robert, Montreal, QC: 1973 WS; 1973 IC

Watt, Gord, trainer, Lethbridge, AB: 1999 PAG

White, Greg, P.R. co-ordinator, Nepean, ON: 1997 WJ

White, Vincent, public relations, Beaconsfield QC: 2003 WJ

Williams, Brad, trainer/equipment manager, Vancouver, BC: 1987 WJ; 1988 WJ; 1990 WJ; 1994 WS; 1995 OQ

Wiwchar, Joe, business manager, Morden, MB: 1999 WJ; 2000 WJ

Younker, Harold, trainer, Langley, BC: 1975 IC; 1987 PAG; 1988 OG; 1988 WS; 1990 WS; 1993 WSG; 1993 WS; 1994 WS; 1995 OQ

Zeman, Joe, business manager, Saskatoon, SK: 1967 PAG

Appendix E

AWARDS & HONORS

MAJOR LEAGUE BASEBALL

Most Valuable Player
Larry Walker, Colorado Rockies, 1997, NL
Cy Young Award
Ferguson Jenkins, Chicago Cubs, 1971, NL
Eric Gagne, Los Angeles Dodgers, 2003, NL
Rookie of the Year
Jason Bay, Pittsburgh Pirates, 2004, NL
Rookie Pitcher of the Year
Reggie Cleveland, St. Louis Cardinals, 1971, NL
Jason Dickson, California Angels, 1997, AL

Rookie Player of the Year
Pete Ward, Chicago White Sox, 1963, AL
Fred Hutchison Memorial Award
John Hiller, Detroit Tigers, 1973
Gold Glove Award
Larry Walker, 1992, 1993, 1997, 1998, 1999, 2001, 2002, NL
Major League Executive of the Year
Doug Melvin, Texas Rangers, 1996

CANADIAN PLAYER OF THE YEAR

James "Tip" O'Neill Award
The James "Tip" O'Neill Award has been presented annually since the Canadian Baseball Hall of Fame's inception in 1983 to the Canadian baseball player "judged to have excelled in individual achievement and team contribution while adhering to the highest ideals of the game of baseball."

1984 – Terry Puhl, Houston Astros
1985 – Dave Shipanoff, Portland (Triple-A) & Philadelphia Phillies
1986 – Rob Ducey, Ventura (Single-A) & Knoxville (Double-A)
1987 – Larry Walker, Jacksonville (Double-A)
1988 – Kevin Reimer, Tulsa (Double-A) & Texas Rangers
1989 – Steve Wilson, Chicago Cubs
1990 – Larry Walker, Montreal Expos
1991 – Daniel Brabant, Team Canada
1992 – Larry Walker, Montreal Expos
1993 – Rob Butler, Syracuse (Triple-A) & Toronto Blue Jays
1994 – Larry Walker, Montreal Expos
1995 – Larry Walker, Colorado Rockies
1996 – Jason Dickson, Midland (Double-A), Vancouver (Triple-A) & California Angels
1997 – Larry Walker, Colorado Rockies
1998 – Larry Walker, Colorado Rockies
1999 – Jeff Zimmerman, Texas Rangers
2000 – Ryan Dempster, Florida Marlins
2001 – Corey Koskie, Minnesota Twins & Larry Walker, Colorado Rockies
2002 – Larry Walker, Colorado Rockies & Eric Gagne, Los Angeles Dodgers
2003 – Eric Gagne, Los Angeles Dodgers
2004 – Jason Bay, Pittsburgh Pirates

James "Tip" O'Neill, who hailed from Woodstock, Ontario, was one of major league baseball's first legitimate stars. With the St. Louis Browns in 1887, the outfielder set major league records in hits, doubles, slugging percentage, and total bases while compiling an astounding .492 batting average (walks were included as hits in 1887, but if his average was calculated by today's standard, it was .435, the second highest in major league history to Hugh Duffy, .438).

INDEX

Jackson, Larry, 47
Jackson, Max, 149
Jackson, Russ, 35
Jansen, Larry, 48
Jarrell, Arnie, 40
Javier, Stan, 205
Jenkins, Delores (mother of Fergie), 44, 46, 48, 52
Jenkins, Ferguson Arthur "Fergie", 2, 4, 42-54, 84, 99, 127, 168
    career stats, 49, 52, 71, 74, 129
    Hall of Fame induction, 42-43, 51-53, 58, 98, 215, 217
Jenkins, Ferguson Holmes (father of Fergie), 43, 44, 46, 51, 52-53
Jenkins, Mary-Anne (wife of Fergie), 51-52
Jenkins, Raymond (son of Fergie), 53
Jenkins, Samantha (daughter of Fergie), 53
Jeter, Derek, 5, 153
Johnson, Deron, 204
Johnson, Jerry, 205
Johnson, Mike, 26
Johnson, Randy, 129
Johnson, Wallace, 207
Johnston, Elwood, 37
Johnston, Rick, 215
Jones, Chipper, 213
Jones, James Earl, 114, 166
Jones, Mack, 202, 205, 209
Jones, Todd, 79
Jordan, Brian, 96
Jorgensen, Mike, 144
Josephson, Duane, 168
Judd, Oscar, 71
Justice, David, 70

Kaline, Al, 117
Kashuba, John, 189
Keane, Johnny, 139, 140, 141
Kelly, Mike, 185-86, 189
Kemp, Steve, 151
Kennedy, Bill, 136
Kenning, Ryan, 13
Kent, Jeff, 96
Kerr, Mel, 119
Killebrew, Harmon, 47, 48, 50
Kingston, Stuart, 197
Kinkade, Mike, 153
Kinsella, John, 166
Kinsella, Ray, 166
Kinsella, W.P., 166

Kjos, Ryan, 104
Klassen, Anna (grandmother of Danny), 150
Klassen, Bryan (brother of Danny), 150, 155
Klassen, Danny, 3, 15, 23, 24, 148-55
Klassen, Helen (née Hamm, mother of Danny), 148, 150, 151-52
Klassen, Vic (father of Danny), 148, 150-52, 153, 154
Klein, Chuck, 60, 75
Kluszewski, Ted, 75
Knight, Bobby, 106
Kook, Shanna, 213
Koonce, Cal, 205
Koosman, Jerry, 142, 143, 145, 146
Koskie, Corey, 1, 3, 5, 14, 83, 87-90, 181
    hockey background, 6
    at National Baseball Institute, 99, 177
Koskie, Leonard (father of Corey), 88
Koskie, Maryann (mother of Corey), 88
Koskie, Shannon (wife of Corey), 89
Koufax, Sandy, 132
Kranepool, Ed, 143
Kreuter, Chad, 167
Krug, David, 191
Kubiszyn, Jack, 139
Kuhn, Bowie, 50
Kurtz, Clyde, 115
Kusiewicz, Mike, 6, 13
Kyle, Billy, 30, 195

Laboy, Coco, 205
Lachance, Andre, 124
Lachemann, Marcel, 168
Lachemann, Rene, 168, 169
LaCoss, Mike, 69
Laforest, Pete, 5, 6, 7, 12-13, 24, 123
Lajoie, Nap, 60
Laliberte, Guy, 203
Lamphere, Tom, 89
Lancaster, Ron, 35
Lanier, Hal, 94
Lannin, J.J., 55-56, 62-63, 213
Larkin, Barry, 74
LaRussa, Tony, 3, 106, 132-33, 168
Lasalle, Moe, 192
Lasorda, Tommy, 18, 47, 86, 128
Lau, Charlie, 215
Lavallee, Brent, 186
Laveay, Blaise, 101, 104
Laverty, Andrew, 198

Tavares, Tony, 201
Taylor, Carole (sister of Ron), 136
Taylor, Chuck, 142
Taylor, Drew (son of Ron), 146-47
Taylor, Eddie, 167
Taylor, Elizabeth (grandmother of Ron), 136
Taylor, Matthew (son of Ron), 146
Taylor, Maude (mother of Ron), 136, 144
Taylor, Ron, 3, 4, 49, 53, 134-46, 205
Taylor, Rona (wife of Ron), 134, 144, 146
Taylor, Russ, 205
Taylor, Walter (grandfather of Ron), 136
Taylor, Wes (father of Ron), 136, 144-45
Tenace, Gene, 59
Terry, Steve, 161
Theodore, Jose, 124
Thigpen, Bobby, 173, 174
Thompson, Ronnie, 197
Thomson, Rob, 213
Thorman, Scott, 10, 177, 214-15
Thorn, John, 57
Tidrow, Dick, 163
Tillman, Bob, 209
Timlin, Mike, 38
Tinkers, Joe, 109
Tomko, Brett, 153
Topolie, Damon, 189
Torrance, Ken, 101
Torre, Joe, 47, 96, 103, 133, 213
Tosca, Carlos, 10, 154-55
Touchette, Serge, 202
Tracy, Chad, 132
Tracy, Jim, 3, 129, 131
Trammell, Alan, 151, 152, 154
Treanor, Dean, 132
Tresh, Tom, 141
Troudart, Vincente, 16
Troutman, George, 208
Tsao, Chin-Hui, 158
Tsukayama, Bobby, 43
Tuck, Darcy, 43
Tunstall, Christopher, 55, 62-63
Turley, Bob, 135
Tyson, Mike, 135

Uecker, Bob, 140, 142, 146
Upstell, Lorne, 66
Urrutia, Osmani, 24

Valcke, Tom, 16, 18, 83, 87, 186
Valentine, Bobby, 172

Valo, Elmer, 115
Van Brabant, Ozzie, 115, 136, 207
Vander Meer, Johnny, 48
Van Horne, Dave, 204, 205
Van Slyke, Andy, 202
Van Tol, Gary, 191
Velez, Higinio, 15, 25
Vernon, Fraser, 113
Vernon, Mickey, 169, 212
Villeneuve, Jacques, 76
Vince, Bert, 27, 31-32, 211, 218
Vincent, Fay, 52
Virdon, Bill, 86
Votto, Joey, 10

Wager, Gerry "Doc", 196
Wainhouse, Dave, 99, 177
Wakabayashi, Mel, 44
Walker, Angela (née Brekken, wife of Larry Jr.), 75
Walker, Barry (brother of Larry Jr.), 66
Walker, Cam, 92
Walker, Carey (brother of Larry Jr.), 66
Walker, Gary (brother of Larry Jr.), 66
Walker, Larry, Jr., 1, 4, 14, 59, 64-82, 105, 107
  awards, 3, 68, 76, 98
  as Canadian role model, 175, 181
  career stats, 86, 99, 133, 173, 215, 217
  hockey background, 6, 64
  minor league play, 177, 186
Walker, Larry, Sr., 64-67, 69, 81-82
Walker, Mary (mother of Larry Jr.), 66
Wallace, Dave, 126
Wallach, Tim, 72-73, 203
Ward, Pete, 144, 173
Wardle, Mr., 85
Ware, Jeremy, 17, 22, 23, 160
Warwick, Carl, 141
Watson, Bob, 86
Watson, Carl, 118
Watts, Elwyn, 196
Webster, R. Howard, 213
Weese, Keith, 30, 40
Weimers, Larry, 194
Weir, Mike, 121, 130
Weiss, Bill, 61
Welke, Don, 129, 132
Wells, David, 43, 146, 181
Wells, Vernon, 16
Westgate, Murray, 109
Westrum, Wes, 142

ACKNOWLEDGEMENTS

Most members of the Red Sox Nation remember Oct. 21, 1986. The Red Sox came to Fenway Park up 2-0 in the best-of-seven World Series. And in the first inning Dennis "Oil Can" Boyd allowed the New York Mets back into the Series, giving up four runs in the first. It was a Series long remembered for Billy Buckner's error in Game 6 and another Mets' comeback in Game 7.

Back then, I was covering baseball for the *Ottawa Citizen*. My memory of the Series is from the afternoon of Game 3: lunch at the Harvard Book Store with Wayne Parrish, new sports editor of the *Toronto Sun*—a job interview. Two months later, after scouring the country for a baseball writer, he settled on me. And that was the start of a beautiful friendship, as Humphrey Bogart said at the end of *Casablanca*.

A friendship with Parrish, a boss ranked with the late Eddie MacCabe and Graham Parley amongst former bosses, led us to a friendship with Sun columnist James O'Leary. Now, Parrish and O'Leary run SPORTClassic Books. It was good that someone as wise as Parrish got out of sports writing. He was giving us a bad name. After all, he is a pianist. Parrish's successor at the Sun was Mike Simpson, a patient, patient man, and a brilliant editor, who was able to muddle through the nightly field of land mines unscathed. Full responsibility for causing most of his grey hair is accepted.

My sincere thanks to all three bosses, as well as the other sports editor, Scotty Morrison, now at Sportsnet, and current boss Pat Grier. Grier proof read *Hard Ball*, the George Bell autobiography I authored in 1990, and was good enough to give me time away from work to write *The Northern Game*.

Thanks to Baseball Canada officials, who helped from day one. Talking to athletes at the Olympics is difficult in the mix zone, athletes on one side of the fence, the media on the other. As Tyler Kepner, of *The New York Times* said at a ball game in Athens: "Every night at Yankee Stadium I show up at 4 o'clock and can talk to Derek Jeter. I show up here and can't speak to Clay Bellinger." Bellinger, the former Yankee back-up infielder, played for Greece. Thankfully, I was able to gain access to the athletes' village four times.

My sister Elizabeth, of Kingston, Ontario was very helpful researching my grandfather's travels, combing through scrapbooks.

Sincere thanks are extended to the likes of Jim Ferguson, director, media relations for Minor League Baseball, formerly with the Cincinnati Reds and the San Diego Padres; Claudette Burke of Hawkesbury, Ontario who is the reference librarian in the A. Bartlett Giamatti Research Library of the Baseball Hall of Fame & Museum in Cooperstown, New York; her boss Jeff Idelson, the Hall's vice-president, and Brad Horn, a former TCU Horned Frog who graduated a year after Jeff Zimmerman.

This project would not have been possible without the help of Bill Weiss of San Mateo, California, and Marshall Wright of Quincy, Massachusetts, historians who compiled Minor League Baseball's top 100 teams in 2001; historian John Thorn of Kingston, New York; Raymond J. Nemec of Naperville, Illinois, researcher and statistician, and Rod Nelson of Denver, SABR co-chair of the Scouts Committee. In addition to the baseball historians, we consulted Doug Betts' scrapbook of the 1991 World Youth championships in Brandon. And we had help rounding up photographs from Honourable Mr. Justice Randall Scott Echlin, Superior Court of Justice (Ontario), as well as Matt Charbonneau of Baseball Canada.

We'd be remiss if we didn't mention those who provided baseball memories wherever we went: Ron Earl, Bobby Gilmour, Elwood Johnston, Greg Orr, Charlie Pester, Billy Pratt, Keith Weese and Guy White in Kingston. Mike Arundel, Billy Courchaine, Phil Franko, Ed Jordan, Jimmy Kent, Greg McNally, Paul Murphy, Clare Osborne, Don Campbell and Gord Hamilton in Ottawa. William Bargel, Corey Berneski, Nick Chisholm, Sammy Elliott and his older brother Matthew, Daniel Fishbein, Billy Hurley, Chris "Cleve" Okrainetz, Rovin Perumal, Thom Pierson, Sean Pisarski, Talib Reid, Chris Rutherford and Kyle Young in Mississauga. The majority of their games were scored by all-world scorekeeper Margaret Fishbein. Or those we listened to and learned from, such as Art Neilsen, Marc Picard, Danny Thompson and Ronnie Thompson. Thanks to Gary Howatt, Bobby Jones and Buddy Bell, who have shown that it can be done. Special thanks to Willie Hugh Nelson of Abbott, Texas, Merle Ronald Haggard of Bakersfield, California, James Robert Wills of Kosse, Texas, and George Harvey Strait of Pleasanton, Texas. They helped us make it through the night.

And finally thanks to my family: Claire, who would go to games and watch one hitter, her son, Bob, who knows far more about the game than I did at the same age, and Alicia, who struck a mean pose in the on-deck circle and sometimes covered third.

As Boston manager John McNamara used to say in 1986 when he finished his daily press briefing, good luck to everyone wherever the night may take you.

And the hat size, as it was in 1970, remains 7 5/8.